M000238312

UNSPEAKABLE

UNSPEAKABLE

A Life beyond Sexual Morality

Rachel Hope Cleves

The University of Chicago CHICAGO AND LONDON

The University of Chicago Press, Chicago 60637
The University of Chicago Press, Ltd., London
© 2020 by The University of Chicago
All rights reserved. No part of this book may be used or reproduced in any
manner whatsoever without written permission, except in the case of brief
quotations in critical articles and reviews. For more information, contact
the University of Chicago Press, 1427 E. 60th St., Chicago, IL 60637.
Published 2020
Printed in the United States of America

29 28 27 26 25 24 23 22 21 20   1 2 3 4 5

ISBN-13: 978-0-226-73353-1 (cloth)
ISBN-13: 978-0-226-73367-8 (e-book)
DOI: https://doi.org/10.7208/chicago/9780226733678.001.0001

LIBRARY OF CONGRESS CATALOGING-IN-PUBLICATION DATA

Names: Cleves, Rachel Hope, 1975– author.
Title: Unspeakable : a life beyond sexual morality / Rachel Hope Cleves.
Description: Chicago : University of Chicago Press, 2020. | Includes
bibliographical references and index.
Identifiers: LCCN 2020020769 | ISBN 9780226733531 (cloth) |
ISBN 9780226733678 (ebook)
Subjects: LCSH: Douglas, Norman, 1868–1952. | Authors, English—
Biography. | Sodomy—England.
Classification: LCC PR6007.O88 Z598 2020 | DDC 823/.912—dc23
LC record available at https://lccn.loc.gov/2020020769

♾ This paper meets the requirements of
ANSI/NISO Z39.48-1992 (Permanence of Paper).

To my children, Eli and Maya, who've listened to their mother talk way more about Norman Douglas than they would have liked.

Let 'em write what they like, my dear—let 'em, let 'em.

NORMAN DOUGLAS

You couldn't write a life of him without bringing up some awful episodes; but as he constantly brought them up himself the biographer can hardly be blamed.

NEIL HOGG

There are still those who ask occasionally: Who is this fellow Douglas?

PHILLIPS TEMPLE

Contents

Introduction

In 1923, when he was fifty-four years old, the writer Norman Douglas boasted that he'd had sex with eleven hundred virgins during his lifetime.[1] Those were just the girls. In his thirties, he had switched mostly to boys. No one knows how many boys there were. And by boys, I mean boys. By present standards he was a monster. During his lifetime he was considered a great man, including by many of the children who had sexual encounters with him. The people who thought him wicked often liked him for that reason. This is not the story of a child abuse scandal. It is a history of the social world of sex between men and children before the 1950s.

Pedophiles crowd our imagination. They are the villains in our headlines, but they occupy very little space in our histories. Norman Douglas was a celebrity in the early twentieth century. He was friends with Joseph Conrad, D. H. Lawrence, Aldous Huxley, and countless other fixtures in the literary pantheon, all of whom knew about his sexual life. Everyone did. He was a central figure in literary circles all the same. The photographer Islay Lyons predicted in 1948 that "a few generations from now, the name of Norman Douglas will be known . . . when D.H. Lawrence will have been forgotten, Huxley remembered only in part, and all the contemporary trash long consigned to the pulp-machine."[2] Lyons was wrong. Douglas died in 1952. After his death, he was briefly infamous, then disappeared from popular memory. Today Douglas is long forgotten, while Lawrence and Huxley still crowd the bookstore shelves. His writing has not held up well to modern tastes. His sexual life has weathered even worse.

Many books about Douglas have been attempted, but almost all those attempts have failed. Writers have found the obstacle of Douglas's sexual history insurmountable. It's not for lack of sources. The problem is the opposite. There are too many sources that cause discomfort: explicit records of sex acts between Douglas and children; letters from children expressing their affection for Douglas; and endless remarks by Douglas's friends describing him as extraordinary.

This superabundance of sources makes a book about Norman Douglas both imperative and impossible. There is no single figure whose life provides richer sources for examining the subject of sex between adults and children from the mid-nineteenth through the mid-twentieth century. And there is no way to write about the extraordinary regard in which he was once held without pitting the present day's violent antipathy to pedophilia against the more ambiguous attitudes of the past. This is no small interpretive dilemma. Pedophilia is the third rail of contemporary culture. Writing or saying anything that might be taken as expressing sympathy for a pedophile is a surefire way to incinerate a career. Only a fool would write Douglas's biography. Think of this, instead, as a history told through the story of a man.

I didn't set out to write this book. It began with a family vacation to Italy. I had bought discount airline tickets to Naples, and a friend recommended we take a day trip to Capri while we were there. I didn't know anything about Capri, so I did a little research and learned that it was an island at the southern tip of the Bay of Naples that was legendary for its sybaritic atmosphere, which had been captured in a famous 1917 novel by Norman Douglas titled *South Wind*.[3] I read the novel during our visit. *South Wind* is a roman à clef about the eccentric community of cosmopolitan expatriates who lived in Capri during the early twentieth century. The book is very funny and completely amoral. The plot, such as it is, involves nudism, free love, adultery, bigamy, whispers of homosexuality, and a premeditated murder you can really get behind. Since I'm a historian of sexuality, I was intrigued. I wanted to know more about the real people who inspired the novel. After our vacation, I tracked down Douglas's 1933 autobiography *Looking Back*, seeking the facts behind the fiction. This was totally naive.

Like every well-trained historian, I was taught in graduate school that self-interest and the passage of time make autobiographies unreliable evidence. Sometimes I overlook this lesson, but Douglas's autobiography wouldn't allow me to make that mistake. *Looking Back: An Autobiographical Excursion* calls attention on every page to the constructedness of memory. Douglas begins with a description of a dog-shaped incense burner that he used over the years to store the calling cards given to him by friends, then he proceeds by figuratively pulling out the cards, one at a time, and free-associating from the printed names. The resulting memories are as mixed up as the pieces of colored glass in a kaleidoscope. The book jumps from 1886 to 1912 to 1904 and so on, back and forth and forth and back. It's not clear if Douglas has arranged the cards in any particular sequence, or whether the structure faithfully replicates the order in which he pulled the cards from the incense burner. Douglas admits to changing certain names. He denies any memory of others, following those cards with a question mark. Most pages include two or three names. Some cards spark memories that extend for several pages. At the end of the first lengthy entry, Douglas reveals that he checked his recollection of a key event against his daily diary and found that he had misremembered the day. "It is a lesson not to trust one's memory," he warns.[4] It's an aviso not to trust his memoir either.

Like all memoirs, *Looking Back* offers a very incomplete account of its author's life. The nature of its oversights, however, are the opposite to what you might expect. Astonishingly, Douglas includes numerous stories about his sexual encounters with children, while excluding any stories about his wife and sons. He explains how he contracted with parents for sexual access to their children. He includes affectionate portraits of several of the children with whom he had long-lasting affairs. He even dedicates the book to one of his former boy lovers. But the nearest he comes to acknowledging his marriage is a single anecdote about the alcoholic lying-in nurse for his first son. I read Douglas's autobiography looking for stories of sexual nonconformists who were disreputable in their own time but seem like visionaries today. What I found was historical evidence about a sexual behavior that is even more taboo today than it was in the past.

Today almost all of Douglas's sexual encounters with children and youth would be defined as assaults, both in the law and in public opinion.[5] Neither legal nor popular definitions were so clear-cut in the past. As Estelle Freedman argues, the meaning of rape is "fluid, rather than transhistorical or static."[6] There was no age of consent for boys in Britain for much of Douglas's life, and the age of criminal responsibility at which boys could be found guilty of "gross indecencies" with men was fourteen. In France and Italy, where sex between males was decriminalized in the nineteenth century, the age of consent for boys was thirteen until the 1920s.[7] Popular attitudes aligned with the law, generally treating boys as capable of consent once they entered puberty.

In short, whether Douglas's sexual encounters with children constituted assault at the time depended on a wide variety of factors including their location, the children's age, their sex, their sexual histories, and whether physical force was involved. For this reason, I use the word *encounter* to describe Douglas's sexual relations with children and youth. The word *encounter* is capacious. Encounters can be violent, coercive, willing, or enthusiastic. The word does not preclude assault, nor does it imply assault.

As for the words *boys, girls,* and *youth,* I use them flexibly since they also have no fixed transhistorical definition. Historians of childhood argue that understandings of childhood have shifted dramatically over time. Chronological age mattered less in defining capacity or maturity during the past than did class, gender, and physical development. Twelve-year-old males were elected to the British Parliament and other offices before the eighteenth century. Ten-year-old females could legally marry. The concept of adolescence only emerged in the late nineteenth century, and the word *teenager* is a mid-twentieth-century neologism.[8] Today, Steven Angelides argues, "sexuality is *the* most highly cherished marker delineating the boundaries between childhood and adulthood."[9] But that's a recent definition of childhood that cannot be projected backward. Roughly speaking, in this book, I use the words *boy* and *girl* for younger teens or preteens, and I use the word *youth* for older teens. I mostly reserve *children* for boys and girls below the age of sixteen. But I use all of these words loosely, with an eye to their historically shifting meanings.

During his own lifetime, the sex of Douglas's boys posed a greater legal risk than did their age. Douglas was more likely to be arrested for gross indecency than for statutory rape. I didn't know that when I first read *Looking Back*. I didn't know much about the recent history of sex between adults and children, despite my expertise as a historian of sexuality. I had never read any twentieth-century English author who wrote so brazenly about having sexual encounters with children. The memoir left me far more curious about how Douglas could publish such a self-incriminating narrative in the 1930s than about the history of the hedonistic island where he once lived. So I followed my curiosity to the archives, where a second discovery persuaded me, against my better judgment, that I had to attempt a book about Douglas even if it was doomed to become more kindling on the bonfire of earlier failures.

In the Berg Collection room at the New York Public Library, I came across Norman Douglas's transcriptions of the travel diaries of Giuseppe "Pino"

Orioli, the publisher of D. H. Lawrence's *Lady Chatterley's Lover*. Orioli and Douglas were boon companions in Florence, where Douglas lived during the 1920s and '30s. The two men went on numerous walking tours together in Italy and abroad. Douglas always insisted that Orioli keep a diary. Later Douglas would transcribe the diaries to share with friends or adapt for publication. Douglas's transcriptions may have cleaned up Orioli's questionable spelling, but they didn't sanitize his accounts of Douglas's paid sexual encounters with the boys they met along the way. Douglas's and Orioli's friends found this material funny, or arousing, or both. Orioli's diaries used words like *fuck* and *cock* that *Looking Back* had avoided in order to escape censorship. A barely there scrim of ambiguity hung over *Looking Back*. Orioli's diaries made Douglas's sexual practices explicit. I had never read anything like them.

Very few historical sources from Douglas's lifetime explicitly describe sex between adults and children. The two primary exceptions are legal records and pornography, both of which have interpretive limitations. Legal records reveal how common intergenerational sexual encounters were in the nineteenth and early twentieth century, but they do a better job capturing the mechanisms of the legal system than the perspectives of the people caught up in it.[10] Pornography offers a fantasy intended to arouse consumers, but says little about real-life practices. Orioli's diaries are unique because they give firsthand accounts of adult-child sexual practices that are graphic but not pornographic.[11] Instead of fantasies of virile handsome men and beautiful willing boys, the diaries describe the men's impotency, the boys' pimples, and the crude commercial calculations involved in the majority of their sexual encounters.

Honest, graphic but not pornographic writing about historical sexuality is rare. Honest, graphic, but not pornographic writing about sexual encounters that were potentially illegal is even rarer. The fact that the diaries survived in the hands of collectors after Douglas, who was perpetually broke, sold them off is extraordinary. As soon as I read Orioli's diaries, I knew that I had to write about them. The diaries were a one-of-a-kind set of sources that opened a window onto a chapter in history that is rarely discussed. Sex between men and children was historically common but has seldom been historicized. Sex between women and children was historically uncommon and is even more rarely discussed by historians. The specter of pedophilia is central to contemporary cultural politics. As distasteful as the subject might be, the history of adult-child sex needs to be reckoned with if we want to understand the sexual past. And we need to understand this history if we want to make sense of our present moment. There is no way to understand the third rail without grabbing hold of it.

In his 2017 book *Disturbing Attachments*, Kadji Amin argues that scholars of sexuality have neglected the history of sex between men and boys because it threatens the project of queer sexual liberation. In his words, "modern pederasty is the detritus of Queer Studies' orientation toward political futurity."[12] According to Amin, "modern pederasty," which he defines as age-differentiated sex, was the dominant form of male same-sex practice until the mid-twentieth century. As he reminds readers:

> Virtually all late nineteenth- and early twentieth-century canonical authors now remembered as "gay"—including Walt Whitman, Oscar Wilde (whose famous "love that dare not speak its name" was pederasty), Marcel Proust, Jean Cocteau, André Gide, Jean Genet, and even James Baldwin—participated in and, in some cases, wrote about age-differentiated same-sex erotic relations.[13]

This history, Amin argues, has posed a dilemma to the fields of queer studies and queer history, both of which emerged as outgrowths of the modern gay rights movement.

The rise of the gay rights movement during the 1970s and '80s prompted attacks by right-wing critics who disparaged homosexuality as a threat to the safety of children.[14] By the 1970s, same-sex relations between relatively equal adults had become the norm within Western countries. Under assault from reactionary critics, activists responded by drawing a strict line between "homosexuality" and "pedophilia."[15] Claims for inclusion were built on pragmatic exclusions, a common story. Richard Yuill and Dean Durber argue that the marginalization of adult-child sex was "a crucial transformative precondition for the flourishing of mainstream sexual minorities."[16] This marginalization was not limited to contemporary politics. The imperatives of the present also shaped the telling of the past, as a rising generation of gay and lesbian historians focused their attention on relations between adults and, for the most part, excluded age-differentiated relations from their definitions of the queer past.

The reluctance of historians to write about adult-child sex is not entirely political. It's also visceral.[17] The topic, because it is taboo, is extremely discomfiting. I've seen proof of that sentiment in people's faces when I've given talks about this project. Elise Chenier remarks that "for most people, the whole topic is either best avoided, or it arouses such a strong reaction that careful contemplation is quite simply not possible." The history of sexuality, however, cannot avoid an entire range of human behavior because it arouses feelings of disgust. The history of sexuality cannot be limited to "the history of what makes historians feel sexy," as Catharine MacKinnon once snidely dismissed the field. MacKinnon criticized historians particularly for disregarding the ubiquitous history of male rape of girls. However, some sexuality scholars have argued that feminist master narratives of child sexual abuse, like MacKinnon's, have hampered the history of intergenerational sex by imposing a desexualized and disempowered understanding of childhood that contradicts the complexities of children's lived experiences. Angelides argues that queer studies, if anything, has offered more productive avenues than feminist studies for understanding intergenerational sex.[18]

Those historians who do not feel hampered by visceral disgust for the subject of adult-child sex may still be reluctant to research the topic from fear that visceral discomfort will lead readers to avoid their work. Writing about a taboo topic without breaking taboos poses a daunting challenge. As Yuill writes, from experience, the "pressure to not conduct research on this topic suggests that even such research itself in some way undermines the very cultural taboos" that surround it.[19] Those who do attempt such research risk overt censorship.

When Yuill was a PhD candidate in sociology at Glasgow University writing his dissertation, "Male Age-Discrepant Intergenerational Sexualities and Relationships," he was subjected to multiple investigations by his university, had his research materials reviewed by the police, was attacked repeatedly in the British press, and had his completed dissertation embargoed for five years. Cognitive psychologist Susan Clancy was blacklisted for her dissertation research at Harvard questioning the trauma model of child sexual abuse, and she was forced to find work outside of the country. Journalist Judith Levine couldn't find a publisher for her work on adolescent sexuality for five years, and when the University of Minnesota signed her book, the Republican-led state legislature threatened to cut the press's funding. Literary scholar James Kincaid's work on the fetishization of childhood sexual innocence during the Victorian era was described as "obscenity" by the British House of Lords, which sought to ban its distribution in the UK. Bruce Rind's interdisciplinary work on pederasty for a special issue of the *Journal of Homosexuality* was removed following intense pressure from critics and wasn't published until eight years later, in a special volume exploring the controversy.[20] Several editors and agents whom I spoke with about this book expressed doubt that any press would risk publishing it.

In addition to political disincentives, visceral discomfort, and cultural taboos, a final challenge has stymied historical research into adult-child sex: the limitation of sources. Although the legal age of sexual consent for boys was low, and sex between adult men and girls was common, many adult-child sexual encounters were vulnerable to criminal sanction because they involved same-sex dynamics, incest, force, payment, violence, or very young children. As a consequence, participants rarely documented their activities. But the police did. I am indebted to the handful of scholars who have used legal records resulting from arrests to piece together an understanding of sex between men and children, boys in particular, in the Anglo world during the nineteenth and twentieth centuries.[21] Their work has been critical to my efforts to contextualize the life of Norman Douglas, who was born in Austria but considered himself Scottish and spent many years living in Britain. Matt Cook's work on turn-of-the-century London has been especially important for understanding Douglas's years spent there before World War I.[22]

Intellectual historians have researched pederasty using literary sources like poetry and art history. Several scholars have examined the connection between pederasty and neo-Hellenism, or the movement venerating the ancient Greeks that was popular in the nineteenth-century English public schools where Douglas was educated.[23] A few scholars have tackled how this neo-Hellenic fascination gave rise to the Uranian school of poetry on the theme of "boy love," which counted among its practitioners Oscar Wilde and his lover Lord Alfred "Bosie" Douglas.[24] Norman Douglas was too young, and too individualistic, to number himself among the Uranians. But he was strongly influenced by the neo-Hellenism of his youth. He liked to think of himself as a *pederast* in the ancient Greek sense. His life span tracks closely with the literary ascendance of this term, before its replacement by the word *pedophile* in the second half of the twentieth century.[25] He often wrote admiringly about the Hellenic legacy in Italy. It was this Greek past that drew Douglas to cities such as Naples (originally Parthenope) and Syracuse.

Douglas spent more of his adult life living in Italy than in any other country, in part because sexual relations between males were not criminalized there during the late nineteenth and early twentieth centuries. He was among a coterie of privileged British and German pederasts who congregated in cities like Florence, Venice, and Taormina. Several Italian scholars have studied the surprisingly tolerant attitudes of Italian families and communities to relationships between local boys and foreign men.[26] Stefania Arcara's work on the neo-Hellenist fantasies of British and German sex tourists has been especially important for my understanding of Douglas's love for Italy.[27] Joseph Allen Boone has looked at the Orientalist pederastic fantasies that inspired sex tourists to travel to the Middle East, another region that Douglas visited throughout his life.[28]

Although Douglas lived and died before contemporary ideas about pedophilia took hold, I never would have been able to imagine writing this history without the work of a handful of scholars who have examined pedophile discourse through a critical lens. James Kincaid attended the infamous Mc-Martin Preschool trials in California during the late 1980s (prosecuting alleged satanic ritual sexual abuse of children), and then investigated the origins of the moral panic around pedophilia. According to Kincaid, the ideals of childhood innocence that emerged during the Victorian era had the double-edged effect of making children perversely desirable.[29] Lewis Carroll's pinafored Alice is just one face of a coin, the flip side of which is Charles Dodgson's erotic photographs of Alice Liddell as a beggar child, with her shift falling off her shoulder. As literary scholar Kathryn Bond Stockton writes, "It's a mistake to take innocence straight." Drawing on Kincaid, she argues that "detailed narratives of child molestation, which the press is full of, allow 'normal' citizens what they seem to seek: 'righteous, guilt-free . . . pornographic fantasies' about the violation of a child's innocence."[30] Expressions of outrage against pedophilia must be situated within a larger affective economy that simultaneously produces untoward emotions like desire.

Just as the fetishization of childhood innocence has had unintended consequences, so has the demonization of adults who have sex with children. The belief that pedophiles are monsters did not become ubiquitous in North America and western Europe until the late 1970s. Critics of the contemporary hysteria over pedophiles don't argue in favor of sex between adults and children, but they express suspicion of the consequences of treating the pedophile as a bogeyman.[31] One problem with the monster narrative of pedophilia is that it blinds us to the everyday child sexual abuse committed by people whom we like or love.[32] The monster narrative can even blind us to abuse committed by people we don't like. Since monsters by definition are not real, the narrative hampers our ability to recognize that any seemingly ordinary person could be committing acts we deem to be monstrous. If someone were a monster, surely they would not walk among us. The monster narrative effaces the prevalence of sex between adults and children.

Despite its problematic effects, the monster narrative exerts enormous power today. Readers are riveted by the stories of men like Jeffrey Epstein, Michael Jackson, and Larry Nassar. The topic of child sexual abuse is personalized in a distinctive way, which is why it makes sense to look at the history of sex between adults and children through the lens of an individual life. The story of how Norman Douglas could be so open about his sexual encounters with children and still be considered a great man—not despite his sexual immorality, but because of it—tells us how much the history of adult-child sex has changed since the first half of the twentieth century. By looking at Douglas's story not as a monster narrative, one gets at the historical ordinariness of pederasty. Douglas did not stand outside his time—he took part in well-developed social practices, including boarding school relationships, concubinage contracts, and child prostitution.

If I'm not writing a monster story, how should I write about Douglas? Certainly not as a "great man." The nineteenth-century philosopher Thomas Carlyle once said that "the History of the world is but the Biography of great men."[33] Even biographies that admit the moral imperfections of their subjects are often based on the premise that their subjects were "great" in terms of their influence within their fields of action. A lot of artists fall into this category. Picasso and Tolstoy were arguably rotten people, but few doubt their creative greatness. Many who knew Douglas considered him to be a great writer. Islay Lyons thought he was "not merely one of the greatest writers of English literature alive, but one of the greatest our language has ever produced. This is no biased claim. It is a very simple fact."[34] Few would go so far as Lyons, but a fundamental faith in Douglas's greatness as a writer does suffuse the handful of short biographical sketches that appeared about him during and immediately after his lifetime, as well as the only comprehensive Douglas biography, by Mark Holloway, published in 1976.[35]

I owe a great deal to Holloway's extensive research, as well as to the editions of Douglas's correspondence produced by an admiring set of Douglas scholars associated with the state library of Vorarlberg, in western Austria.[36] These resources have been enormously helpful to my work, but I don't share their creators' mostly unreserved enthusiasm for our common subject. I have my favorite Douglas books. I love *Looking Back* and *Together*. I think some of the essays in *Old Calabria* are beautiful. I highly recommend *South Wind* to anyone looking to read a philosophical, dialogue-driven, light comedy about early twentieth-century sexual mores. On the other hand, I think *They Went* is boring and *Paneros* is lightweight. But these are personal preferences. This book is not grounded in any objective claim to Douglas's greatness as an author. I stand with the reviewer for *Punch* magazine, who a few years after Douglas's death summed up his career by saying he had "realized himself more as a man, and a figure of his time, than a writer."[37] Douglas's fans see his sexual history as a distraction from the central story of his literary accomplishments. For my part, I take Douglas's sexuality as my main subject and treat his writing as a window onto that history. I was intrigued by *South Wind*, but I wrote this book because of Orioli's diaries.

I follow more in the footsteps of A. J. A. Symons than Thomas Carlyle. Bored of reading too many great man biographies, Symons announced in 1929 that he was seeking a new way to write biography, a "fresh and attainable alternative to the dry imbecility of the ordinary life."[38] Five years later he published *The Quest for Corvo*, an experimental biography of the writer Frederick Rolfe, better known by his nom de plume, Baron Corvo. Symons's biographical endeavor began, like mine, with a novel and a set of documents, both loaned to him by his friend Christopher Millard. The novel was Corvo's *Hadrian the Seventh*, which Symons read and loved; the documents were a passel of letters written by Rolfe in 1909–10, describing his sexual encounters with the young male gondoliers who plied the waterways of Venice. "What shocked me about these letters," Symons explained in the opening chapter of his biography, "was not the confession they made of perverse sexual indulgence: that phenomenon surprises no historian. But that a man of education, ideas, something near genius should have enjoyed without remorse the destruction of the innocence of youth."[39] The discovery of those letters launched Symons on his "quest" to understand their author (who had died in 1913).

Douglas loved *The Quest for Corvo*, which Symons sent him as a gift. Douglas wrote back thanking Symons and saying it was "a fascinating book, written just as I think such things ought to be written." Symons had written the biography in the first person, narrating his strenuous efforts to track down former friends of Rolfe willing to tell him about the writer's strange history. "What troubles all your researches must have given you. But also—what a worthy object!" Douglas wrote to Symons.[40] The worthy object Douglas had in mind wasn't Corvo, whom he dismissed as a "wicked fairy," a "horrible creature," a "cochon," a "worm," and a "canaille."[41] The worthy object was the book itself, which reimagined biography as a mystery story rather than a parable, with Symons playing the role of detective.[42] I share Symons's suspicions of turning history into a parable, because I worry that our moralizing will prove as faulty as that of earlier generations. So, inspired by Symons, I've constructed Douglas's story with the seams turned outward. I offer a full retelling of Norman Douglas's life, highlighting the historical and interpretive questions that his life provokes, as a window onto the past.

By now, thanks in part to Symons (who was himself a questionable person), the story of the artist behaving badly is old news.[43] Douglas appears to be a familiar type: the privileged man who used his personal charisma and social power to exploit vulnerable people. The puzzle is not how could such an unappealing man have created such appealing art; it's how could such an unappealing man once have been so appealing?

What do we learn about the history of sexuality from the fact (and it is a fact) that so many of his former child lovers held him in such high esteem? Eric Wolton, the boy to whom *Looking Back* was dedicated, called Douglas "my God" in a letter he wrote when he was in his twenties.[44] Wolton never rejected his childhood relationship with Douglas. After settling in British colonial East Africa and becoming chief of police in Tanganyika, he brought his family on return visits to see Douglas, the last time in 1951. Wolton's story provides uncomfortable evidence that there were boys in the early twentieth century who simply did not view sex with adult men as traumatic, even after they had come of age. Sex between men and boys may have been exploitative and predicated on power inequities, but so were many other types of sexual encounters in the early twentieth century, making pederasty less far outside the norm than pedophilia appears to us today. By studying Douglas's life in close detail, we can unearth a social world where pederasty was not that aberrant.

Douglas's appeal extended beyond his boy lovers. He also attracted many pathbreaking queer and feminist women who regarded him as a sexual role model. What do we learn about the history of sexuality from this surprising affinity? When the food writer Elizabeth David was a young woman just setting out in the world, Douglas advised her: "Always do as you please, and send everybody to Hell, and take the consequences." His words became a motto by which she lived her life unapologetically. She wasn't the only one. As David put it, there were an "uncommonly large number of men and women of all ages, classes and nationalities who took Norman Douglas to their hearts and will hold him there so long as they live."[45] Douglas's philosophy appealed to a lot of sexual nonconformists, not just fellow pederasts. By studying Douglas's life, we can illuminate a world where the "charmed circle" of sexuality, as theorist Gayle Rubin puts it, was so narrow that those who were cast outside its limits shared common ground. Identity categories that are distant from each other today—like loose women, lesbians, and pederasts—were more proximate when they were all outside the charmed circle. Pederasty was less taboo before the 1950s, in effect, because so many other behaviors were disreputable as well. Pederasty was less distinct from other types of sexual nonconformity.[46]

Writing in the midst of a surging moral panic during the early 1980s, Rubin predicted that in twenty years the smoke would clear and pedophiles would be recognized as "victims of a savage and undeserved witch hunt."[47] Despite her perspicacity, Rubin's prediction has proven just as wrong as Lyons's prediction about the longevity of Douglas's reputation. The taboos against sex between adults and young people have become more strenuous with each passing year, to the point that many people now profess revulsion at cross-generational encounters involving young adults and older adults, which seldom raised moral hackles in the past. Studying Douglas's life engages a philosophical question embedded at the core of the history of sexuality. To what extent is sexual morality historically constructed? When we trace the arc of historical change from repression to tolerance, as in the expansion of gay rights, we have no problem arguing for sexual morality as a construct. When we trace the arc of historical change from tolerance to repression, as in the heightening taboo against sex between adults and young people, we are more inclined to see it as evidence of moral progress.

Douglas spent his career decrying all morality as a false construction, which is what made so many readers in the 1920s and '30s regard him as a philosophical mentor. He made his name by ridiculing sexual morality in *South Wind*. The Scottish author Moray McLaren, born in 1901, recalled the effect that *South Wind* had on students who entered university immediately after World War I: "It showed us a way of life, a philosophy of pleasure." Graham Greene, born in 1904, said that "my generation was brought up on *South Wind*."[48] Eventually, Greene and Douglas became dear friends, and when Douglas died, Greene was one of his fiercest defenders. During his lifetime, Douglas's friends accepted, indulged, and even celebrated his sexual amorality. Today we celebrate the authors who adored Douglas for the radical challenges they posed to Victorian morality, but only insofar as those challenges abide by our own current moral code, which limits appropriate sexual encounters to those between two adults of roughly equal status. The story of how Douglas fit into his social world forces readers to grapple with a central tenet in the history of sexuality, by confronting what the historical contingency of sexual morality means when it comes to a behavior that we now regard as a transhistorical moral wrong.

PART I

George Norman Douglass

Crocodiles

In 1941, when Norman Douglas was seventy-two years old, he cobbled together an almanac of aphorisms from his earlier writings. Age was taking its toll. He had rheumatism and a heart condition that made him dizzy. His creative capacities were exhausted. But he had plenty of old writing he could recycle, including pithy observations like "you may cram a truth into an epigram; the truth, never," which he assigned to December 29. For his birthday, December 8, Douglas selected the line: "Give love to the young, who requite you with kisses; take no thought of *hic iacet*, which takes no thought of you."[1] The extract suited him. Even in his old age, Douglas paid little attention to death. He was too consumed with childhood.

Douglas loved children. He loved the idea of childhood, as well as children in the flesh and blood. He affected a world-weary tone about most matters, but he was earnest about youth. "A child is ready to embrace the universe. And, unlike adults, he is never afraid to face his own limitations," he wrote in his 1921 book *Alone*, recounting his travels through Italy at the end of the First World War. The title, he admitted, was a misnomer since he devoted much of the book to describing the children he met along the way. Children, he wrote, "are more generous in their appreciations, more sensitive to pure ideas, more impersonal. Their curiosity is disinterested." Children had the "passionless outlook of the sage." But Douglas's interest in children was not passionless. He loved their bodies in addition to their spirits. "To be in contact with physical health—it would alone suffice to render their society a dear delight, quite apart from the fact that if you are wise and humble you may tiptoe yourself, by inches, into fairyland."[2]

Lytton Strachey, a central figure in the Bloomsbury group, had "a special love" of *Alone*.[3] Sigmund Freud, the father of psychoanalysis, preferred Douglas's 1923 book *Together*, about his travels through Vorarlberg.[4] Douglas went to Austria with a young lover named René Mari, who was around eighteen at the time. Douglas delighted in depicting Mari's boyish exuberance, his bottomless appetite for milk and eggs, his innocent flirtations with innkeepers' daughters, and his affinity for wild spaces. Reflecting on an afternoon spent exploring a ruined castle in the woods, Douglas wrote, "These are the surroundings in which children ought to grow up." Fields, gardens, orchards, meadows, forests, rocks, and rivulets. "Keep them off the street-pavement. Impermanent things, like pavements and what they stand for, stimulate the adult; they overstimulate children, who should be in contact with eternities."[5]

The quasi-mystical tone of Douglas's prescriptions for a healthy childhood could have come from the pen of another Austrian writer of the same generation, Rudolf Steiner, founder of the Waldorf education movement. Both Steiner and Douglas shared the belief that nature was the best school for children's self-development. Douglas thought it was harmful "to withhold from our children the contemplation of woodland marvels, with their tender symbolism of leaf and flower, birth and decay." But he was not a programmatic thinker, like Steiner was. Douglas opposed the "standardization of youth."[6] He was fiercely dedicated to individualism. Douglas had no interest in pedagogy beyond the instruction of the boys he loved.

Much of what we know about Douglas's early years comes from *Together*. He wove memories of his childhood into the narrative, taking Mari to visit places that had been important to him, such as a streamlet that used to be dammed in the summer to water the fields. Douglas remembered a hot day when he and his younger sister, Mary, chased butterflies through the field, getting so sticky that Mary decided they should wade into the flooded river to cool off. Afterward they went to the house of the gardener, who "lighted an immense fire at which our scanty summer garments were dried, one by one." The combination of nostalgic and erotic undertones in passages like this seduced Douglas's readers. The novelist E. M. Forster thought *Together* "very beautiful," and "unlike anything that you or any one else has done." Lytton Strachey wrote to Douglas, after reading *Together*, that "the slightest of your phrases gets me into the right key at once, and the thrill that only you give me goes down my back." Strachey's description evokes the unique sexual charge that he got from reading Douglas.[7]

The unfettered childhood that Douglas described in *Together* was predicated on a terrible loss. In September 1874, when Douglas was five years old, his father, John Sholto Douglass, fell a thousand feet to his death while hunting chamois in the mountains. "There was nothing about him that was not shattered; his gun, his watch, were broken into fragments," Douglas wrote. He took Mari to see the heights where the accident had taken place. Mari wanted to scramble about the shale looking for chamois, but Douglas resisted. The terrain scared him. Almost half a century after the accident, Douglas could not make sense of why his father had chosen such a risky route: "Vainly I ask myself along what lines he would have developed had his life been spared."[8] This is a question we must ask about Douglas himself. To what extent did his father's death shape his later development? Did Douglas end up the way he did because of trauma?

Certainly, it was his father's sudden death that enabled Douglas to run so wild when he was a boy. In the aftermath of tragedy, the family fell apart and the children roamed unsupervised. Take, for example, a memory Douglas relates in *Together* about a time that he and Mary snuck into the vault beneath their house where barrels of alcoholic apple cider were stored. They turned the tap of one of the barrels, he wrote, "and the liquid began to trickle deliciously down our throats, while we egged each other on to drink more and more. I have no idea how long we stayed down there." When a farm laborer came to refill his jug, he discovered the two children, passed out senseless, and carried them to their beds. Douglas joked that Mary "was three years old at the time; the suggestion, therefore, can only have come from her."[9] Two years older than Mary, he would have been five. And since he stated that the escapade took place during the cider-harvesting season, it was likely in fall, probably weeks after his father's death. Douglas didn't say as much, however, probably because it would have spoiled the idyllic memory.

Douglas was similarly withholding about any possible connection between his father's death and the loss of his religious faith. He brought Mari to a spot along the river running through the Lutz forest where, when he was seven years old, he shouted out loud that there was no God. "Who can tell what previous internal broodings had led to this explosive utterance! None at all, very likely," Douglas mused.[10] His offhand dismissal seems unlikely. It's probable that the death of his father, a devout Presbyterian, contributed to Douglas's rejection of religion. The event was traumatic enough to shatter a child's faith. His older brother, John, who was nine when their father died, remained devout throughout his life, but Douglas came to consider religion a pernicious absurdity.

Freed from internal obligations to religious authority, Douglas rejected

1. John Sholto Douglass and Vanda Douglass with their sons, John William (*left*) and George Norman (*right*), on the front steps of their home, Falkenhorst, ca. 1870. Douglas dropped the second *s* from his last name as an adult. Norman Douglas Forschungsstelle, Bregenz.

conventional moral restraints from a young age. He liked to joke, "I have been subject to temptations from earliest childhood, and always know beforehand whether I shall yield or not. I always yield."[11] He regarded this as evidence of his strength of character. As Douglas saw it, his early years left loose to wander the Alpine landscape had allowed him to develop into his own person. The problem with raising children in cities and schools, Douglas thought, was that it enslaved them to social norms. His feral childhood had set him loose from the deluded belief in good and evil. "Morality is the property of the crowd," Douglas wrote.[12] He was an individual.

Douglas's overt rejection of conventional morality thrilled his readers who came of age amidst the repressive hypocrisy of late Victorianism and then lived through the horrible bloodshed of World War I. Douglas's refusal to bow to other people's opinions earned readers' admiration. Perhaps Douglas's independent-mindedness would be attractive to modern readers, if only he hadn't been so doggedly consistent about his amorality. He made no exception to the rule of yielding to temptations when those temptations came in the form of children's bodies. This pattern likely traced back to his early childhood as well.

In the 1930s, Douglas told his close friend Martha Gordon Crotch that he had been erotically fixated on children all his life. His interest in sex began when he was six years old. On occasion, he implied that his earliest sexual encounters were with his sister.[13] "Some people have an absurd objection to incest," Douglas scoffed in a letter to Elizabeth David.[14] He rejected this moral rule along with the rest. He may have just been trying to shock, as he was wont to do. Or he may have been speaking honestly, which he was also wont to do. In *Together*, Douglas depicted Mary as an enthusiastic partner in crime. Not only did they get drunk off purloined cider, but they also broke into a local crypt and played skittles with the skulls. When the children got in trouble, they would hide together under a bed that was so enormous the adults couldn't reach them.[15] Douglas and Mary remained friends when they were adults. But neither Douglas's romanticized account of their childhood relationship nor their ongoing adult intimacy can answer the question of whether Mary felt victimized by her brother.

Very little has been written about the history of incest, and most of what has been written focuses on father-daughter sexual relations rather than relations between siblings.[16] Catharine MacKinnon lumped incest among the many examples of male sexual abuse of girls and women that historians of sexuality avoided out of preference to discuss subjects that "make them feel sexy."[17] MacKinnon's argument fits into a general tendency within feminist theory since the 1980s to regard incest as an expression of male hegemony.[18] It's difficult to read about Douglas's possible childhood sexual encounters with his younger sister without this framework in mind, especially since his later life might be regarded as a master class in the misuse of male power. But Douglas was not a powerful man at the time he first became interested in sex and possibly engaged in sibling incest. The loving infatuation between Douglas and his sister fit quite well into Victorian family ideals.[19] Both siblings may have regarded any sexual encounters as merely another form of mischief.

Their mother, Vanda, did little to intervene in her children's carryings-on. She was distracted. Around the time of her husband's death, she fell passion-

2. Norman Douglas, age six, with Mary Douglass, age four. Norman Douglas Forschungsstelle, Bregenz.

ately in love with her painting teacher, a young man named Jakob Jehly. They became engaged in 1876, when Vanda was thirty-five and Jehly was twenty-two. The relationship produced howls of protest from Vanda's parents and her former in-laws. It wasn't their age difference that primarily concerned the older generation; it was the gulf in class.

Vanda had been born at Windsor Castle. Queen Victoria was her godmother. At the time of Vanda's birth, her father, Baron von Poellnitz, was serving as a chamberlain to Prince Albert. Her mother, Isabella Drummond Forbes, was the daughter of the 17th Lord Forbes, of Aberdeenshire, a general who had served in the Napoleonic Wars. He was one of Scotland's most notable men, although he preferred to live in Bregenz, an Austrian city on the shores of Lake Constance, than in Castle Forbes, in the Vale of Alford. The Douglass family was also noteworthy, if somewhat less lofty. John Sholto Douglass was the 15th Laird of Tilquhillie, an ancestral estate in Banchory, Scotland. Debts on the estate had led to its sale in the early nineteenth century, but John Sholto's father had married the daughter of a wealthy Manchester mill owner, and with his father-in-law's help, he established a cotton mill in the Austrian village of Thüringen, earning capital to buy back the family estate.[20] John Sholto and his children were born at Falkenhorst, the family home in Thüringen. However, they considered themselves Scottish by nationality and took pride in being "the oldest country-family in Kincardineshire," even if they chose not to live in their gloomy old castle.

Neither the Poellnitzes nor the Douglasses wished to be brought down by association with a common housepainter by profession like Jakob Jehly. It was this concern that ultimately brought an end to Douglas's idyllic childhood. After Vanda and Jehly were engaged, Baron von Poellnitz banned his daughter from his home in Bregenz, and John Sholto's mother, Jane Kennedy Douglass, wrote letters demanding custody of the grandchildren. Vanda resisted, but without support from her own family, she was ultimately pressured into a compromise. She kept Mary, while the two boys were sent to school in England.[21]

Douglas wrote extensively about his school years in his 1933 memoir *Looking Back*. He recalled them bitterly. As he saw it, he was cast out of golden paradise into gray purgatory. In his memories, it was perpetually gloomy in Staffordshire, where his first school, Yarlet Hall, was located. But the weather wasn't his main complaint. Douglas hated the conformity and bullying that defined the English boarding school system. When he arrived at Yarlet Hall,

3. Norman Douglas, age six. Private collection of Deirdre Sholto Douglas. Photograph by author.

he spoke English haltingly with an Austrian accent, which made him the tar-
get of fellow students. The schoolmaster at Yarlet Hall was a violent man, a
"worm in human form." Half a century later, Douglas confessed that "if some-
body were to assure me officially that he had died of a lingering and painful
disease I should rejoice from the bottom of my heart." Life improved in 1879,
when Douglas moved to private tutelage at Mowsley Rectory, in Leicester-
shire. At Mowsley he had time to be alone, wandering the small valley where
the rectory was set, bird-watching and collecting stones. In his memories, "it
was always summer at Mowsley." Then in 1881, at age twelve, Douglas was sent
to join his older brother at Uppingham School in Rutland, which was just as
brutalizing as Yarlet.[22] "I wonder how much they would have to pay me to be
an English private-school boy again," Douglas wrote with distaste. He used
the line for his August 12 entry in *An Almanac*.[23]

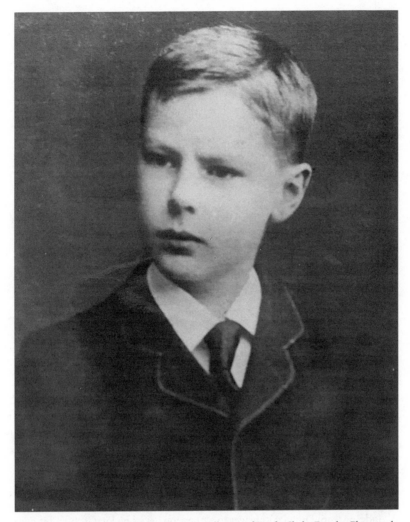

4. Norman Douglas, Uppingham period. Private collection of Deirdre Sholto Douglas. Photograph by author.

And yet, Douglas's school years were not without their pleasures. Some were intellectual, such as his investigations into natural history—an interest that would occupy him into his thirties. Others were intimate, to be found in connection with fellow students. Douglas told Constantine FitzGibbon, who worked on a biography about him during the late 1940s, that the boys' main form of recreation at Uppingham was "sexual malpractice."[24]

One scholar has described schoolboy encounters as "perhaps *the* formative sexual experience for middle-class men" in nineteenth-century England.[25] Relationships between schoolboys were often age-structured, with older, more sexually mature boys forming intimacies with younger, less sexually mature boys.[26] Douglas had a "familiar" friendship at Uppingham with an older boy named Harry S. Collier. The two boys took long walks together through the fields and woods surrounding Uppingham, and may have used those private times for erotic encounters.[27] Such relationships provoked little public concern until the late nineteenth century.[28]

The sexual dynamics in schoolboy relationships tended toward touching and mutual masturbation rather than anal penetration.[29] That was likely the experience of Douglas, who decades later jokingly referred to Uppingham as "Suckingham."[30] Pornographic representations of boarding school relationships spun fantastic stories of penetrative daisy chains. The year that Douglas was sent to Uppingham, the first gay pornographic novel ever published in English appeared, featuring tales of boarding school orgies. *The Sins of the Cities of the Plain* was the ostensibly real-life story of Jack Saul, who worked as a rent boy in London during the 1870s. It begins with the hero's first night in boarding school, at age ten, when he is initiated into anal sex by his fourteen-year-old bedmate. The book continues with Saul's sexual adventures in a wide variety of locations—the milking shed, the gentleman's club, et cetera—before finishing up with an appendix that returns to the boarding school setting.[31] Boarding school romances also inspired more literary works, such as the early gay novel *Tim* (1891), which the author Howard Overing Sturgis set at Eton, his alma mater. His heroes, a younger boy and his older friend, never consummate their love beyond a single kiss. Sturgis's novel was delicate enough to attract the admiration of Edith Wharton and Henry James.[32] Douglas's experiences probably fell somewhere in between those of Jack Saul and Tim.

Judging from Douglas's answer to a question asked by FitzGibbon, his own erotic experiences at Uppingham involved touching but not anal sex. Douglas told FitzGibbon that he hated Uppingham so much that after two years he wrote to his mother threatening to get himself expelled if she wouldn't let him leave voluntarily. FitzGibbon pressed Douglas: "Was sodomy the threat?" No, Douglas answered, it was "sexual malpractice. Not sodomy."[33] It's ambiguous how Douglas or FitzGibbon defined sodomy in this exchange, or whether they defined the word the same way. FitzGibbon, who was born in the twentieth century, probably understood sodomy in contemporary terms to mean anal penetration. Douglas may have shared this understanding, and by answering "sexual malpractice," he could have meant that he intended to get caught engaging in mutual masturbation or another non-penetrative act like intercrural (thigh) sex.

On the other hand, Douglas may have hewed to an older definition of sodomy as extending to any non-reproductive sex, including mutual mastur-bation.[34] In that case, his answer to FitzGibbon that he didn't mean to be caught for sodomy might have meant he intended to be caught committing a non-physical offense. For example, Douglas could have planned to be dis-covered with a suggestive letter. In 1858 the future homosexual rights advo-cate John Addington Symonds, then a student at Harrow School, revealed suggestive letters that the headmaster Charles Vaughan had sent to another student, forcing Vaughan to resign.[35] If Douglas's plan was simply to incrim-inate himself with a letter, it's possible that he didn't actually participate in Uppingham's culture of sexual malpractice. But knowing Douglas, it's hard to imagine. His policy was always to yield.

As the Vaughan affair suggests, sexual encounters between students and teachers, as well, were a familiar element of nineteenth-century English school culture. Local newspapers carried stories of British grammar school teachers prosecuted for sexual misconduct with their pupils.[36] Elite boarding schools took more private measures against teachers to avoid public scandal. It's likely that Douglas witnessed encounters between teachers and students at Yarlet Hall. He told FitzGibbon that the teachers there were "sex-starved" and so "miserably underpaid" that they couldn't even afford prostitutes.[37] His implication was that the teachers turned to their students for sex, although FitzGibbon's notes are not clear on the matter (perhaps intentionally).

Some elite male teachers idealized their erotic attraction to young male students within the Hellenic framework of *pederasty*, defined as a romantic mentor-mentee relationship between teacher and student.[38] According to this logic, a teacher's love for his student was integral to the educative process. The Hellenic ideal erased the potential violence within teacher-student sexual re-lations, by depicting the pederastic dynamic as primarily emotional rather than physical. Douglas likely encountered this pederastic ideal during his English school years and absorbed its ethos. As an adult, Douglas became friendly with several people who were closely connected to the nineteenth-century Eton schoolteacher most responsible for romanticizing classical ped-erasty, the poet William Johnson Cory.

In 1872 Eton dismissed Cory because of suspicions that had arisen about his relationships with pupils. His niece Faith Compton Mackenzie, who was a close friend of Douglas, wrote a biography of Cory in which she discussed the scandal. She acknowledged that he had loved his students, "perhaps, too well." His relationships with students were "romantic" and "brimming with sentiment," but Mackenzie chalked it up to the soft emotionalism of the era. Back then "a letter could be headed 'Beloved' and mean less than 'Darling' does now." Unfortunately, a parent who "did not understand Platonic friendship" complained and Cory was dismissed.[39] After he left Eton, Cory became famous for his neo-Hellenic poetry. His writings contributed to a queer English subculture that idealized the ancient Greeks.[40] Douglas had several male friends who had been influenced by their youthful friendships with Cory, including the writers Edward Hutton and E. F. Benson and the politician Lord Rosebery.[41] When Douglas died, several of his friends thought it fitting to eulogize him by quoting Cory's most famous poem, a translation of Heraclitus's epitaph.[42]

In the Hellenic model, pederastic relationships between older men and younger boys operated within a framework of heterosexual socialization. The relationships began at the onset of puberty. As boys reached sexual maturity, signaled by the development of body hair, their older lovers were supposed to encourage them to form erotic relationships with women. A similar logic operated in the nineteenth century, situating boys' same-sex encounters as a stage to be followed by mature sexual encounters with girls and women. In Looking Back, Douglas depicted his own sexual development as following this model.

After Douglas left Uppingham in 1883, he enrolled at a gymnasium in Karlsruhe, the lively capital of the Grand Duchy of Baden. Initially, he lived with his mother, stepfather, sister, and new baby half-sister, who had all moved to Karlsruhe along with him. Later, when his family moved back to Vorarlberg, he migrated through a series of boardinghouses, eventually settling in a pension run by two old Prussian women, one of whom had a drinking problem that left Douglas free to do as he pleased. Liberated from the stifling atmosphere of the British boarding school, Douglas threw himself into romances with the city's girls and women.

Douglas boasts about his youthful affairs in Looking Back, which engages in a fair amount of self-mythologizing. The memoir is nothing like the torrid pornographic autobiography privately printed by his friend, the notorious journalist Frank Harris, and passed from hand to hand between the world wars.[43] Harris took his career as a lothario extremely seriously. He described

5. Norman Douglas, Karlsruhe period, 1885. From *Looking Back* (1933).

himself, from earliest childhood, as an earnest devotee at the altar of the female body. Douglas, on the other hand, regarded his younger self with a sense of humor. He had been a good-looking kid, clear-skinned, thick-haired, and well-built. He had money, manners, and a name. In short, he had all the qualities that might make a young man insufferable to be around. "Such was my vanity in those days that I expected all girls to fall in love with me," he confessed.[44] In *Looking Back*, Douglas did not hide the fact that he had been a callow youth.

As might be expected for a young man of his elite status, Douglas felt entitled to pursue erotic encounters with girls and women all along the social spectrum. He flirted with female students who attended several of the elite girls' schools in Karlsruhe. He also met girls at the boardinghouses where well-to-do young ladies stayed. He suffered a terrible put-down from Elsie Macleod, the daughter of the celebrity clergyman Norman Macleod, who had served as a chaplain to Queen Victoria.[45] Another aristocratic girl, Violet Sherbrooke, was more receptive to his overtures. When their relationship became too physically intense, Douglas broke it off, for fear of getting into a situation from which he couldn't extricate himself. The two remained on friendly terms, however, and he visited Sherbrooke later when she was married.[46]

A third relationship with an elite girl resulted in an engagement. At Karlsruhe, Douglas became intimate friends with an Italian student named Luigi Guerrieri-Gonzaga, who was a member of the noble family of Mantua. Their relationship inspired Douglas to take Italian lessons. He traveled home with Guerrieri-Gonzaga on numerous occasions, visiting the family's historic palazzo in Lombardy, as well as their home on the Via Venti Settembre in Rome. During these visits, he met Luigi's two younger sisters, Sofia and Maria, who were considered great beauties. Douglas and Sofia became engaged in 1889, when she was fifteen and he was twenty.

Throughout his life, Douglas held on to a photograph of Sofia as a young girl—probably taken around the time he first met her. Dressed for a masquerade, Sofia appears in a Grecian tunic, wearing a headdress of flowers and holding a lute. The photograph, which captures her dress slipping off one shoulder, mixes innocence and eroticism, echoing Charles Dodgson's photos of Alice Liddell.[47] Sofia's personification of this Victorian aesthetic of desirable childhood attracted several adult male admirers besides Douglas. Around the time that she and Douglas were engaged, she was also courted by the future Nobel Prize–winning French writer Romain Rolland, who was two years older than Douglas.[48] Sofia resisted Rolland's overtures. She and Douglas remained engaged until 1895.[49] Douglas never explained why it ended. Afterward, Sofia married a notable Italian statesman, Pietro Bertolini, who was twenty years her senior.

Whatever his desires, Douglas's physical relations with elite girls could only go so far. For sex, privileged young men like Douglas turned to lower-class girls whom they met in shops and brothels. *Looking Back* also includes stories of Douglas's experiences with Karlsruhe's working women. For ex-

6. Sofia Guerrieri-Gonzaga. Private collection of Deirdre Sholto Douglas. Photograph by author.

ample, he and his friend Arthur Baumstark had relationships with two sisters who worked at a grocery opposite the gymnasium. The women were in their late twenties, a full decade older than the boys. Since the sisters shared a room and had little time off, both couples often used the room for sex at the same time, which Douglas called "a sound education."[50] Although he didn't explicitly say as much in his memoir, the arrangement probably involved an exchange of cash or gifts.

Douglas denied visiting Karlsruhe's regulated prostitutes, who worked from brothels located on Kleine Spitalstrasse. Baumstark told him they weren't suitable for "a gentleman." Douglas knew the street well enough, calling it "really a horrible hole."[51] Students were frequent visitors there, and often made lots of noise, upsetting the neighbors.[52] But if Douglas can be believed, he wasn't a customer. He did admit to visiting a brothel once on his way home from school for Christmas vacation, but he was so obnoxious that the prostitutes kicked him out. It's possible, he wrote, that "I gave myself airs, which was not unlikely at my age."[53] Douglas didn't soft-pedal his self-portrait of the artist as a young man. He typified the Victorian double standard that demanded sexual continence of privileged young women, while licensing privileged young men to exploit poor girls and women.

Douglas broke from his peers, however, by not aging out of his erotic attraction to boys, even as he expanded his erotic repertoire to include girls and women. At Karlsruhe he continued to form intimacies with other boys, like H. Wohlgemut, "a slender child" with "lively dark eyes." The two were "joined by one of those sterile but exquisite attachments of boyhood, when nothing is done, nothing even said; and everything taken for granted."[54] They took long bicycle rides together through the Rhine woods northwest of the city. During their explorations, Douglas kept notes on the wildlife, which would later become the basis of his earliest publications in scientific magazines.[55] Douglas held on to a photograph taken in Karlsruhe labeled "Henry," which might be H. Wohlgemut as an adult. He kept the photograph with pictures of his lovers.

There were other boys at Karlsruhe whom Douglas desired. Hermann Gilg, "a sturdy fair-haired lad," was a great athlete, and Douglas recalled that "we were all in love with him." Another boy, Ruthven Wilshire, was "a good-looking young fellow." On the other hand, Wilhelm Händel, who shared Douglas's interest in the natural sciences, was "of no interest to me from the aesthetic point of view." As Douglas entered his late adolescence, he was self-aware about his ongoing attraction to boys.[56]

The first memory that Douglas included in *Looking Back* suggests that he began feeling a sense of queer kinship around the time he was seventeen. The memory was triggered by the calling card of Frau Stephanie Schenkh, his Italian teacher.[57] According to his recollection, Douglas was at Schenkh's house in June 1886 when he heard news that King Ludwig II of Bavaria had drowned. Ludwig, "the Swan King," was a famous bachelor aesthete who surrounded himself with male friends instead of marrying. After his death, rumors spread that he had been murdered. The news made a strong impression on Douglas, but, as he confessed at the close of the passage, his memory of being at Schenkh's house when he heard about Ludwig was false. His daily diary from 1886 revealed he was somewhere else at the time. Douglas's placement of this false memory at the beginning of his memoir pointed toward a figurative truth, rather than a literal one. The key to Douglas's life lay in the connection between Ludwig and Italian, between his queerness and his choice to immerse himself in a Mediterranean culture that was more tolerant of sex between males than northern Europe, where a monarch could be murdered for his tastes.[58]

Douglas graduated from gymnasium in 1889, when he was twenty years old, and left Karlsruhe for good. He never chose to live in a German-speaking country again, but he never left Karlsruhe entirely behind. Memories of those years overwhelm his memoir, despite his long and eventful life. To judge from the pages of *Looking Back*, Douglas admitted, "I might have spent a third of my life as a schoolboy in Karlsruhe."[59] The intellectual interests that he developed there—in the Italian language, the natural sciences, and the classical world—continued to absorb him after he graduated. So did his early erotic interests. After graduation, he moved without interruption from having youthful affairs with young people into adult affairs with young people.[60] And not only did Douglas remain drawn to children, but he continued to describe his desires in the same language that he had used when he was a student.

One last story from *Looking Back*, as illustration: Among Douglas's many flirtations in Karlsruhe was a girl named Mabel Ninds, who attended the same school as his sister, Mary. When the schoolgirls went outside, their teacher made them walk two-by-two in a long line, a formation known in British slang as a "crocodile."[61] Douglas would watch the crocodile go by and whistle for Mabel. The girls were not supposed to look up from the sidewalk when they were out in public, so Mabel had to be sneaky when she smiled back at Douglas. This game made all the girls laugh.[62] Douglas recounted this story with great humor, Ninds thought. She wrote Douglas a fan letter after *Looking Back* was published, telling him, "My daughter joined me in a good laugh over the 'crocodile episode' which I remember well."[63] She might have been less inclined to laugh if she knew that ever since those days, Douglas had called the children he had sex with *crocodiles*, a semantic choice that was pleasing to Douglas both because of his childhood associations and also, probably, because in Italy (where many of his crocodilian affairs took place), the word for the overgrown reptile is *coccodrillo*, inspiring an obvious pun for dirty-minded Anglophones.

Here lies the challenge to writing about Douglas's childhood. Everything is overshadowed by what came later. It would be easy to construct a sympathetic narrative about how Douglas, as a boy, was left to his own devices after the death of his father and the remarriage of his mother, and consequently became a radical independent thinker. But Douglas's radical independent thinking led to his adult refusal to be bound by moral sexual injunctions. The youthful flirtations that Douglas included in *Looking Back* could be stitched together into an engaging narrative of the coming of age of a sexual radical. But Douglas continued seeking sex with children and youths throughout his adult life, which casts his earlier romances in a dark light. In essence, it's impossible to laugh with Ninds and her daughter over the crocodile episode, if you know that Douglas later called the ten-year-old boys he was attracted to "crocodiles."

The story of Douglas the man overshadows the story of Douglas the boy, but it was the experiences of the boy that determined the life of the man. It's fair to say that throughout his life Douglas remained not just fixated on his childhood, but fixed in it. When he was growing up, it was normal for sex to be structured by inequality, whether of class, gender, age, ethnicity, race, or some combination of all of the former. Even erotic encounters between children were structured by age inequalities. Attitudes began shifting around the time Douglas reached adulthood. At the end of the nineteenth century, John Addington Symonds and other early advocates of homosexual rights embraced a new model of same-sex love structured by ideals of equality and reciprocity as part of a strategy to win acceptance. "We cannot be Greeks now," Symonds wrote.[64] But Douglas remained enamored of the past. He refused to abandon the pleasures of childhood, or children.

CHAPTER TWO

Lizards

The *Podarcis sicula coerulea* is a very distinctive lizard. Unlike its green cousin *Podarcis muralis*, the ordinary wall lizard, *P. sicula coerulea* is a shocking blue. The blue of its underbelly has an electric tint like the blue of the Mediterranean Sea that laps the rock where it lives. *P. sicula coerulea* can only be found on the outermost of the Faraglioni, the three looming rocks that emerge from the waters off Capri's southernmost point, la Punta di Tragara. Gustav Heinrich Theodor Eimer, professor of zoology at the University of Tübingen, first observed *P. sicula coerulea* when he was invalided in Capri in 1870, following his service in the Franco-Prussian War. Eimer theorized that the lizard's blue color was an adaptation to the rock island's lack of vegetation. The color camouflaged the lizard within its setting of rock and sea.[1]

Douglas bought Eimer's book on the variations of wall lizards in February 1887.[2] He was at the height of his mania for naturalism, and Eimer's work enthralled him, despite the denseness of the writing. Douglas was especially intrigued by Eimer's application of Darwinian theory to an isolate species inhabiting an archipelago far closer to home than the Galápagos. Longing to lay eyes on the *P. Sicula coerulea* for himself, Douglas embarked on his first trip to Italy in March 1888 in the company of his older brother, John.

Before Douglas left, he wrote to his grandmother Jane Douglass, "I have been studying my Baedeker very diligently and already <u>seem</u> to know my way about Naples quite well."[3] Baedeker published the best-known travel guides of the nineteenth century. They steered wealthy travelers to critical works of art and architecture.[4] It was Baedeker's advice that led Douglas to visit the Vatican Museum in Rome. There he "gloated" at one of the treasures of the Vatican's classical collection, a marble sculpture of Laocoön and his sons that had been praised by Pliny the Elder.[5] Another sculpture in the collection also caught his eye. Douglas was curious to see the *Apollo Sauroctonus*, which was mentioned in Eimer's work. The complicated story of the significance that the *Apollo Sauroctonus* had for Douglas shines a light onto the rich cultural framework of pederasty during the late nineteenth century.

Carved from marble, in imitation of an earlier bronze cast by the legendary Greek sculptor Praxiteles, the Vatican's *Apollo Sauroctonus* depicts a graceful male youth leaning against a tree trunk, watching a lizard crawl upward to his left hand. Archaeologists thought that the statue once held an arrow that the youthful Apollo intended to use to stab the lizard and then divine the future. However the arms in the Vatican's copy were later restorations. In a passage concerning the *Lacerta muralis coerulea*, Eimer hypothesized that the *Apollo Sauroctonus* depicted the god in the act of capturing a lizard with a grass noose, a method still used by boys in Capri at the time of Eimer's writing. He justified his theory by quoting a Greek epigram by the ancient poet Martial that referred to the Praxiteles statue.[6]

The Martial epigram came from a collection of ancient poetry known as *The Greek Anthology*, which spanned the classical and Byzantine periods of Greek literature. The *Anthology* was ubiquitous to the nineteenth-century gentleman's education. It was also a favorite book for well-educated pederasts because its twelfth volume, subtitled *The Musa Paedika* or *Musa Puerilis*, contained 258 epigrams on the subject of erotic encounters between boys and men. The *Paedika* poems remained untranslated in the nineteenth century, which allowed those in the know to use references to the Greek text as a shorthand to allude to pederasty without broaching public decorum. This is the approach that Eimer took in the footnote to his passage on the *Apollo Sauroctonus*, which quoted the relevant lines from the *Paedika* only in the ancient Greek.

Douglas understood and appreciated Eimer's reference to the *Paedika*. Forty years after he first laid eyes on the *Apollo Sauroctonus* at the Vatican Museum, he returned to the statue in a 1928 work titled *Birds and Beasts of the Greek Anthology*. In this whimsical catalog of all the animals mentioned in the ancient poetry collection, Douglas questioned whether the statue represented Apollo at all, or was just meant to depict an ordinary boy in the act of catching a lizard. To support his own interpretation, Douglas also quoted Martial's epigram about the statue: "Ad te reptanti, puer insidiose, lacertae / Parce; cupit *digitis* illa perire tuis."[7] Douglas, like Eimer, didn't translate the

7. *Apollo Sauroctonus*. Roman copy after a bronze original ca. 360 BCE by Praxiteles. Louvre Museum. Wikimedia Commons.

lines. But in a later book, *Late Harvest* (1946), he offered readers instructions on where they could find a translation of Martial that would unlock the meaning of the statue: "The correct, and improper, interpretation of these lines is given on p. 194 and its footnote of H. Licht's *Sexual Life in Ancient Greece* (Routledge, 1932)."[8]

Hans Licht was the pseudonym of Paul Brandt, a professor at Leipzig University and the author of *Sexual Life in Ancient Greece*, first published in England in 1932. This history argued that sex played a central role within Hellenic culture. Writing under the protection of a pseudonym, Brandt openly discussed classical pederasty. To illustrate his discussion, he included a photograph of the Vatican's copy of *Apollo Sauroctonus* and translated Martial in full: "Spare the lizard creeping towards you; it desires to fade away in your fingers." According to Brandt, the statue did not represent Apollo hunting a lizard, but enticing it into play, "until it perishes from desire and love under his coaxing finger." The verb *perire*, according to Brandt, meant "to pass away in love, to be madly in love." Moreover, the Greek word for lizard referred to the penis, "and by preference that of a boy or young man."[9] In short, the sculpture of the beautiful youth leaning against a tree being climbed by a lizard was a representation, on many levels, of the erotic allure of male youths.

Douglas's trip to Italy in 1888, he said later, marked an "epoch" for him: "But for this episode, decided upon at a moment's notice, my subsequent life would have been different."[10] His search for a species of lizard brought Douglas to an island, Capri, that had been notorious since ancient times for the sexual availability of its children.[11] Eimer had observed that the boys of Capri still used grass nooses to catch lizards. Douglas would discover that the island's boys were still amenable to encounters with adult men. For the rest of his life, Douglas linked lizards and boys and Italy together. Visiting Italy exposed him to a dense network of pederastic cultural associations that attracted great numbers of northern European male tourists during the late nineteenth century. His first trip to Capri was short, but it guaranteed that he would return.

At the end of his spring break, Douglas returned to Karlsruhe for his exams. The next year he moved to Paris to study French in preparation for applying to the British Foreign Office.[12] While in Paris, Douglas had an opportunity to examine the Louvre's copy of the *Apollo Sauroctonus*, listed in Baedeker's along with the morgue, another popular tourist attraction.[13] In 1890 Douglas moved to London to continue his studies for the Foreign Office examination. Meanwhile, he set to work preparing his research on lizards for publication. He had already contributed a handful of brief notes on color variation within corvid species to the *Zoologist*, a monthly naturalist journal printed in London.[14] The new essay was far longer—so extensive that it had to be published serially over seven issues of the *Zoologist* throughout 1891. "On the Herpetology of the Grand Duchy of Baden" shared his earlier notes' central concerns.

Douglas counted himself a strong "evolutionist," but he questioned Charles Darwin's theory of sexual selection and thought that observation of the color variations among lizards supported his doubts.[15] External environments, Douglas argued, rather than female sexual choice, explained where lizards got their hues. "The Herpetology of the Grand Duchy of Baden" took the form of a catalog—which became one of Douglas's favorite genres. It proceeded species by species through the lizards and snakes of Baden, scrutinizing the color variations between males and females within each species. Not until the third installment did Douglas tip his hand about the purpose of his catalog. In a section on Colubrine snakes, Douglas staked his claim: "I am disinclined to call to aid the cumulative effects of female preference, for it can hardly be supposed that a simultaneous and almost identical change of aesthetic tastes should be taking place in many of the females of several distinct species."[16] Not yet ready to launch a direct attack on Darwin's theory of sexual selection, Douglas returned in the following essays to simply describing the evidence. Later, Douglas would write more extensively about his opposition to the theory of female-guided sexual selection, extending his critique to humans as well as reptiles. Research into the natural sciences was deeply entangled with ideas about sex and sexuality in the eighteenth and nineteenth centuries.[17] Douglas participated in this tradition.

Amid his studies for the Foreign Office exam, and his research trips to collect lizard samples for scientific inquiries, Douglas kept up a busy social life, attending dinners, operas, concerts, and dances, as well as rendezvous with a variety of women.[18] "I often found it difficult to remain faithful to a single person, where women are concerned," Douglas admitted.[19] As in Karlsruhe, Douglas pursued affairs at all points along the social spectrum. He expressed enthusiastic appreciation for the girls and young women who worked the city's retail counters. "Shopgirls" were the subject of great sexual fascination in late Victorian London.[20] This emerging class of working women, who labored in the city's swiftly multiplying stores, figured prominently in the era's novels and plays. Romances often pictured the shopgirl as a young woman from refined but straitened circumstances who was waiting for a well-off male customer to marry her and restore her to domestic bliss.[21] In actuality, many shopgirls were working-class young women who saw their wealthier male customers as tickets to the city's new entertainments, like pleasure gardens, which they couldn't afford on their own meager wages. Men's invitations often came with the expectation of sexual favors. This quid pro quo arrangement was known as "treating."[22] It was an arrangement that suited Douglas.

In spring 1892, Douglas picked up a girl named Cora who worked at a milliner's shop in Richmond. Their relationship began as a light flirtation, a mere "joke" in Douglas's words, but he soon began acting like the hero of a sentimental romance, meeting Cora three times a week at Ellerker Gardens Road so they could go for walks together through Richmond's Terrace Gardens. In Douglas's eyes, Cora personified all the romantic qualities of the archetypal shopgirl. "She was so pretty, so different from the society girls one ran after! She talked so endearingly!" Douglas reminisced. Despite his romantic self-stylings, Douglas had no intention of committing to Cora. He was still engaged at that point to Sofia Guerrieri-Gonzaga. Fearful that the affair with Cora would soon lead him "into serious trouble"—by which he likely meant pregnancy—Douglas left for a trip to Greece without a word of farewell.[23]

Douglas's told this story in *Looking Back* as a conventional seduction narrative. The affair typified the cavalier sexual exploitation of working-class women that was routine among young men of means in late Victorian London. It established Douglas's claim to a type of ultra-masculinity defined by sexual adventuring. In the context of today's sexual system, which organizes sexual identity according to gender and age preferences, Douglas's affair with Cora seems to conflict with his later preference for boys. One might be tempted to view the Cora affair as evidence that during his early twenties Douglas had either not yet developed, or not yet acknowledged, his orientation toward children. By the standards of the 1890s, however, sexual identity could still be organized according to scale rather than gender or age preference. There were people who had a lot of sexual encounters, of various types, and people who contained their sexual desire within strict boundaries, defined by marriage. The Cora affair showed Douglas to be one of the former types, a sexual libertine.

His model of sexual libertinage owed more to robust romantics, like Lord Byron, than to sickly late nineteenth-century aesthetes, like Aubrey

8. Norman Douglas, 1892. Photo taken in Richmond. Perhaps a gift for Cora? From *Looking Back* (1933).

Beardsley.[24] While Douglas was living in London in the early 1890s, a literary movement known as Decadence was in full swing, associated with Beardsley, Oscar Wilde, and other contributors to the infamous literary quarterly the *Yellow Book*. The Decadent aesthetic was morbid, anti-naturalist, highly mannered, and sexually perverse. Douglas, while an aspiring libertine, did not mingle with the Decadents. His interests remained entirely scientific for the time, rather than literary. He didn't identify with Beardsley as a man who stood apart from society. Douglas's hedonism, as Constantine FitzGibbon argued, was "that of the Victorian gentleman, not of the eighteenth century diabolist or of the twentieth century experimenter." He was "never anti-social," but rather a man of his society.[25]

Douglas substantiated his identity as a developing libertine in other stories of seduction he told from the early 1890s. He chased after a fourteen-year-old cousin, the daughter of the Irish art collector and politician William Massey-Mainwaring. "Here was a *pièce de musée* after my own heart," he waxed nostalgic in *Looking Back*. "She was inclined to be a little fast, and I tried my utmost to make her still faster, but, haphazard as the family was, nobody ever knowing what anybody else was doing or going to do, the mother, alas, was too sharp for me."[26] Not to be discouraged, Douglas also flirted with another member of the family, a girl of twenty. His casual disregard for the incest taboo fit within the libertine model. The pornography of the Marquis de Sade, which Douglas read, was full of incest stories.[27]

Not so surprisingly, Douglas's sexual misadventures led him to contract syphilis in 1892. He told his onetime literary executor William "Willie" King that he caught the disease "from a lady in Radclyffe Square and it lasted off + on till his marriage."[28] But he told FitzGibbon that he had contracted it in a hackney carriage on the Albert Bridge, coming back from the races.[29] It's possible that these two accounts refer to the same event, since the Albert Bridge lies not far from Chelsea's "Redcliffe Square," which then, as now, was an expensive address appropriate to a "lady." Despite the disease's deleterious neurological effects, Douglas successfully passed the Foreign Office exam in January 1893.[30] After a year of further training in London, he requested a posting to St. Petersburg.

Is it any surprise that the motivation for going to Russia was a lizard? Not just any lizard, but the sheltopusik, a legless lizard also known as a glass snake. "But for the Sheltopusik my whole life might have been different," Douglas speculated.[31] It's a minor irony that a creature as phallic as a legless lizard played such an important role in determining Douglas's life course. He had wanted to collect a sheltopusik ever since he was fifteen and first read about the unusual reptile in the German zoologist Peter Simon Pallas's three-volume account of his travels through Russia during the 1770s. It was this book that inspired Douglas to take Russian lessons in Karlsruhe, and which later qualified him for a posting to Russia. Soon after his arrival in St. Peters-burg, in March 1894, he embarked on a series of naturalist journeys, through Finland, eastern Europe, and Anatolia, in search of specimens.

Douglas combined his lizard hunting with prowling for sex. In *Looking Back*, Douglas included the calling card of a British officer who joined him on his specimen-collecting trip to Anatolia, which prompted a memory of a restaurant in Smyrna where "you could pick up a girl or anything else you fancied." In Willie King's annotated copy of the memoir, a penciled excla-mation mark follows this observation.[32] Such offhand allusions to noncon-ventional sexual tastes indicate that Douglas's sexuality was never limited by gender, even during the height of his womanizing. The city of Smyrna was associated with a famous story of classical pederasty, as like-minded readers of *Looking Back* would have known. The city was home in the seventh cen-tury BCE to a beautiful youth named Magnes, who was the *paidika* (boy fa-vorite) of the Lydian king Gyges, founder of the Mermnad dynasty. The rela-tionship between Magnes and Gyges was described by Nicolaus of Damascus and retold later in nineteenth-century scholarship.[33] The pederastic implica-tions of Douglas's reference to the availability of "anything else you fancied" in Smyrna were reinforced by Orientalist narratives of the era, by authors like Sir Richard Burton, which linked the Middle East with beautiful boys.[34] Ac-cording to Burton, Turkey and the Middle East fell within the "Sotadic Zone," where boy love was common.[35] Douglas admired Burton, who died in 1890, and he bemoaned the fact that Burton's small-minded wife, Isabel, had disin-terred his body from Trieste, where he died, and transported it beyond the Sotadic Zone to be buried in Mortlake Catholic cemetery, in southwest Lon-don.[36]

Douglas's scientific and sexual adventuring inspired further scholarly out-put. In fall 1895, he published two essays in *Natural Science* elaborating his ar-gument against the theory of sexual selection. As evidence of the mechanism's irrelevancy among humans, Douglas observed that the "gradual diminution of the xanthous complexion to the advantage of a darker stock" could not be explained through the "cumulative action of female preferences."[37] In other

words, women weren't choosing darker-skinned lovers over light-skinned lovers. This tidbit of racialism was fairly atypical for Douglas, if entirely in keeping with the times. Douglas's dogged pursuit of affairs with girls and women
likely influenced his skepticism about the impact of female preference on evolution. He was too committed to his own self-image as a seducer to accept a
theory that emphasized female choice. One young girl he flirted with during
his Russian posting later recalled, "I think he regarded love as a sort of campaign."[38] In Russia, he collected lovers like lizards.

One of the most important of his affairs resulted from Douglas's unhappy
discovery that his Russian-language skills lacked the idiomatic finesse required of a skilled diplomat. His friend General Nikolai Obruchev, governor
of Transcaucasia, suggested a pleasurable means to improve his fluency. In
Looking Back, Douglas alludes to this method by saying that "the French have
coined a vulgar but expressive phrase" for the technique. He later supplied
that phrase to Willie King: *coucher avec son dictionnaire*.[39] To sleep with one's
dictionary. Obruchev had recommended that Douglas learn the language
from a mistress.

Not just any mistress. Obruchev suggested that Douglas follow a local
practice of contracting with a family for the sexual services of one of their
daughters. According to Obruchev, "You pay so much a year to the parents,
quite a small sum, and they set her aside for you, and for you alone, till she
has reached the proper age." When the arrangement concluded, "you could
pass her on afterwards to some husband, or send her back to the family."[40]
Late nineteenth-century Russian literature includes numerous stories of families selling girls into prostitution, and of women using prostitution to earn
dowries. Once again, Douglas was taking part in well-established social practices.[41] Before Obruchev made his suggestion, Douglas had pursued affairs in
St. Petersburg with upper-class Russian women and the daughters of diplo-
mats. But those romances were conducted in French or German or English,
not in idiomatic Russian. Douglas agreed to Obruchev's suggestion, and the
general set out to procure a girl. A week later, Anyuta Ponomareva presented
herself at Douglas's house.[42]

How old was Ponomareva? Douglas, who was twenty-six when the affair
took place, described Ponomareva as his "little Russian girl."[43] Ponomareva
was young enough to be considered a girl, but old enough for her family to
consider her a suitable age to become a man's mistress. According to an 1889
study, 39 percent of brothel prostitutes in Russia were under the age of twenty.
The legal minimum age at the time for licensed prostitutes was sixteen, but

many younger children, including prepubescent girls, also earned a living from selling sex. A physician who worked at a St. Petersburg hospital claimed that, at the turn of the century, child prostitution was "no longer considered perverse or unusual."[44] Judging from a photo given by Ponomareva to Douglas, however, she was post-pubescent at the time their relationship began and very likely in her late teens. The photo of Ponomareva shows that she was not a young child, but it is impossible to know if she was a mature fourteen or a youthful twenty-four. She was young enough to call Douglas "little daddy" as a nickname (Pusin'ka in Russian), but old enough to be considered a desirable lover by several other men, as she revealed in a couple of Russian-language letters to Douglas written during and after their affair.[45]

Douglas's biographer Mark Holloway called Ponomareva's letters "charming and affecting."[46] That depends on perspective. The letters, which expressed Ponomareva's affection for Douglas, might be charming at first glance, but on reflection they're disturbing. As historians of letter-writing have argued, the expression of affection within letters frequently functioned as a tool to achieve specific ends.[47] And there can be no doubt that Ponomareva had material needs that she hoped Douglas would fulfill. On the other hand, historians should be cautious about imposing their own attitudes on their historical subjects. It's possible that Ponomareva's expressions of affections were sincere as well as utilitarian, and that a girl raised in a culture where contractual relations, like the one she had with Douglas, were typical might have positive feelings for her partner, especially when those relations were sanctioned by her family.

Ponomareva's two surviving letters suggest a relationship with Douglas that was both mercenary and warm. In one of the letters, Ponomareva asked Douglas for a bicycle. In another she remarked on the poverty of her lover, perhaps hinting that Douglas should send money.[48] During the late 1890s, Douglas was quite flush, combining income received from the family mill with his Foreign Office salary. But this evidence that Ponomareva sought gifts from Douglas doesn't mean she didn't also have feelings for him. Quite the opposite, Ponomareva may have wanted the gifts as proof of Douglas's affection for her. That's how he regarded a gift she gave to him, of a silver-topped Malacca walking stick engraved with a Chinese scene of a gathering of Mandarins beneath the trees. Douglas held on to the cane for decades, as a tender reminder of this "endearing companion" whom he claimed to have made "happy" during their time together.[49]

"You ask me whether I am happy now," Ponomareva wrote to Douglas after he left St. Petersburg. "I am happy only because I have everything, I do not need stuff, but my heart is broken." She wrote the undated letter no more than a year after Douglas's departure, since in its pages she recalled how a year before she had broken up with her lover and "I remember how I cried those days at your place." After Douglas left, Ponomareva wrote, "I do not love anyone, and this is why I often think about the past." She was being kept by a new man, who gave her two hundred rubles a month (the modern equivalent of several thousand dollars) and made only a handful of visits. But she missed the intimacy of her connection with Douglas. The new lover, she complained, "is kind to me, but I have no idea what he really thinks. I'd prefer to know his heart than to receive money."[50] She begged Douglas to keep her letter private, giving the impression that she was unburdening her heart to someone she trusted.

If anything, the letters convey a sense that Ponomareva's feelings for Douglas were stronger than his for her. Both of her letters expressed longing to see Douglas, and disappointment that he had not made an effort to meet her. In one letter, Ponomareva told him about her travels in Sweden, Denmark, and Germany, and reprimanded Douglas for not inviting her abroad to see him, remonstrating, "You probably thought that I would come and never leave, but I would never do that. I only thought that I could see you for a few days and tell you everything about myself." The other letter she wrote to him after a trip to Switzerland, where she had visited Douglas's friend Campo Alegre, secretary to the Spanish Embassy in St. Petersburg. Ponomareva complained that Douglas hadn't arranged to see her during her visit. "Please next time arrange for us to see each other at least for a day, I'd want this very much."[51] In what would become a pattern, Douglas's younger sexual partner wanted more than he was willing to give. It was this unequal dynamic that so often required Douglas, in his words, to put "a slice of sea" between himself and his former lovers.[52]

A different sexual affair with a riskier partner was responsible for driving Douglas out of Russia permanently. In Looking Back, he referred to this lover by the first name Helen and mentioned that she was bosom friends with Princess Aurore Karageorgevitch. King's annotated edition of the memoir contains Helen's last name as well, Demidoff. The Demidov family was second only to the Romanovs in terms of wealth and included a young woman named Aurora Pavlovna Karađorđević, who married the prince of Serbia. Aurora Karađorđević had a sister named Helen, but she was too young to be Douglas's lover, judging by a picture he saved.[53] Holloway theorizes that Douglas's Helen was Elena Alexandrovna Demidoff, who later married Prince Katkov-Kalikov, escaped the Russian Revolution, and lived out her days in Paris.[54] This theory is hard to reconcile with Douglas's assertion that he had no knowledge of what became of Helen after he left Russia, considering that he was a frequent visitor to Paris between the wars.

Wherever she fell on the family tree, Helen's membership in the powerful Demidov family meant trouble for Douglas when she became pregnant. He begged the Foreign Office to let him take a two-year unpaid leave and fled immediately after the request was granted. One unreliable source claims that Douglas escaped just ahead of the secret police and would have been put to death if he'd been captured. This seems unlikely, as does the story that before his departure Douglas received a telegram from Helen that he could not read, and which he learned decades later was written in transliterated "Siamese."[55] It seems more plausible to accept Douglas's claim that he never heard from Helen again. He never returned to Russia, either.

Douglas's desire to collect a sheltopusik led to a chain of events that ended his diplomatic career, changing the course of his life. When he left the foreign office *en disponibilité*, Douglas threw off the vestiges of respectability that until then had shielded his sexual behavior as youthful escapades, appropriate to a young man of his status. In St. Petersburg, he had picked up a French translation of Apuleius's *Golden Ass*, a pornographic classic of the ancient world. The edition included an excerpt of Apuleius's treatise on the "Daemon of Socrates," which inspired a new obsession for Douglas, into the idea of "attendant demons."[56] Abandoning his professional position, Douglas embarked on a new life following the dictates of his own demon, lust.

CHAPTER THREE

Annetta and Michele

The street that climbed up from the Riviera di Chiaia into the hills behind the Neapolitan waterfront was dark with the settling evening. No streetlamps illuminated the stone steps that negotiated the steep ascent into one of the city's poorest neighborhoods. Norman Douglas never saw the blow coming. It struck his head with all the passion a fourteen-year-old boy could deliver. What sort of passion depends on which telling of the story you believe. Whether it was motivated by righteous anger or sexual jealousy, the blow forced Douglas to sit on a nearby doorstep until he recovered from his dizziness. When he was well enough to stand, Douglas walked back to the apartment of the girl he had just been visiting so he could confront his assailant. He had heard a great deal about Annetta's brother Michele. At last, the two had met.

From his first visit in 1888, Douglas loved the Bay of Naples. The striking landscape of stony cliffs, blue water, and bright sun were far more beautiful to him than England's pastoral landscape. "English nature is too green, and that green too monotonous in shade and outline; it is (*entre nous*) a salad landscape," Douglas liked to joke.[1] During his time in the cold northwest of Russia, Douglas dreamed of Naples. In 1896 he asked a German friend who worked at Naples's zoological station to find him a house in Il Posillipo, a peninsula on the north end of the bay. The friend arranged for Douglas to buy a property at Il Posillipo's tip, known as Gaiola, across the water from the Isola di Gaiola, a small rocky outcropping. Gaiola was familiar to Douglas because it was the site of a ruin called the Scuola di Virgilio, or Virgil's School, a popular stop on the itinerary of British tourists. According to medieval legends, the ancient poet Virgil had directed a school of magic there.

9. Postcard of Il Posillipo, Naples. Library of Congress Prints and Photographs Division.

Percy Bysshe Shelley visited Gaiola in 1818 and wrote a letter about it to his friend the writer Thomas Love Peacock, whose conversational novels are often likened to Douglas's fiction. In *Looking Back*, Douglas quoted from Shelley's letter to Peacock, describing Gaiola's "lofty rocks and craggy islets, with arches and portals of precipice standing in the sea, and enormous caverns, which echoed faintly with the murmur of the languid tide."[2] Douglas could resist neither the landscape nor the literary associations.

Douglas bought his property in Il Posillipo from an Irish naval architect named Nelson Foley, who was the inventor of the collapsible umbrella, as well as a brother-in-law of Sir Arthur Conan Doyle.[3] When Douglas fled St. Petersburg in the fall of 1896, he traveled directly to Naples and took possession of the house. He renamed his new home the Villa Maya, a word meaning illusion in Sanskrit. The name was Douglas's nod toward the house's proximity to Virgil's school of magic. In Italian, which doesn't use the letter *y*, it was known as the Villa Maia. This name pleased Douglas as well, since in Greek mythology Maia is a nymph, the daughter of Atlas, and the mother of Hermes. This sort of layering of ancient and medieval histories had a powerful appeal for Douglas, especially as his scholarly interests were shifting from the natural world to the classical world.

History was not the only attraction that drew him to Naples. In the late nineteenth century, many queer British visitors traveled to Naples because of its reputation for tolerating sex between men, as well as for its robust culture of male prostitution. That reputation dated back to the days of the "Grand Tour," when wealthy, young British men traveled to the Continent ostensibly to expand their aesthetic sensibilities. The opportunity to expand their sexual experiences proved just as alluring for many travelers. Young travelers took advantage of the sexual opportunities presented by the female *grisettes* of Paris and by the male *gondoliere* of Venice. Grand Tour travelers regarded Italy, in particular, as a sexual draw, and they associated the country especially with sex between men.[4]

Throughout the nineteenth century, same-sex acts were not legally punished in southern Italy. In 1889, when a unified Italy enacted the Zanardelli Code, sex between males was decriminalized nationally.[5] According to Italian historians, the southern regions of the nation were particularly tolerant of boys' homosexuality. Southern Italian culture was intensely patriarchal and carefully guarded female virginity by segregating the sexes. Since boys and girls were not allowed to socialize, sexual encounters between boys, or between boys and men, were seen as a form of compensation and only a minor evil.[6] Mario Bolognari explains, "Adolescent homosexuality was traditionally tolerated as a prevention strategy."[7] This attitude stood contrasted to sentiments in Britain, where proscriptions against sex between men and boys were hardening during the late nineteenth century, and harsher punishments were being meted out.

In 1885, four years before Italy enacted the Zanardelli Code, Britain had passed the Labouchere Amendment, making it easier to prosecute queer men for "gross indecency" without the evidence of anal sex that had previously been required for a sodomy conviction. The Labouchere Amendment also raised the age of criminal responsibility for boys (which functioned as an age of consent) to fourteen. The Labouchere Amendment led to increased state scrutiny of consensual sexual relations. Oscar Wilde is one of the most famous victims of the Labouchere Amendment. According to Frank Harris, after Wilde's conviction, queer men fled the nation and "every steamer to Calais thronged with members of the aristocratic and leisured classes."[8] Harris exaggerated, but it was true that after Wilde's trial, Italy became a particular haven for queer British men with the means to live abroad. Sir Richard Burton famously remarked that "England sent her pederasts to Italy, and especially to Naples."[9]

Douglas was familiar with several men from this wave of British exiles. One friend and neighbor in Il Posillipo, for example, was Archibald Philip Primrose, Lord Rosebery, the former prime minister of England from March 1894 to June 1895. Rosebery was rumored to have had a sexual relationship with his secretary, Francis Douglas, Viscount Drumlanrig—the older brother of Lord Alfred "Bosie" Douglas, Oscar Wilde's lover.[10] A year after Norman Douglas moved into Villa Maya, Bosie and Wilde, who had recently been released from prison, rented a home in Il Posillipo called the Villa Guidice.[11] An Italian newspaper at the time misreported this event saying that Wilde was visiting the Villa Maya, mixing up Alfred Douglas and Norman Douglas.[12]

Naples also had a specific local sexual tradition that made it attractive to queer male visitors. The city was home to a gender and sexual minority known as *femminielli*, biological males who lived as females, dressing in women's clothing and performing women's work, including prostitution. *Femminielli* were believed to bring good luck in Neapolitan culture.[13] Douglas, who became fluent in the Neapolitan dialect during his years of residence in the city, used the word *femminielli* more generally to refer to effeminate gay men, not necessarily cross-dressers. He once called the American poet Walt Whitman "a typical 'feminella'" and remarked that he was "surprised that anyone should ever has [*sic*] doubted his homosexuality."[14] In addition to its *femminielli*, Naples was also notorious for its boy prostitutes.[15]

Naples's appeal to Douglas owed as much to its prostitutes, male and female, as to its scenery and classical history. After he moved to the Villa Maya, Douglas became a frequent client of a legendary local pimp named Raffaele Amoroso, who served a clientele of visiting noblemen and gentry, including such luminaries as the Duke of Edinburgh, according to Douglas. Amoroso was known for fulfilling his clients' "most freakish demands." Affiliated with the Camorra (local organized crime), he was above the law and took as his motto "*la libidine non ha fine*," or "the libido has no limits." Amoroso nicknamed Douglas "Lo Sposo." In *Looking Back*, Douglas wrote that the nickname "requires no commentary."[16] This was typical of the rhetorical dodges he favored, making the nature of his sexual tastes clear, while maintaining just enough discretion that those who preferred to turn a blind eye could preserve their ignorance, in a fashion that the anthropologist Monica Konrad describes as "active not knowing."[17] In plain language, Lo Sposo

10. Nude boy bathing on Naples waterfront, 1890s. Wikimedia Commons.

translates to the bridegroom and referred to Douglas's insistence on having sex only with virgins.[18]

This preference for virgins may have been motivated by Douglas's desire not to catch venereal diseases from his sexual encounters, following his earlier syphilis infection, from which he still suffered. He does not mention whether he took any precautions not to infect the girls whom Amoroso supplied, which probably answers that question. Douglas's preference for virgins also spoke to his attraction to children and youths. Most of the "virgins" procured

for him by Amoroso were likely young. The fetish for virgins was a preoccupa-
tion in eighteenth- and nineteenth-century pornography, which often dwelled
in gory detail on the bloody defloration of young girls.[19] Reform literature
of the era harped on the same theme. William Stead's infamous 1885 newspaper exposé, "The Maiden Tribute of Modern Babylon," recounted in sensational terms the supposed sex trafficking of young English girls to brothels on
the Continent.[20] The multipart series, which sold in vast numbers, described
child rapes in a style that blurred the line between reportage and pornography. Stead's exposé was a major influence on the movement to raise the age of
consent for girls in England, and a contributing factor to the hostile climate
that inspired Douglas to live instead in Italy. Although Douglas boasted about
his taste for virgins, he never fetishized pain or bloodshed in his writing. He
also broke from the Steadian model by extending his taste for virgins to boys
as well as girls. His sexual philosophy was that "to get proper fucking, one
must <u>bring them up oneself</u>. And the same applies to the other thing. Nothing like a virgin, when all is said and done, male or female."[21] Douglas sought
enthusiasm from his sexual encounters, not terror.

Amoroso procured many virgins for Douglas, but it wasn't through Amoroso that Douglas met Annetta, whose brother Michele attacked him with
a stick in a dark alley near the waterfront. They met through the children's
aunt, Maria Spasiano, a dressmaker, who had a shop on the Corso Garibaldi,
the broad thoroughfare that linked the harbor to the train station. Douglas
hesitated to call Spasiano a professional procuress, insisting that she set him
up with lovers "for sport" and maybe a "small commission."[22] In the case of
Annetta, Spasiano was likely motivated by family interest as well. Spasiano
saw Douglas, a young and wealthy foreigner, as a desirable patron for her impoverished niece, whose father had died, leaving her without the money for
a dowry.

Annetta was originally from the nearby city of Afragola, but after her father's death, she and her mother and her younger brother had moved to Naples. Spasiano introduced Douglas to Annetta's mother first, and the two
quickly agreed on the terms of the proposed relationship. Douglas recalled
Annetta's mother as "dusky" and noted that she didn't wear a hat, which
he claimed was a sign that the widow belonged to that class of people who
settled their disputes with knives rather than the law. Afragola's coat of arms
depicted a hand bearing a bouquet of red strawberries, the fruit for which the
city was named, but by reputation Afragola was associated with the red of

444
444

bloodshed. The city was known to be controlled by the Camorra, and its citizens had a reputation for violence. For Douglas, this association sweetened the deal. Northern Europeans, like Douglas, characterized southern Europeans, like the citizens of Afragola, as wild and passionate, qualities that made them sexually desirable. Annetta's roots in Afragola sharpened her differentiation from the elite aristocratic women Douglas was supposed to court, and helped him to rationalize his purchase of her sexual labor as an arrangement that could be justified as normal in southern Italy.

"Such contracts for girls, I may say, were quite a regular thing," Douglas explained in *Looking Back*, "they enabled them to gain a little money which afterwards constituted, or helped to constitute, their marriage portion." If a man seduced a girl without her parents' consent, he was sure to suffer violent retribution. But "once that consent was obtained, nobody, not even the nearest member of the family, had another word to say in the matter. The age of the girl was not taken into account; she might be a minor or even a child; she generally was." Douglas's claim about local indifference to the age at which girls became sexually active was both self-serving and borne out by evidence. An 1877 report on Neapolitan poverty repeated the testimony of a local morgue physician that "there are no virgins among girls over the age of 12."[23] Annetta, who was sixteen when Douglas met her, was older than many prostituted girls.

Douglas was pleased by what he saw when they met. Annetta had dark eyes, a pale complexion, and full lips. Annetta's impression of Douglas is not recorded in the sources. She may have been repulsed by the tall, stocky, mustached, tweed-suited man who was contracting her sexual labor. By 1897, the year of their encounter, Douglas had lost the boyishness of his Karlsruhe days and grown into a big fleshy man. Yet his wealth, status, and experience may have appealed to Annetta. Douglas never had difficulty finding lovers, even when he wasn't paying, and the sixteen-year-old might have appreciated his charms. It's impossible to know. The sources don't record Annetta's feelings. That silence is itself a record, which reveals a key aspect of the history of youth prostitution in late nineteenth-century Italy. The youths themselves often had little voice in the matter. Annetta at sixteen likely had more voice than many younger working-class Neapolitan prostitutes, but her only words that Douglas recorded were a warning about her hot-tempered and reckless younger brother: "Something awful will happen, she used to say, if he finds out about us."

Michele was an engraver's apprentice. As Douglas told the story in *Looking Back*, when Michele found out about his sister's contract, he followed Douglas from the apartment one evening and clubbed him in the back of the head. When Douglas recovered his wits and returned to the apartment to confront him, the children's mother took Douglas's side. Angry at her son's disrespect for her authority, Michele's mother forced the boy to apologize on his knees. Douglas related this episode as a classic "meet cute" story, in which the lovers' negative first impressions are later reversed and they fall in love, like Mr. Darcy and Elizabeth Bennet. During Michele's apology, Douglas took notice of Michele's looks: "He was like his sister, and even prettier; the same red lips and pale cheeks, but the chiseling and pencilling were more thoughtfully done." According to Douglas, Michele likewise found something to admire, "for not long afterwards the boy fell in love with me desperately, as only a southern boy of his age can do; so blindly that at a hint from myself he would have abandoned his work and family and everything else."

This is not the only version of their encounter that Douglas told. Douglas loved to tell risqué stories. "He enjoyed shocking people," the literary hostess and novelist Brigit Patmore recalled. Probably many of the stories in *Looking Back* were honed from repeated retellings before he set them down in print. Patmore heard the story of Annetta and Michele from Douglas, with a slightly different spin. In the version she recorded, Michele hit Douglas in the first place because he was already in love with the writer and he was jealous of Annetta.[24] Douglas could have told Patmore the story this way to rattle her sensibilities. A proper Englishwoman like Patmore, born in the late Victorian era, might be shocked to hear of such sexual depravity on the part of a young teen. Actually, Patmore was rumored to have been lovers with the female poet H.D.; she abandoned her husband for H.D.'s former lover Richard Aldington, who later abandoned her for her older son Michael's wife, Netta; and she was very close to her younger son, Derek, who was gay, so she probably wasn't that easily shocked.

If Brigit Patmore wasn't shocked, many of the readers of *Looking Back* were. A review of the memoir noted that Douglas had admitted to actions "assorted, named, and ranged in the admonishment of a civil code, which is commonly accepted."[25] Douglas's passages about his affairs with Anyuta, Annetta, and Michele inspired the British literary critic Raymond Mortimer to observe that Douglas "coolly admits to odious conduct that anyone else would try to forget."[26] Douglas's descriptions of contracting with parents for sexual access to their children flew in the face of even the most liberated ideal of British sexual morality. Mortimer, a member of the Bloomsbury group, was a self-professed hedonist and a longtime lover of Sir Harold Nicolson, who was married to Vita Sackville-West, the lover of Virginia Woolf. Members of the Bloomsbury group shared a belief in open marriages and same-sex relationships, and several—including Mortimer, E. M. Forster, Lytton Strachey, and Virginia Woolf—were friends of Douglas or fans of his writing. But Douglas's boasts about how he paid parents for sexual access to their children went too far, at least for Mortimer.

Douglas claimed, in his defense, that affairs like the ones he had with Michele were commonly accepted in Italy. "The queer thing is (queer, at least, to our English way of thinking), that his mother and sister were not in the least surprised; they thought it the most natural thing in the world. 'L'avete svegliato,' the mother said; you have woken him up." This defense didn't sway all readers. According to one of Douglas's defenders, "It would have been impossible to persuade English-speaking countries that it was quite common practice for poor Italian families to 'loan' their older children, girls and boys, to rich (as they thought) foreigners, in exchange for money which went to their dowries, or their education."[27] It's probably equally impossible to persuade English-speaking readers today, but Italian historians have upheld Douglas's claims.

Giovanni Dall'Orto argues that parents tolerated their sons' connections with wealthy foreigners: "The boys could devote a few years to exchange his sexual impetuosity with capital, which is useful to get married and start a business, and then, once he had become officially an adult, forget everything." Mario Bolognari agrees that in the Sicilian city of Taormina, which also attracted many foreign pederasts, the community accepted the men's connections with their sons as largely beneficial. "People at that time were less stupid and less naive than they are portrayed by today's historians," Bolognari writes. They saw value in tolerating youthful prostitution, and when religious leaders or political leaders attacked the foreigners, the community defended them.[28] Chiara Beccalossi draws on Bolognari's research and concurs that "the fact that local communities recognised a temporary homosexual phase as normal made it easier for families to condone male prostitution on the part of boys as a resource that could complement a family income."[29] Overall, these Italian historians paint a picture of Italian society in the late nineteenth and early twentieth centuries, particularly in the south, as accepting prostitution as a legitimate means for children to earn money for themselves and their families.

In some ways, there was nothing remarkable about Italian parents contracting their children for sexual labor. During a period of large families and widespread poverty, parents contracted their children for all sorts of labor, much of it more dangerous than sex. Italian parents signed contracts with labor procurers who transported children as young as five or six years old to work as wandering musicians in the streets of London and Paris. Parents also sent their young children to work in glass factories in southeastern France, where they were exposed to deadly temperatures and explosions.[30] Impoverished Italian children experienced dangers just as grave at home as abroad. In Lipari, an island off the coast of northern Sicily, young children were subjected to terrible conditions in the pumice mines. During his time in the Foreign Office, Douglas wrote a report condemning child labor in Lipari, which generated enough outrage among London buyers to pressure the mine owners to eliminate the practice.[31]

Douglas was both a sexual exploiter of children and a defender of children. He didn't view his relationships with Michele and Annetta as incompatible with his critique of the Lipari mine owners. Beccalossi has argued that many foreign men, like Douglas, who were drawn to Italy because of the sexual opportunities it presented also contributed to the nation's well-being because of their love for Italian culture and people. "British homosexual tourism in Italy defies any over-simplified and homogenising binary interpretation, whereby the British homosexuals are seen simply as part of an imperialistic project and the Italians as victims of an Orientalist practice," Beccalossi argues.[32] Italians, including Italian youths, had agency within sex tourism.

Several narratives of Douglas's life treat his relationship with Michele as a turning point, the moment at which his erotic inclinations shifted definitively toward boys.[33] But Douglas had been having relationships with boys since he was a boy. And long after his relationship with Michele, Douglas continued to have relationships with girls and women. In fact, the year that he met Michele, Douglas pursued several significant relationships with women, including at least one who was older than he was.

In May, Douglas traveled from Naples north to Merano, a village in the Italian Alps close to the Austrian border, to meet a "sultry" widow he had known since the early 1890s. The lady had been married at age sixteen to an older British officer "who expired not long afterwards in the arms of a Parisian cocotte." This was the woman who had given Douglas the *brûle-parfum* he used to collect his calling cards. In Willie King's annotated copy of *Looking Back*, the name of the widow is given as Effie Wallace Carpenter, and an explanatory note states that her husband died "while being sucked off." Major Wallace Carpenter was an amateur actor and chairman of London's "Lyric Club," as well as a collector of Oriental artifacts and a spiritualist. He died in 1891, when his wife, Euphemia, was twenty-seven, which was about the time that Douglas, then twenty-two, first met her.[34] The fact that the two had been engaged in an affair for six years points to Douglas's capacity for sustained sexual interest in a diverse range of lovers. His connection with Michele hardly marked a new discovery, nor did it put an end to old pleasures. It fit within Douglas's identity as a rapacious sexual libertine who pursued as many diverse encounters as possible.

Another relationship Douglas pursued in 1897 did lead to an indisputable turning point in his bachelor existence. Douglas had likely arranged to meet Effie Carpenter in Merano because of its proximity to Vorarlberg, where his mother was once again living. In March of that year, she had been widowed by her second husband, and Douglas needed to pay his respects. While there he made the rounds of all his relations in the area, including one cousin who had attracted his sexual interest even longer than Effie Wallace Carpenter. Her name was Elsa FitzGibbon.

CHAPTER FOUR

Elsa

There's a story from Norman Douglas's marriage that appears three times in the sources. Each time it's a terrible story, but the degree of Douglas's moral culpability varies in each rendition.

In the first version, Douglas and Elsa are living together in the Villa Maya, expecting their second child. They watch a bird build a nest and raise her chicks on their terrace. Then one day they wake up and find that the nest has been destroyed by a stray cat. Elsa is distraught, so after dinner Douglas helps her to lay down poison, hoping to kill the cat. The next morning they wake up to find four dead dogs. The dogs are a bad omen, but not a judgment on Douglas. The reader can sympathize with his desire to protect the fragile feelings of his nesting wife.[1]

In the second version of the story, while Douglas and Elsa are living in the Villa Maya, he lures a neighbor's big dog into his garden shed and hacks it to death with a hatchet because the dog has been harassing the birds who visit the terrace. In this version, the killing of the dog symbolizes the hot silent anger at the core of Douglas's personality that will eventually destroy his relationship with his wife.[2]

In the third version of the story, there is no mention of Elsa. Douglas is living at the Villa Maya, devoted to his garden. He takes particular pleasure in watching the fourteen blackcap nests on his terrace. To protect the songbirds, he mercilessly shoots the cats who hunt the birds, and he periodically puts down poisoned pâté, killing six to eight stray dogs at a time—but he always warns his neighbors to keep their pets inside on those nights. Douglas, who has no pregnant wife to exculpate his actions in this version, comes across as coldhearted, but he has reasons for his actions. He is not bloodthirsty.[3]

They say there are three sides to every story: his, hers, and the truth. This anecdote from Norman Douglas's marriage to Elsa FitzGibbon would seem to support that aphorism. Douglas shifts in the three renditions from a loving husband, to a brutal villain, to a flawed man. The accounts, however, don't align as we might expect. The first version, which paints Douglas in the most sympathetic light, was written by Elsa in her diary at the time of the events. The second, which paints him in the most brutal light, was written by Hans Fischer, a novelist who knew Elsa a few years after she divorced Douglas. The third, which saddles Douglas with the highest death count, comes from the pages of *Looking Back*, where instead of defending himself as a concerned husband, Douglas erases Elsa from the tale altogether.

Recounting the history of Douglas's marriage to Elsa is not as simple as sorting through "he said, she said." For one thing, Douglas never told his side of the story. He expunged all mentions of Elsa from his published writings and intimate correspondence. He regaled audiences with tales of his affairs with children, but he maintained a stony silence about his marriage. He couldn't totally erase the evidence of their relationship. They had two children together. Their divorce generated legal records and newspaper headlines. Later their struggle over the custody of their sons generated more legal records. But almost nothing remains in Douglas's own words. His silence might be seen as self-serving, since the history of the relationship reflected badly on him. On the other hand, the absence of Douglas's voice allows for the worst interpretation of his motives. No matter how the story is told, the history of Douglas's marriage gives a sad demonstration of the gendered inequalities that structured marriage at the turn of the twentieth century, even for elite women. Taking seriously the power differential between husbands and wives at that time puts the power differential within sexual relationships involving adults and children in a new light. There was not then the same gulf between intergenerational relationships and marital relationships that there is today.

Elizabeth Louisa Theobaldina FitzGibbon, Elsa for short, was the daughter of Douglas's mother Vanda's youngest sister, Adèle, making them first cousins. In Hans Fischer's novel *Violet* (published under the pseudonym Kurt Aram), the character modeled after Douglas, Herbert von Strehlen, falls in love with the character modeled after Elsa, Violet Fitzalan, when he is fifteen and she is eight. Strehlen thinks he has "never seen a more beautiful little girl."[4] Violet has big silver-gray eyes and lovely reddish-gold hair, as well as a fiercely independent character. This account of the origins of Douglas and Elsa's relationship is believable. It echoes the circumstances of Douglas's relationship with Sofia Guerrieri-Gonzaga. And, as aberrant as it sounds today, it was not scandalous for its era. The archbishop of Canterbury at the time, Edward White Benson, began courting his cousin, Mary "Minnie" Sidgwick, when he was twenty-three and she was eleven. They were engaged when she was twelve and married when she turned eighteen.[5]

In Fischer's novel, Strehlen and Violet also don't become lovers until she has turned eighteen. This may or may not have been the case for Douglas and Elsa. Douglas's would-be biographer Constantine FitzGibbon, who was related to Elsa on her father's side, pressed Douglas for the history of their relationship. According to FitzGibbon's notes, Douglas and Elsa were "adolescent" lovers.[6] For the relationship to have begun while Douglas was still a youth, Elsa could hardly have been older than thirteen. But FitzGibbon might have been using loose language, and perhaps it was just Elsa who was an "adolescent" when their romantic relationship began.

In Fischer's novel, by her late adolescence Violet has grown into an introspective, curious, spiritual, otherworldly, and very beautiful young woman. Douglas's mother, Vanda, recorded a rather less laudatory impression of her niece in her 1894 diary. Vanda complained that eighteen-year-old Elsa was spoiled and inconsiderate. She had done nothing during the past year but "read novels and play the piano." Elsa refused to offer any help to her grandmother, with whom she lived. Vanda wrote that Elsa was "missing simple understanding," and she worried about the girl's lack of judgment. When Elsa began talking about converting to Catholicism, Vanda's worst fears were confirmed.[7] In her 1894 diary, Vanda only mentioned Douglas, who was living in Russia at the time, when he sent her letters or gifts, or when she was struck by a fond memory from his childhood. There's no evidence that he did begin courting Elsa at that time. Rather, their adult flirtation likely began the following year, when Douglas visited home.

In *Violet*, Strehlen courts Violet through her mind. He begins to leave books by Charles Darwin and Herbert Spencer for Elsa to find. "After a few days," the novel explains, "she started to ask him about the content of what she had read. After a few weeks she lost all her interest in the mystics."[8] Violet comes to respect Strehlen as an intellectual guide. Strehlen falls passionately in love with Violet, but she doesn't reciprocate. She looks on his courtship with the same disdain that she views the attention of the other young men she encounters in her aristocratic social circles. So Strehlen travels away for a while, hoping that his absence will bring Violet to recognize her feelings for him.

Douglas did, in fact, leave Vorarlberg after his 1895 visit, to return to St. Petersburg. The novel describes how Strehlen manipulates Violet's feelings by writing long letters to her mother but only short postcards to her. Strehlen's correspondence with Violet's mother also allows him to keep track of the men who are courting his cousin. When he learns that Violet is becoming attached to a young Dutch painter, he rushes home "as if it was for life and death." The family opposes his courtship, but Violet, who cannot be told what to do, is antagonized by her mother's opposition to Strehlen, and "before she even knew she was his fiancée."[9]

In *Looking Back*, Douglas gave no indication that he was romantically preoccupied with Elsa during his final year in Russia. This was the period of his affairs with Helen and Anyuta. The daughter of an English diplomat who knew Douglas in St. Petersburg wrote to him, after reading the memoir, "But how did you find time for so much activity? I took at least six hours per week of your valuable time. Did you ever eat and sleep?"[10] Furthermore, in Douglas's rendition of those years, it was not love for Elsa that eventually drove him from Russia, but the pregnancy of his lover Helen. When he left Russia, he traveled by his own account straight to the Bay of Naples. He plunged into a life of deflowering virgins, before the death of his stepfather forced Douglas to visit home the next spring. Even then, he managed to combine his trip to Vorarlberg with a side journey to the Italian Alps, where he met up with his longtime lover Effie Carpenter.

Douglas arrived in Bregenz in the spring of 1897 not as a lovesick suitor, but as a sexual adventurer. He flirted with Elsa, attracted by her golden hair and her open manner. According to FitzGibbon, Elsa was amused to see how Douglas's "ribald attitude towards the proprieties tended to shock the older generation."[11] Her mother, Adèle, called Douglas "the anti-Christ," but since Elsa didn't get along with her mother, she viewed this as a point in his favor.[12] Adèle tried to stop the flirtation. She was, Douglas said, "the only woman who has moved Heaven and Earth to pain me in every possible way." She would have killed him, if she could have, Douglas claimed.[13] A flirtation with Douglas gave Elsa the perfect opportunity to break from her overbearing mother.

In early 1898, Elsa left Vorarlberg to visit her relatives, the Massey-Mainwarings, in London. Douglas made a trip to Britain at the same time. When Elsa returned to Vorarlberg, Douglas secretly followed, taking rooms in a village on Lake Constance. Soon they eloped together to England, marrying in a registry office on June 25, 1898. Elsa was twenty-two and Douglas was twenty-nine. They returned to the Continent the next day and presented their marriage as a fait accompli. Their son Louis Archibald (Archie) was born seven and a half months later, on February 2, 1899. By then, Douglas and Elsa were living together in the Villa Maya.

Since Douglas left no record of his feelings, it's impossible to know whether he intended to marry Elsa all along, or whether her pregnancy forced his hand. Did he purposefully get her pregnant so that she would have to marry him, manipulating her as Strehlen had in Fischer's novel? Or did Douglas accidentally impregnate Elsa, then find himself trapped into marriage? Elsa wasn't the first woman he had gotten pregnant, but she was the first he couldn't abandon by putting "a slice of sea" between them.

Douglas's actions suggest he had reservations about the marriage from the beginning. Rather than marry Elsa in Austria, he delayed the legalities until they reached England. The most likely explanation is that Douglas knew British law gave husbands preference in matters of custody, while Austrian law favored mothers. In other words, at the time Douglas married his pregnant cousin, he was already laying the groundwork for their eventual divorce.

An anecdote from the couple's honeymoon in Ischia, an island in the northern part of the Bay of Naples, suggests that Elsa may have also anticipated the marriage's eventual dissolution from the outset. Constantine Fitz-Gibbon claimed that in Ischia, Elsa gave Douglas a copy of Benjamin Constant's novel *Adolphe*, a bitter retelling of the author's failed love affair with the famous French saloniste Madame de Staël. A strange choice of a wedding gift, FitzGibbon noted.[14] Douglas kept ahold of the book throughout all his relocations in the decades that followed, perhaps in appreciation of the irony.

FitzGibbon attributed this anecdote to Douglas's friend Arthur Johnson. But Johnson's widow, Viola, claimed FitzGibbon got the details wrong. According to Viola, almost every day of their honeymoon, Douglas and Elsa visited a used bookstore on Ischia that had a battered old copy of *Adolphe* that Douglas admired. As a surprise, Elsa purchased the book and had it rebound, placing hearts down the book's spine. Elsa, according to Viola, had no knowledge of the book's contents. In fact, "the gift had charmed Norman, and that had been sufficient reason for keeping it all those years."[15] But FitzGibbon rejected Johnson's version of this story, insisting that Elsa, who was an aspiring writer, could not have been unaware of the contents of the book, which was one of the most famous novels of the nineteenth century.[16]

It's possible that the marriage took place neither by design nor under

11. A silver fish pill box, given by Elsa Douglas to Norman Douglas as a wedding gift. Private collection of Deirdre Sholto Douglas. Photograph by author.

duress, but was a happy accident. Douglas held on to another gift that Elsa had given him early in their marriage, a small silver sculpture of a fish whose mouth opened to reveal a secret compartment, possibly designed to be used as a pill box. This gift didn't ironically gesture to the marriage's end. It was simply a pretty object, a curio, that may have recalled for Douglas the marriage's brief happy period.

A scrapbook that Elsa started in spring 1899, not long after Archie's birth, shows pleasure in her new life. It opens with a quotation from Ouida (Maria Louise Ramé), the couple's favorite living novelist: "Water is the living joy of Rome." There are photographs of Elsa's and Douglas's childhood homes and other scenic locations in Vorarlberg. There are further poetic excerpts, including verses from Rumi and *The Ramayana*, which suggest that Elsa hadn't entirely forsaken mysticism. A page of pictures shows Douglas and Elsa standing together on a pier, hiking with friends on the islet of Vivara near Ischia, and bicycling along a flat road with mountains in the background.[17]

Douglas "followed her about all over the place" during the first two years of their marriage, he told his friend Muriel Draper.[18] Draper believed that "he had loved her deeply" during this period. Elsa finally was freed from her mother's narrow worldview, and Douglas gave her a chance to see the world. They traveled together to India, Ceylon, Tunisia, Scotland, and England—all places significant to him. But according to Douglas, their travels were more for Elsa's benefit than his own. Perhaps this added to his sense of betrayal when Elsa had an affair with an Austrian officer she met in Ceylon.[19]

On the other hand, Douglas never was faithful to Elsa, so he had little justification to feel betrayed. As FitzGibbon put it, "Monogamy made no appeal whatever to Norman Douglas, nor, apparently, did monandry to his wife."[20] In *Looking Back*, Douglas includes anecdotes that shed light onto some of his extramarital activities during their travels. A card from Mr. Horace Drummond Deane, a tea planter he met in Ceylon in 1900, leads Douglas to a memory of the excursion he took to Dondra Head, a cape off the southern tip of the island, where he watched "native children, so mild-eyed and graceful, so naked and frolicsome, that one longs to steal half a dozen of them and carry them home as keepsakes."[21] And in Delhi he slept with a "hermaphrodite," an accomplishment he boasted of years later as "great fun" and "full of surprises!"[22] Even after his marriage, Douglas remained very much the libertine.

Douglas's sexual infidelity may have contributed to Elsa's affair, which she insisted went unconsummated. Douglas didn't believe her. FitzGibbon claimed that Douglas always wondered whether his second son, Robert (Robin) Sholto Douglas, was actually the Austrian officer's son.[23] But Robin not only looked like Douglas, he was also conceived well after Ceylon. Viola Johnson said that Douglas told her that Robin was the "result of an attempt at reconciliation with Elsa."[24] He told the writer Robin Maugham, nephew of W. Somerset Maugham, that Robin was conceived "as the result of a bottle of *strega*."[25] The Italian liqueur was one of his favorite drinks.

Elsa's diary from this period of reconciliation survives. Her entries from July 1901 to July 1902 give no indication that her marriage was anything but loving.[26] The first entries in the diary describe life at the Villa Maya. She spent her days swimming at the beach beside the house, soaking in the beauty of the scenery, sailing on adventures with the couple's friends, and playing with her toddler. A nurse and a servant and a washerwoman did all the hard labor. The diary then describes Elsa and Archie's trip to England (she spent the passage flirting and gossiping) to meet Douglas, who had gone ahead to arrange for the publication of a book of stories they had coauthored. After their reunion in London, the family traveled north to Scotland for the summer. Elsa

12. Norman Douglas at Bregenz, ca. 1900. Private collection of Deirdre Sholto Douglas. Photograph by author.

and Douglas went on daily walks together and bicycle rides, paying visits to family and friends. Some entries suggest that she might have gotten pregnant during this period and later suffered a miscarriage.[27]

In September the couple received copies of their book. *Unprofessional Tales* by Normyx, their nom de plume, is a collection of supernatural short stories for which Elsa supposedly supplied the ideas and plots, and Douglas the writing. Later Douglas would express embarrassment about this amateur production. He had 750 copies printed in London, but he joked that only eight copies of the book were sold. The true number may have been closer to 150. The rest of the copies were pulped, he claimed with relief.[28] Elsa's diary, however, expressed only pleasure in the arrival of the books, which she called "quite delicious."[29] This was a favorite adjective Douglas used over the decades.

The couple returned to Villa Maya in late October and threw themselves back into the life of leisure Elsa described before leaving for England. In November, Elsa must have gotten pregnant again. She mentions fainting in early December, although that may have been an adverse reaction to the smallpox vaccines the family received. Douglas's vaccine made him so ill that he had to be transported to the hospital, where he had an operation of some sort, before finally returning home in early January. Soon Douglas recovered and the couple recommenced their routine. They took trips to Capri and Ischia. They socialized with guests (including Sir Arthur Conan Doyle, who got stuck in a Roman tunnel on Douglas's property and had to be pulled out). They started work on a terrace with extended views of the sea and discovered Roman relics buried on their grounds. When Douglas went to Capri without Elsa in mid-May, she felt lonely and depressed by his absence. Elsa's diary gives the impression that the two were inseparable. And yet, the marriage was about to end.

The dead dogs were the omen. As Elsa told the story in her diary, she and Douglas were walking in the garden when they found a birds' nest that they had "been watching with such interest and affection, destroyed, and all the little newly hatched birds gone. I couldn't help howling it made me so miserable." After supper, she and Douglas put down poison "for those infernal cats."[30] The next day, they discovered that four dogs had died from eating the poison. Elsa wrote no more about the subject in her diary, but in her mind the event must have become associated with the end of the marriage. *Violet*—which is primarily about the divorce, not the marriage—opens with this episode. The very first sentences read, "Baron Strehlen kam mit einem Beil aus dem Gartenschuppen. Er hielt das Beil weit von sich, denn es war rot von Blut."[31] (Baron Strehlen came out of the garden shed with a hatchet. He held the ax far away, for it was red with blood.) The scene foreshadows the death of the marriage.

In late June, the family traveled to Vorarlberg to escape the heat. Soon after their arrival, Douglas's mother, Vanda, died of a heart attack. Elsa mourned her aunt, but she and Douglas seemed to continue together happily. In July, they went for a walk in the woods and found "some delicious orchids." When Douglas had to return to Italy to handle their property, Elsa "felt awfully blue and miserable."[32] The diary ended while Douglas was still away. He returned before August 20, 1902, when the couple's second son, Robin, was born. No diary survives to describe what happened to end the marriage after his return. Douglas told FitzGibbon that Elsa "informed him one day quite openly that a certain Austrian officer was her lover," so he decided to divorce her.[33] Fischer's novel and the divorce court proceedings offer more details, but the two narratives tell opposing stories, neither of which can be relied upon.

In Fischer's retelling, Violet feels alienated by Strehlen's angry and cold character she leaves him in Naples, taking her sole child "Archi" to her mother's house in Austria. Her decision to break from Strehlen is precipitated by her love for another man, but their feelings remain unconsummated. However, when Violet announces her decision to end the marriage, Strehlen begins to scheme for revenge and control. He agrees to divorce her on the condition that she assume fault by confessing to adultery, despite her innocence. Violet, far less worldly than Strehlen, agrees to his condition, unaware that it will undermine her claim for custody of Archi.

The divorce proceedings paint Elsa in a more negative light. According to the court papers, in February 1903, when Robin was six months old, Douglas returned to Italy to oversee the construction of a new house in Capri. Douglas tried to get Elsa and the children to come with him to Italy, but she insisted on staying in Bludenz. During his absence, Elsa began an affair with Baron Arnhold von Stengel, a lieutenant in the Twentieth Bavarian Infantry Regiment. Stengel would take the late train to Bludenz and climb into Elsa's ground-floor bedroom by the window. When Douglas returned to Bludenz to collect Elsa and the children, she rushed off to a friend's house in Strasbourg. She didn't return until after miscarrying Stengel's baby. At that point she confessed to the affair. Soon afterward, Douglas intercepted a letter from Stengel to Elsa that confirmed the story. Since the couple had married in Britain, Douglas was able to use his Scottish "domicile" to file for divorce in Edinburgh, where the courts were favorable to fathers.[34] The Court of Sessions granted the decree.[35] The divorce was a public scandal—the details that came out in the proceedings were reported as far away as New Zealand.[36]

If the divorce had ended with Elsa building a new life for herself, it might be plausible to see both parties as equally at fault. Douglas's ongoing infidelities, some with children, were repaid by Elsa with her own infidelities, and

13. Norman Douglas with his sons, Archie and Robin, ca. 1903. Private collection of Deirdre Sholto Douglas. Photograph by author.

her decision to end the marriage. As FitzGibbon put it, "They were two strong characters, and when the marriage soured they nearly smashed each other to pieces." But the outcome was not equal for both parties. FitzGibbon wrote, "He was the stronger. He survived it, just."[37] Elsa did not.

What happened after the divorce puts Douglas in a terrible light. In Fischer's retelling, Violet moves to Munich and brings the children, but

Strehlen hires an investigator who observes men visiting Violet. Strehlen then arranges a kidnapping of Archi and brings the boy back to Capri. His goal is to force Violet to return to him. Violet tries to get Archi back, but Strehlen uses the Camorra to hide the boy. Later Strehlen moves Archi to a British boarding school. But Violet triumphs in the end, when her longtime admirer, the Dutch painter, re-kidnaps Archi and brings him back to Munich. They all live happier ever after, except for Strehlen, who is stabbed to death after trying to stop a man from beating a donkey.

The plotline of *Violet* represents Elsa's fantasy of how her divorce might have ended. The truth was almost entirely the opposite. Douglas kept custody of the children, while Elsa died early in tragic circumstances. Douglas was granted legal custody from the beginning, because Elsa admitted to adultery. At first, Douglas was willing to let Elsa see the children. In 1905 he sent Robin to visit her in Munich, where she had moved to start a new life. However, when she brought Robin back to Capri, she became convinced that Douglas was treating Archie "in an immoral way." Elsa instigated legal proceedings both in the Italian courts and with the British consul in Naples to regain custody, but Douglas seized both boys and hid Robin in a nunnery.

Again Douglas used his Scottish domicile to contest Elsa in the British courts. In March 1908, the courts found in his favor and secured his custody of the children, despite the ongoing legal battle in the Italian courts.[38] Douglas had brought both children to live with friends in England, where their mother had no rights to them. He returned alone to Italy. "I left my father's home and guardianship forever in 1906," Archie wrote to Douglas's biographer Mark Holloway. "He wrote me quite often, yet I only saw him on comparatively rare occasions until the inter WW1–WW2 period."[39] He only saw his younger brother six more times in his life. He never saw his mother again.

Douglas celebrated his legal victory by taking a vacation in Ischia, where he had honeymooned a decade before. This time he traveled in the company of his half-sister Grete and her husband, Olaf Gulbransson. "We spent a lovely week together," he recalled in *Looking Back*, "I was still simmering with joy at the recent turn of events; bubbling in tranquil fashion, all to myself, day and night." In taverns Douglas toasted "to the damnation of our enemies." He felt elated. "This was precisely what kept me in such high spirits all the time. Certain folks had been damned; it was enough to make anybody bubble with contentment." One night, he was so overcome with joy that he left the

hotel where they were staying and wandered down the road until he found a
heap of stones, where he sat down and began to laugh:

> I laughed through the whole of that moonless night; the more I re-
> viewed the situation, the more laughable it proved to be, the comi-
> cality consisting in a fact which had never struck me till then, that it
> was they, the others, who should have laughed. In the bubbling ex-
> uberance of my glee at the turn of events, I had forgotten what this
> signified to them. They had expected to laugh, and rightly. Instead
> of that, they had been damned, damned for good and all—yes, and
> wrongly damned! This was the divine joke. How I laughed. . . . That
> April night was surely one of the most blissfull of my life.[40]

This remark about how his enemies were "wrongly damned" was as close as
Douglas ever came to a confession that he did molest Archie, as Elsa alleged.

It was a happy ending for Douglas, but not for Elsa or the boys, who never
saw their mother again. Living alone in Munich, with barely enough money
to survive, Elsa fell into a deep depression and became an alcoholic. In 1916
she died in a bed fire, likely sparked by a cigarette. Elsa's sister Violet later told
Archie that the "bed sheets were glued to her back by the fire." According to
Violet, Elsa's last words were "my children in England."[41]

Norman Douglas destroyed Elsa FitzGibbon's life. In the worst interpretation, he groomed her from a young age, manipulated her into marriage, laid
the groundwork to keep custody of their children in the eventuality of their
divorce, sought a divorce on terms that he knew would favor his custody, molested his oldest son, then punished her efforts to regain custody by guaran-
teeing that she never saw her children again. He laughed at the injustice of it,
and to cap it off, he laughed at her death. His friend Martha Gordon Crotch
described one drunken evening in 1937 when Douglas broke his habitual silence about the marriage. She recorded the details of his screed in her diary,
detailing "how he hated her, what a fiend she was, the terrible death she died.
A dipsomaniac, hopeless. She set her bed alight when she was smoking and
was burned to death." He said it "served her right."[42] The decades had not lessened his vindictiveness.

Another friend, Muriel Draper, wrote in a postmortem tribute to Douglas
that when he described the circumstances of Elsa's death, "his eyes flamed for

14. Elizabeth (Elsa) Louisa Theobaldina FitzGibbon Douglas. Munich, March 1907. Norman Douglas Forschungsstelle, Bregenz.

a second, his lips smiled into ashes," and he said, "Burned to death in a hotel somewhere in Germany." In her original draft, Draper added another remark from Douglas: "'God is not always stupid, you know, though,' and he smiled a real smile this time as he put his fingers around the neck of the wine bottle, 'I could have managed it better,' and he poured wine into his glass. Very kind, Douglas, really, though you might not believe it."[43] Draper struck out these lines before the piece was published in *Harper's Magazine*. No wonder. Who would believe Douglas was kind after hearing how he celebrated his ex-wife's death?

Maybe this is where I should have begun. This is true villainy: to destroy a woman and then to laugh at her death. Douglas's family, who were Fitz-Gibbon's family as well, never forgave him. One English cousin wrote, "I was, like many of the family, never allowed to meet Norman Douglas because of his reputation and the way he treated his wife and children."[44] The family opinion was that Douglas had treated his wife "abominably."[45] I suppose, in the light of contemporary taboos, Douglas would be judged most harshly for his treatment of Archie. Both Archie and Robin bore the scars of their wrecked childhoods throughout their unhappy lives. Yet Archie and Robin lived. They even venerated their father, for what it's worth. Archie never mentioned any memory of sexual abuse by his father. As an old man, he refused to condemn his father's sexual proclivities. He told Holloway, "I gave little or no thought that ND was happy with young people of either sex."[46]

It could be argued that Douglas mistreated Elsa more gravely than he mistreated many of the boys he picked up later. He caused her more serious and lasting injury. The tendency to categorize sexuality by types, as good or bad, can obscure the specific contexts that define individual relationships. Married sexuality falls into the good category, or as the sociologist Gayle Rubin puts it, the "charmed circle."[47] But the most acceptable sexual relationship of Douglas's life, the one that he shared with his wife, was perhaps also his most abusive.

Douglas felt that it was Elsa who had ruined *his* life. According to Richard Aldington, whenever Douglas did mention his wife, he would preface his remarks by saying, "to give the devil her due."[48] It's hard to know for certain how Douglas felt because for the most part he refused to talk about Elsa. He had ample incentive to tell his side. Fischer's novel was a bestseller in Germany and Austria. And the book wasn't a flash in the pan; it had staying power. In 1921 the director Artur Holz adapted *Violet* into a silent movie, which screened at Berlin's famous Tauentzien Palast theater.[49] The book and film thoroughly befouled Douglas's reputation in both the country where he grew up and the country where he had completed his education. Judging from the erratic way that Douglas repeatedly stamped his initials into his own copy of the book, Fischer's representation of the marriage enraged him.

Yet Douglas refrained from offering his own counternarrative. Even long after Elsa's death, when Constantine FitzGibbon interviewed Douglas about his life, he would discuss the marriage only hesitantly.[50] At the end of his life, he destroyed all evidence of their relationship within his own papers. There are no letters from her, let alone letters mentioning her, among the thousands that he left behind at his death.[51] The most generous interpretation is that Douglas imposed this silence out of consideration for Archie and Robin. Or maybe, half a century later, the memories of the marriage and its dissolution were still so painful to Douglas that he could not bring himself to talk about it. There are less generous interpretations as well. Maybe he remained so consumed with hatred for his ex-wife that he wanted to erase her memory. Or maybe Douglas had no defense to offer.

CHAPTER FIVE

Capri

Capri's charm is inseparable from its association with the pagan past. Its whitewashed loggia climbing with scarlet bougainvillea set on sheer cliffs overhanging the sapphire sea look like walkways into ancient history. The German historian Ferdinand Gregorovius, who first visited in 1853, witnessed a parade of briar-crowned figures on the island who "had such a pagan look" that they reminded him of "a procession of votaries of Bacchus."[1] Douglas was enchanted by Gregorovius's account, which he read as a student at Karlsruhe. Later he suggested to his sister, Mary, that she translate the book into English. Her edition, *Island of Capri: A Mediterranean Idyll*, appeared in 1896 to warm reviews.[2] Mary made her literary debut before her brother, but it was Douglas who made his fame from the island. He became, according to the Italian author Raffaele La Capria, "the greatest . . . of all the writers who wrote about Capri."[3] Douglas, more than any other twentieth-century writer, gave Capri the reputation it has today.

It's unclear whether Mary ever had a chance to visit Capri. Life did not treat her well. Constantine FitzGibbon's brief research notes from his Douglas biography includes the sentence: "Sister: younger than N.D., translates Gregorovius; married to a shit. Takes to drink."[4] A shitty husband and an inclination to drink were not the sum total of Mary's problems. She also suffered from tuberculosis. By the time that Douglas moved to Capri in 1903, Mary was too sick to get out of bed. She wrote to her brother from a sanatorium in Switzerland, "I . . . do nothing but lie in the sun on the terrace or a sofa. . . . I feel so irritable that I could simply murder anyone who even asks 'how I feel?'"[5] Two months later she was dead.

They say bad luck comes in threes. Swift on the heels of his acrimonious divorce and his sister's death came a third crisis that destroyed the last vestiges of Douglas's former life. He lost his fortune. Douglas had long been supported by a yearly income from the family business, supplied by the generosity of his older brother, John, who had inherited the mill in entirety from their father. Douglas was supposed to have received a legacy from a childless great-aunt, but she had disinherited him when she heard about his dissolute lifestyle. (Douglas claimed it was all a misunderstanding.) Then in 1903, John decided to sell the mill. There may have been solid economic reasons to do so, but Douglas claimed that John's wife, Olga de Reuter (daughter of the founder of Reuters news), made him sell the property because she thought that her father-in-law's ghost haunted it.[6] The sale had devastating consequences for Douglas. He received a payout, but it was barely enough to cover the debts he already had. Douglas was forced to sell the Villa Maya back to its prior owner. He affected indifference, claiming that the house reminded him of his failed marriage, but it must have been a bitter pill to part with this spectacular property. That wasn't the end of his losses. Financial need soon forced him to sell his property on Capri and resort to renting.

And yet Douglas described his post-divorce years in Capri as "a serene period on the whole, with blissful streaks in between." The destruction of his fortune, his marriage, and his reputation, did not destroy him as a person. If anything, these trials served as the crucible that forged the persona that made him famous. Freed from the constraints of marriage, wealth, and position, Douglas embraced the philosophy that "the business of life is to enjoy oneself; everything else is a mockery."[7] He decided to follow the example of his friend Campo Alegre, a Spanish diplomat he had first met back in St. Petersburg, who refused to be a "slave to taboos." Campo Alegre had passed away shortly after visiting Douglas and Elsa at the Villa Maya in 1901.[8] Douglas was hit hard by the death, which proved the truth of his old friend's advice that "life was too short" to put off seeking pleasure. Campo Alegre had seized life by the throat and "made it yield every pleasure, legitimate or otherwise, which it had to offer." Douglas chose to do the same. On Capri, Douglas constructed a new identity as a modern pagan. The island's classical allure settled on him like a laurel crown. From the beginning, Douglas's erotic interest in boys was a core ingredient of his pagan persona. Rather than a shameful secret, Douglas's pederasty was central to his public appeal.

According to the lesbian modernist painter Romaine Brooks, who also spent long stretches in Capri during the early twentieth century, Douglas was notorious at the time for his "faunesque liking and pursuit of young boys" on the island.[9] The adjective "faunesque" linked Douglas's sexual encounters with the island's boys to pagan traditions. The island's girls also received Douglas's attentions. In his later writings, he recalled several such affairs. There was Enrichetta, "a little maid from the neighbouring farm," who devoted herself to his happiness in the years following the divorce.[10] She died during the typhoid epidemic of 1913, but Douglas immortalized her by giving her name to a character in *South Wind*. Another affair with "a Capri girl" in 1906 was so "all-consuming" that Douglas claimed he remained faithful to her even when a wealthy seventeen-year-old girl from Naples tried to lure him into betrayal.[11] Maybe Douglas's notoriety made him an object of desire to some of the youths he encountered.

That seems to have been the case for the bohemian writer Muriel Draper. Douglas had built such a reputation as a danger to youths that when Draper first visited Capri in 1906, at age twenty, her chaperones tried desperately to protect her from his evil influence. They did so despite the fact that one of her chaperones, Annie Bertram Webb, was Douglas's main financial benefactor. Webb purchased Douglas's library of rare books about Capri (which she donated to Harvard University) and also helped Douglas by pulling strings in his divorce battles. He thanked her by making fun of her in his memoir and by seducing her charge. Actually, by Draper's own account, it was she who, seeing her chaperones' reservations, first invited Douglas to tea. She plunged into their relationship enthusiastically, grateful for Douglas's life instructions. Her friendship with Douglas launched her down a path filled with lovers and conversation. The two maintained a lifelong correspondence rich in filthy language and ribald humor.[12]

Douglas's notoriety for sexual adventurism with Capri's children also attracted negative attention. The British consular agent on the island, Harold Trower, was so dismayed by Douglas's affairs that he tried to drive him from Capri, an insult for which Douglas never forgave him.[13] Trower failed in his efforts. However much Douglas outraged the moral sensibilities of the British agent, most Capriotes appear to have tolerated Douglas's behavior. Capri had a long reputation for offering shelter to pederasts, which was probably why Douglas had moved there in the first place. As the Italian historian Eugenio Zito explains, during the nineteenth and early twentieth centuries, Capri was famous as a "refuge" for pederasts, who for the most part experienced a culture of "tacit social tolerance and relative legal safety."[14]

Accounts of the sexual availability of the island's children had drawn tourists to Capri for a long time. As one seventeenth-century visitor commented, "The women are very beautiful, just like the boys, and both gladly do good turns."[15] In the late 1890s, when Douglas first began to spend significant time on the island, the coterie of foreigners who moved to Capri for its girls and boys was growing. There was the German artist Christian Wilhelm Allers, who painted neo-Hellenist erotic images of local boys, before the Neapolitan police threatened to arrest him and he fled to Samoa. There was also the German munitions manufacturer Friedrich Krupp, who more than once conveyed Douglas from Naples to Capri in his yacht. Krupp's great wealth and generosity helped smooth the way for him in Capri, but his sexual predilections caused trouble back home. In 1902 the German socialist magazine *Vorwärts* exposed Krupp's Capri affairs. Shortly afterward, the industrialist died suddenly, likely from suicide.

Krupp's suicide pained Douglas even decades later. In *Looking Back*, he described Krupp as a kind man, who had been unfairly attacked by a local teacher who resented Krupp's generosity to a rival language instructor. "If Krupp, in a burst of Teutonic idealism and demonstrativeness, placed his arm on the shoulder of some young sailor like Silvestro, that was so far as it ever went," Douglas insisted. Even so, Douglas said he wouldn't care a tuppence if the insinuations had been true. "I should think it rather sporting of the old gentleman to have indulged in love-affairs of any kind, at his time of life."[16] Douglas was far more willing to admit in print to his own immorality than to reveal the truth about his friends. According to a historian of the Krupp family, Friedrich Krupp hosted parties at a grotto on his Capri property where boys were served wine and encouraged to engage in public sex acts (rockets were set off when they orgasmed) while a local photographer snapped shots that were later sold by a pornographer.[17] It's more than likely that Douglas attended as a guest along with other friends from the island.

Another infamous pederast who made his home on the island in the early twentieth century, the French poet Jacques d'Adelswärd-Fersen, settled in Capri at Douglas's own suggestion. Fersen was arrested in Paris in 1903 for modeling naked schoolboys in *tableaux vivants* at his salon, then taking them into the bathroom and masturbating them or performing oral sex on them.[18] After his release from La Santé prison, Fersen visited Capri, looking for a place to live. Douglas showed him an appealing spot where he could build a villa. Later Douglas regretted his helpfulness, not because he disapproved of Fersen's pederasty, but because the poet's presence became a source of discord within the exile community.[19] His regrets did not stop Douglas, however, from capitalizing on Fersen's notoriety. According to Martin Birnbaum, Douglas loved to gossip about "all the scandalous details of the life of Fersen."[20] Later Fersen became the subject of two classic novels about Capri.[21]

There were also Englishmen among the island's notorious pederasts. Douglas was close friends with John Ellingham Brooks, a Cambridge University graduate and student of the classics who lived in Capri for most of his life, at times sharing his house with the popular writer W. Somerset Maugham, whom Brooks had first seduced when he was twenty-six and Maugham was only sixteen.[22] Once he grew up, Maugham shared his former lover's sexual orientation toward male youths. His longtime companion Gerald Haxton "produced young boys" for Maugham to sleep with, according to Maugham's nephew, who was fond of boys himself.[23] Maugham and Douglas were not close friends, nonetheless Maugham helped Douglas financially for many years, according to Alan Searle, Maugham's last lover. Searle, who was a teenager when he first met Douglas, recalled him as "a really wicked man and wonderful company."[24]

Brooks and Maugham also shared their villa with the writer E. F. Benson, the son of Edward Benson, the archbishop of Canterbury who had courted his own eleven-year-old cousin Minnie. E. F. Benson's sexual history remains obscure, but his erotic inclinations are clear enough from his ownership of many translations of the "Musa Paidika."[25] According to Faith Mackenzie, who was friends with the two men, Brooks and Benson "had tastes in common besides literature, which made Capri a desirable retreat for them both." Their joint residence wasn't based on friendship or even mutual respect. In fact, Brooks was dismissive of Benson's popular "Mapp and Lucia" novels, calling them "deplorable trash" and saying he turned the pages but couldn't read them. Benson, for his part, scoffed at Brooks's endless "pathetic pains with translations of Greek epigrams" that never yielded any books.[26]

But Douglas appreciated the translations, which he used in his 1927 book *Birds and Beasts of the Greek Anthology*, dedicated to Brooks.[27] The translations weren't very good, but Douglas liked the idea of Brooks spending his days in Capri devoting endless hours to translations of the *Greek Anthology* for no greater purpose than the pleasure of it. Brooks embodied the Hellenic spirit of Capri that Douglas had first glimpsed in Gregorovius's account. The island's evocation of the ancient past was as forceful an attractor, for Douglas, as the sexual availability of its youths. The two were inextricably related in the person of Brooks.

Once Douglas became well known as a writer, Capri's pagan spirit and pederastic opportunities would be linked in his person as well. Douglas came to be seen by many as a modern-day iteration of Tiberius, the Roman emperor who had retired to Capri in 36 AD and was notorious for organizing pederastic orgies involving the island's youths. A bit of doggerel written by a poet on Capri asked, "Was there a sin Tiberius committed / Which would one moment find N.D. outwitted?" There were famous Tiberian dinners held on Capri where Douglas appeared as a guest of honor.[28]

Douglas contributed to this conflation of himself and Tiberius through his writings. His blissful years on Capri following his divorce were not entirely given over to sexual affairs with youths. Douglas also took pleasure in the recondite joys of research and writing. Campo Alegre had once given Douglas a copy of the dialogues of Petrarch, the fourteenth-century father of humanism. Campo Alegre enchanted Douglas with stories of how Petrarch had explored "a trackless world and rediscover[ed] the old landmarks" and made himself "lord of all the buried past."[29] When he moved to Capri, Douglas was determined to follow in Petrarch's footsteps. He began researching the ancient history of the island and writing about his discoveries. Later he confessed that he had "seldom enjoyed myself more than while writing with infinite trouble a series of dull monographs" about the island.[30] The eight pamphlets Douglas published about Capri between 1904 and 1907 (a ninth appeared in 1915) marked a turning point in his writing life. In their pages he began to find his voice.

Douglas's research for the pamphlets began in Naples's Biblioteca Nazionale, where he read hundreds of old books in Italian, German, English, and French, taking close notes in small leather-bound lined journals that he later indexed.[31] On Capri, he continued his explorations by foot, boat, and donkey. Martin Birnbaum recalled that Douglas was a "tireless walker," who was indefatigable in his exploration of every corner of the island. Together, they "rowed into every grotto, blue, red, or green; we explored the great caves and climbed at low tide through the pitch-dark chimney-like passage to the top of the Monacone, one of the *faraglioni*, where traces of the rifled tomb of the architect of Tiberius could still be examined." All the while, Douglas regaled Birnbaum with stories of the island's scandals. "There was never a dull moment in Douglas's company," Birnbaum said. "To know Douglas during those days was a rare privilege."[32]

The pamphlets that resulted from these researches capture Douglas's transformation from gentleman scholar to literary wit. Whereas his earlier pamphlets had sought to make contributions to scientific knowledge, these new pamphlets were intended to amuse. Douglas's writing began to take on the narrative quality of fiction. In *The Blue Grotto and Its Literature* (1904), he described the Capriote fisherman who first told a visiting Polish tourist about the island's most famous sea cave: "At the departure of Kopisch from Capri in 1829, Angelo Ferraro woke up to find himself famous."[33] It's a sentence that tells a story.

Douglas's research remained unimpeachable, but his presentation became playful. In his journals he carefully entered the full bibliographical information for each of his sources, as well as important details, with the page numbers cited. But in his pamphlets, he wore his learning lightly. The scholars he so studiously consulted appeared as characters of fun. He took pages of notes on the eighteenth-century author Antonio Parrino's many volumes, only to teasingly dismiss the historian as a "cantankerous and inaccurate scribbler."[34] A seventeenth-century author came in for even worse treatment. Douglas called him "an industrious but indiscriminate compiler," and complained that he "seems to have lacked all sense of the necessity of subordinating his laboriously accumulated data, he quotes from parchments which no one save himself has seen, his references are inadequate, his indices incomplete or wholly wanting."[35] One detects a note of self-deprecation in this description. Didn't Douglas's notebooks reveal his own indiscriminate industry? Didn't he quote from authorities no one had ever read?

Douglas was clearly writing in the ironical mode in his fourth pamphlet, *The Lost Literature of Capri* (1906), when he observed of another author: "We are told that the cause of Giraldi's sojourn on Capri was his wife, who passed as a beautiful and intelligent woman, but who *'poisoned his life'* and drove him to take refuge there with his son."[36] Readers of the pamphlet, which was privately distributed to friends, would surely have observed the implicit parallel between Giraldi's and Douglas's biographies.

Douglas identified most strongly with Tiberius, whom he wrote about frequently. According to the Roman historian Suetonius, Tiberius had devoted his life on Capri to perverse pleasures. Adults were not enough to sate his appetites. He taught the little children of the island to play between his legs when he was in the bath, and "those which had not yet been weaned, but were strong and hearty, he set at fellatio." He called these children his little fish.[37] Suetonius's scandalous account made Tiberius's name a byword for vice. He appeared as a character in pornography.[38] Tiberius's misdeeds became part of the lore of Capri peddled by tour guides, or *cicerones*, to gentlemen on the Grand Tour. Locals liked to point out the spot at the mountaintop ruins of Villa Jovis, Tiberius's residence on Capri, where the perverted emperor had supposedly pushed his enemies off the cliff to their deaths. Capri's notoriety for pederasty was appealing even to visitors who didn't share an erotic appetite for youths.

Before his divorce, Douglas accepted the common narrative about Tiberius as fact. His 1901 short story "Nerinda" describes Tiberius as having shown an "inhuman lust of cruelty."[39] But the first of Douglas's Capri pamphlets indicated a shift in his thinking. He insisted that allegations about Tiberius's frolics in the Blue Grotto "with the fair nymphs of his harem" were invented by the *cicerones*.[40] The fifth pamphlet in the Capri series, published after Elsa accused him of molesting Archie, delivered a defense of Tiberius that spoke loudly of his sense of identification with the slandered emperor. Tiberius, according to Douglas, was "embittered in his family and marital relations" when he moved to Capri. But Douglas denied that the end of the emperor's life was characterized by "cruelty and lust." He laughed off allegations that Tiberius was a "prototype of the Marquis de Sade." Suetonius was not a neutral observer. His mischaracterizations were designed to bolster Tiberius's political enemies. Plus, Douglas objected, his account was internally inconsistent. "The love of drunkenness, with which [Tiberius] is credited, would effectively preclude certain others." In other words, if Tiberius were drunk all the time, he would hardly be able to get erections.[41] Not everyone was happy to see Tiberius rehabilitated. Lytton Strachey wrote to Douglas, "I had hoped some flaws might have been found in the modern theory—but no doubt you are right. Only I am sorry to exchange that dramatic monster for such a respectable old person."[42]

Tiberius was only one of Douglas's classical pederast avatars. Friends and acquaintances also associated Douglas with the Greek satirist Lucian of Samosata, whose works included a dialogue, "Erotes," which one scholar has described as "the swan song of the Greek pederastic tradition."[43] Another of Lucian's works retold the story of Hyacinth, a beautiful Spartan prince who was beloved by both Apollo and Zephyrus. Douglas quoted from Lucian's Hyacinth dialogue in a book he helped his friend Edward Hutton to write about their travels together in Greece.[44] Douglas and Lucian held another point in common. Lucian was infamous for scoffing at religion and the supernatural. Douglas delighted in satirizing the absurdities of Christianity and other faiths. The seventh pamphlet in his Capri series, which appeared in 1907, retold the life of "the venerable Suor Serafina di Dio," a seventeenth-century religious figure from Capri. But Douglas's retelling didn't offer much veneration. Instead, Douglas attributed Suor Serafina's religious ecstasies to the sublimation of "misguided sexual yearnings into a sub-carnal passion for the Son of God," and quoted from the sexologist Havelock Ellis for support.[45]

Douglas was also likened by friends and acquaintances to Silenus, a satyr who was tutor to Bacchus, the god of wine. Compton Mackenzie used this analogy when describing Duncan Maxwell, the character modeled after Douglas in his novel about Capri, *Vestal Fire*.[46] Compton's wife, Faith Mackenzie, who first visited Capri at Douglas's invitation in 1914, described how that spring Douglas rode around the island by donkey, "like Silenus on his ass."[47] Silenus had to be carried by ass because he was so frequently drunk. Douglas had to be carried by ass because he had twisted his ankle, an injury that he probably sustained while stumbling home drunk along Capri's narrow hillside streets after an evening of *strega* on the piazzetta. Douglas gave the impression of Silenus even when he wasn't mounted. His friend Viva King said she used to think of Douglas as old Silenus and sometimes would check under the table for his goat's feet.[48] Douglas's association with the island of Capri made the image stick. A notice published after Douglas's death called him "a Caledonian Silenus" who had "helped make Capri the most notorious island."[49]

It's hard to imagine a more unlikely pairing than the words "Caledonian" and "Silenus." The Scotland of Douglas's ancestry was dour and bleak. Aberdeen, the nearest city to Tilquhillie, is nicknamed the Grey City for the shadowy granite from which its stone buildings were hewed. It evokes none of the classical aura of Capri's whitewashed villas and pillared colonnades. Edwin Cerio, mayor of Capri in the early 1920s, once commented on how his friend Douglas, a "faun of Scotland," came to "acquire the citizenship of Paganism."[50] After World War II, Cerio engineered honorary Capri citizenship for Douglas. Even in the early 1950s, the Capriotes celebrated the notorious pederast.

"You are the last of the pagans! The modern Petronius Arbiter," the author Oscar Levy wrote to Douglas. Levy's remark connected Douglas to another classical satirist, the purported author of the *Satyricon*, a comic novel recounting the misadventures of Encolpius and his boy lover, Giton. Although the title of Petronius's novel does not derive from the word *satyr*, the two were often associated, including by Levy, who commiserated in the same letter, "We two are the only surviving Satyrs."[51] Levy, an enthusiastic womanizer, identified with Douglas's embrace of sexual pleasure. Levy was a Nietzschean who financed the translation of the German philosopher's complete works into English, and he saw a kinship between his own Nietzschean rejection of the tenets of good and evil and Douglas's strident amoralism.[52] For his part, Douglas had no appetite for modern philosophy.

Eventually Douglas moved away from Capri, but he never abandoned the island's pagan spirit. The ancient world held an inseverable attraction for Douglas because it sanctioned his sexual relations with children to a degree that modern Nietzscheanism could not rival. According to John Addington Symonds and Walter Pater—the two late nineteenth-century authors whose writings most influenced Douglas's understandings of the ancient world—the Greeks viewed the pederastic relationship, in which an older man inspired by the beauty of a younger male took on his education, as a positive good. The rediscovery of the pederastic tradition by British scholars like Symonds and Pater laid the groundwork on which a positive view of homosexuality would be built in the twentieth century. Oscar Wilde quoted from Pater and called on the Greek tradition in his closing remarks at his first 1895 trial for gross indecency.[53]

It's not simply that neo-Hellenism provided a context for pederasts like Douglas to rationalize their sexual relationships with children. The existence of the Greek pederastic tradition made neo-Hellenism an attractive cultural tradition in the first place. Men like Pater and Symonds adored the Greeks because of the ancients' appreciation for love between older and younger males. The romance of the pederastic tradition was baked into the reputation that Douglas acquired as a modern pagan. It was an essential part of his allure when, following his move to Capri, he began to build his reputation as a writer.

Reflection I

Even before Norman Douglas became famous as a writer, people regarded him as extraordinary. It was a rare privilege to know him during those early days, in Martin Birnbaum's wistful words. The traces of Douglas's charisma still cling to the archive, but his seductive powers have been diminished by time. In today's light, his charms appear tawdry: his scholarly wit, just the gilding of a gentleman's education; his sexual rapacity no longer daring, but the unbridled expression of inherited privilege. From today's perspective, Norman Douglas seems all too predictable, not worth caring about—except that his willingness to trespass the bounds of Victorian politesse has left a documentary record of a routine but disreputable variety of sexual behavior that most people then and now would rather not discuss.

Contemporary logic dictates that something is profoundly wrong with a person if they are sexually drawn to children and youths. They must be broken inside. It's easy to slot Douglas into this narrative. His early childhood was traumatic. His father died in a horrible accident, plunging to his death from a mountainside. Or possibly, the death was a suicide. Douglas expressed suspicions about why his father chose to travel by such a dangerous route. In the family chaos that followed, Douglas acted out sexually and in other ways, experimenting with alcohol before he was six. Then he was sent to a boarding school where the children were beaten, and he may have either witnessed or been subjected to sexual abuse by the teachers. Meanwhile, his mother remarried and had a new baby, emotionally replacing him. Freud would have had a lot to say. But Douglas wouldn't have any of it. "They could just as well psychoanalyse me as circumcise me!" he liked to scoff.[1] Douglas thought Freudian theory was just another variety of mumbo-jumbo, no more meaningful than theology.

Douglas didn't think there was anything broken about himself. Quite the opposite. As he saw it, his early childhood in Vorarlberg had laid the foundations for a rare independence of character that made him disdainful of hypocrisy. He refused to be bound by false morality. It was the rest of the world who were damaged by their monotheistic delusion in good and evil. Most readers won't agree with Douglas that taboos against sex between adults and young people signify a false morality. But he had a point about society's hypocrisy. Real or false, this moral injunction was frequently broken. As in other regards, Douglas was not extraordinary in pursuing sexual encounters with children and youths, but rather predictable. The most unusual aspect of his sexuality was his taste for self-disclosure. Douglas's predictable life and unusual openness lay bare the unpleasant truth that sex between young people and adults, far from an aberration, fit into established cultural and social norms during his childhood and early adulthood.

A rich tradition of Western scholarship and art positively described intergenerational encounters. As a student, Douglas read works by modern German and British authors who celebrated the pederastic poetry and sculpture of the ancient world. Additionally, child prostitution was widespread. As a young man, Douglas paid for sex with children and youths in Russia, Italy, India, and the Ottoman Empire. He visited and lived in places that were known to be amenable to his sexual desires. Eventually, Douglas began to craft a public persona as a pederast. His sexual honesty drew admirers who found his evocation of the pagan ideal to be romantic. Many of his friends likely engaged in active not-knowing about his sexual predilections. They knew he was a pederast, but they chose not to think about the raw mechanics of the acts that were involved. Turn-of-the-century Anglophone culture did not ideologically tolerate sex between adults and children. It was proscribed then, as it is now. But lots of things were proscribed, and people engaged in a lot of active not-knowing for the sake of convenience. The fact that gross power imbalances structured most types of sexual encounters at the turn of the century, including those between husbands and wives, made the power imbalance between adults and young people less distinctive than it is today.

Sex between adults and children was more normal during Douglas's early adulthood than it is now. That's troubling to read because "normal" sounds like a moral judgment. I'm using the term as a statement of fact. If I don't use the word "normal" to describe a widespread social practice set within a well-elaborated cultural framework, whose interest am I serving? Whose interest does it serve to insist that only broken people want sex with children and youths? There is plenty of evidence that in times and places where sex with young people was considered normative, many adult men engaged in sex with young people. The capacity for this sexual expression must be widespread. Insisting that only monsters could desire children is a form of active not-knowing that does more to exculpate ordinary adults from suspicion than it does to protect children from harm. The monster narrative casts children's ordinary experiences as unbelievable or unspeakable.

Protectionist discourse about the sexuality of women has long been scrutinized by historians who spy the iron fist of social control hiding beneath its ostensible tendernesses. Some scholars express a similar suspicion of protectionist discourse about children's sexuality. "Cultural values ebb and flow at various periods, and ideas about the sexual child are no different," write Emma Renold, Jessica Ringrose, and R. Danielle Egan in their introduction to a coedited volume on children and sexuality. But, they point out, the scholarship on childhood sexuality is different because it's plagued by "fear, projection, fascination, and consternation." As ideas about modern childhood took shape in the Anglophone West, the social construction of the child was "inextricably tied to the education, regulation and normalization of its sexuality." That makes it almost impossible to discuss children's sex and sexuality except through the lens of abuse and exploitation.[2] Childhood, a historically shifting category, is today defined by the negation of sexual agency.[3] Children are those persons who by reason of chronological age cannot consent to sex.

The Douglas archive is extraordinary because it includes the voices of children who described their encounters with Douglas in terms that challenge protectionist discourse and force a reckoning with the history of children's agentic sexuality. Following the breakup of his marriage, Douglas entered into a series of long-lasting relationships with boys that broke from the pattern of ephemeral and transactional encounters he had pursued beforehand. The boys remained bound to Douglas throughout their adult lives. Douglas's early ephemeral sexual encounters left few sources that captured the perspective of the children. Annetta and Michele are silenced in the record. The sustained relationships that Douglas entered into during his forties onward produced letters, diaries, and remembrances by the children. These primary sources allow for a sustained engagement with questions around consent and agency that is typically impossible to derive from the sources. The children's writings are the most singular source in the Douglas archive, rarer even than Orioli's ribald diaries, and perhaps even harder to read and reconcile.

PART II
Norman Douglas

CHAPTER SIX

Norman Douglas

"It is obvious to me that you have a distinguished future before you as a Writer. And also some hard times before you get known. Think seriously of writing a novel."[1] Joseph Conrad's letter of advice to Douglas arrived in February 1908. By December of that year, Douglas had placed his first piece of commercial fiction in a popular magazine and signed his name "Norman Douglas" for the first time.[2] The man had just turned forty. The writer was newborn.

Over the course of his life, Douglas went by several names. He was George Norman Douglass when he was christened. He was "G. N. Douglass" in the flyleaves of his schoolbooks.[3] He was Von. G. Norman Douglass in 1892 when he published an essay, in German, on the wildlife of the Greek island of Santorini. And he was plain G. Norman Douglass when he wrote his essays in English on the birdlife and herpetology of Baden. He was one-half of Normyx when he coauthored *Unprofessional Tales* with Elsa in 1901. He signed his series of privately printed pamphlets on the history and geography of Capri with the initials N.D. Only in 1908, when he began writing for the commercial market, did he become Norman Douglas, the name he'd be known by for the remainder of his life.[4]

Writing for money wasn't a choice but a necessity. By 1908 Douglas was out of cash, and out of properties and libraries to liquidate. His past acquaintance with several popular writers, including Sir Arthur Conan Doyle and F. Marion Crawford—a best-selling American novelist who lived in Sorrento across the Bay of Naples—persuaded Douglas that there was money to be made in fiction.[5] At least this is the explanation Douglas gave in *Looking Back* for his decision to become a professional writer. He neglects to mention that he had just as many writer acquaintances who were perpetually short on cash.

Before he lost his fortune, Douglas had repeatedly loaned money to the novelist Maria Louise Ramé, known as Ouida. Despite the success of her novels, the author had little to live off by the turn of the twentieth century, when Douglas and Elsa wrote to ask whether they might dedicate *Unprofessional Tales* to her. Ouida's influence on their collection extended from the plotting and writing, to the use of a one-name pen name. When Ouida responded to Douglas and Elsa's letters with a request for a helping hand, the couple were happy to oblige. They even offered to host her in the Villa Maya. Douglas continued to offer Ouida what help he could until his own well ran dry. The experience should have been a warning to him about the perils of pinning his financial hopes on a writing career.

Conrad too, despite his *succès d'estime*, had difficulty making ends meet. He borrowed money from Douglas more than once. The two writers first met in Capri in early 1905, when Conrad visited the island with his wife, Jessie, and their son Borys. He was broke at the time and in poor health, conditions that he did not disguise from Douglas.[6] From their first meetings, Conrad was impressed by Douglas's intelligence. He described Douglas in a letter to H. G. Wells as a man "who can not only think but write."[7]

Conrad's feelings for his new friend went beyond intellectual respect to something more intimate. Conrad seemed to regard Douglas as an echo of himself, almost a doppelganger, a theme that intrigued him as a writer.[8] Like Conrad, Douglas had not spoken English as his mother tongue, yet he had made himself into a master of the language. Like Conrad, Douglas had pursued a prior career before trying to reinvent himself as a writer in his late thirties.[9] Conrad's identification with Douglas led him to take "the matter to heart" of advancing Douglas's writing career.[10] Over time, he also helped Douglas in his personal life, by taking Douglas's younger son, Robin, into his household after the custody battle between Norman and Elsa. Conrad remained a steady presence in Robin's life for many years, providing a home to the boy when he wasn't in school. But letters between Douglas and Conrad focused more attention on what Conrad was doing to advance his friend's career than to help his friend's son.

Immediately after they first met, Conrad wrote to his literary agent, J. B. Pinker, recommending that he take Douglas as a client. Pinker wasn't just any literary agent, but a man who has been credited with inventing the profession.

15. Robin Douglas (*left*) and John Conrad (*right*). 1911. Private collection of Deirdre Sholto Douglas. Photograph by author.

The writers he represented included James Joyce, Henry James, H. G. Wells, D. H. Lawrence, Ford Madox Ford, Katherine Mansfield, and Stephen Crane. Conrad told Pinker that he thought "Mr Douglass" had a promising future as a magazine writer, and that "the handling of his stuff you will find easy and so far profitable." Douglas was even amenable to writing on suggested subjects, Conrad promised, although "of course it will be no hack work as a glance at the pages I send will make clear."[11] Douglas's prose was learned with a wry touch. At its best, his writing gave the seductive impression of passing time with the smart and funny rebel who sat in the back of class. It was a voice that a reader could fall in love with. Well, it was a voice that a smart, skeptical, educated reader with a desire to laugh at conventions could fall in love with. But for all of Conrad's assurances to J. B. Pinker about Douglas's commercial potential, it wasn't a voice that appealed to everyone.

When Conrad sent Pinker a brief bio of Douglas, he let slip that his new friend's first book had sold only three copies.[12] Conrad blamed the poor sales on the publisher. He accused them of swindling Douglas and suggested to

Pinker that maybe something could still be done with the remainders. But Pinker wasn't sold. Soon Conrad began sending Douglas's writings to editors himself. It wasn't an easy sell. By July 1905, he was telling Douglas that he needed to make his voice more accessible: "You don't allow enough for the imbecility of human nature."[13]

It can take a long time to catch a break. Three years later Conrad consoled Douglas, "Its weary slow work at best this trying to get a footing in the world of scribblers and publishers. Yet it can be done—with patience."[14] Douglas managed to place two pieces with American magazines in 1908: a nonfiction article in the *Atlantic Monthly* alleging that Milton had cribbed *Paradise Lost* from an Italian author; and a short supernatural story in the *Cavalier*, which he extracted from *Unprofessional Tales* and published under the name "Norman Douglas."

He was not yet committed to his new pen name. Douglas later sold stories from *Unprofessional Tales* under the names Wilfrid Hale, Edward Morris, E. F. Lyubin, and Albany Clifford.[15] The last name combined an allusion to Douglas's London address at the time, an apartment building called Albany Mansions, and the name of a famous atheist philosopher, W. K. Clifford, who wrote, "It is wrong always, everywhere, and for anyone, to believe anything upon insufficient evidence."[16] Douglas may have taken "Lyubin" from a popular Ivan Turgenev play, which featured a roué character by that name. Turgenev was a favorite writer of Conrad's.[17] Douglas's inspirations for using the names Wilfrid Hale and Edward Morris are lost to time. Rumors have circulated about other pseudonyms.[18] Many thought Douglas to be the author of a 1906 collection of supernatural tales titled *Stories of Strange Women*, published under the name "J. Y. F. Cooke." But Douglas told the bibliographer Cecil Woolf that he never used this name.[19] In fact, J. Y. F. Cooke was the real name of a railway engineer who retired in 1899, and considering that the first story in *Strange Women* is narrated by a railway engineer, it seems likely that the book was authored by this man.[20]

If Douglas was primarily motivated by the desire to make money from writing, then writing supernatural stories for the era's popular pulp magazines would have made sense. Many of Douglas's author friends made more money from short stories than from their novels. D. H. Lawrence wrote to Pinker in November 1916 that he was finishing his most recent novel and "I *do* hope, now, we can begin to make a little money, on stories, etc. in America." Echoing authors throughout the ages, Lawrence moaned that he was "tired of being always pinched and penniless."[21] Literary fiction did not pay well. Literary nonfiction paid even worse. When Douglas showed Conrad a short piece he had drafted about a devastating 1908 earthquake in southern Italy that killed as many as 200,000 people, Conrad replied, "I entreat you earnestly to try and throw your impressions of Messina into the *form of a story.* Do try my dear fellow. I believe you would get both money and kudos that way. Where as an article or a small book would bring very little."[22] Douglas failed to take Conrad's advice and published his essay, "Land of Chaos," in the *Cornhill Magazine* in September 1910.[23]

"Land of Chaos" interwove Douglas's memories of visits to the city of Messina in September 1908, before the earthquake, with glimpses of the destruction that followed, which he had witnessed firsthand when he traveled there in June 1909 to deliver contributions he'd raised from the expatriate community in Capri. The essay combined the astute attention to detail familiar from his naturalist essays with the personal narrative voice he had developed in his Capri pamphlets, and took an innovative approach to chronology, jumbling past and present together with the same kaleidoscopic effect that he later perfected in *Looking Back.*

Recounting his satisfaction in a meal enjoyed during his September 1908 visit, Douglas wrote: "No prophetic visions of the Messina of to-day, with its minute sheds perched among a wilderness of ruins and haunted by sacred shadows in sable vestements of mourning, arose in my mind that evening as I sat at the little marble evening table, sipping my coffee over-roasted, like all Italian coffee, by exactly two minutes and puffing contentedly at my cigar."[24] The description mixed past and present in a jumbled slurry while at the same time carving the flow of time into discrete pieces ("exactly two minutes"). The disordered chronology of "Land of Chaos" mimetically reproduced the upheavals wreaked by the quake itself, which Douglas captured best in a metaphorical description of a fallen house:

> The house with its inmates and all it contained was lying among the high-piled wreckage within, under my feet; masonry mostly— entire fragments of walls interspersed with crumbling mortar and convulsed iron girders that writhed over the surface or plunged sullenly into the depths; fetid rents and gullies in between, their flanks affording glimpses of broken vases, candelabras, hats, bottles, birdcages, writing-books, brass pipes, sofas, picture-frames, tablecloths,

and all the paltry paraphernalia of every day life. No attempt at stratification, horizontal, vertical, or inclined; it was as if the objects had
been thrown up by some playful volcano and allowed to settle where
they pleased.[25]

The description was a tragic counterpoint to Douglas's earlier scholarship,
with its ordered lists of snakes, birds, and books. In "Land of Chaos," all the
objects Douglas observed were jumbled together, the writing books next to
the brass pipes, the conjunction so unexpected that it takes a moment to realize he isn't referring to pipes for smoking, but for plumbing. The chaos of
the quake obliterated all stratification. Time's layers collapsed. Douglas was
crushed by the devastation he witnessed. A Catholic newspaper's attempt to
blame the quake on Messina's spiritual failings made him spitting mad. He
saw no such "divine message" in the quake; "the just were entombed with
the unjust" amid much "heart-breaking."[26] His own heartbreak resonated
throughout the piece.

"Land of Chaos" is an emotionally moving, formally innovative, exquisite
miniature that engages readers in communal mourning for the lives lost to
the earthquake. It was the best thing that Douglas had yet written. As such,
it raises one of the unavoidable questions haunting this book: What can be
done with the work of artists whose life histories offend contemporary moral
standards? Or, as Claire Dederer puts the question: "What do we do with the
art of monstrous men?"[27] Can readers appreciate Douglas's art if they know
about his life? This question is germane to "Land of Chaos," because Douglas's mournful eulogy for Messina is impassioned by his erotic sensibility.

At its surface, the essay operates in the best humanist tradition, seeking to
expand the boundaries of empathetic sensibility. The essay sought to make
faraway English readers, who had little regard for the slum-dwellers of southern Italy, feel the tragedy of the staggering loss of life in Messina and open
their pockets to lessen the post-quake suffering. A century later, the essay produces a similar effect in bridging the gap of time, cutting through the numb-
ing enormity of a historic death toll measured in the hundreds of thousands
to convey the individual humanity of each soul lost in the destruction.

But can the rights of the piece countervail the wrongs of its author?
One of the major draws that brought Douglas to Messina before the
quake was its boys. Sicily stood alongside Capri as an Italian destination
notorious for its child sex trade. To Englishmen of the era, Sicily represented ancient Greece on Italian soil. Its rocky landscape was studded with

16. *Hypnos* by Wilhelm von Gloeden. Wikimedia Commons.

grand ruins of the Hellenic past, and its youths were supposedly amenable to pederastic traditions. Some of the grandest ruins could be found in Taormina, thirty miles from Messina, where the German photographer Wilhelm von Gloeden set up his studio, taking photographs of well-endowed Sicilian youths posed like Grecian statuary.[28] These pictures were bought by luminaries of the homosexual rights movement, including Symonds and Wilde. One of the first modern English public expressions of homosexual desire was Theodore Wratislaw's 1893 poem "To a Sicilian Boy," which is considered a pivotal text in queer history. Alfred Douglas followed months later with his own homoerotic poem "Sicilian Love Song."[29]

Traces of this pederastic sensibility can be found in "Land of Chaos," alongside the humanism of its guiding ethos. Douglas's description of two "handsome lads" and their uncle whom he befriended at the city gardens before the quake echoed Gloeden's imagery. "I can see them still, the two boys, their grave demeanour belied by mobile lips and mischievous fair curls." Douglas had a thing for boys with curls. "Land of Chaos" recounted the beauty of these lads for erotic purposes, and to evoke the reader's empathy. After the quake, Douglas visited the family's address and found their home in ruins. This was the house whose contents Douglas had seen thrown into disarray, books and copper pipes side by side.

When he looked on the devastation, Douglas "thought of the two nephews, their decent limbs all distorted and mangled under a heap of foul rubbish, waiting for brutal disinterment and a nameless grave. This is no legitimate death, this hideous violation of life. How inconceivably odious is such a leave-taking, and all that follows after! To picture a fair young body, that exquisite engine of delights, crushed into an unsightly heap; once loved, now loathed of all men, and thrust at last, with abhorrence, into some common festering pit of abominations! . . ." Douglas's words trailed off, as if the horror were too great for him to contemplate.[30]

This is the alchemy of art. It transmutes base into gold. Douglas's erotic appreciation for the physical beauty of the Sicilian youths generated the passion of his grief over their loss. It was his horror at the image of "a fair young body, that exquisite instrument of delights, crushed," that inspired Douglas to write "Land of Chaos." Douglas's voice in the piece is both objectifying and empathizing. Many neo-Hellenists, like Symonds and Pater, idealized pederasty as spiritually elevating. It's easy to dismiss these pretensions as lipstick on a pig. But Douglas's sexual desire for children and youths did inspire much of the humanity of his writing.

Conrad advised Douglas to turn his piece on Messina into a story so he could sell it. Despite Douglas's claims that he became a professional writer because he needed the money, he rejected Conrad's sound advice. Selling "Land of Chaos" to the *Cornhill* likely didn't pay, but at least the essay caught the eye of publishers. Reg Smith, editor at the *Cornhill*, began discussing the prospect of publishing a book by Douglas. Before Smith and Douglas could reach terms, another publisher, J. M. Dent, stepped in with a firm offer of a forty-pound advance to publish a book of Douglas's essays on Capri and the Sorrentine Peninsula, a handful of which had appeared the previous year in the *English Review*, edited by Ford Madox Hueffer (who had not yet anglicized his last name to Ford). Hueffer called one of the essays, which was about sirens, the best thing he ever published in the *English Review*. Douglas titled his book *Siren Land* after this essay. The book came out in 1911.

Douglas often said that each of his books was inspired by falling in love. In the case of *Siren Land*, the object of his affections was Pasqualino Amitrano, nicknamed Nico, a "small but efficient peasant boy" who lived with Douglas in spring 1908 at the Casa degli Spiriti in Nerano, at the tip of the Sorrentine Peninsula, working as his houseboy while Douglas wrote. Amitrano and Douglas spent several months in each other's solitary company, wandering the local trails, down to the deserted beach at Recomone, and up to the crumbling Martello tower at the peak of Ierate, a wilderness overgrown with aromatic evergreen shrubs. These wanderings involved sexual encounters that established Nerano as a "sacred spot" for Douglas, and one he would return to often throughout his life. Pino Orioli, who visited Nerano several times with Douglas in the 1930s, wrote in his idiosyncratic English that the area was "full of indementicable memoires" for Douglas from his times with Amitrano.[31]

Amitrano came from the nearby town of Termini, and he supplied Douglas with many of the local legends that give magic to the pages of *Siren Land*.[32] His influence extended beyond the folklore of *Siren Land*. He, along with the other local boys whom Douglas hired to guide his explorations of the peninsula, inspired one of the book's most wistful passages, celebrating the youths of the region:

> It is not praising them unduly to say that their minds, like their limbs, grow straight without schooling, and that they possess an inborn sobriety which would be sought in vain among the corresponding class in the North. It is the quality which the Greeks called "sophrosyne." Inured to patriarchal discipline from earliest childhood and familiar with every phenomenon of life from birth to death, they view their surroundings objectively and glide through adolescence without any of the periodical convulsions and catastrophes of more introspective races. Their entire vocabulary consists, I should think, of scarce three hundred words, many of which would bring a blush to the cheek of Rabelais; yet their conversation is refreshingly healthy, and many subjects, popular enough elsewhere, are tacitly ignored or tabooed. Not Puritans, by any means, nor yet the reverse; they will bend either way, but, the strain relaxed, they forthwith straighten like a willow wand.[33]

The eroticism of this passage didn't alienate readers of *Siren Land*. It won him fans. Lytton Strachey wrote to Douglas, "I should like to know more about the conversation of the young Sirenlander which was calculated to bring a blush to Rabelais' cheek—and many other things."[34] Other readers, who didn't share Douglas's erotic inclinations, read his description of the boys of the Sorrentine Peninsula as evidence of his deep love for children.

Amitrano, like many of the boys with whom Douglas grew close, remained a friend for long afterward. Eight years later, in 1916, Douglas hired him to work as his cook at the Villa Behring in Capri, while he was writing *South Wind*. This was only fitting, since Douglas claimed that the earliest seeds for *South Wind* had been sewn during their hikes together in 1908. Amitrano, who was married by that time, probably was no longer Douglas's lover. But their friendship retained its "Rabelaisian" humor, judging from a brief note addressed to Amitrano that Douglas held on to throughout his life. The letter— instructions for Amitrano to come to Capri's Hotel Morgano dressed in his best clothes—included at its bottom a naughty sketch of a reclining tomcat, testicles facing outward, drawn by Douglas's brother-in-law, Olaf Gulbransson. No one, it seemed—not Amitrano, not Douglas, not Douglas's relatives— was overly concerned about the sexual history between the man and the boy.

It's easy to be skeptical about Douglas's claim to have fallen in love with Amitrano and the boys who followed. Contemporary sexual morality views love as incompatible with child sexual abuse. Historical systems of sexual morality thought differently. How can one know whether Douglas loved Amitrano? He certainly mourned Amitrano when he died from injuries in the Great War. Douglas memorialized him in later books, refusing to let his memories of this "laughter-loving child" fade into obscurity.[35] And he continued to visit Amitrano's widow and child. In April 1937 he found the pair in comfortable circumstances, but angrily concluded, "They would be faring better, if he were still alive."[36]

Many fans consider *Siren Land* to be Douglas's best book. Compton Mackenzie wrote that he was "as much bewitched by it as any mariner of long ago by the Sirens' song."[37] But critical success did not translate into commercial success. *Siren Land* earned Douglas little income beyond the initial advance. Many of the prints in the original run were pulped, although the book went through multiple subsequent reprints. The problem, according to Conrad, was that Douglas's writing was too smart to be accessible. "You haven't plumbed the vapid depths of public imbecility," Conrad advised his protégé. Typical readers, he explained, "have neither minds nor gullets. You must di-

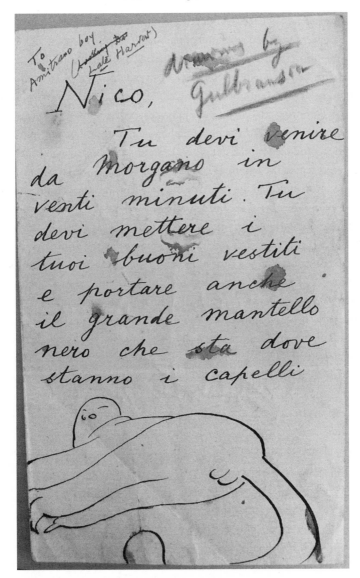

17. Note to Nico, probably written by Olaf Gulbransson. Norman Douglas Collection, Beinecke Rare Book and Manuscript Library, Yale University. Photograph by author.

lute your stuff. I am perfectly serious. It's like too strong Bovril. Nine people out of ten won't get it down and the tenth man will feel qualmish."[38] Conrad was right that Douglas's nonfiction had little commercial appeal. But *Siren Land* did make Douglas's literary reputation.

Martin Secker, an ambitious young publisher who printed many early works by modernist authors, offered Douglas a contract for his next book. In 1912 Secker published *Fountains in the Sand*, Douglas's account of his travels throughout Tunisia in 1910. Tunisia had similar attractions to Sicily and Naples. The boys there were reputed to be friendly to men's sexual advances. At the turn of the twentieth century, Wilhelm von Gloeden moved his studio to neighboring Algeria for a season to execute a series of eroticized images of Arab youths. Other photographers, like Rudolf Lehnert and Ernst Landrock, produced similar images in Tunis and Cairo. Orientalist literature often represented the bathhouse as a site for pederastic sexual encounters.[39] This tradition informed the very title of Douglas's *Fountains*. Amid accounts of the rocks and ruins of the French colony, Douglas included evocative descriptions of the Arab boys who jumped into the Roman baths in the city of Gafsa in exchange for a sou, and he wrote longingly of the Tunisian girls who washed their clothes at the oasis of Leila and were "frolicsome as gazelles but far less timid."[40] Gazelle-like limbs were a standard trope of Islamic pederastic poetry, suggesting Douglas's familiarity with this literature.[41]

Fountains in the Sand succumbs more to cliché than Douglas's books about Italy. It's also more freighted by prejudice—against Arabs, against Islam, against Jews, and even against Corsicans. That didn't bother readers at the time. Conrad judged the book to be "first rate" and admired its "unmistakable masculinity," even though he worried that a "hermaphroditic public" might object to the book's sexual content.[42] Sexual norms before World War I still regarded the sexualization of youths as evidence of hypermasculinity. Douglas's rapacious sexual appetite was proof of his manhood, rather than evidence of a monstrous sexual identity. His erotic inclinations were likely to offend un-sexed hermaphrodites—or prudes, in other words—but not readers with healthy appetites.

Unfortunately for Douglas, the British readership was full of prudes. The book didn't sell well, but it won him praise in the quarters that mattered, which softened the blow. In October 1912, Austin Harrison, the editor of the *English Review*, invited Douglas to step in as sub-editor.[43] Douglas had been writing reviews for the journal, based in Covent Garden, for a year. He quickly agreed to Harrison's job offer. The promise of a steady salary must have been very persuasive, but that wasn't Douglas's only reason for accepting a job in London. He was in love again, this time with a Camden Town boy named Eric Wolton.

CHAPTER SEVEN

London Street Games

Thirteen-year-old Eric Wolton loved Norman Douglas's "dear old face." At least, that's what he wrote to the forty-two-year-old author when the two were separated during a brief period in the summer of 1911. He wrote that he was "longing" to see Douglas again and signed the letter "your loving friend." The letter had its intended impact. Shortly afterward, Douglas came to collect Wolton from his parents' house and the two were reunited.[1]

Douglas's writings offer a rare firsthand glimpse into the attitudes of pederasts at the turn of the twentieth century. The letters that his juvenile lovers wrote him back offer a rarer insight still. The history of childhood is bedeviled by the problem that almost all its sources were written by adults. Historian Peter N. Stearns calls the absence of sources created by children "the granddaddy issue" in the field. Retrieving the child's voice from the past is difficult. The absence in the sources has opened the door for historians to fill in the silences with their own projections. In the absence of sources by Douglas's child lovers, it would be easy to speculate that the children experienced their encounters with the writer solely as damaging. But in Douglas's case, the sources do exist, and that presents a different dilemma. The letters and diaries written by the children often show affection for Douglas, upturning contemporary moral expectations. Stearns speaks to this issue of value judgments in the history of childhood as well, noting that those historical sources that do exist often reveal "features of childhoods past" that "seem unpleasant or bizarre." Historians must try to address this issue, he argues, by reexamining their own assumptions.[2]

Judging by what they wrote, many of the children who had sexual encounters with Douglas adored him. They adored him because he was old and a mentor and maybe because they enjoyed the sex. They adored him when they were children, and they continued to adore him after they had grown up, when their relationships had transformed into friendship or kinship. Some contemporary social scientists argue that adults who express ongoing affection for their childhood abusers are suffering from Stockholm syndrome.[3] Psychological explanations for human behaviors, however, are tricky to project backward, or laterally, onto times and places with different cultural norms in place. There have been many times and places where pederasty has been viewed as normative. How might the affection between boys and men be viewed in those contexts? Can we know for certain that a boy like Eric Wolton was suffering from Stockholm syndrome, as opposed to operating according to a set of cultural norms that are unfamiliar today?

Eric Wolton believed that Norman Douglas was the best thing that ever happened to him. The two first met at the Guy Fawkes celebration at London's Crystal Palace on November 5, 1910.[4] The Crystal Palace was an enormous glass-and-iron structure initially built for the Great Exhibition of 1851 in Hyde Park, then disassembled and rebuilt south of the Thames at Sydenham in 1854. By the turn of the century, the Crystal Palace was in disrepair, a decidedly down-market attraction. The writer John Davidson painted a word picture of the boisterous working-class youths who flocked to the Crystal Palace in a 1909 poem. The crowd had "hatless heads," "torn coats," "ragged skirts," "starved faces," and "heavy-shod" feet, yet these "solemn youths" and "ravished donahs" possessed a radiant beauty that drew the attention of more privileged men, like Davidson and Douglas.[5]

Wolton was one of those heavy-shod youth when he first met Douglas. A poor kid from Camden Town, he was, in his own words, a delinquent. "Had it not been for him I would have been doomed for all times," Wolton later told Douglas's friend Martha Gordon Crotch. "When he rescued me, I had already got into the frame of mind when I thought only dishonesty and violence could get me any share in the things I craved."[6] His parents had given up hope and planned to send him to reform school. Wolton's delinquency may have extended to prostitution. In the early twentieth century, sex work was a quasi-tolerated means for male youths to earn money in poor London neighborhoods. Moral arbiters and authorities expressed alarm about boy prostitution, but the boys themselves and many of their family members were more sanguine about the practice. Popular culture often depicted boys as the aggressors in intergenerational encounters, rather than the victims. The *Illus-*

trated Police News carried numerous stories of delinquent boys and youths who made unwanted advances on men. Concerns about children as the victims of predatory adults focused largely on girls before the 1920s.[7]

Odds are the initial encounter between Wolton and Douglas was both sexual and transactional. Douglas marked the date in his pocket diary with an *X*. He had made *X* marks on two previous dates in his 1910 calendar, using the symbol to keep track of some periodic occurrence that he didn't wish to spell out. In general, he filled his daily diary with the names of people he wrote letters to or met for meals. The *X* suggested another variety of personal interaction that Douglas thought should go unnamed. After Douglas met Wolton, the *X* marks in his diary proliferated. About a third of the days in November and more than half the days in December are marked with *X*'s.[8] If Douglas was using this symbol to record his sexual encounters, not all of them were with Wolton, since in late November, Douglas returned to Capri. But Douglas longed for Wolton, and in early 1911 he returned to London to invite the boy to join him on a journey through southern Italy.

Although it may seem strange to modern parenting sensibilities, it makes sense that when a fine gentleman showed up at the Woltons' door offering to educate their turbulent son by bringing him to Italy, they readily agreed. Even if they understood that Douglas's offer of mentorship came at a sexual price, Wolton's parents likely saw Douglas's interest in the boy as promising a far better payoff than the more fleeting encounters Wolton may have engaged in. It's possible that Douglas paid Wolton's parents directly for their son's sexual companionship, or that they hoped to extract money from him later. His 1914 diary includes a series of payments to "Camden" that likely went to the Woltons.[9] The 1911 calendar entries for the dates of Douglas and Wolton's trip, from April 12 to August 8, don't note any monetary transactions, but they are a riot of *X*'s. Some days Douglas marked with two or even three *X*'s. A few he marked with asterisks or *X*'s in circles. These variant marks may have been used by Douglas to mark out-of-the-ordinary sexual acts. There's no way to know.[10]

That Douglas's interest in Wolton was sexual is undoubted. Despite the risks, Douglas held on throughout his life to a nude picture of Wolton that he had snapped on a beach in Crotone, during their first visit to Calabria in 1911. The photo shows Wolton sitting on an empty stretch of sand. His is a child's body. He looks no older than his age. His knees are bent, left thigh hiding his genitals from view, his face turned directly to the camera,

18. Eric Wolton in Crotone, 1911. Norman Douglas Forschungsstelle, Bregenz.

eyes squinting in the bright sun. It's not a candid shot of a boy at play. The photo is carefully posed by an eye attuned to the beauty of boys' bodies. The photo might distress readers as visual evidence of Wolton's sexual abuse by Douglas. And yet classical statuary, or even neoclassical statuary, guided by the same aesthetic appreciation of boys' beauty, doesn't upset people. Take, for example, Hiram Powers's sculpture *Fisher Boy*, which shows a boy "of eight or nine years," in the sculptor's words, at roughly the same stage of physical development as Wolton in 1911. A model of *Fisher Boy* was displayed at the Crystal Palace Exhibition in 1851, and several marble replicates were later commissioned from Powers.[11] The *Fisher Boy* is representative of the cultural context that shaped Douglas's appreciation of boys' beauty. But contemporary culture values the work of an artist like Powers, who carved his appreciation into white marble, while revolting against the same eros imprinted onto film. One could argue there is a difference in the photograph's representation of a specific person, versus the statue's representation of a generalized boy, but Powers likely worked from a living model.

In addition to his love for Wolton's body, Douglas cared about Wolton's

19. *Fisher Boy,* by Hiram Powers, 1857. Metropolitan Museum of History.

mind. In his role as tutor, Douglas insisted that the boy keep a diary during their trip to Calabria. The diary captures Wolton's childish sensibility. Take, for example, his record of their visit to the beach at Crotone. Setting out along the Royal Hill Road, Wolton writes, "we got to a castle built by some noble man. After having our bathe we came back and on our way bought a water mellon the rest of the day we were writing and doing things." After Douglas corrected the first draft of Wolton's journal, the boy copied it out in slightly neater handwriting into a second journal, adding "and" following the word *mellon*. Wolton didn't correct his misspelling of the word *melon*. Nor did Wolton mention the photo session on the beach at Crotone, or clarify what sorts of *things* he and Douglas did together after their time at the beach.[12]

Douglas wasn't a strict taskmaster, but he took his role seriously. He fulfilled his promise to Wolton's parents to educate their son. In addition to making Wolton keep a diary, he had the boy work on lists of vocabulary words and practice his writing by composing formal letters to his friends back home. "Dear Harry, I am just writing a line to tell you one of my places in Italy where I went to this place is a jolly long way from Naples and it is called Cotrone," Wolton wrote in his letter describing that day at the beach.[13] (Cotrone was the pre-Italianate spelling of the city, which changed its name to Crotone in 1928.)[14] Wolton's vocabulary lists are ambitious, including abstractions, rare words, and difficult-to-spell words like *unelucidated, holus bolus,* and *naphtha*. Douglas was particularly fond of burdening the boy with words of four syllables or more, including *somnambulist, inexplicable, unenthusiastic,* and *dilapidated*. Many of the words were taken from the books that Douglas made Wolton read, classics like *Captain Cook's Voyages of Discovery* and the poetry of John Milton. Sophisticated reading for a thirteen-year-old.

Taking Wolton to Italy was not just an excuse to spend interrupted private time together; it was also an essential aspect of Douglas's educative program. "The boy of the streets, who sees nothing of the protean witchery of flowers and living waters, is not a veritable boy at any time, since his youth is ended ere it began," Douglas argued in an essay published just after he met Wolton. The ancient Greeks, he wrote, had understood the necessity for communion with nature.[15] They also understood how pedagogy and eros intertwined in the relationship between teacher and student. As Douglas saw it, his cultivation of Wolton's mind and his enjoyment of Wolton's body fit together naturally within the classical tradition of pederasty. By taking responsibility for Wolton's education, Douglas styled himself as a modern-day *erastes*, the adult male within the pederastic bond. It was a popular mode of identity among early twentieth-century homophiles like André Gide and John Henry Mackay, who in turn were influenced by earlier Hellenic enthusiasts, like August von Platen and Johann Winckelmann.[16]

Douglas relished the opportunity to educate Wolton. After the fact, he also found a practical use for at least one product of Wolton's studies. Wolton's daily diary served as an *aide-mémoire* to Douglas in the composition of his third book, *Old Calabria*, which follows the itinerary of Douglas and Wolton's 1911 trip through southern Italy. The narration often uses the collective *we*. "We are on a hill." "We reached the town of Sant'Angelo." "We glide into the sunshine of Hellenic days."[17] But Douglas never specifies the identity of his companion. "Calabria is not a land to traverse alone," he states simply in the book's final chapter, which describes a Doric column that stood near the beach in Crotone. The column was all that remained from the forty-eight pillars of the Temple of the Lacinian Hera, which had once been erected in the Achaean colony of Magna Graecia that preceded modern Calabria. "I took a picture of the survivor," Douglas wrote. The picture did not make it into the book, but Douglas held on to it, along with his picture of Wolton naked on the beach. Perhaps both shots were taken on the same day. The photo of the column captures the ruin's shadowy fluting and erect demeanor. It's possible to read the photo of the column as a phallic self-portrait, Douglas's identification with a last "survivor" of a pagan age. In *Old Calabria*, he described how he wandered around the column, picking up fragments of ancient statuary, and dreaming of an era in which the "disharmonies of our age" had no place. "How fair they are, these moments of golden equipoise!" he wrote.[18]

Douglas began work on *Old Calabria* soon after he and Wolton returned from Italy. It was not a moment of golden equipoise. During the final days of their trip, Douglas and Wolton both caught malaria. When they reached England in August 1911, Douglas delivered Wolton back to his parents and then holed up in a rented room on Museum Street. His skin turned yellow and his body raged with fever.[19] The X marks in his diary stopped. Realizing that he could not take care of himself, Douglas dragged himself to the Conrads' house in Kent. He showed up on their doorstep more dead than alive. Conrad and his wife, Jessie, did not receive Douglas graciously. A letter that Douglas sent from Calabria had upset the couple, apparently by making a joking allusion to his sexual misadventures with Wolton.[20] The Conrads were sexually straitlaced, even if many of their friends—including Ford Madox Hueffer, H. G. Wells, and John Galsworthy—were not. Practitioners of the art of active not-knowing, they were happy turning a blind eye to Douglas's transgressions, but being asked to laugh at them was beyond the pale.

Already upset by the untoward letter, the couple did not appreciate Douglas's infectious disruption to their daily routine. Conrad required strict order and quiet for his writing. Robin Douglas remembered how the writer would

shout and holler when he and their son Borys made too much noise.[21] The
disruption from Douglas's malarial visit far exceeded Robin and Borys's noisy
play. Conrad wrote to Galsworthy describing the unpleasant scene:

> He does not recognise anybody, his temp after most appalling ups
> and downs has reached 105.—and here we are. . . . All we know *for*
> *certain* of D's illness is that it is not typhoid. At first we thought it
> was a heat-stroke. Now we doubt it. The doctor says—how can
> I tell? There are no other symptoms but fever. And suppose it is
> brain fever. He can't be moved and indeed where could one move
> him? One can hear him moaning and muttering all over the house.
> We keep Jack outside all day—or as much as we can. Borys begins
> to look hollow-eyed—his room is just across the passage—six feet
> from the sick man's door which is kept open for air. . . . Should he die
> I shall have to bury him I suppose. But even if he recovers (which we
> still hope for) it will be a matter of weeks. All my work, all our plans
> and our little pitiful hopes seem knocked on the head. I have seen
> and tended white men dying in the Congo but I have never felt so
> abominably helpless as in this case. As Jessie said last night—this is
> like a nightmare.[22]

The next day the Conrads moved him out of their home and into Ashford
Hospital, where his malaria was diagnosed and treated with quinine. Within
the week he was well enough to leave Kent, collect Wolton, and move to the
seaside. Both were still very sick and remained so for weeks, but the X marks
in his pocket diary resumed. In a letter to a friend, Wolton wrote about the
terrible shivering fits he suffered and the sudden bouts of vomiting.[23] As
Douglas put it, the boy "developed a disconcerting trick of being sea-sick,
without a moment's notice, in the middle of a street or wherever else he might
happen to be."[24] Wolton's hair fell out, and his spleen was so enlarged that a
doctor joked he should be put on display.

While they convalesced, Douglas worked on *Old Calabria*. He was in a
state of "acute financial depression."[25] He had run out of funds entirely during
the Calabria trip, and only a well-timed check from Annie Bertram Webb had
provided the means to leave Taranto.[26] Douglas desperately needed to publish. Unfortunately, he was also questioning his talent as a writer. "Don't give
way to the feeling of having written yourself out," Conrad wrote to him in

October.[27] The two were back on good terms after Douglas's recovery. Conrad had reassumed his role as writing mentor, dispensing good advice to his struggling friend. Even better than that, he used his connections to help get Douglas work as a reviewer for the *English Review*. Douglas's desire to remain close to Wolton probably played as influential a role in his accepting the offer of steady employment in London as did the promise of an income.

Douglas rented a flat in Richmond where Wolton stayed with him. Wolton's mother, his sister Violet, and his brother Percy visited frequently.[28] Douglas had long disparaged London as a cold mercenary city, but in Wolton's company his eyes opened to the city's vibrant youth culture. He became fascinated by the creativity of the games that the city's children invented. Douglas turned his naturalist gaze to the subject. Traveling through the Cockney neighborhoods of Finsbury, Hackney, Islington, Whitechapel, Stepney, Limehouse, Poplar, Shoreditch, Bethnal Green, Deptford, Camberwell, Kennington, Bermondsey, Rotherhithe, and Shadwell, he recorded the countless names that the local children gave to their sports.[29] His research material includes notes in children's handwriting, suggesting that Douglas brought along a pen and paper to the streets and asked the kids to write down what they knew. Altogether there are thousands of poems, songs, and descriptions of games.[30] "It required time, days and weeks, to stalk these children and win their confidence," he later recalled.[31] No doubt having Wolton beside him was an asset, as were the chocolates, toy pistols, cheap watches, small dolls, pennies, cigarettes, and snuff he carried in his pockets to compensate the children.[32] Wolton's sister Violet recalled Douglas paid her ten shillings to collect street games and promised to buy her a pair of butterfly corsets when she grew up.[33]

In November 1913, Douglas published "In Our Alley," a ten-page article in the *English Review* that presented the first fruits of his research. Adopting the voice of a genial working-class Londoner, Douglas recounted how the city's children *larked about*. They played Egg-in-Cap, Monday-Tuesday, Quinine, Tommy All Round, Throwing the Nickers, Tin Can Copper, High Bobbery, I Spy — Spit in Your Eye, Deliver Up Those Golden Jewels, All the Way to London, Cut-a-Lump, French Touch, Touching Iron, Witty, Non-Stop Touch, Postman, Cat on Hot Bricks, Papers, Writing Letters to Punch, All Hands on Deck, Stiff-Legged Copper, Charge of the Light Brigade, Hopping All the Way to Church, Shooting the Moon, Flies Round the Jam-Pot, All the Winkles, Shoeing the Wild Horse, Stags, Release, Rounders, Broken Bottles, One-

Two-Three, Steps, Sly Fox, Honey-Pots, We Have Come to Work a Trade, Hop-Scotch, Chalk Chase, Roman Candles, Shunting Engines, Egg in a Duck's Belly, Salmon Fishing, Hot and Cold Pies, Touch Wood and Whistle, King John Says So, Chinese Orders, Showing No Ivory, Follow My Leader, Tibby Cat, Picking the Crow's Nest, and Knocking Ginger Out of Bed.[34] The names of the games are pure poetry. It's no surprise that Douglas's research was an inspiration for James Joyce while he was writing his masterpiece of wordplay, *Finnegans Wake*.[35]

Douglas quoted from his informants to describe how some of the games worked, taking as much joy from their use of language as from the content of their explanations. Take, for example, this account of how to play Monday-Tuesday: "After clipping the throer calls out the name of the day in the weke and the chap whats taken that day has to catch if he misses it they all run away and shout no egg if I move—becose if they dont the throer can say a egg if you move—& that helps to make the quantity of the eggs."[36] The explanation continues to the end of the page. Douglas took special pleasure in the dirty games. To play Deliver Up Those Golden Jewels, a boy and his confederates went up to a "soft boy" and instructed him to serve as a judge interrogating a prisoner. The judge was instructed to tell the prisoner to "deliver up them Golden Jools." What happened then? "I can't tell you any more about that game. It's rather rude."[37] Considering that jewels have served as a synonym for testicles since the medieval era, one can imagine the answer.[38]

In 1916 Douglas expanded the essay into a short book titled *London Street Games*. The book included more dirty games, including one called Touching the King's Sceptre. The game was not nice at all, Douglas said, instructing readers to go ask for the rules themselves. "If you can get that out of them, you can get anything."[39] But the rules of the games didn't really interest Douglas. It was the inventiveness of the children's vocabularies that he admired. The book, like the article, was a breathless catalog of names, with only limited explanations and no analysis. *London Street Games* was a tribute to youth culture. It was an act of memorialization motivated by the same nostalgia for a disappearing world that had inspired his rhapsodies about the last Doric column of Crotone. Douglas saw the threat of routinization hanging like a sword of Damocles over the youth culture of London. "The standardization of youth proceeds relentlessly," Douglas bemoaned in the preface to his 1931 edition. "How many of these games are still played?"[40] His pessimism proved justified. Folklorists today are grateful for Douglas's passion for collecting children's culture a century ago.

Douglas spent time with adults as well as children during the years following his trip to Calabria. Working at the *English Review* placed him in the center of London literary life at the height of the modernist era. He frequented Muriel Draper's musical salon at her Edith Grove apartment, often in the company of his friend, the pianist Arthur Rubinstein. He had long literary lunches at Soho restaurants. On Tuesdays he joined the writers who gathered at the Mont Blanc Restaurant, the walls of which were painted with romantic frescos of Swiss landscapes. Edward Garnett, the preeminent publishers' reader of the day who was known for spotting literary talent, headed a table that often included John Galsworthy, D. H. Lawrence, Ford Madox Hueffer, W. H. Hudson, Hilaire Belloc, Stephen Reynolds, Thomas Seccombe, and—when he came to town—Joseph Conrad.[41]

Douglas didn't keep his sexual life secret from his literary friends. It was public knowledge. Some merely tolerated Douglas's relationships with boys; others found it amusing. Garnett shared Douglas's relish for the risqué, but he wouldn't let his teenaged son be alone with Douglas.[42] Douglas attracted many sexually nonconformist writers. The writer Eden Phillpotts, who according to his daughter molested her throughout her childhood, befriended Douglas at this time.[43] So did the gay novelist Hugh Walpole, who wrote in his diary, "Norman Douglas to lunch. Most amusing. Has been everywhere and done everything, including I should imagine many things he should not."[44] Afterward, Walpole invited Douglas to Cornwall for a visit.[45] The talented young Scottish author Compton Mackenzie, whose early novel *Sinister Street* explored the subject of illicit schoolboy relationships, was drawn to Douglas's pagan charm when the two first met in a restaurant in Soho in 1912.[46] He compared Douglas to "a satyr who had been dressed up in conventional attire and set to work in a London office."[47] Lawrence became friends with Douglas in 1913, the same year that he published his homoerotic novel *Sons and Lovers*.[48]

Douglas encouraged many young writers during his post at the *English Review*.[49] Neil Bell met Douglas in 1912, when, in his own words, he was "little more than a boy." (He was twenty-five.) Douglas was kind, generous, and magnanimous to Bell, lavishing him with praise and encouragement, which evidently paid off in a prolific career writing science fiction and literary novels.[50] According to Douglas, the *Review*'s lead editor, Austin Harrison, was often unresponsive and unsupportive. Douglas went out of his way to help upcoming writers whom he thought had been treated shabbily by Harrison, such as James Elroy Flecker, an impoverished tubercular poet who submitted a long poem to the *Review* and was left waiting to hear back for over a year and a half. After Flecker died at Davos, Douglas continued a decades-long, often scandalous, correspondence with his widow, Hellé Flecker.[51]

Despite his interest in the young, Douglas rarely took advantage of his time in London to see either of his own sons, who were attending schools in England. Robin recalled traveling to London to see his father once during a school break in 1913, when he was ten. He showed up at St. Pancras Station to find no sign of his father. Instead, a large policeman approached him asking, "Is your name 'Douglas'?" and handed over a slip of paper with directions to meet his father at the *Review* offices. When Robin reached the offices, he found another note, this time directing him to Gennaro's Restaurant. At Gennaro's he found a note directing him to Douglas's apartment, 63 Albany Mansions, across from Battersea Park.[52] After Robin finally caught up with his father, Douglas fobbed him off. Throughout the holiday, Douglas would hand him pocket change and direct him to go to the movies or stay out till dark. As Robin acknowledged later, "On those rare occasions when I was a guest of my father's he must have felt seriously discommoded. . . . He had plenty to think of and to do without having the inconvenience of a small boy around the place."[53]

In fact, Douglas did have a boy living in his place for much of this time, Eric Wolton. Douglas and Wolton were so inseparable that many people thought the boy might be his illegitimate son. Douglas even tried to legally adopt Wolton, although Wolton's mother would not agree. She did agree to allow Douglas to take Wolton with him on return trips to Italy. In May 1913 they traveled together to Sant'Agata then spent a week in Ischia. Douglas took another photo of Wolton on the beach in an alluring poise, this time at Nerano. Wolton was fifteen, and not so childlike as he had been two years before. Douglas's time with Wolton in Sant'Agata helped fix the village as another "sacred" spot, one that he revisited frequently over the subsequent decades. Later he remembered his repeated trips to Italy with Wolton as some of the happiest moments in his life. In 1933 he dedicated *Looking Back* to "my dear Eric," writing in an open letter to his now adult friend, "We lived with greater zest than the present generation seems able to do. We had more fun—of that

I am convinced."[54] One would expect Wolton to remember the trips differently, as passages of extended abuse. But Wolton shared Douglas's perspective.

Writing from a hospital bed in Dar es Salaam in 1922, while he was recovering from typhoid, Wolton waxed nostalgic about the good times he and Douglas had once shared. "Doug, I have wanted Italy and you as bad as anything last week. All the old times flash back in my memory."[55] Perhaps the typhoid had reminded him of the malaria he contracted on their first trip together to Calabria, but he had no unhappy associations with Italy. "How I should love St Agata now, the walks and all the happy times," Wolton reminisced.

When Wolton wrote "all the happy times," he meant the sex as well as the sightseeing. He knew that his childhood sexual relationship with Douglas was considered immoral, but he refused to condemn their relationship. "They were happy times too Doug wer'nt they, I have no evil thoughts about them although I am different today than I was then," he wrote, several weeks later. As an adult, Wolton was sexually attracted to women not men. He was "different" than he had been. But he still enjoyed the memory of his adventures with Douglas. "I want you to understand Doug that you are more to me than ever you were," he wrote, "the difference is now that I am old enough to realise it." A few weeks later, he wrote again. He had just read one of Douglas's books, which was inspired by a new boyfriend, and he admitted to feeling jealous. "You are my god Doug," Wolton wrote. "I am pleased I have been able to give you a little pleasure during the whole time of our friendship."[56]

Wolton's positive adult memories of his childhood sexual relationship with Douglas were not that unusual. Sociologist Bruce Rind has argued from his review of the social science literature that many adult men have positive recollections of unforced boyhood sexual experiences with adults. For example, a 1988 study of Dutch male subjects found 69 percent positive memories for "willing participants" (versus 31 percent positive for unwilling participants). Rind also cites case studies of adults who positively recalled their boyhood sexual experiences with men. For example, the psychoanalyst Heinz Kohut (1913–1981) and the writer Gavin Lambert (1924–2005) both wrote positively about sexual experiences with adult men that took place beginning when they were eleven years old.[57] Other scholars of youth sexuality, such as Joseph Fischel and Kathryn Bond Stockton, have cited Rind's work.[58] But the social science literature on this topic is controversial to say the least. Works by

Rind and by Susan Clancy, who has also challenged the assumption that children are inherently traumatized by sex with adults, have come under heavy criticism by those who see their work as justifying child sexual abuse. Critics point out the unreliability of autobiographical sources, and ascribe any positive feelings to abusers' psychological manipulation of their child victims.[59]

It's possible that Wolton's positive memories of his relationship with Douglas were unreliable and manipulated. It's also possible that his letters protested too much. Maybe his repeated assertions that he had no evil thoughts about his sexual encounters with Douglas were attempts to persuade himself of that. It's possible to explain Wolton's words as false consciousness, or the effects of lingering trauma, or instrumental because he still wanted Douglas's mentorship. But if so, the instrumentalism continued even after Wolton had ascended through the British colonial hierarchy to become chief of police in Tanganyika, then public prosecutor (jobs that he was qualified for as a consequence of Douglas's tutoring). Wolton never changed his mind about Douglas. Rather, the two remained close friends for the remainder of their lives, both traveling repeatedly across continents to spend time together. Wolton swore to the end that Douglas had been the most important relationship of his life. One must at least consider taking him at his word.[60]

CHAPTER EIGHT

Keeping Faith

Faith Mackenzie met Norman Douglas in 1912 through her husband, Compton, but the two swiftly became friends on their own terms. In fact, they became closer friends than the two men. Like her husband, Faith Mackenzie was not the judgmental type. A former professional actress, she had an open marriage, taking both male and female lovers. From childhood onward, she had loved listening to dirty talk, which made her a perfect audience for Douglas, who loved talking dirty. "Ribaldry was the basis of our friendship, and I don't know a better one," Mackenzie explained in her memoirs. "The tang of his salty conversation delighted me."[1]

Douglas was just as filthy in his writing. They exchanged hundreds of letters, in a correspondence that lasted forty years. Faith Mackenzie's side of the exchange has disappeared, but Douglas's side remains, and makes for eye-opening reading. In the first surviving letter, mailed in December 1915, Douglas set the tone for the hundreds that followed. "I have to give an address in a Swedenborgian Chapel this afternoon, on 'Chastity for Minors'—a delicate subject, about which I know nothing," he joked.[2] Mackenzie's tolerance of Douglas's ribaldry evidently extended to humor about his fondness for having sex with "minors."

It was this sort of humor that had irritated Joseph Conrad back in 1911. According to Conrad, Douglas was becoming more indiscreet with each passing year. He began really going "downhill" in 1914, carelessly intermixing his sexual life with his professional life.[3] He made the grievous error of bringing the journalist and pornographer Frank Harris to Conrad's house for a visit in 1914, a breach of taste for which the upright Polish author did not forgive him.[4] When Conrad tried to advise Douglas to "consider his position," his warnings had no effect.[5] Douglas went so far as to sleep with one of the office "boys" at the *English Review*.[6] A new initial began to appear in his pocket diary in 1915, a simple penciled R. On February 24, the R was followed by an X mark, the first time he had used that notation since 1911. Perhaps this was the office boy.[7] It's unclear if the affair played any role in Douglas's resignation from his sub-editorial position in March 1916. He might have quit over money that was owed to him, but if so the departure didn't help his strapped finances. In one of his weekly letters to Archie, who was attending school at Uppingham, Douglas warned: "You must now be prepared for very lean years."[8]

Douglas tried to replace his lost editorial income with wartime work for the British government, but no one would hire him, despite his former position in the Foreign Office and his fluency in German, Russian, Italian, and French. Douglas wrote humorously about this failed bid to contribute his services, recalling how he "lingered in long queues, and stamped up and down, and sat about crowded, stuffy halls, waiting."[9] He tried the War Office, the Foreign Office, the Education Office, the Censorship Department, Munitions, and the Board of Trade Labour Emergency Bureau. After months of applications, Douglas finally received an offer of employment: in a factory at Gretna Green, Scotland, working for 17 shillings and 6 pence a week. By that point it was too late. He had already made plans to leave the country the next day.

The basic outline of Douglas's story is true. He did apply for government work during World War I. But his retelling neglected to acknowledge the reason why he couldn't get hired or the events that drove him from the country. Others have been more forthcoming. In Douglas's saga of failed interviews, he mentioned an interview at the Ministry of Munitions with Mr. W, a civil servant and aspiring poet who had once submitted a manuscript to the *English Review*. Mr. W, "a nice-looking young Hebrew," was "freezingly noncommittal," Douglas remarked.[10] The identity of Mr. W was later supplied by the man himself, Humbert Wolfe, who became a best-selling writer during the 1920s. In Wolfe's memoir, he explained why he didn't give Douglas a job: "It had been indicated to me that at that particular moment in England he would not be a success."[11] In other words, Wolfe was under direct orders to give Douglas the runaround.

Wolfe was even more explicit in personal conversation, telling the writer Richard Aldington that Douglas had been given the "sod's push" from England because of widespread knowledge about his disreputable sexual life.[12]

The writer H. Montgomery Hyde claimed that Wolfe had been deputed by his higher-ups to tell Douglas to get out of England or face arrest on a "certain charge."[13] Wolfe, who had been insulted by Douglas's anti-Semitic insinuation that he connived his way out of military service, might have told these stories to get back at Douglas. But Wolfe claimed in his memoir to be a devoted fan of Douglas's work.

Wolfe's story is also buttressed by Compton Mackenzie's account of his own failure to get Douglas a post with British Intelligence. Mackenzie worked in counterespionage during the Gallipoli campaign and then in Athens. In Greece he approached his commander, Colonel Fairholme, to see about hiring Douglas. He didn't know that Fairholme was Douglas's cousin on the maternal side, and thus Elsa's cousin as well. Only weeks earlier, news had reached England that Elsa had died in a bed fire in Munich.[14] When Mackenzie raised Douglas's name, Fairholme turned purple and raged, "Never! Do you know I've just heard that his unhappy wife whom he treated so abominably was burnt to death recently in a Munich brothel?" Denouncing Douglas as a blackguard, Fairholme promised, "I'll see to it that *he* never comes out to Greece."[15]

Douglas's increasing indiscretion during the early years of the war may have been, in part, a consequence of Eric Wolton growing up. Douglas had a strong preference for boys in their early adolescence, before they developed underarm hair. This was the period of development that ancient Greek literature identified as ideal for pederastic relations. Contemporary pederasts, like Baron Corvo, also sang the praises of boys with "milky armpits."[16] Wolton, who turned sixteen in 1914, was aging out of Douglas's ideal range. In June 1916, after Wolton turned eighteen, he was drafted into the British Army.[17] Douglas was away in Capri at the time, but when he returned to London in late July, he went cruising for new boys. He befriended one student who attended the Battersea Polytechnic Secondary School nearby his flat in Albany Mansions.[18] Other flirtations proved less successful. In late November 1916, Douglas was arrested outside the South Kensington tube station, a popular cruising spot in walking distance from Douglas's apartment. A couple days later he appeared before the Westminster Police Court and was charged with two counts: one for "loitering with intent there to commit a felony," and one for having made an "indecent assault" on a sixteen-year old named Edward Carey Riggall.[19]

Reports of the arrest and subsequent hearings appeared in the *Times*, as well as in two neighborhood papers, the *Chelsea News and General Advertiser* and the *Fulham Chronicle*. The local papers reported the courtroom testimony in close detail. Riggall testified that on the afternoon of Saturday, November 18, he had attended a lecture at the Natural History Museum in South Kensington (a block from the tube station). At four, when the lecture ended, the museum closed its doors. Riggall was on his way out when Douglas approached him and said that it was a pity the museum shut so early. He began to ask Riggall about his ambitions and suggested he could help Riggall find a job connected with natural history. They stopped in at the A.B.C., a chain of tea shops. Douglas bought Riggall some cakes and invited him home to eat the cakes and talk over job prospects. He told Riggall that he was lonely as his wife was out. He also asked Riggall whether "his people were hard to manage, meaning his parents, and whether they would let him go in for natural history."

Once they reached the apartment, Douglas lit the fire, sat on a chair, and pulled Riggall onto his lap. Riggall tried to get away, but Douglas pulled him back and kissed him. Then he gave Riggall a shilling and a screwdriver as a "keepsake," and asked Riggall to meet him again the following week. He also asked Riggall not to tell anyone about their encounter. Despite Douglas's request, as soon as Riggall returned to school, he told his teacher Mr. White what had happened. The two then went together to speak to a police constable, Detective-Sergeant Goggin.

The following Saturday, November 25, Riggall met Douglas at the museum. Goggin followed the man and the boy as they walked around the exhibits. They left together, returning to the A.B.C. so Douglas could buy Riggall cakes. When they left the A.B.C., Detective-Sergeant Goggin arrested Douglas. According to Goggin, he approached Douglas and said, "I am a police officer. What are you doing with that boy?" Douglas answered, "I have just been with him to a lecture." Goggin said, "This boy says you took him home last Saturday and assaulted him." Douglas denied it, claiming, "I only took him there to find an address," then remarked, "I suppose it is not good my saying anything." Douglas's lawyer, Roland Oliver, questioned Riggall, asking whether he resisted Douglas's advances. Riggall said he did struggle with him but did not call out. When asked why he had agreed to meet Douglas a second time, Riggall answered that he was worried Douglas would not let him leave the flat otherwise.[20]

Riggall's testimony is the only intimation in the archival evidence that

Douglas ever used force to coerce sex from minors. More typically, he seduced young people with gifts and by showering them with attention and affection. Douglas clearly tried both these tactics with Riggall as well, picking up cakes for him at a tea shop, asking him about his ambitions, and offering to help him find work. At the same time, Douglas, who was tall and heavily built, intimidated the youth, giving the impression he would not let him leave without a promise of another meeting. This may have been a common practice for Douglas. It's possible that Douglas used his physical size to intimidate other youths he picked up, even if those threats have not left traces in the archives.

It's also possible that Riggall's testimony that he was physically intimidated by Douglas was intended to dispel any impression that he had consented to their initial encounter. Admitting consent would not just undermine the assault charge against Douglas, but it might also lead to the prosecution of Riggall, since any consensual sexual intimacy between males was illegal. Historically, in English law, there had been no age of consent for boys. The age of criminal responsibility was set at fourteen, which functioned as a de facto age of consent. Sexual relations between adults and boys under fourteen might be considered statutory assaults. In 1922 the age of consent for boys was raised to sixteen years old. Historian Louise Jackson argues that these shifts in statute law effectively brought new groups of children into being.[21] As Foucault famously argued, power is not just repressive; it produces meaning.[22] The quality of being unable to consent to sexual encounters is not descriptive of childhood, in this reading, but is itself the condition that produces what we understand as childhood. This distinction matters to the history of modern pederasty, since it suggests that what has changed over time is not attitudes to sex involving children, but attitudes toward childhood as defined through sex.

In 1916, the sixteen-year-old Riggall was well within the bounds of the age of criminal responsibility, and thus could be convicted under the Labouchere Amendment's definition of gross indecency, unless he was able to prove to the court that he had been violently assaulted. A lot rode on Riggall's success in persuading the court that he had not consented to Douglas's sexual overtures. The typical criminal penalty for consensual sex between males was months of hard labor. When Henry Rowe and William Wells were arrested in January 1917 for "loitering at South Kensington Station and at Knightsbridge with intent to commit a felony," they were sentenced to twelve months and six months hard labor, respectively.[23] Rowe and Wells were repeat offenders, which aggravated their sentences. But even first-time offenders like Maurice

Cohen and Abraham Samuels, who appeared before the Westminster Police Court charged with being "suspected persons loitering at Knightsbridge with intent there to commit a felony," were treated harshly. Both Cohen and Samuels were sentenced to three months hard labor.[24]

The charge of assault against Douglas meant he was likely facing severe punishment. Douglas's lawyer, Roland Oliver, tried to get Douglas released by arguing that Riggall's story was uncorroborated, but Detective-Sergeant Goggin told the court that he had been instructed by higher-ups to recommend against bail because there might be further serious developments in the case. The court denied bail at the first hearing. A week later, when Douglas reappeared, his bail was set at one hundred pounds. (He had to provide a surety for the whole, or two sureties of fifty pounds, to gain release.) This was more than two times the yearly salary he had been offered at Gretna Green.[25] The bail was far beyond Douglas's means.

Douglas reached out to his friends for money. At least twice in the past he had loaned Conrad money, but the author was unsympathetic, to put it mildly. Conrad wrote to his agent, J. B. Pinker, after learning of the arrest: "I wish to goodness the fellow had blown his brains out." Conrad wasn't surprised by the charge. It was "of the kind you may guess," he wrote.[26] After news of Douglas's arrest, the two friends never spoke again. Douglas later said that he had "no correspondence whatever with Conrad after November 1916."[27] Conrad did, however, continue to support Douglas's younger son, Robin, throughout the ordeal, welcoming the boy to his house during the Christmas 1916 holidays and trying to keep the papers from him so he wouldn't read his father's name in their pages.[28]

Other friends were more accommodating than Conrad, whom Douglas described as the "greatest stickler for uprightness I have ever known."[29] Two friends stood bail for Douglas. Faith Mackenzie provided him an alibi.[30] In As Much as I Dare, the first volume of her memoirs, Mackenzie told the saga of Douglas's arrest without mentioning him by name. "Seeing in the paper that a friend whom I respected and admired had been arrested on a peculiar charge, I wrote to him in prison assuring him of my belief in his innocence," she began.[31] In fact, Mackenzie was well aware of Douglas's sexual interest in children, which he had joked about in his letters to her. She acknowledged as much in a fictionalized account of Douglas's arrest that she included in a collection of short stories. The story's narrator recalls sitting down to dinner with an author shortly before his arrest. She tells him, "You are an ass. You'll be run in one day." He laughs off her warning.[32] Mackenzie's letter to Douglas in prison reassured him of her friendship. When he was released on bail, he went to her apartment asking for help.

On January 2, 1917, Douglas was charged with two more indecent assaults, against Robert Duncan Knight, age twelve, and Esmond Penington Knight, age ten. Both alleged assaults had taken place on July 5, 1916, at the Natural History Museum.[33] According to the boys, who were cousins, Douglas "improperly caught hold of them at the museum" and was "personally indecent to them."[34] Afterward he took them to a shop and bought them sweets. In short, the police had pinned a second earlier set of assaults on Douglas. They intended to lock Douglas up and throw away the key. Without Faith Mackenzie's intervention, they may have succeeded (for better or worse).

Mackenzie accompanied Douglas to police court for his hearing after he was charged with the second set of assaults. Most of the charges that came up were against deserters and "young girls of fourteen and fifteen hauled up for soliciting." Interestingly, despite the fact that the age of consent for girls had been raised to sixteen, the court apparently still prosecuted girls below that threshold for prostitution. However disreputable, prostitution continued to be a routine means for London youth to earn money in the 1910s. When it came time for Douglas's case to be heard, an usher approached Mackenzie, who looked like a respectable lady, and advised her to leave the courtroom. "I'm a witness in this case," she informed the usher, to his chagrin.[35]

When Mackenzie took the stand, she testified that on the July day when Douglas was purported to have assaulted the two cousins in London, she had dined with him in Capri. She had an entry in her personal diary to prove it. Mackenzie's testimony alone may not have been sufficient, but Douglas's passport backed up her story. Exit and entry stamps supported his claim that he had left England in May 1916 and did not return until mid-August. He had spent the summer in Capri, living off the generosity of friends. (Letters to Archie in July, postmarked from Capri, also confirm this claim.) The justice believed Douglas's alibi and vacated the new charges.

Had the police fabricated the second charges against Douglas? The boys' testimony could have been coached. As it happened, the younger of the two boys, Esmond Penington Knight, would later become a famous actor, best known for continuing his stage career after a World War II injury blinded him nearly completely. When Knight wrote his autobiography, *Seeking the Bubble*, he told a number of stories about the hijinks he and his cousin got up to in

20. Faith Mackenzie and Norman Douglas in Capri, 1925. Private collection of Deirdre Sholto Douglas. Photograph by author.

London during World War I, but he made no mention of being assaulted at the museum or of testifying in court against the man who assaulted him.[36] It's also possible that the boys testified honestly, but were mistaken about the identity of their assailant. This possibility points, once again, to the ordinariness of sexual encounters between adults and children in the early twentieth century. Douglas was not the only man cruising the Natural History Museum, picking up boys, and buying them cakes in exchange for sexual encounters.

While Douglas had an unimpeachable alibi that exonerated him from the assaults against the cousins, he still faced the initial charge of assault against Riggall. That one charge was enough to get Douglas sentenced to hard labor. Rather than test his luck at trial, Douglas jumped bail and fled the country. Maybe Humbert Wolfe or another government emissary advised him to leave. It's possible that there were members of the government who did not fancy the prospect of a highly publicized trial against a moderately prominent author, for a charge that boiled down to unwelcome kissing. It had all the makings of a cause célèbre and was a potential source of embarrassment for a government already struggling with the burden of an increasingly unpopular war. Douglas applied for and received visas to travel to Italy and France on January 11–12. His seventeen-year-old son Archie helped him pack his bags. He fled London on January 13.[37] Two weeks later, the *Police Gazette* included Douglas in an "apprehensions sought" column, but the British government hadn't made any significant effort to prevent him from leaving the country.[38]

Faith Mackenzie remained proud, throughout her life, of her role in saving Douglas from prosecution. "That was my 'war work,' I thought it was worth doing, because I happened to be the only person who could do it, and it would be absurd to pretend that it was anything but interesting and exciting," she wrote in her memoir.[39] Compton Mackenzie was also proud of his wife's loyalty to their friend. Douglas's other so-called friends, who abandoned him during his time of need, were rats in Mackenzie's estimation.[40] Douglas had a good scare from this episode. He erased evidence of what had taken place, destroying letters from the period of the crisis. But he soon wove the event into his personal mythology, treating it as yet another subject of the ribald humor that had drawn Faith Mackenzie to him in the first place. "I left England under a cloud no bigger than a boy's hand," he liked to say.[41] It was the sort of witticism that his friends appreciated.

CHAPTER NINE

Alone

If Norman Douglas had put an end to his troubles by shooting himself in 1916, as Joseph Conrad so uncharitably suggested, he would swiftly have faded from memory. Nothing that Douglas had written to date had enjoyed any significant popularity. Fame came for Douglas in the summer of 1917 when he published *South Wind*, his scandalous novel about the hedonist expatriates who crowded Capri before the First World War. Douglas said that *South Wind* resulted from his desire to "write a novel with all the sins in it that have ever been committed and some that have never been committed before."[1] The novel appeared at a timely moment, when the Victorian code of morals had been fatally weakened by the horrors of the Great War. Cynical readers embraced the book's strident immorality, and Douglas's personal notoriety only added to their pleasure. Sexual immorality didn't end Norman Douglas's career—it made him into a literary celebrity.

The first inspiration for the novel came from Conrad, who wrote to Douglas in 1908 after reading his essay about Ischia:

> It is obvious to me that you have a distinguished future before you as a Writer. And also some hard times before you get known. Think seriously of writing a novel. Write your fiction in the *tone* of this very excellent article if you like. Place it in S. Italy if that will help.... Place *European* personalities in Italian frame. European here means an international crowd.[2]

Conrad likely had Capri in mind as a setting. It was where the two men met, and there was no better spot for observing "European personalities" in an Italian frame.

Douglas didn't take Conrad's advice right away. He first developed his theories about Italy's effects on northern visitors via nonfiction. In a 1910 essay, he praised the benefits of spending "a period of *katharsis*, of purgation and readjustment" in the Mediterranean, "for we do get sadly out of perspective with our environment in the fevered North."[3] The distinction that Conrad and Douglas drew between northern and southern Europeans was typical at the time, but Douglas confounded expectations by praising the superiority of the south. The fevered pace of life in the industrialized north, he wrote, had turned men into drudges. The attitude to living was healthier in Mediterranean countries, where "sexuality and every other physiological fact is taken for granted by the smallest children."[4] From the beginning, Douglas was up front about the attractions that drew him and many other northern visitors to the Mediterranean. He proselytized these pleasures to his readers, writing, "Many of us would do well to *mediterraneanise* ourselves for a season."[5]

In spring 1916, after leaving the *English Review*, Douglas finally followed Conrad's advice and adapted his theories to fiction. A friend had offered Douglas room and board in Capri. He traveled to the island in May and began working ten hours a day on a novel.[6] Faith Mackenzie, who was in Capri as well, met him each afternoon to type out his handwritten manuscript pages. By July, he had completed thirty-five of a projected fifty chapters. He estimated that it would take two more months to finish the book. Douglas returned to England in August. Before his arrest in November, he managed to finish the book. When he was released from jail, he immediately delivered the draft of *South Wind* to his editor, Martin Secker. He needed an advance to pay for passage out of the country.

As soon as he arrived in Italy, Douglas wrote to Secker, enclosing an address where the proofs could be sent.[7] Over the next several months, as Douglas traveled through Italy in search of a place to settle, he sent Secker letters discussing the proofs and begging for advances. The money wasn't just for himself but for his sons.[8] Robin, who wanted to be a sailor, had failed the admiralty exam and was training for the navy on the HMS *Worcester*. He needed warm clothes. Archie, recently turned seventeen, was struggling to figure out how to earn a living now that his father couldn't pay for Uppingham. Douglas was desperate for information about when the book would come out.[9] He needed the sales.

Fortunately, he had finally come up with a bestseller. *South Wind* tells the story of a very proper Anglican bishop, Thomas Heard, whose ideas of morality are transformed by a visit to a Capri-like island called Nepenthe. Douglas said the plot of the novel was to explain "how to make murder palatable to a bishop."[10] Heard travels to Nepenthe to meet his cousin, Mrs. Meadows, and escort her to England. During the twelve days Heard spends on Nepenthe, a strong "south wind" blows through, metaphorically sweeping away most of his fixed ideas. "Northern minds seem to become fluid here, impressionable, unstable, unbalanced—what you please," says Mr. Keith, an island resident who is a stand-in for the author.[11] The effect of the island is so powerful, Mr. Keith explains, that two or three English visitors a year throw themselves to their deaths off the island's highest cliff. At the end of his visit, Heard witnesses Mrs. Meadows push her scheming ex-husband off the cliff to stop him from blackmailing her about her bigamous second marriage. By the time of the murder, Heard's northern morality has been so Mediterraneanized that he is able to condone his cousin's actions.

It might involve a murder, but the story of *South Wind* is secondary to its appeal. Many reviewers knocked the book for its lack of plotting, a critique that annoyed Douglas to no end.[12] The book's real draw is the conversation conducted among its "ultra-cosmopolitan" cast of characters—British, Italian, German, Russian, and American—almost all of whom have succumbed to the island's tendency toward "excessive lechery and alcohol." The animating spirit of Nepenthe is the aforementioned Keith, whose Villa Khismet bears a strong resemblance to Douglas's lost Villa Maya, located at the end of a torturous path and surrounded by gardens overlooking the sea. Keith's views on life also bear a striking resemblance to Douglas's own. Keith stands for "paganism and nudity and laughter." He is described as "oozing paganism at every pore" and dancing "faun-like measures to the sound of rustic flutes." Keith is a self-proclaimed follower of the Greek philosopher Epicurus. He rejects Christian notions of morality, even disclaiming "any objection, on principle, to incest." He defends individual sexual freedom, speaking out on behalf of a friend accused of immorality: "Why should I approve or disapprove? Old Koppen's activities do not impinge on mine."[13]

Old Koppen is Cornelius van Koppen, an American millionaire who has made his fortune selling condoms, and who passes several weeks a year sailing off the coast of Nepenthe on his yacht, the *Flutterby*. His transmuted nationality does little to disguise Koppen's resemblance to Douglas's deceased friend Friedrich Krupp, the German munitions millionaire who used to carry him by yacht from Il Posillipo to Capri. In *South Wind*, Keith defends Koppen from rumors that the millionaire keeps "a bevy of light-hearted nymphs" aboard the *Flutterby*.[14] In real life, Douglas was unable to protect Krupp from the impact of German newspaper reporting about his sexual encounters with Capriote youths, which prompted Krupp to commit suicide in 1902. Douglas resurrected his friend in *South Wind* to protest the dictates of sexual morality, by which strangers imposed judgments on the lives of others. Let each person be responsible for himself, *South Wind* argued.

Koppen is just one of the novel's many characters based on authentic Capri characters. After publication, Eden Philpotts wrote to Douglas, "You'll have to give Capri a wide berth, won't you? Or do they all feel flattered & appreciated?"[15] Douglas expected most of his friends on the island to feel appreciated. He recommended the book to Muriel Draper, saying, "You may laugh a little, and it will certainly remind you of old Capri times."[16] Douglas took care to disguise the queerness of his friends. He turned Krupp's boys into Koppen's nymphs. He recast his friend John Ellingham Brooks as Earnest Eames, and refashioned his pederasty into love for a grotesquely fat woman. Douglas's friend Vernon Andrews, a beautiful young gay man, contributed to the character of Denis Phipps, whom he described with a wink and a nod as a "queer boy," "full of gay irresponsibility," who was fond of reading Baudelaire and Beardsley. But to counter this suggestive description, Douglas makes Phipps lust after a girl named Angelina.

Douglas was less kind with characters based on individuals he did not like. He transformed his old enemy Harold Trower, who tried to have Douglas removed from Capri, into the repellent Freddy Parker, purveyor of doctored whisky. And he turned Trower's ally, the local magistrate Signor Capolozzi, into Signor Malipizzo, a portmanteau of the Italian words *mal*, or bad, and *pizzo*, or extortion money. As Douglas confessed, he disliked Capolozzi since the man "very nearly had me in the lock-up once or twice."[17] The first time was likely during Douglas's stay on the island after his divorce. The second time was in 1917, when someone tipped off Capolozzi about Douglas's London arrest. Capolozzi questioned Faith Mackenzie, who had recently returned to Capri. She then complained to her friend the consul general at Naples, who sent over an emissary to reprimand Capolozzi. Douglas remained free to visit Capri without fear of arrest.[18] Italian authorities were aware of Douglas's sexual encounters with local children, but with the exception of Capolozzi, they chose to tolerate his behavior as falling within the boundaries appropriate to Capri. Douglas's friend Edwin Cerio, who came from one of the most powerful families on the island, adored Douglas and shielded him from interference.[19] This was the Mediterranean attitude that Douglas admired.

South Wind hit the shelves in early June 1917.[20] The public response was immediate. The book went through four printings in a year.[21] Douglas went from pariah to literary celebrity overnight. This transformation was aided by Virginia Woolf's glowing review in the *Times Literary Supplement*. Woolf described the book as an instant classic based on an obvious recipe:

> Take all the interesting and eccentric people you can think of, put them on an island in the Mediterranean beyond the realms of humdrum but not in those of fantasy: bid them say shamelessly whatever comes into their heads: let them range over every topic and bring forth whatever fancy, fact, or prejudice happens to occur to them: add, whenever the wish moves you, dissertations upon medieval dukes, Christianity, cookery, education, fountains, Greek art, millionaires, morality, the sexes: enclose the whole in an exquisite atmosphere of pumice rocks and deep blue waves, air with the warm and stimulating breath of the South Wind—the prescription begins something in this way.

The formula was simple, but not anyone could pull it off. According to Woolf, Douglas had a quality of mind akin to the spirit of Oscar Wilde, or the forgotten English satirical novelist Thomas Peacock, yet uniquely his own, that made the book "surprisingly and delightfully successful."[22]

The queen of Bloomsbury's opinion shaped the response of others in her high circle. Raymond Mortimer said Woolf's review influenced him to buy *South Wind*, and he soon grouped himself among Douglas's most ardent admirers.[23] E. M. Forster, a close friend of Woolf, was similarly enthusiastic. He wrote to Douglas in November 1917, "South Wind has at last reached me and I would like to thank you for it: down more agreeable paths to crime I have never been led." Forster, who was living in Egypt at that time, compared the relaxation of principles in Nepenthe to what he witnessed in the British community in Alexandria, with the difference that the flatness of the Egyptian city meant "if a lady when peevish with a gentleman should give him a push he can never fall further than fifteen feet and then upon sand."[24] The painter Dora Carrington also loved *South Wind* and shared it with Lytton Strachey, who became a passionate fan and bought all Douglas's books. Carrington and Strachey spent evenings together reading aloud from Douglas.[25]

The book had its fans outside of Bloomsbury as well. The American cartoonist H. T. Webster recalled that in the 1920s, "everybody who thought of himself as belonging to the cognoscenti, the intelligentsia, the sophisticates, or even the intelligent minority, admired *South Wind*."[26] Despite the nasty things Douglas wrote about him, Humbert Wolfe professed he would "almost as soon have written 'South Wind' as Shelley's 'Ode to the West Wind.'" *South Wind* inspired Wolfe's poem "The Locri Faun," which he dedicated to Douglas.[27]

Although Douglas was no *enfant terrible* at forty-eight, *South Wind* had popularity among the young. Its urbane disenchanted voice perfectly suited the sensibilities of British youths raised during the last gasps of Victorianism and coming of age in a time of senseless total warfare. When Charles Ryder, the hero of Evelyn Waugh's *Brideshead Revisited*, arrives at Oxford in 1923, Douglas's *South Wind* is one of three books that he stacks on his shelf. Critics have credited *South Wind* with inspiring a raft of new novels by young authors, including *Crome Yellow* (1921) and *Those Barren Leaves* (1925) by Aldous Huxley, and *The Rock Pool* (1936) by Cyril Connolly.[28] The literary critic Lewis Leary, born in 1906, claimed that Douglas "invented the lost generation."[29]

It was the immorality of *South Wind* that made the book a hit. The rumored immorality of its author added to that appeal. These rumors circulated far beyond London literary circles. "There are all sorts of stories that go about regarding you," a fan from Edinburgh wrote to Douglas in 1922.[30] *South Wind* cemented Douglas's reputation as a hedonist who lived his life for pleasure. The reality in 1917 was rather bleaker. Despite *South Wind*'s success, Douglas still had little money to live off and was depending on the charity of friends like Maurice Magnus, a gay man who had once been the theatrical agent for the bohemian modern dancer Isadora Duncan. Magnus took pleasure in Douglas's sexual disreputability, and he was happy to put the writer up in his Rome apartment during the summer.[31]

Another friend who came to Douglas's rescue was the writer Edward Hutton. Like Douglas, Hutton had a passion for Italy. In 1917 Hutton helped to establish the British Institute of Florence, which became a key meeting place for the city's Anglo colony. Publicly, Hutton was a sexual conformist. His own son said that "he would in my opinion have found any discussion of sexual matters, serious or comic, personal or general, not merely distasteful but quite impossible."[32] However, Hutton's correspondence with Douglas reveals a different side of the man. He was, it appears, a ladies' man. Douglas teased Hutton about seeing him "engaged, as usual, in flirting with cosmopolitans of the female persuasion."[33] The London hostess Viva King described Hutton as "very attractive."[34] Hutton was also a collector of erotic books, which he loaned to Douglas.[35] The two men kept a running discussion about these books, including René Guyon's *Sex Life and Ethics* and Hans Licht's *Sexual Life in Ancient Greece*, both of which took a positive view of Hellenic pederasty.[36] Hutton's receptivity to this point of view may have been a consequence of his childhood friendship with William Cory, the poet who was dismissed from Eton for having inappropriate relations with the students. It was Cory who had first introduced the classics to Hutton, when he was eight years old, by taking him for long walks on Hampstead Heath and telling him stories of ancient Rome.[37] Hutton tolerated Douglas's sexual leanings. In Douglas's many letters to Hutton, he freely acknowledged his sexual attraction to boys. In one letter he effused about the town of Sant'Agata, "where all the boys look like angels and mostly are!"[38] Another postcard that he sent to Hutton featured a Greek bas-relief of a nude boy.[39]

In May 1918, Hutton launched a new magazine, the *Anglo-Italian Review*, and invited Douglas to contribute.[40] Hutton showed the same tolerance for Douglas's pederastic enthusiasms on the printed page that he showed within their private correspondence. Between August 1918 and August 1920, Douglas contributed fifteen pieces to the *Review*, detailing his travels throughout Italy following his flight from England. He described these pieces as a "Rabelaisian account of my wanderings."[41] The essays were full of descriptions of the charming boys and girls who warmed Douglas's heart during his lonely travels.

In his essay about Olevano, published in the September 1918 issue of the *Anglo-Italian Review*, Douglas described getting drunk in a wine shop with a curly-haired boy named Giulio. "While I confined myself to the minor part of Silenus—my native role—this youngster gave a noteworthy representation of the Drunken Faun," Douglas reminisced.[42] Later the two paid a visit to the family farm, where Douglas met Giulio's brothers, including "Alberto, an adorable cherub of five, the pickle of the family." Douglas ingratiated himself with the boy, who soon curled up "comfortably on my knee." "It appears you like children," the boys' mother remarked. "I like this one," Douglas answered. "I shall steal him one of these days and carry him off." The boys' mother retorted that Douglas couldn't have Alberto because he was too small. Douglas regretted that he couldn't risk a kidnapping during a time of war "when a foreigner is liable to be arrested at every moment."[43] The interchange skated perilously close to revealing the criminal nature of Douglas's affection for boys.

Later essays took similar risks. In his essay about Levanto, published in June 1919, Douglas confessed his preference for children over adults. "The onward march of years," Douglas wrote, had a "cramping effect" that encrusted adults with a veneer of hypocrisy. Children were more generous, sensitive, and curious.[44] In Levanto, Douglas spent time with two children: "a small mason-boy" named Attilio and a "young girl" named Ninetta. Douglas met Ninetta in the shop where she worked as a seamstress, which he visited repeatedly to pursue "an elaborate, classical flirtation." Since Ninetta was "still a child," their acquaintance couldn't leave the shop. It would have been impossible to take a walk with her, Douglas explained, since "to be seen together for five minutes in any public place might injure her reputation."[45]

Boys in Levanto didn't face the same restrictions on their movements, luckily for Douglas. He met Attilio while the boy was carrying bricks along the road outside Levanto and asked him to become his guide. Attilio was "observant and tranquil, tinged with a gravity beyond his years . . . and with uncommon sweetness of disposition," he wrote; "a pleasanter companion could not be found." Attilio brought Douglas to meet his mother in their small village over an hour and a half from Levanto, a walk he made twice a day for work. "Do you wonder," Attilio asked, "at my preferring to be with you?" His question hinted at the brutal conditions underlying the culture of child sex commerce in early twentieth-century Italy. Attilio had many sisters, and a father who had vanished to America, reducing the family to a state of such severe poverty that despite the boy's small size, he was forced to earn money shouldering bricks over rough paths. Working as a guide for a wealthy traveler, even if the job involved selling sex, was preferable to his ordinary daily labor. "Everything depends on me," Attilio told Douglas. The family's need for money was so severe that when Douglas offered to hire Attilio for a week to accompany him on a visit to the marble mines of Carrara, the boy's mother readily agreed.[46]

On the way back to Levanto, Douglas and Attilio got caught in a snowstorm and took shelter in a stone hut, getting tipsy together from a bottle of wine. Douglas elegized this exquisite moment: "So passed an hour of glad confidences in that abandoned shelter with the snowflakes drifting in upon us — one of those hours that sweeten life and compensate for months of dreary harassment."[47] The passage exemplifies Douglas's ability to seduce readers into accepting the unacceptable. What reader wouldn't long for this moment in time — to be tucked safe within the shelter of a stone hut, warmed by Italian wine, watching the snowflakes fall outside, while sharing confidences with an enchanting companion? The trick of Douglas's prose was his ability to communicate his erotic life while leaving space for plausible deniability. Readers could share the feeling of Douglas's longings and pleasures while turning a blind eye to the base facts.

After their time in the stone hut, Douglas quizzed Attilio about whether he had a sweetheart. "Certainly I have. But it is not a man's affair. We are only children, you understand—siamo ancora piccoli." Douglas pressed the boy, "Did you ever give her a kiss?" Attilio denied it. Kissing his sweetheart would be disrespectful. "She is not like you and me," Attilio explained. "Not like us? How so?" Again, Douglas's prose skates to the edge of the obscene. If Attilio's relations with his sweetheart were not physical, because his sweetheart was not like himself and Douglas, then by implication his relationship with Douglas was physical. The essay ends a few lines later. Douglas brings his reader to the edge of obscenity but no further.

Achieving this effect required great care. Douglas wished he could have written more openly about his flirtations. He told a friend that he resented that "come what may, I shall never really be able to say what I think on any of the important questions of life. That damned public—those blasted librarians!" In his own estimation, he "sailed pretty close to the wind, here and there."[48] But he kept on the safe side of censorship. The essays in the *Anglo-Italian Review* amplified the reputation for hedonism that he had cultivated in *Siren Land, Old Calabria*, and *South Wind*. His notoriety, in turn, laid the basis for his popularity. His portrayal of himself as a dissolute satyr wasn't just canny marketing. Douglas felt a strong compulsion to write about his erotic desire for children, and boys in particular. That drive toward self-exposure differentiated him from other men of his time more than anything.

He could have written more popular fare. He could have followed the example of Ouida and written additional novels and stories set among the cosmopolitan elite he encountered on his travels. For example, Douglas visited Levanto because a friend had recommended the fine hotel in the town where a friendly international crowd gathered. Douglas could have set a novel in Levanto, rather than written a travel essay about the place. Many of the books that *South Wind* inspired, like *Those Barren Leaves* and *The Rock Pool*, were set within Anglo expatriate colonies along the Mediterranean.

Instead of imitating Ouida, Douglas followed in the footsteps of John Addington Symonds, who channeled his desires into travel writing, such as his *Sketches in Italy and Greece* (1874). Symonds, most often remembered as a homosexual rights crusader, was a defender of the pederastic tradition, which he described as "a passionate and enthusiastic attachment subsisting between man and youth."[49] Small wonder Douglas was a fan of Symonds. When Douglas collected his *Review* essays into a 1921 book, he described the volume as "my Italian sketches."[50] Symonds's *Sketches* began in Menton, a town on the border between France and Italy. Douglas's sketches, which he titled *Alone*, also began in Menton, a choice determined not by his actual itinerary but by his desire to pay homage to Symonds, whose book Douglas acknowledged in the first paragraph: "Discovered, in a local library . . . those two volumes of sketches by J. A. Symonds, and forthwith set to comparing the Mentone of his day with that of ours."[51]

Symonds's travels took him to Siena, Rome, and Florence. Douglas visited many of the same places. Symonds devoted a chapter of his sketches to the songs of Tuscany. Douglas claimed to have made a "scientific collection" of Tuscan curse words, "abusive, vituperative, or profane expletives."[52] The critic Stefania Arcara has argued that the locations on Symonds's itinerary were less important as travel destinations than as spaces that allowed him to write in positive terms about the classical homosexual tradition.[53] Douglas's travel destinations likewise allowed him to write positively about pederasty. A visit to Pisa, for example, allowed Douglas to expound his theory that pederasty produced a healthier adult masculinity than did the repressive sexual regime in England. In Italy "the rainbow period of youth" led to a mature sex binary that was preferable to the "iridescence and ambiguity" of English sex roles.[54]

At heart, Douglas was a storyteller rather than a theorizer. He used the genre of travel writing less as an opportunity to develop arguments than to express his desires. *Alone* added even more tales of flirtatious encounters with children to those that first appeared in the *Review*. In Sant'Agata, Douglas took a delightful stroll "with a wild youngster." In Alatri, Douglas had an encounter with two goatherds, "aboriginal fauns of the thickets, who told me, amid ribald laughter, a few personal experiences which nothing would induce me to set down here." In Rome, Douglas got "lost in a maze of vulgar love-adventures, several of which came nigh to making me play a part in the police-courts of Rome." That sailed pretty close to the wind. He sailed even closer in his chapter on Viareggio. There Douglas watched boys playing soccer, their "figures of consummate grace and strength, and clothed moreover in a costume which leaves little to the imagination. Those shorts fully deserve their name. They are shortness itself, and their brevity is only equaled by their tightness. One wonders how they can squeeze themselves into such an out-fit." Douglas engaged one of the soccer players, "a superb specimen, all dewy with perspiration," in a discussion of the war, only to beg off with the excuse: "On some other day, I would like to discuss the matter with you point by point—some other day, that is, when you are not playing football and have just a few clothes on. I am now at a disadvantage." Arguing with the boy was like "haggling with Apollo Belvedere." Douglas shifted to asking the boy about how he got into his tight shorts.[55]

This passage comes the closest of any in the book to trespassing the boundary between plausible deniability and outright obscenity. Similar stories crowded the pages of *Alone* to the very end. The book's final passages recounted a visit to a lake outside Alatri, between Rome and Naples, with an unnamed companion, presumably a child. It was a perfect June day, and so Douglas and his companion took their time along the trail until at long last they reached the lake: "We took our ease. We ate and drank, we slumbered awhile, then joked and frolicked for five hours on end, or possibly six.*" The last line of the book addressed the asterisk mark: "The title *Alone* strikes me, on reflection, as rather an inapt one for this volume. Let it stand!"[56]

Douglas had many transitory encounters during his wartime travels through Italy. But the title wasn't as inapt as Douglas claimed. He was plagued with loneliness following his exile from London. That feeling wouldn't dissipate until the very end of 1918, when he fell in love again.

CHAPTER TEN

Together

There's another story from Norman Douglas's life that appears in the sources three times, like the story of the murdered dogs at Villa Maya, but this is the story of a perfect moment.

The first version is from the 1922 travel diary of René Mari, an eighteen-year-old Corsican youth who was then Douglas's lover. On the morning of July 22, Mari and Douglas walked through the Austrian countryside from Thüringen to the ruins of Blumenegg castle. In the diary that Mari kept at Douglas's request, he recorded the day's events: "We rested in the middle of the castle. I played some music on the moss which was perfectly dry. The spot is very beautiful. Of the castle which seems to have been very large there remain only some decayed walls, windows and some pieces of wood here and there. In the interior, there is moss and large firs."[1] After their rest in this serene spot, they took the road back to Thüringen, ate dinner, had another stroll along the road to Bludesch, and then went back to the inn to sleep.

The next version of the story appeared in Douglas's 1923 travel book, *Together*, describing his and René's travels through Vorarlberg in the summers of 1921 and 1922. Douglas devoted an entire chapter to Blumenegg. In his typical scholarly fashion, he explained the etymology of the castle's name and the castle's history dating back to 1265. These facts were less significant to Douglas than the castle's timeless beauty. Blumenegg, he wrote, was "one of the fairest places on earth." He drew on Mari's diary entry to describe the ruin:

It is desolation itself, a harmonious desolation, among its dreamy firs and beeches; firs within, firs and beeches without. The roof is gone, and so are nearly all the internal partitions; nothing but the

shell survives. This shell, this massive outer wall of blocks partly
hewn and partly in the rough—waterworn bowlders, dragged up
from the Lutz-bed below—is encrusted with moss wherever moss
can grow; out of that moss sprout little firs and little beeches, drawing what nourishment they can from the old stones. They garnish
the ruin. So Blumenegg is invaded by nature; and nature, here, has
been left untouched. A castle in a tale!

It was here, amid the moss and beeches and firs, that Douglas experienced
a perfect moment. He and "Mr. R" made themselves "comfortable within
the enclosure, on that soft carpet." He watched the light filter through the
fir branches. Hours passed and the light faded, as Mari lay flat on his back
"playing tunes on that mouth-organ—that talisman which I, in a moment of
inspiration, presented to him." They didn't begin the descent to Thüringen
until dark.[2]

This memory of visiting Blumenegg was so precious to Douglas that he
returned to it a third time, a decade later, in an entry about Mari in *Looking Back*. By that time, Mari was sick with the tuberculosis that would soon
end his life. Knowledge of Mari's illness infected Douglas's portrait with an
unmistakable poignancy. During the heyday of their relationship, they had
traveled together throughout much of Italy as well as Vorarlberg, but Douglas's thoughts kept returning to their visit to Blumenegg. In *Looking Back*,
Douglas described how he combed through Mari's 1921 and 1922 diaries
searching for each mention of the ruins. They had first visited the ruins together on September 15, 1921, when Mari described the castle in French.[3] They
returned on July 22, 1922, when Mari played his mouth organ; and again on
August 10, 1922, when they had a late picnic and Mari played music again.[4]
In *Together*, Douglas had compressed these three visits into one. In *Looking
Back*, Douglas paused to appreciate each visit on its own terms. But he left out
a fourth mention of the ruins in Mari's diary, when they visited the castle to
take photographs.[5] This erasure wasn't a simple oversight. Douglas treasured
those photographs of Mari at Blumenegg, preserving them in an envelope
separate from his general collection of photos of lovers. Perhaps the photographs, which captured Mari's beauty, were too transparently erotic for sharing. Or perhaps Douglas simply wanted to hold something back for himself.
He didn't need the photos to communicate the beauty of the moment.

Together's account of Mari lying in the moss playing his harmonica is one of Douglas's most evocative passages of writing. The passage elicits the sense memory of a perfect moment. Isn't this power to communicate shared truths—to access the universal through the specific—the definition of good writing? Like his essay "Land of Chaos," the Blumenegg chapter raises questions about the relationship between the art and the artist. It forces readers to consider the ethics of accessing the sublime through reading a passage written by a man about his boy lover. Douglas's inspiration was hardly unique. For example, many of Shakespeare's love sonnets were inspired by a young male known to scholars as the "Fair Youth." Shakespeare's sonnets include a dedication to "Mr. W. H.," who may have been the fair youth, and whose term of address is echoed by the name Douglas used for Mari, "Mr. R." Oscar Wilde theorized that the Fair Youth was a boy young enough to act the female roles in Shakespeare's company, in his story "The Portrait of Mr. W. H.," which Douglas likely read.[6] Since no one knows for certain who or how old Shakespeare's Fair Youth was, or whether their relationship was sexual, the poems seem unobjectionable. Ambiguity allows readers to engage in active not-knowing. No such ambiguities protect Douglas's writing.

The fact that Mari was eighteen on the afternoon at Blumenegg only goes so far in exculpating Douglas. Mari was fourteen when Douglas first picked him up, on December 15, 1918.[7] And considering Mari's youthful appearance at age eighteen, one can imagine how innocent he must have looked four years earlier. Douglas, who had just turned fifty when they met, was sick, starving, and seedy.

He had passed much of the year in France, lonely and broke. In February 1918, Douglas wrote from Paris to his old friend Muriel Draper, "I live in conditions more like a pig than a human being; as to food, you wouldn't believe what I have to eat." Draper and Douglas shared a love of good food. Now, he wrote, "I cook my own breakfast and luncheons over a spirit lamp; my room is full of bugs."[8] He was looking for a handout. Draper's old guardian Annie Webb was in Paris, and Douglas hit the old lady up for meals. Sometimes she even obliged with checks, although Douglas complained that "there were not nearly enough of them, nor were they nearly big enough." An ungrateful remark, but "it was a question of money or starve."[9] When Paris was shelled in spring 1918, he moved to Saint-Malo, a fortified city on the Brittany coast. A friend of Webb's who lived there fed Douglas dinners of bacon and eggs or cold fish and meat. He worked on the manuscript for a novel based on a Breton folktale about a drowned city, but he gave up writing the book "owing

21. René Mari at Blumenegg, 1922. Private collection of Dierdre Sholto Douglas. Photograph by author.

to lack of food."[10] After returning to Paris in fall, Douglas taught French to American officers. He lodged in Montmartre and dined in cheap restaurants, where they served sorrel instead of spinach. Sometimes his lunches were made up of no more than a handful of roasted chestnuts. (At least he starved in style!) On one occasion his friend Edward Hutton came to Paris and took him out to dinner. Douglas ordered a porterhouse, but his stomach couldn't tolerate the rich meat and he threw it all up. Later Douglas complained how his writing suffered as he found it "impossible to warm my imagination to the required pitch on an insufficient dietary."[11]

Hunger may have hampered his literary output, but it didn't stifle his libido. "There was a thread of scarlet running through my dun existence," Douglas recalled of these months. This included a "convulsive love-episode" at Amiens, where Douglas went to visit his son Archie, who had been gassed while fighting in France. Douglas didn't detail this "love episode" in *Looking Back,* but Willie King annotated his copy of the memoir: "On the way the author encountered a Madagascar soldier who was lying dead-drunk in the gutter and who if he is still alive is unlikely to realize that he was once buggered by the writer of *South Wind*."[12] At face value, this is a horrible confession about raping an unconscious man, but that wasn't Douglas's point. The story fit into Douglas's earlier mode of self-presentation as a libertine, who pursued as many and as various sexual encounters as possible. The point in Douglas's telling was that he had added a man from Madagascar to his lengthy list of sexual conquests. In truth, by 1918 Douglas's sexual appetites seemed to focus more and more exclusively on boys. His well-rehearsed shocking tales about having sex with a variety of unlikely subjects, including an unconscious Malagasy soldier, seem intended to distract from his growing monomania.

Far more important to Douglas than the brief encounter in Amiens was his ongoing connection in Paris with a youth named Marcel, "a plump but ragged *voyou*—almost a child; a product of the underworld." Marcel was adorned with the "thick-clustering curls" that Douglas liked best. He "looked like an angel in disgrace, and I learned from him more than any angel could have taught me. He was amusing and pretty, unstable of temperament, and liable to fits of passion or else of prodigal generosity, during which he insisted on standing me drinks, taking me to a circus or two, and showing me other marks of affection."[13] Douglas claimed he didn't ask where Marcel got his money, but he described meeting the boy in the rue de l'Agent Bailly, which runs behind the church of Notre-Dame-de-Lorette, a popular site for prostitution (giving rise to the slang word *lorettes,* for prostitutes).[14] Marcel also frequented the rue de Vert-Bois and the passage du Caire, additional locales associated with prostitution.[15]

After the Armistice in November, Douglas's language lessons dried up. Once again, he starved. He got sick in December 1918. Marcel ran off with a hundred-franc note Douglas gave him to purchase medicine. Finally, Douglas decided to leave Paris for the Riviera, where he hoped the sun would improve his health. He sold everything in Paris. Marcel came to say goodbye at the train station on the day of his departure. According to Douglas, Marcel grieved over this separation. When it was time for Douglas to board the train, "he set up a terrific howl. Nothing I could say in the way of consolation had the slightest effect, and his chubby little face, all streaming with tears, attracted more attention than I cared about."[16] Marcel begged to be taken along. Douglas declined. Is it possible the boy felt grief over their separation? Was he just hoping for one more hundred-franc note? There is no way to know, since there are no archival traces in Marcel's hand. Douglas didn't even record his last name. He did, however, carry something away from their last embrace. Douglas arrived in Menton with a bad case of scabies.

The trip took three days on a third-class ticket that compelled Douglas to stand the whole way. When he reached his destination, Douglas was in a disastrous state. He was sick. He had scabies. He had injured his leg in a collision with a taxicab on the way to the Gare de Lyon. He couldn't even carry his bags from the station to the nearest cheap hotel. This was the nadir at which Douglas first caught sight of René Quilicus Mari. The fourteen-year-old was a student at a local *collège* (middle school) and had come to the Menton station to see off a school friend. The only account of this meeting is from *Looking Back*. If Douglas is to be believed, he asked Mari if he would carry his bag to a nearby hotel. "Something inspired him to say 'Je veux bien.'" Their meeting marked "a turn of the wheel," the return of Douglas's good fortune. Mari recommended the Hotel d'Italie, which was run by a friend of his father, who lived across the Italian border in Ventimiglia. Douglas wrote a note to Mari's parents expressing gratitude for their son's assistance. Mari's parents came by the next day to introduce themselves. Afterward, Mari stopped by whenever he could.[17]

Once he was sufficiently recovered, Douglas and Mari began taking excursions around Menton. One of their first walks was to a hilltop cemetery where the consumptive foreigners who traveled to Menton for the recuperative effects of its warm climate were buried when all treatments failed. Douglas was looking for the tomb of Aubrey Beardsley, the Decadent illustrator who had died of tuberculosis in 1898. The cemetery is filled with curious monuments to young victims of the disease, cut down before their time. Douglas and Mari studied the tombs, reading the sepulchral inscriptions, and deducing from age and nationality how many of those who were buried had died from tuberculosis.[18]

Eventually, Douglas rented an apartment in town. Mari's parents agreed to let their son live with Douglas so he wouldn't have to commute from

Ventimiglia. Mari's parents were Corsican, and his father worked in a public administrative post in Italy, but they wanted Mari to attend school in France. Unlike Douglas's previous child lovers, René Mari came from a middle-class family. It seems extraordinary that privileged parents would allow their school-aged son to move in with a middle-aged man of questionable intentions, or that a boy like Mari would want to make such a move. But the Mari family had vulnerabilities, other than poverty, which created opportunities for Douglas. René's father wanted his son to perform well in *collège* and pass the *baccalauréat* exam so he could secure a good job. Unfortunately, René hated *collège* and did poorly at his schoolwork. Douglas appealed to René's father by offering to tutor his son and appealed to René by offering freedom from his father.[19]

Douglas appreciated Mari exactly for those "brigand strains" that most frustrated the boy's father, an admiration which in turn must have ingratiated him with the boy.[20] He admired Mari's physical ease in the natural world, his ability to lie in the moss of a ruined castle for hours without discomfort, his interest in birds and small creatures. Mari was Douglas's dream companion on his rambles through the countryside. Although Douglas moved to Florence in the fall of 1919, he spent spring and summer holidays with Mari for the next four years. They traveled together to Provence in 1919 and Italy in 1920. The latter adventures found their way into the manuscript of *Alone*, which Douglas completed after meeting René (one more reason that the book's title was inapt, as Douglas put it).[21]

The relationship with Mari renewed Douglas's creative energies. In letters to his friend John Mavrogordato, Douglas referred to Mari as his "Insp," an abbreviation for "inspiration," but also perhaps for "inspirer."[22] According to Hans Licht's *Sex Life in Ancient Greece*, the word for "lover" in the Doric dialect was *inspirer*.[23] Mavrogordato, the Bywater and Sotheby Professor of Byzantine and Modern Greek Language and Literature at Oxford, would have recognized the classical reference. While living with Mari, Douglas finished his drowned-city novel, *They Went*, which was published in 1920.[24] The novel features a brigand boy named Harré, around the age of twelve, who is frequently naked.[25] Harré likely owes a debt to Mari. But however inspiring Mari was, the novel itself is dull. Maybe some of its vague quality can be attributed to light-headedness brought on by the starvation that afflicted Douglas during its initial composition. In 1921 Douglas began work on a new book about his travels with Mari in Vorarlberg.

As with Wolton, Douglas asked Mari to keep journals of their travels together that he later used as source material. Mari's first journal is written primarily in French and records their visit from August 27 to September 23, 1921. The second journal is written primarily in English, a language that Douglas was helping Mari to study for his *baccalauréat*, and records their travels from July 21 to September 6, 1922. Both diaries are filled with Mari's enthusiastic observations of the landscape and the food in Austria. Mari also noted a couple encounters with girls he met during their travels. At the Adler Inn in Schnifis, Mari spoke with the innkeeper's daughter, a "rather pretty" thirteen-year-old.[26] At the Krone Inn, he took notice of a serving girl named Antonia.[27] But overall, Mari showed far more interest in the meals he ate than in any romantic adventures. Mari made no reference to any sexual encounters between himself and Douglas, although he acknowledged that they slept together. When they went to the Weisses Kreuz hotel in Bregenz, Mari noted, they were given "two well-furnished rooms, but as always we slept only in one of them."[28] Douglas was rather more explicit. In the midst of their second trip to Vorarlberg, he wrote to Archie, who was then working in Port Sudan, to decline an offered gift of ostrich feathers, telling his son: "My bottom-hole has other things to do just now than to decorate itself so uselessly."[29]

Douglas's rendering of his travels with Mari paid far greater attention to the boy's flirtations than the diaries did. *Together* is equal parts appreciation of the Vorarlberg landscape and appreciation of Mari's lusty appetites. Each morning, for breakfast at half-past seven, he enjoyed two eggs and no less than a liter of milk; "he is a milk-and-egg maniac."[30] At dinner, Mari was overawed by the generosity of the menus. Every night the inn served a different local delicacy, beefsteaks too large to finish, four vegetables with every meat course.[31] In Douglas's account, Mari's appetite for the local girls matched his appetite for the Austrian cuisine. He was at "an inflammable age," although "far more decent-minded than I used to be."[32] At "Tiefis" (Schnifis), Mari took notice of the innkeeper's "pretty fair-haired child," who had "the sweetest smile" and "mysterious golden-gray" eyes. Douglas sought to engineer their flirtation by inviting the girl to sit beside Mari while he distracted the mother with a discussion about the cost of wine. Douglas coached Mari on how to make an impression on the girl: "look straight into her face and smile; put your soul into it." Douglas brought Mari back to Tiefis a second time so he could resume his flirtation. Mari begged Douglas to distract the mother again, so he could have a chance to kiss the daughter, but the mother would not be put off.

When they returned a third time to Tiefis, the inn was crowded with peasant folk drinking beer and smoking and chatting. Douglas engineered a plan to get Mari the kiss he'd been longing for. He told the boy to wait at the orchard. Douglas would order eggs for him, and then send the girl to the orchard to let him know they'd been served. The two would have thirty seconds together before the mother became suspicious. Douglas advised Mari to "clasp her firmly if you get the chance, or you may bungle the whole affair."[33] When the eggs arrived at the table, Douglas briefly distracted the mother with a discussion about the price of *Kirschwasser*, and soon Mari returned with an air of insouciance that could not hide his self-satisfaction. Cultivating Mari's erotic faculties was as important to Douglas as instructing him in English. Ultimately, Mari failed his *baccalauréat* exam twice, but he succeeded as a lover, an accomplishment in which Douglas found satisfaction.

Douglas wrote to Mavrogordato that his goal in *Together* was to evoke a pederastic sensibility while preserving deniability. "What I want to avoid is any definitive phrase for the reviewers to catch hold of; and I think I have avoided this. If they object vaguely to its general tone—why, that will help to sell the book, especially if they say why they object." In fact, Douglas thought that *Alone* had sold much better than *Old Calabria* because there was more pederasty in it.[34] For sophisticated readers between the world wars, pederasty was disreputable enough to be titillating, without being so monstrous that it was repellent. It was immoral but not entirely taboo. Douglas didn't have to disguise his erotic inclinations entirely, but it helped if he couched his love for boys within a libertine persona.

Although *Together* is a love song to Mari, Douglas dedicated the book to his sons, Archie and Robin. It's hard to imagine how they received this tribute. Both sons were at loose ends in the early 1920s. Archie, who turned twenty-two in 1921, was struggling to build a career in civil service—a journey that would take him from London, to Port Sudan, to Prague, and back to London again. He kept in close touch with his father, writing weekly. Douglas was familiar in his letters to Archie, and blunt. He wrote about Mari frequently, referring to the boy as his "Insp."[35] Since Archie had helped his father to escape jail time in London for assaulting a schoolboy, there was nothing to hide. Douglas's letters to Archie were loving and full of advice, but he did little to materially advance Archie's welfare during those years he spent doting on Mari.

Douglas's relationship with his younger son, Robin, who was only two years older than Mari, was more strained. Douglas frequently sought news of Robin, but Robin only wrote erratically. During 1920 and 1921, while Douglas and Mari explored Vorarlberg together, Robin was down and out. He was kicked out of naval training after an accusation of stealing. Then he had what may have been a psychotic break while studying engineering in Scotland. In November 1921, Robin was so hard up that he nearly starved to death on the streets of London, and he contemplated throwing himself into the Thames to end his life.

During this period, a friend arranged for Robin to have lunch with the wealthy writer W. Somerset Maugham, who was sexually interested in boys and youths. Maugham knew Douglas from Capri, but he remarked to Robin that he hadn't known Douglas had sons. "It's strange you should turn out to be his son. You m-m-must be very proud of him; he is a genius," Maugham said. Robin answered, "I've heard it so often. But he's never helped me at all, and he might have done such a lot for me." Maugham agreed but justified Douglas's neglect, saying, "But after all, he's not like any other living man." Then he handed Robin five pounds and suggested that he start a band.[36] Robin may have left out some significant details of his meeting with Maugham. A couple years later, Douglas warned Archie off spending time with Maugham's lover Gerald Haxton, who was reputed to be his pander. Douglas wouldn't say why, just that the reason concerned Robin and that Archie should give Haxton a wide berth.[37]

The contrast between Douglas's material neglect of his sons and his devoted attention to his boy lovers who were near their ages raises an interpretive question: Who had it better or worse? The sons he loved and neglected, or the boys he loved and had sex with? The current taboo treats child sexual abuse as uniquely damaging, an attitude that goes with the presumption that pedophiles are uniquely monstrous. This belief, however, is not supported by contemporary social science, which finds the damage wrought by physical abuse, emotional abuse, and neglect to be equally profound.[38] Historically, during a time when intergenerational sex and child prostitution was more normative than it is today, the comparative effects on children and youths of parental neglect versus sexual encounters with adults are even harder to judge. The Douglas archive provides anecdotal evidence to answer this question. Of all the youths in Douglas's life, the one who expressed the strongest sense of resentment against him was his younger son, Robin. Robin and Archie both suffered tremendously from being separated from their mother, neglected by their father, and farmed out to friends, relatives, and boarding schools. Both men lived unhappy lives. And yet, ultimately, both Robin and Archie, as well as Douglas's long-term boy companions, like Eric Wolton and René Mari, remained loyal to him throughout their lives.

When he grew up, Mari visited Douglas in Florence as often as he could. According to Pino Orioli, who called Mari "one of the most companionable and delightful youngsters I have met in my life," the young man loved to reminisce about the trips that he and Douglas had taken to Vorarlberg.[39] They were a highlight of his youth. His family life had been unhappy. He hated school. But he had loved hiking through the Alps, feasting at mountain inns, flirting with the local girls, and playing his harmonica in the ruins of ancient castles. As Douglas explained, Mari had been "so systematically thwarted by his parents, and demoralized by them, that I have always had my work cut out for me straightening him out again during his holidays."[40]

Mari finally broke from his father's control in 1924. He traveled straight to Douglas's apartment in Florence and looked for work in Italy. "I'd do anything except whoring," he wrote. "I know three languages (more or less . . . it's true)."[41] Douglas lined up a job for him in Guernsey. The next year Mari returned to France, got married, and moved to Vence, a medieval mountain village not far from Menton, where he took a job teaching sports in the local *collège*. But his good fortune did not last long. By the early 1930s, he had developed tuberculosis. His marriage ended. Douglas visited him in Vence and helped to arrange his admission to the sanatorium where D. H. Lawrence had been treated. Douglas kept in close contact throughout Mari's final days — visiting, sending letters and books, asking his friend Martha Gordon Crotch, who lived nearby, to check in on the dying young man, and trying to pressure Mari's father to spend more money on his son's care. Mari appreciated his efforts. He sent Douglas a letter in June 1933 that included a sketch of Douglas as an owl and Mari as his little friend.[42] (Douglas frequently signed his letters with a sketch of an owl, perhaps in tribute to his Athenian propensities.) Mari's affection for Douglas seems to have persisted undiminished into adulthood, just as Wolton's did. He relied on Douglas as a friend and mentor until the end.

Unfortunately, the end came very quickly. Mari wrote to Douglas in early

February 1934, "I think I really am done for." He couldn't write anymore because it tired him out. "Ah là là," he sighed, "I do nothing but curse all day long."[43] The letter must have reminded Douglas of his sister Mary's final missives. Douglas wrote to many of his friends about his concerns for Mari's well-being. But nothing could be done. Mari died in early March. "There are some people who ought never to have died. René was one of them," Orioli eulogized, in *Adventures of a Bookseller*.[44] Douglas often claimed to have written the book for Orioli. The lines about Mari sound like they came from Douglas's pen. René Mari had personified the qualities of boyhood that Douglas most admired. He was generous, sensitive, open, and the vigorous embodiment of physical health. To see him sicken and die overturned the natural order of the universe. In Mari's company, during their afternoons at Blumenegg, Douglas had tiptoed into fairyland. He kept the memory of that moment alive long after Mari's body was laid to rest in the ground.

Reflection II

What should we make of René Mari's and Eric Wolton's expressions of affection for Douglas? Can we take them at their word? Their feelings challenge contemporary assumptions that sex with adults is inherently traumatic for children and therefore abusive by definition. Neither Mari's nor Wolton's writings or actions give evidence that either considered their long-lasting relationships with Douglas to be traumatic or abusive. Both seem to have looked on their experiences within the positive framework of pederasty that held meaning during their own time, rather than through the negative framework of pedophilia that predominates today. In the pederastic model, sexual relationships between men and boys were seen as a loving and healthy form of erotic mentorship. It's one thing for historians of sexuality to accept that people separated from us in time by 2,500 years, like the ancient Athenians, lived in a context where sex between men and boys could be defined by love rather than abuse, but it's harder to wrap our minds around the possibility that this historical context could define people's affective experiences in the twentieth century.

There are other ways to read the evidence. Mari's and Wolton's affectionate letters might be interpreted as utilitarian efforts to extract personal favors and material support from Douglas. Although Douglas was not himself wealthy, he knew plenty of wealthy people, and he had powerful connections who would come in handy to a young man on the make. A roughshod London youth like Wolton benefited from having Douglas pave his way by writing letters to people with job opportunities to offer. The fact that Wolton continued to visit Douglas long after he was ensconced in the upper reaches of the British colonial government in East Africa might have been the result of habit.

Why burn bridges at the end? As for Mari, he had no sooner established himself on his own two feet then he fell sick. Mari's affectionate letters prompted Douglas to work on his behalf to get him proper medical care and sufficient family support. Both young men profited from continuing their relationships with Douglas into adulthood.

Or the letters could be read as evidence of Douglas's emotional manipulation of the boys during their childhoods. As an adult with superior understanding, he was able to persuade the naive boys that their relationships were loving and mutual, when in truth they were exploitative and one-sided. When they grew up, Wolton and Mari remained committed to the narrative that Douglas had constructed during their youths, perhaps because challenging that narrative would have unleashed trauma they had long been suppressing. In this reading, Wolton and Mari both suffered from false consciousness. They cannot be taken at their word because youths don't have the emotional capacity to consent to sexual relationships with adults. The power imbalance between adults and youths is too vast, and adult knowledge of sexual relations too superior to that of children, for children to be competent to make the decision to have sex with adults. Even if children consider themselves willing and have positive feelings about their adult sexual partners, the truth is that they are victims of those adults. Whether they acknowledge that truth as adults or not has no bearing on the emotional dynamics of their earlier experiences.

This third reading would not satisfy all historians of sexuality. First of all, many historians are skeptical of any historical explanation that depends on the premise of false consciousness. The concept of false consciousness derives from Marxist theory, where it is used to explain, among other things, why the proletariat does not recognize that the overthrow of the capitalist system is in its best interests.[1] False consciousness is a troubling theory to apply at the level of the individual, where it must rest on ungrounded presumptions about the operations of the psyche. In sexuality studies, the concept of false consciousness poses problems when it is used to invalidate the apparent consent of persons or communities to forms of sex that are deemed problematic or perverse within mainstream thought. For example, the concept of false consciousness has been applied to women who, within the context of a patriarchal system, engage willingly in sadomasochism.[2] Can the concept of false consciousness be used more safely in regard to children who, within the context of age hierarchy, willingly agree to sexual encounters with adults?

To suggest that Eric Wolton and René Mari *willingly agreed* to sexual encounters with Douglas (and we have no evidence that they did not) is not
equivalent to saying that the boys *consented*. This is the distinction embedded
in age of consent laws, which define any sexual encounters between adults
and children under a certain age threshold to be statutory rape. Historically,
that threshold tended to be conceived of in developmental terms. When children entered puberty, they became capable of consent. In the nineteenth century, as childhood became "standardized," in Douglas's terms, the law shifted
to a threshold determined by calendar age. Thirteen years old. Fourteen years
old. Ages rose as the nineteenth century advanced, and then lowered in the
twentieth century with the spread of sexual liberalism.[3]

The category of consent has its critics, and not just among defenders of intergenerational sexual relations. In *Screw Consent* (2019), legal scholar Joseph
Fischel argues that the focus on consent is not helpful for present-day sexual
justice activism, because consent is insufficient, inapposite, and contradictory.
The fact that children cannot consent to sex with adults, Fischel argues, is not
the reason why such sex should be proscribed. Children's need for supervi-
sion means that there are all sorts of physical things they cannot consent to,
such as vaccinations, that are still done to them for their own benefit.[4] Other
critics see affirmative consent discourse, which presumes women's victimiza-
tion, as problematic because it operates, in tandem with paternalism, to undermine women's autonomy.[5] To extend this logic to children, some sexuality
scholars argue that consent discourse undermines youths' sexual autonomy,
by figuring any expression of child sexuality as denoting abuse or exploitation.[6]

Using modern definitions of consent as a standard by which to judge sexual relations in the past raises further problems. If consent is defined according to contemporary understandings as predicated on a relatively equal distribution of power between two agentic individuals—the understanding that
drives rules against sexual encounters involving professors and students, or
bosses and employees—then pretty much all historic sexual encounters involving men and women are precluded. Contemporary definitions of consent
do little to help historians differentiate the sexual landscape of the past, which
was defined by inequalities, and at the same time capacitated a wide range of
interactions from violent assault through enthusiastic mutuality. Historians
need a better metric than consent to elucidate those differences.

If historians of intergenerational sex assume that all such encounters, by failing to meet contemporary definitions of consent, constitute assault, then we sacrifice the ability to distinguish the meaning of those interactions within the framework of the past. Eric Wolton's and René Mari's diaries, letters, and life histories give evidence that they viewed their relationships with Douglas as beneficial on the whole. They may have enjoyed the sexual aspects of the relationships; they may have been indifferent to the sex; or they may have seen the sex as a necessary price for other aspects of the relationship that benefited them. Their precise feelings are unknowable from the sources, but Wolton's and Mari's warm regard for Douglas is certain. Douglas always claimed that he had made a positive impact on his boy lovers. He told Constantine Fitz-Gibbon, "No boy I have cared for has failed to profit from our relationship."[7] He made a similar remark to Martha Gordon Crotch, describing how he had nurtured the boys' health and education. "He swears he has done many boys the world of good," Crotch wrote in her diary.[8] She was dubious then, as readers will be now, but Mari and Wolton seemingly agreed with Douglas.

PART III
Uncle Norman

CHAPTER ELEVEN

The Pederastic Congress

Florence seems an odd place for Norman Douglas to have wound up. True, the city had a long-established Anglo-American expatriate "colony" dating back to the mid-nineteenth century. Perhaps 10 percent of Florence's residents in the early twentieth century were British or American. Many leading families within this community, like the Berensons and the Actons, were drawn to Florence for its Renaissance art and architecture. Douglas disdained such enthusiasts as "cinquecento Charlies," and he refused to waste his time in churches and museums.[1] When he passed through Florence soon after fleeing London, he wrote to Martin Secker, "I don't much care about the place; never did. I don't like the Tuscan character."[2] He preferred sunny southern Italy. After a few years of restless peregrinations, however, it was Florence where he chose to settle down.

Douglas's decision to make Florence his home owed not to its art but to a lesser-known facet of its history: the city's long association with pederasty.[3] This reputation preceded Florence's Renaissance fame. During the late Middle Ages, Middle High German had a verb, *florenzen*, which meant "to sodomize." In Florence, sodomy almost always took the form of sexual relations between men over eighteen and male youths between the ages of twelve and twenty. Typically, adult men took the active penetrative role and boys took the passive receptive role in sexual acts including anal sex and intercrural sex. Judging from the legal records, adult men rarely had sex together. On the other hand, pederastic relations were so common in fifteenth-century Florence that a special court was established just to handle these cases. Historian Michael Rocke has calculated that between 1459 and 1502, at least one of every two youths in the city of Florence was formally implicated in sodomy by the age of thirty. Savonarola's infamous campaign against the city's sinners at the end of the fifteenth century targeted pederasts with particular savagery.[4]

Florence's scandalous historical reputation was a subject of great amusement to Douglas. When his brilliant but dilettantish young friend Harold Acton was looking for a writing project, Douglas suggested that he translate a scandalous seventeenth-century biography of the last grand duke of the Medici family, Gian Gastone, who was notorious for his voracious sexual appetite for the city's boys. Douglas wrote the introduction to Acton's translation. In his typical mocking manner, Douglas warned that he "should hesitate to recommend it to any boy under twelve years of age."[5] (Douglas also blamed the duke's preference for pederasty on his having an ugly German wife.) Acton's *The Last of the Medici* (1930) was published in Italy by Pino Orioli in a limited private edition. Even so, the book caused problems for Orioli with the British Home Office, who contacted the Italian government. Three detectives were sent to Orioli's shop to seize all copies of the book that hadn't yet been sold.[6]

The heyday of Florentine pederasty had passed by the early twentieth century, but there were plenty of British men still attracted to the city for its boys. John Addington Symonds wrote about the beautiful Florentine lads who strolled the Lungarno, the city's main avenue fronting the river.[7] The boys who went swimming in the Arno attracted even more fervent admirers. Lytton Strachey described how "in Florence . . . large crowds collect every day to see the young aristocrats bathe in the Arno—and they are 18 or so. As each one steps out of the water a murmur of approbation or the reverse rises from the crowd. They criticise details—that young man's legs are too fat—oh! the beautiful torso! etc. I long to go and live there, or at any rate stay there a week."[8] Many queer British men numbered among the swimmers' admirers. The writer Ronald Firbank satirized his compatriots in his play *The Princess Zoubaroff*, in which the character Lord Orkish, based on Oscar Wilde, remarks, "I don't know at all what the Arno is coming to. I was leaning on my window-sill and there were some youths who appeared to be bathing without false modesty of *any* kind." Another character remarks, "How dreadful." Lord Orkish replies, "I'm sure if I looked it was quite involuntary."[9]

Douglas shared Firbank's sense of humor about Florence's appeal to men like himself. In September 1918, he wrote to Muriel Draper that he was traveling to the city for its "annual paederastic congress, which, as you know, opens on the 16th at the Palazzo Vecchio."[10] He made the same joke to his friend

22. *The Bathers at San Niccolò*, by Domenico Passignano, 1600. Depicting youths swimming in the river Arno in Florence. Private collection. Wikimedia Commons.

John Mavrogordato in the fall of 1921, shortly after he'd settled in the city. "Are you going to the Paederastic Congress here next month? I understand they are counting on you for a little speech: is that so? What is the subject? '<u>Coit. Int. Fem.</u> during the Magalenian Period?'" The abbreviation stood for *coitus inter femora*, or intercrural sex.[11] He had no particular event in mind when he made these jokes, he was just referring to the seasonal migration of expatriates back to the city following the hot summer.

Douglas rented a "microscopic" apartment at the top of the Albergo Nardini, in the Piazza del Duomo, in spring 1921. The apartment looked south toward the Baptistery of St. John and east toward Brunelleschi's Dome. He had his tin trunk of valuables that he'd packed up in London delivered to the new apartment, and he planted poppy seeds in flowerpots that lined his tiny balcony. For the first time in four years, he made a home for himself. Perhaps he had delayed so long because he still entertained hopes of returning to England after the war. In 1920 he discussed the idea of making a visit to London, but he must have gotten the message that he would not be welcomed back by the British government.[12] The 1920s marked a turning point in Britain, when

authorities began to take the issue of the sexual corruption of boys more seriously. In 1925 British law shifted to treating any boys under the age of sixteen
as victims of abuse rather than complicit parties in sexual encounters with
adult men.[13] As a result, Douglas wrote to E. M. Forster, "I am more or less of
a fixture here, at Florence; there are drawbacks to the town, but, on the whole,
it suits me better than any other—and I have tried a good many."[14]

The drawbacks included broiling hot summers and gloomy gray win-
ters. Those unpleasant seasons inspired Douglas to take frequent trips out of
the city. Just because he had settled down didn't mean he had expended his
wanderlust. Sant'Agata, a few miles outside Sorrento, drew Douglas back repeatedly. A sympathetic female innkeeper in the town kept him well supplied
with boys. Child prostitution remained a thriving business in Italy between
the world wars. The nation entered a severe recession in 1920, and countless families were impoverished by the wartime loss of their men or by postwar male immigration. Living conditions in the south, especially, worsened
during the 1920s.[15] There was strong financial incentive for families to engage
in prostitution as a survival strategy. Douglas took full advantage of this need.
During a visit to Sant'Agata in March 1923, Douglas took up with a local "infant" whom he hoped to bring back to Florence to work as his cook.[16] When
he returned again in March 1924, he reported to Mavrogordato that he was
enjoying "a most marvellous Hellenic mutual-and-at-first-sight love affair."[17]
But Sant'Agata was a small village, with little to offer besides its boys and the
landscape. Soon enough Douglas always returned to Florence.

Even if Douglas scorned Florence's cinquecento Charlies, the city's rich
expatriate social life suited him, as he acknowledged. "The town is full of English people," Douglas wrote to Archie soon after he rented his apartment.[18]
Many of these English people—like his friends H. G. Wells, Rebecca West,
D. H. Lawrence, Aldous Huxley, Harold Acton, Ronald Firbank, and Reggie
Turner—either shared his predilection for boys or were sexual radicals who
did not judge him for his tastes. Douglas avoided socializing with the more
stuffy reaches of the Anglo colony, for example, staying far away from the sa-
lons organized by his Scottish compatriot Janet Ross at her estate in the hills
above the city.[19]

The bookseller Giuseppe "Pino" Orioli was Douglas's most steady companion during this period. Born in Emilia Romagna in 1884, Orioli was a sau-
sage maker's son who apprenticed to a barber at age twelve. After his manda-
tory military service, Orioli traveled to London, where he got a job teaching

Italian at a language school. There Orioli met Irving Davis, a Cambridge student who was school friends with Philip and Cecil Woolf, the younger brothers of Virginia Woolf's husband, Leonard. Davis and Orioli became lovers and moved together to Florence, opening a bookshop in 1910. In 1913 Orioli and Davis opened another bookshop in London, which specialized in rare and antique books. Orioli had to return to Italy for military service at the beginning of World War I, but the Italian government later sent him back to London, where he met Christopher Millard, a book collector who wrote the first bibliography of Oscar Wilde's works, and who also collected the pederastic letters of the writer Baron Corvo.

After the war, Orioli returned to Florence and opened his own antiquarian bookshop, remaining in partnership with Davis, although the two were no longer lovers. Acton described Orioli's bookstore as a meeting ground for the city's queer expatriates, who gathered there to pass the time in "scandalmongering."[20] Wilde's friend Reggie Turner was a constant customer and became a close friend of Orioli. Oscar Browning, a retired Cambridge professor, also frequented the shop in the company of a young man whom he referred to as his "secretary." According to Orioli, once the secretary opened his mouth, "you could guess what he was—an uneducated Cockney boy, and a pleasant one." Orioli himself liked males in their late teens. He shared his customers' appreciation for the sexual charms of Florentine boys and spoke fondly of how they tailored their gaberdine trousers specially to show off their assets.[21]

Orioli and Douglas first met in 1921, at a small party hosted by a rich old woman.[22] Orioli told Douglas how much he had enjoyed reading *Alone*, and the two men shared a bottle of strega, stolen from the liquor cabinet. They connected over their mutual love of ribaldry. Orioli was a shameless clown who liked to whip out his penis for a laugh. He was also an epicure, a bon vivant, and an intellectual. The Scottish writer Eric Linklater described Orioli as "a kindly and exuberant man who offered, as freely as windfalls from an abundant orchard, anecdotes and tales of his unusual life for the entertainment of all his companions. Many of the anecdotes were scandalous, but as gay and lively as a horde of little boys in a swimming-pool, and in his voice, as he told them, was a recurrent splash of laughter."[23] The choice of metaphor was intentional.

Eventually, the two men bought neighboring apartments in a small building on the Lungarno delle Grazie, on the north side of the river. Their south-facing windows looked straight across the Arno to the Piazzale Michelangelo, where a large statue of the *David* was erected. Orioli and Douglas were a study in contrasts. The publisher Charles Prentice, who was friends with both, described watching them walk together along the Lungarno Corsini. Orioli, who was much shorter than Douglas, looked like "a frog that would awooing go" as "he beamed up with such an appealing ingratiating air into the angular Voltairean face of his friend, and waggled his square little stern." Derek Patmore called Orioli "a marvellous foil," who played the part of Sancho Panza to Douglas's Don Quixote. The writer, activist, and heiress Nancy Cunard believed "no one else could have been so well suited [to Douglas] as this wise, gay, well-rounded, witty little man, of so Italian an essence."[24]

Others looked less favorably on the friendship. Osbert Sitwell, the British aesthete, likened Douglas and Orioli to characters from *Volpone*, a seventeenth-century play by Ben Jonson about a sinister aristocrat and his buzzing fly of a servant. (Douglas didn't like Sitwell much either, dismissing him in letters as "Osbert Shitwell.")[25] Martin Birnbaum thought Orioli was a bad influence on Douglas. But D. H. Lawrence had the opposite perspective, blaming Douglas for encouraging Orioli to "razzle and drink."[26] Birnbaum and Lawrence both felt that Douglas and Orioli together made an unwholesome combination. Everyone agreed on the two men's significance to each other. There is no evidence that they were lovers, but they behaved like a married couple. They ate together, traveled together, and frequently gave accounts of each other in letters to mutual friends, sometimes even signing postcards to friends with the portmanteau *Pinorman*.

Despite the ordering of their combined nickname, it was Douglas who dominated the friendship. Orioli catered to Douglas's whims. Douglas was constantly plaguing Orioli with requests of one sort or another. "Dear Pino, I am all alone and Can't go out. Send some one to cheer me up. Yours ND," Douglas beseeched Orioli in a typical brief note to his friend. Orioli scribbled at the bottom, "I sent a bottle of whisky to cheer him up."[27] Orioli often acted as a wingman in Douglas's sexual affairs. Douglas wrote to Orioli all the time seeking assistance with his boys. He would ask Orioli to help him keep the existence of one boy secret from another, or to smooth over sticky situations with parents and authorities.[28]

Douglas's interactions with the boys of Florence went far beyond watching them swim in the Arno. He employed countless boys to carry messages for him. Friends who met Douglas for drinks or meals in the city's caffès and trattorias witnessed his fondness for these youths, many of whom likely supplemented their income by also exchanging sexual favors for cash or presents. These ephemeral encounters were numerous, but left only occasional traces in the archives. For example, Mavrogordato stopped by Douglas's apartment on a summer afternoon and found his friend "very cheerful qui stamattina Marcellum fellaverat et Italum fratrem postea Paedicaverat."[29] In translation, Douglas was happy because he had fellated Marcello and afterward had pederastic relations with Marcello's brother Italo. A couple more entries in Mavrogordato's diary are the only evidence of Douglas's encounters with Italo and Marcello. Neither boy developed into a full-blown affair. They were two of many youths who breezed in and out of Douglas's life.

There were other boys from his Florence years who stayed longer. Several moved in with Douglas for a spell, taking on the role of cook. He initiated this pattern early in 1923, when he brought the "infant" he had met in Sant'Agata, who was named Mario, back to Florence. Mario eventually learned to cook "after a fashion."[30] But by spring of 1924, Douglas grew tired of him. As was so often the case, Douglas's affection expired before the affection, or material need, of his lover did. Douglas arranged for Mario to join the Italian merchant marine, which suggests he was not that infantile.[31] But Mario soon left the service and came looking for Douglas. "Don't tell Mario where I am!" Douglas wrote urgently to Orioli in June 1924.[32] If Mario caught up with him, he worried, "I shall never shake him off again!"[33]

By the summer of 1924, Douglas had a new boy named Silvio living with him as his cook. Douglas wrote to Mavrogordato, "I do all my cooking at home now with my cook—vide photograph; the consequence being that my meals are of Arcadian simplicity and heart-rending monotony. But oh, so healthy."[34] In July, Douglas brought Silvio with him on a visit to his friends Bryher and H.D., queer feminist writers who were living in Territet, Switzerland. Bryher described Silvio as having "skin like wild cyclamen spread over yellow roses. O—quel vie!" Of Douglas, she remarked, "Does anyone ever have such combinations of sordid and exctatic [sic] taste?"[35] Yet if Bryher disapproved, she did so most faintly. Douglas frequently wrote to her about his sexual misadventures and introduced her to his new lovers.

Nancy Cunard met Silvio in Bologna, when Douglas brought the boy along to a dinner she organized with her lover Tristan Tzara, the founder of Dada. "Never had I seen a better-mannered small boy," Cunard noted. She was pleased when Silvio told her he "thought I would look like an asparagus with my clothes off; I seemed to him that long and slim."[36] Douglas was also

23. Emilio Papa in 1925 or 1926. Norman Douglas Forschungsstelle, Bregenz.

enamored of Silvio and grew upset when authorities forced Silvio to return to school in Rome in November 1924. "His family is furious, and so is he, and so am I!" Douglas complained. "That ridiculous education! I am all alone."[37] He wouldn't be for long.

Shortly after Silvio's departure Douglas met Emilio Papa, the most important of all his Florentine boys. Douglas first recorded Papa's name in his pocket diary on December 27, 1924, when Papa was around twelve.[38] He took Papa to Vorarlberg the following summer. Papa's mother and father both died in 1927.[39] Douglas took responsibility for him, although by that time his sexual attentions had moved on to other subjects. In 1928 Douglas took Papa and his younger brother on a summer trip to Abruzzi. "The boys are flourishing," he told Orioli.[40]

Douglas's attentions to Papa continued as the boy matured. As with Wolton and Mari, Douglas encouraged Papa's female love affairs. He heartily approved of Papa's marriage in 1933 to a young woman named Nella. The affection was reciprocated. Nella treated Douglas as family. He ate Sunday lunch with them each week. When Papa and Nella had a daughter, Elena, Douglas became a godfather of sorts. In 1937, when Douglas had to leave Florence, he worried about the effect his absence would have on Papa. He told Bryher that Papa "suffers more than I do, at not seeing me and being able to look after me. He is in despair."[41] The remark sounds self-aggrandizing, but surviving letters from Papa suggest it was not off-base. During their separation, Papa sent many loving, longing letters to Douglas. On Christmas Day, 1937, Papa wrote, he pored over old photographs and diaries from their trips together to Calabria, Tirolo, and Ischia, recalling those "wonderful days."[42] The next fall found him reminiscing again about their excursions. In 1939, Papa wrote to Douglas about a dream he'd had of spending time together; "this morning I told Nella that last night, as happens often to me, I dreamt of being in your company. Believe me, I felt happy."[43]

To believe Papa, he looked back on his childhood experiences with Douglas fondly throughout his adult life, just as Wolton and Mari did. Cunard, who regarded Papa as "by far the nicest" of Douglas's Italian lovers, thought that Douglas had "instructed, and materially helped" Papa, and that Papa in return was "perfectly devoted" to Douglas.[44] For Papa, who grew up in a city where sex between boys and men was routine, the sexual elements of his relationship with Douglas did not stand out as aberrant. The care Douglas took for his well-being, especially after he was orphaned, was more unusual and notable.

Looking at the relationship from Papa's point of view, it's possible to see how this young man might have adored Douglas. But looking at the relationship from a broader perspective, it's equally possible to see how Papa was just one of many boys whose bodies Douglas plowed through during his years in Florence. His sexual rapacity led to dangers as well as pleasures, as in the case of his affair with a boy named Luciano.[45] Douglas likely met twelve-year-old Luciano in the summer of 1924, when he mentioned using the boy to carry an invitation to Muriel Draper for a dinner party with Orioli, the translator C. K. Scott Moncrieff, and a South African artist named Teddy Wolfe.[46] After the dinner, Wolfe sent Douglas a letter illustrated with watercolors of naked boys and asked him, "How is your new little boy and are you quite well and happy?" Wolfe also sent Douglas sketches of farting cupids performing fellatio on men with large erect penises.[47] Pederasty was a source of humor, not horror, to queer society in Florence between the wars.

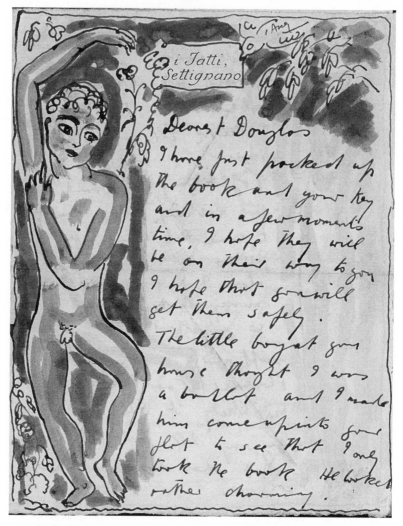

24. Teddy Wolfe letter to Norman Douglas, ca. 1924. Beinecke Rare Book and Manuscript Library, Yale University.

Luciano's parents, who were separated, were divided in their opinions about Douglas's relationship with their son. Douglas had a warm relationship with Luciano's father, whom he described as "a very jovial person (man of business)."[48] But Luciano's mother, whom Douglas thought half-mad, disliked him and alerted the authorities in 1927. The Fascists, who had taken control of Italy, lowered the age of consent as part of their pro-natalist policies.[49] Prostitution and same-sex sex remained legal. However, under the morality campaign known as *epurazione*, Fascist police hassled people who did not keep their homosexuality quiet and hidden, such as effeminate men and notorious foreigners like Douglas. Authorities charged queer men with crimes including scandalous behavior, offense to sense of decency, obscene acts in public, and assault.[50] Douglas had to exercise caution where the law was concerned.

After Luciano's mother alerted the authorities, Douglas skipped town, first to Milan to confer with Luciano's father, and then to France. By the end of March, the danger had passed and Douglas returned to Florence. But still feeling anxious, Douglas worked out a plan to have Luciano's father bring the boy to Pistoia. On April 25, Douglas wrote triumphantly from Pistoia. "The battle is won (the toughest of all my life, and I have had a good few)." The new affair restored his sense of well-being. He felt twenty years younger.[51] Douglas and Luciano traveled together around Italy. They went to Monza, where Luciano's father lived. Douglas wanted to take Luciano to Vorarlberg, but the boy's passport didn't come through. Instead, they went to Sant'Agata and Ischia, where Douglas drank the "amber-coloured wine" while Luciano bathed in the ocean.[52] By the end of fall, the affair had run its course. Douglas was tired of Luciano. He began his typical routine of avoiding his discarded lover. But the affair left a positive impression. Douglas and Luciano remained on good terms. Douglas continued to mention Luciano in his letters for years afterward, even noting his birthday in 1939.[53]

Again, he moved onto new boys. There were always new boys in Florence. When Douglas was out of the city, he complained about how much he missed his "Florentine pleasures." Sex was far more uncertain a proposition in other towns. But it wasn't simply a matter of sex. Affairs with boys were critical to Douglas's creative life. As he wrote to Archie, if he managed to conduct an affair with Luciano, then his "novel and all future novels are assured."[54] Douglas's Florentine pleasures paid off on the page. His voracious sex life during his Florentine years resulted in the most prolific output of books during his lifetime.

CHAPTER TWELVE

A Hymn to Copulation

"I can only write if I have this," Douglas said, grabbing Brigit Patmore by the upper arm. Words didn't come easy. "Every sentence is like having a baby," he told Algernon Islay de Courcy Lyons. "I've never written anything before without having a tangible inspiration."[1] He told Harold Acton the same thing: to write, he needed to be in love. Or, at least, he needed to be in the state of giddy lust and infatuation that he called a "love-affair." There were a lot of love affairs during his Florentine years. "I am loaded up with love-affairs as never before!" he bragged to Archie.[2] The pace of his publishing demonstrated the happy effects. Between 1921 and 1933, Douglas published ten original works and at least six repackaged editions of works formerly published in pamphlet or periodical form. When he wasn't writing, he was working with publishers to produce special editions for the collectors' market, which was a major source of income to Douglas, whose latter books never achieved the popularity of South Wind. This frenetic pace of production led him to complain about feeling overworked, but he kept it up, both because he needed the money and because he was inspired.

His topic was sex. After the publication of Together in 1922, Douglas shifted from idiosyncratic travel writing to books that dealt more forthrightly with his favorite pursuit. In the spring of 1922, he began work on a new "hot and exotic" novel. It was "an orgy of fucking," he said, inspired by his relationship with René Mari.[3] But when Douglas was alone, he complained that he couldn't write. After he and Mari parted following their 1922 summer trip to Vorarlberg, Douglas wrote, "I can't get on with my work like Austria, and that makes me sick. Lack in insp: solitary nights are bad for me." The deprivation took its toll on his writing. "The quality of the work suffers."[4]

He must have swiftly found someone new to distract him. Douglas was feeling bullish about the manuscript in January 1923. He promised Mavrogordato that there would be "plenty of straightforward normal fucking" in his next novel, although he worried that the book would have to be printed in Florence to avoid British censorship laws.[5] Douglas's concerns about censorship eventually overpowered his optimism about the project, and he put the book aside.

In the early 1920s, strict obscenity laws governed British publishing. The growing frankness of the modernist literary movement hadn't led to a relaxation of censorship, but to a renewed desire among authorities to stamp out sexual writing. Courts, customs officers, postmen, publishers, printers, and typists all conspired in the effort to suppress sex.[6] Douglas had bucked against this system from the start of his professional writing career. While still an editor at the *English Review*, he struck out against censorship in his review of a romance novel called *The Night of Temptation* by Victoria Cross. Douglas fumed that censorship codes allowed women like Cross to publish "libidinous balderdash" while they stifled "man-writers" who strained for the same freedom.[7] Actually, Cross had faced censorship attempts during her writing career and had fought them successfully in court. Perhaps Douglas was simply jealous of her success. Cross's best-selling 1901 novel *Anna Lombard* sold more than six million copies.[8]

As long as he continued trying to publish in Britain, Douglas would feel the effects of censorship. He wrote to his friend W. H. D. Rouse, a famous classicist, that he feared "I shall never really be able to say what I think on any of the important questions of life."[9] Some authors, like James Joyce, tried to evade censorship by publishing abroad. British customs agents and postal workers looked out for foreign publications that fell afoul of British obscenity laws, impounding even classic titles like Aristophanes's *Lysistrata* and Ovid's *Ars amatoria*. But publishing abroad still held potential. In 1922 the Satanist necromancer Aleister Crowley suggested to Douglas that they launch a literary magazine together in Italy because "in this country we should not be hampered by considerations of the laws about libel, blasphemy, indecency and all that nonsense, which emasculate Anglo-Saxon publications."[10]

Douglas appears to have dismissed this invitation. He didn't share Crowley's self-seriousness. Douglas saw sex as funny.[11] That sense of humor compounded his struggles with censorship. He didn't want to write serious books about the "sex problem," as it was known at the turn of the twentieth century. Douglas read all the major sexual scientists of his day: Richard von Krafft-Ebing, Havelock Ellis, Magnus Hirschfeld, Edvard Westermarck, René Guyon, Xavier Mayne (Edward Irenaeus Prime-Stevenson), and so on. But he had no desire to reproduce their style. Sometimes he joked about sexology in his writing, but by the early 1920s he professed himself tired of the subject.[12] When Bryher first struck up a correspondence with Douglas in 1921, he dismissed her interest in scientific theories of sexuality: "I know of Westermarck's book; that is, I read it ages ago. Don't dream of sending it here. I am sick of marriage, and sex, and homosexuality, and fornication, and paederasty, and all the rest of that damned tribe."[13] He wasn't sick of the acts. He was just sick of sociology on the subject. It was "all balls!"[14] Later, when Bryher became enamored of Sigmund Freud's theories, she engineered a meeting in Vienna between Douglas and the father of psychoanalysis. They appeared to get on "famously" and exchanged several letters, but Douglas scoffed at the great man's work.[15]

Douglas preferred old-fashioned words and concepts. He rarely used sexological terms like "homosexual" or "invert." He favored "sodomite," or "sod" for short. Sometimes he'd use the word "lesbian," but he was just as likely to call queer women "sapphists" or "saphs."[16] Along with old-fashioned language, Douglas preferred old-fashioned books. "I simply love pornographical stuff," he told Hellé Flecker.[17] He read Casanova's diaries and the works of the Marquis de Sade in the original French. He appreciated the English classics, like *Fanny Hill* and *The Memoirs of Cora Pearl*. And he was well versed in ancient naughty books, like the *Kama Sutra* and Apuleius's *The Golden Ass*, which Douglas recommended as a must-read for all schoolboys.[18]

Classic texts were a natural launching point for Douglas as he began his shift to erotic writing. After setting aside his dirty novel, Douglas tried a different approach to writing on explicitly sexual themes by compiling a naturalist catalog of all the animals that were mentioned in *The Greek Anthology*, with a particular focus on its twelfth volume, the "Musa Paidika." In *Birds and Beasts of the Greek Anthology* (1927), Douglas resumed the tongue-in-cheek scholarly voice of his early works on Capri.[19] The pederastic subthemes of his commentary sailed closer to the wind than ever.

Under the subject of wolves, for example, Douglas mentioned that "Strato, on a certain disreputable occasion, compares himself to a wolf that finds a lamb standing at the door and waiting for him."[20] Douglas was highlighting a common erotic motif in the *Greek Anthology*, likening adult male pederasts to wolves and their boy lovers to lambs.[21] The reference would have been clear to like-minded readers, since the terms "wolf" and "lamb" were still used in the twentieth century to describe adult men and their boy lovers.[22] Douglas took a similar approach in discussing dolphins, when he referred to how "Rufinus, alluding to his sudden and almost incredible change of taste in matters erotical, talks of dolphins browsing on the slopes of Erymanthus and deer in the grey billowy ocean."[23] Rufinus's sudden erotical shift was from boys to women, which anyone consulting the poem in question would discover.

In other passages, Douglas took a more explicit approach. On the subject of vultures, he quoted from a Strato poem that likened purple-clad youths to "ripe figs" waiting to be devoured by the eaters of carrion. On the subject of quails, Douglas explained how the birds were given as presents to boys with the "alleged object" of enabling boys to fight the birds. Douglas pointedly declined to speculate about the real object of such gift-giving, but made it obvious in a subsequent entry, which explained that the gift of a wryneck bird tied to a four-spoked wheel could be used to lure boys or girls to a lover.[24] In sum, *Birds and Beasts* was suffused with Douglas's appreciation for the pederastic culture of ancient Greece, but took an esoteric approach designed to avoid the pitfalls of censorship.

Unsurprisingly, the book's esoteric approach also undercut its popularity. By October, Douglas had declared the book to be in a "hopeless slump."[25] In need of money, and inspired by his affair with Luciano, Douglas decided to take a chance and return to the abandoned dirty novel that he described as "a hymn to copulation."[26] Douglas worked hard during the summer of 1927, waking up each day at six a.m. to write.[27] At the end of July, he wrote to Mavrogordato, "I have at last finished that bloody book of which you read the first chapters in Florence about 15 years ago." A touch of exaggeration, but the book had been a long time brewing. Since he knew "no publisher would touch it as it stands," he decided to print the novel privately.[28] In November, Douglas sent the manuscript of *In the Beginning* to Tipografia Giuntina, a Florentine printer he had been working with since 1925 to prepare collectors' editions of his works.[29] The typesetters' limited command of English made them ideal for the job because they wouldn't complain about the book's obscene contents. Buyers in Florence had the book by December 1927. The first editions arrived in Britain in spring 1928, but were impounded at the border.[30]

Douglas called *In the Beginning* his favorite of his novels. Like *Birds and Beasts*, the novel was built on classical foundations: in this case, a retelling of the myth of the founders of ancient Nineveh, King Ninus and Queen Semiramis. Douglas said he had "consulted everything that classical writers, and not a few of their modern commentators, have told us about this remarkable couple."[31] He also made liberal use of his erotic imagination. The novel is set before the rise of monotheism, when "the thing called Sin had not yet been invented." It opens with a scene of two pubescent youths, Linus and Ayra, frolicking in a stream. Ayra is described as a "tender girl" who had just "blossomed into maidenhood a few months ago, and her swelling breasts could be hidden within her own small hands." Linus is described as "on the borderland of youth; no down had appeared on his smooth cheek." Linus tries to wrestle Ayra to the ground. While they struggle, "the world went out. It was as if some star had burst within him, its fragments invading every limb with a torrent of delight."[32] In short, the youth experiences his first orgasm. At least that's how the censors read this line. When the book was republished in London by Chatto & Windus the following year, the sentence was cut from the manuscript.[33]

As Douglas promised Mavrogordato, the rest of the novel contained plenty of fucking. Linus is seduced by the fish goddess Derco. She appears to him as Ayra and soon her mouth "overran every inch of that smooth body, softly at first, like the quivering touch of a butterfly's wing, soon in a wayward and scalding torrent that drove a succession of rapid tremors through his flesh."[34] When the book appeared in London, the words "every inch of" were cut out.[35] Linus returns to teach Ayra the new tricks he has learned. Derco, who has been made pregnant by Linus, takes revenge, killing Ayra and trying to kill Linus, whom she doesn't know is actually the immortal son of the Earth God. Derco, who is supposed to be a virgin, is abandoned by her believers, but her priest Babramolok defends Derco, saying, "Nobody should be a virgin. Nobody!" That night he "calls loudly for six little virgins and then and there accomplished what would have taxed the powers of his sturdy great-grandsons, had any of them still been alive," after which he dies happy.[36] Chatto & Windus ended the sentence with Babramolok's call for virgins, cutting Douglas's explanation of what followed.

The plot grows more complicated when Linus matures into a mighty ruler, but is captured by his daughter with Derco, Symira, who has become a warrior queen. Linus and Symira don't know their relation to each other and rule together as king and queen. Both become consumed by sexual adventures in a brothel called the House of the Doves. The two half-gods are insatiable.

But Linus grows sick from too much sex with women, and an old female physician suggests that he distract himself with a troupe of dancing boys. "He might take a fancy to one or more of the boys, she argued, and console himself in this fashion for the loss of the other sex."[37] This sentence was also cut from the Chatto & Windus edition.[38] Symira begins to cavort "with dwarfs, and apes, and horses, and other abominations."[39] (This sentence also was cut.) The Earth God becomes so annoyed that he sends down a blight which infects humanity "with preposterous ideas concerning good and evil." As a consequence, "men lost their capacity for joy; they forgot how blithely they used to live." At the end of the book, two satyrs named Nea-huni and Azdhubal mourn the new human obsession with good and evil. "What have they done? They have invented two words," Nea-huni concludes.[40]

The satyrs spoke for Douglas, who despised the moralism that led Chatto & Windus to censor *In the Beginning*. He thought the cuts "emasculated" the novel.[41] Historians tend to treat the struggle against censorship in the early twentieth century as a heroic story, in which sexual liberationists like D. H. Lawrence defended the cause of intellectual freedom against the small-minded priggery of post-Victorian authorities. But Douglas does not fit comfortably into this framework, because the freedom of speech he demanded was for the purpose of expressing a sexuality that is now more anathematized than it was a century ago.

Nineteen twenty-eight was a banner year in the battle over censorship. The English authorities waged a legal campaign to suppress Radclyffe Hall's *The Well of Loneliness*, a novel about lesbianism, and Lawrence's *Lady Chatterley's Lover*, with its explicit accounts of adulterous sex. The effort to suppress *In the Beginning* was less intensive, which makes sense considering the novel's relative lack of popularity in contrast to *The Well* and *Lady Chatterley*. But the censorship campaign against it is more challenging to historicize, because nearly a century later sensitivity about the sexualization of pubescent bodies has grown more intense, rather than diminished. The passages eroticizing Ayra's breast buds and Linus's hairless body, which weren't censored in 1928, might generate attempts at censorship today.

Some of the critics at the time who drew comparisons between Douglas and his fellow censored authors saw Douglas as the most appealing of the bunch. Lord David Cecil, writing in the *Spectator*, favorably compared Douglas's humorous take on erotic writing to James Joyce's and Lawrence's "long, laborious, conscientious, humourless descriptions of the details of life in marriage-bed and brothel." Jack Lindsay, the editor of the *London Aphrodite*, wrote that "Shakespeare might have been more interested technically and personally in the work of Joyce and Lawrence if he were alive to-day than in that of Douglas; but he would have looked on Douglas as a brother, and the others as part of his untamed menagerie." Robin Chanter, the former librarian at the British Institute of Florence, described Douglas's prose as "clean, clear, crisp, quite different from D. H. Lawrence's turgid stuff."[42]

Comparisons between Lawrence and Douglas made sense because the two authors knew each other well and commented on each other's works and characters, often viciously. They met during Douglas's *English Review* days and went out for meals whenever Lawrence visited Florence during the 1920s, although their relationship was strained by several spats. Lawrence was living in Scandicci, four miles south of Florence, when he wrote *Lady Chatterley's Lover*, at the same time that Douglas was working on *In the Beginning*. From the start, Lawrence described the novel to his publisher Martin Secker as "very improper" and "impossible to print."[43] Lawrence and Douglas saw each other several times while each was working on his dirty novel.[44] Some readers even saw shades of Douglas in Lawrence's portrait of Lady Chatterley's sensualist father, Sir Malcolm Reid.[45] In the fall, Lawrence conferred with Pino Orioli and Reggie Turner about the possibility of privately printing *Chatterley* in Italy. Orioli recommended that Lawrence use the same Italian printer Douglas used to print *In the Beginning*. Lawrence agreed. When Tipografia Giuntina began work on *Lady Chatterley's Lover* in the spring of 1928, Orioli oversaw the production.

Douglas read *Chatterley* in proofs. He didn't think much of the novel as a work of literature, but he appreciated its obscenity. He liked to call the book *Lady Cocksuck*. Douglas wrote to Muriel Draper that *Chatterley* was "one of the filthiest books I ever read. The word 'fuck' occurs eight times on the last page." To Mavrogordato, he wrote that the book was "the limit of smuttiness."[46] From Douglas this was high praise. As Draper observed, Douglas was very fond of "good old Anglo-Saxon words of one syllable." His letters to her were filled with sign-offs like "No more, my dear. I am fucked out" and "Must now go and shit." Douglas's letters to Archie were equally filled with obscenities. His fatherly words of advice included gems such as "Women in the '40/50' regime require more fucking than young girls; so much is certain"; and, regarding a lover in Rome whom Archie didn't want to marry: "If she becomes troublesome, you should get a man to fuck her and to pay her for this. After that, having accepted money, she is legally a whore, and can

25. Collingwood Gee painting of Norman Douglas, Pino Orioli, and Reggie Turner listening to D. H. Lawrence read aloud from the manuscript of *Lady Chatterley's Lover*. Reproduction from private collection of Deirdre Sholto Douglas. Photograph by author.

have no claims on you."[47] Douglas's knowledge of dirty words also reached beyond the Anglo-Saxon to a broad variety of ancient and modern languages. Douglas's friend Martha Gordon Crotch said that whenever he got drunk, he started "swearing in all languages, and 'f*****g' everything, but keen-witted and terribly amusing."[48] However accomplished he was as a linguist, Douglas's passion for crude language was never academic. His *fucks*, *shits*, and *cunts* were intended to provoke a laugh.

Fans who shared Douglas's sense of humor were delighted by his next book after his dirty novel, an annotated collection of filthy limericks. Douglas had a long-standing affection for limericks. Nancy Cunard remembered Douglas reciting the dirty five-line poems at their dinner together in Bologna in 1924 to make everybody laugh.[49] He included them in his letters too, for example, writing to Archie asking after a family friend who had moved to Ealing: "Once at Ealing, they will doubtless meet that young lady who had a peculiar feeling, and piddled all over the ceiling. I hope so; at least."[50] He began keeping a written collection of the verse form in 1923.[51] The idea of bringing it to print percolated for years.

In 1927 Douglas started assembling his rhymes into a book.[52] Lawrence warned Orioli off helping Douglas publish his limericks with Tipografia Giuntina. Lawrence predicted that Douglas's book, which exceeded his own in obscenity, would "bring the hounds down on all Florence books."[53] However, Orioli saw the project as a moneymaker.[54] Many of Douglas's writer friends were more enthusiastic than Lawrence about the project, sending him limericks in their letters as he requested. "Send me some more limericks, you lazy bitch, and let them be as filthy and profane as possible," Douglas wrote to Draper.[55] He sent her a couple of examples to give a clear idea of what he was looking for, including a pederastic variation:

> There was an old man of Stamboul
> With a varicose vein in his tool
> In attempting to come
> Up a little boy's bum
> It burst, and he did look a fool.[56]

Friends tried to accommodate his requests. When Lytton Strachey planned a visit to Paris to meet up with Douglas, he promised to bring along his new boyfriend Roger Senhouse, who had "a vast knowledge (so he says) of limericks."[57] The three ate at Prunier's, a restaurant near the Arc de Triomphe that was much loved by visiting English writers. Strachey reported back to his friend Mary Hutchinson that Douglas had worn a somber black coat that contrasted with the scatological limericks he recited in his amusing pseudo-Scottish accent during the meal.[58]

The book went to the printers in October and was ready for distribution by the middle of November 1928. *Some Limericks* included fifty dirty verses, accompanied by a scholarly apparatus of introduction and footnotes. On the opening page, Douglas acknowledged, "I may be abused on the ground that the pieces are coarse, obscene, and so forth. Why, so they are; and whoever suffers from that trying form of degeneracy which is horrified by coarseness had better close the book at once." Douglas refused to limit his humor. The footnotes were just as obscene. Take, for example, a pederastic limerick that Douglas included:

> There was an old man of Madrid
> Who cast loving eyes on a kid.
> He said: "Oh, my joy!
> I'll buggar that boy,
> You see if I don't"—and he did.

In a footnote, Douglas mentioned that there was a variant to the last line—
"and he out with his cock, and he did." He found it to be "a little gross," but
"nothing venture, nothing win; moreover, to the pure all things are pure, and
none but the brave deserve the fair. It takes a brave man to act like this in
broad daylight."[59] By that standard, Douglas was a brave man.

The collection included blasphemous limericks as well. One called the
Virgin Mary a whore, and Christ a fairy. Another limerick rhymed "Jesus"
with "contagious diseases." Douglas included limericks about heterosexual
sex, where the humor derived from references to anal penetration, venereal
disease, and unintended pregnancy. There were limericks about lesbian sex
and incest. In a verse about "naughty old Sappho of Greece," the old poetess
declared her preference "to have my pudenda / rubbed hard by the enda / the
little pink nose of my niece." The footnote clarified that Sappho was not born
in Greece. Bestiality also made its appearance in the collection. A limerick,
about "an old man of the Cape / who buggered a Barbary ape," footnoted the
sexologist Xavier Mayne, who had written on "simili-sexual habits" among
primates. Other limericks described sex acts between men and swans, gan-
ders, and parrots.[60]

According to Douglas, his book was printed for "the Dirty-Minded
Elect."[61] Many of his friends were eager to count themselves within this
group, that's why they were fans. "I am longing to read the Limericks," Harold
Acton wrote to Douglas, "so is everyone."[62] Copies were mailed out to England before the end of the year. Bryher received a copy. So did W. Somerset
Maugham.[63] Douglas pleaded with Draper not to show her copy to journalists
or booksellers or any sort of officials, so that he wouldn't get in trouble with
British customs. He made the same request of Archie, warning him to open
the parcel by himself and to "be very careful to whom you mention the book,
else I shall have trouble with customs + police."[64] It was a lost cause. The book
attracted the attention of the authorities soon enough. One friend of Douglas reported that the "Lord Chief of police" had visited him to ask about the
book. According to another source, Lytton Strachey was almost prosecuted
for having a copy.[65]

The book proved a big success with readers, but Douglas reaped few of the
benefits. Pirated copies appeared in the United States, France, and Germany,
with no compensation to Douglas.[66] The success of *Some Limericks* was long-
lasting. During World War II, pirated editions were popular among American GIs. In 1957 a group of limerick enthusiasts in Chicago calling themselves

"The Society of the Fifth Line" began holding annual "Norman Douglas Memorial Lectures" to celebrate the genre. New American editions came out in 1967 and 1969, to entertain the counterculture generation. As recently as 2009, an alternative London publisher released yet another edition of the book, with an introduction by the English comedy legend Stephen Fry.[67] As a writer, Douglas didn't just draw on the classical pederastic tradition; he also innovated the tradition. His books were foundational for a new twentieth-century pederastic subculture that thrived until the sea change of the 1960s. Even after the rise of modern sexual politics, *Some Limericks* continued to speak to a wide readership.

The great burst of creativity unleashed by Douglas's busy erotic life in Florence came to a conclusion in 1930 with his publication of a book on the subject of aphrodisiacs, titled *Paneros*. This work was a denouement in more than one sense. *Paneros* was Douglas's elegy to his fading virility. Having reached his early sixties, he was suffering from a range of infirmities, including erysipelas, rheumatism, and toothaches, which required the extraction of all his *tusks*, as he put it. Even worse, Douglas claimed he was beginning to grow impotent: "slowly and gracefully, but surely."[68] *Paneros*, as he explained to Rouse, was a "reaction to the approach of old age." Despite its lighthearted subject, the book captured "the real torture of old age," in the words of Martha Gordon Crotch.[69]

The project originated in 1928, when Orioli asked Faith Mackenzie to translate an Italian aphrodisiac cookbook for publication, and Douglas agreed to write the introduction. Mackenzie's translation had to be abandoned due to copyright concerns, so Douglas redirected his efforts to writing an original work on the subject of aphrodisiacs.[70] As before, he reached out to his learned friends for information. He asked Edward Hutton whether there were any mentions of aphrodisiacs in the books in his "private case."[71] He turned to his friend Oscar Levy for works on aphrodisiacs in German.[72] He asked Mavrogordato about the aphrodisiac literature from antiquity.[73] These researches led Douglas to consult obscure authors like Helmontius, Varignana, Weckerus, Leminius, Pisanelli, and Gattinaria, whose names were so unknown that many friends accused him of making them up. Their suspicions were also provoked by Douglas's return to his mock-scholarly voice.

Orioli printed the finished work, *Paneros*, as the fifth volume in his new publishing imprint, the Lungarno Series. Predicting a small readership, like *Birds and Beasts* had, Douglas and Orioli opted for quality over quantity. The first edition, bound in gold lamé vermiculated cloth boards with black leather on the spine lettered in gold, was sold at three guineas. It was an "outrageous price," Douglas confessed.[74] The frontispiece, opposite the title page, was adorned with a painting of a beautiful child, labeled as a portrait of Douglas when he was an infant. In fact, the portrait was of his sister, Mary.[75] This opening deceit was a good indicator of Douglas's attitude toward the reliability of the book's contents.

The book proceeded ingredient by ingredient, taking the form of a catalog. As usual, he reveled in the odd detail. The Arabs, he wrote, had devoured "the relics of the skink," salted and pounded together with herbs and drunk in wine. Juvenal and Ovid recommended the "fleshly excrescence on the head of a newborn foal." But the ancient authorities also recommended more common items to perform sympathetic magic, such as "the upright asparagus," "the root Satyrion," and mushrooms, morels, agarics, and truffles. Birds of a "richly amorous disposition" like pigeons, partridges, and turtledoves, were thought to convey venereal power. Seafood also had the reputation for increasing virility, as did minerals produced by the sea, like pearls and coral. Douglas recommended against artificial stimulants. Through "diligent experimentation" he had discovered that "coca will transport you into a Paradise where Venus may be seen, but not touched" (in other words, cocaine produced erections, but interfered with ejaculation). Alcohol was similarly ineffective, "kindling passion and thwarting the performance." Ultimately, the skeptical Douglas cast doubt on the ability of any food or stimulant to serve as an effective aphrodisiac. "To lovers we therefore say: devour partridge and oyster and asparagus for their pleasurable taste, rather than in the hope of performing prodigies with the beloved." But if the powers of the aphrodisiacs Douglas itemized in the pages of *Paneros* were suspect, the sentiment that inspired his search for such magical ingredients was very much real. "Why prolong life save to prolong pleasure?" Douglas asked. As he grew older, Douglas feared being forced to give up the sexual pleasures that had dominated his life since early boyhood.[76]

"What pleasures are comparable to those of youth? And what ecstasy, of all of them, is more fervid than that of young lovers locked in voluptuous embracement," he asked in *Paneros*.[77] In an early draft, he used the word *children* instead of *youth*, but an advance reader suggested he tone it down.[78] For Douglas, no sexual experience could match the rapture of the earliest encounters of childhood. When the body grew old, a person had to do his best to recapture that vitality. Many searched for restorative medicine in plants and minerals, but the true answer, as far as Douglas was concerned, lay in surrounding oneself with children. "Would you be young? Then live with the young, and flee the old with their aches and pains, fretfulness and valetudinarian makeshifts."[79] Forget about the search for magical ingredients. In the remaining two decades of his life, Douglas would follow his own advice, pursuing children with increasing fervency as he became more and more decrepit.

CHAPTER THIRTEEN

Diavolo Incarnato

Rumors preceded him, like a herald before a king. Stories were passed around about his wickedness. Innocent youths were warned to steer clear of him. The truly daring sought him out in the trattorias and caffès he was known to haunt. During the 1920s, Norman Douglas's books made him infamous. He did his best to burnish this reputation. It was key to his financial success.

Nancy Cunard first met Douglas on a visit to Florence in 1923. At twenty-six, she had not yet acquired her own later notorious reputation. She was at dinner with Osbert and Sacheverell Sitwell, when the wealthy literary brothers began making mysterious remarks about Douglas, who was soon to join their party. Cunard begged the Sitwells to tell her more, but they refused to explain the "aureole of legend" around the writer, except to warn Cunard, "I should be *careful* if I were you—hmh, hmh!" The throat-clearing was as near as the Sitwells would come to naming the nature of Douglas's misdeeds. Cunard understood that Douglas had a reputation for being dangerous, but "dangerous at what, and to whom?" she wondered.[1]

Victor Cunard, Nancy's cousin, had been so thoroughly warned against Douglas that when he met the writer in the 1920s he "expected the diavolo incarnato of the Italian proverb." He was surprised to discover that the man he joined for lunch at Betti's trattoria in Florence was kindly, offering him sage advice on what to order from the menu.[2] Arthur Johnson thought that Douglas had "something of the 'Diavolo incarnato' about him," but declared that "it was such a loveable and kindly one as to endear the whole species."[3] Derek Patmore insisted that Douglas was "at the heart the kindest of men." He only liked "to make the world think he is thoroughly wicked." Timid fools chattered about his hedonism, but Patmore insisted that anyone who visited

Douglas at his austere apartment in Florence would soon realize how false the legend was.[4]

Not everyone had the chance to make the discovery of Douglas's kindness. The painter Arthur Lett-Haines, who knew the Sitwells and the Cunards, had many opportunities to meet Douglas in the early 1920s, "but was never allowed to do so by my immediate entourage."[5] By the '20s, Lett-Haines had been twice married and had embarked on a lifelong (open) relationship with the painter Cedric Morris, so it's hard to imagine why his friends believed he needed protection from Douglas. The incongruity suggests how awful Douglas's reputation was. The American writer Harold Witter Bynner was warned away from meeting Douglas by D. H. Lawrence's wife, Frieda Lawrence. Lawrence told Bynner, who was planning a holiday in Europe, that Douglas was "brilliant fun" but "wicked." Bynner, a queer man who was nearly seventy years old at the time of his planned trip, again seems an unlikely candidate to have required such a warning. But Lawrence thought it necessary. She told another friend, Dudley Nichols, that Douglas was "the only wicked man I have known, in a medieval sense."[6]

Even Douglas's staunchest allies thought him a wicked man. Faith Mackenzie recalled asking him one evening over dinner, "Are you Satan, perhaps?" "Perhaps," Douglas answered coyly.[7] It wasn't in his interest to dispel his sinister reputation. Martha Gordon Crotch also acknowledged her dear friend's bad character. "Uncle N is a very bad man really," she wrote in her journal, using the avuncular nickname that Douglas acquired during his years in Florence. "Judging by the standards one has been taught and exhorted to uphold, he is really a wicked debauchee, steeped in vice," Crotch wrote.[8] Yet she loved him nonetheless. He was, she ultimately concluded after much consideration, "the world's best bad man."[9] Crotch put into words the paradox of Douglas's reputation. He made wickedness look appealing. As the bohemian Viva King told Douglas, "You're the best advertisement for the evil life."[10] The line was so good that more than one friend laid claim to it. Nancy Cunard insisted it was Osbert Sitwell who called Douglas "a very good advertisement for the evil life." Douglas responded, "Yes, I know! It's uphill work now; still, I try to do my best."[11]

The idea that a person could be a "good advertisement for the evil life" belongs to the past. This formulation comes from the era before the rise of sexual liberalism, when the gap between prescriptive sexual morality and the unspoken rules that governed actual sexual behavior was a fixation to cultural bohemians. The blatant hypocrisy of mainstream sexual conservatism created space to appreciate the renegades who bucked the rules, even to the extreme of having sex with children and youths. Mark Holloway tried to explain the nature of Douglas's seductive evil appeal to Valerie Cuthbert, Eric Wolton's daughter, in a 1968 letter:

> As a man, he was one way and another what the strait-laced would call a black sheep, a "wicked" but fascinating uncle, a self-confessed reprobate; but he also had a zest and vitality, an intelligence and an intellectual ability much in excess of the average. In addition, he was both frank and reticent, and although normally courteous and what used to be called well-bred, could also behave as uninhibitedly and as passionately as a gipsy. This combination of qualities made him irresistibly attractive to a great many people, and the subject of a good deal of scandalous gossip and speculation.[12]

Douglas had no interest in shaking this reputation, because his notoriety was the source of his success. Douglas's "reputation for evil contributed to his enormous fame as a writer," Constantine FitzGibbon argued.[13] Readers were drawn to Douglas because of his wicked reputation. "It is the freedom, the seemingly reckless freedom and license, in which we revel," explained the English publisher Roger Senhouse.[14] The appeal of Douglas's sinister reputation was in the way it rubbed off on the reader, like body glitter from a lap dancer. Reading Douglas "marked you out as a free spirit who had broken the bonds of Anglo-Saxon Puritan conformity," the writer Alan Massie elaborated.[15]

Meeting Douglas was even better. You could dine out on the stories for life. The gay novelist Angus Wilson, who knew Douglas during World War II, was a "great raconteur" of Douglas tales. So was the writer Michael Davidson, who spent just three days with Douglas, yet told "wildly amusing stories and anecdotes" about him for years afterward.[16] Many of these brief acquaintances wrote about their encounters with Douglas, earning royalties from their brush with infamy. In his 1962 memoir, *The World, the Flesh and Myself*, Davidson recorded Douglas joking that he had always liked "a very small possessor attached to a very large possession."[17] Davidson, who was a self-described "lover of boys," sympathized with Douglas. But even men and women who didn't share Douglas's sexual tastes took a vicarious thrill from bearing witness to his wicked ways.

In his 1924 travel book *Sunward*, Louis Golding wrote about feasting with Douglas in Capri in the early 1920s, then joining him for a day hike in the Sorrentine Peninsula, guided by an eleven-year-old boy named Luigi. This encounter with one of Douglas's boys added to the thrill of the day.[18] Eric Linklater's 1953 memoir included the story of a scandalous dinner with Douglas and Orioli at Betti's. Douglas gave him a copy of *Paneros*, with its effusions about the seductive properties of children. Linklater was flattered and felt "overawed" by the breadth of the older man's experience.[19]

As perverse as it sounds, Douglas's sexual immorality was a major attraction to his friends and fans. His openness, the unvarnished nature of his indiscretion, compelled people, regardless of the specific nature of his misdeeds. It's hard today to imagine the appeal of a notorious pedophile, but that's a reflection of how sexual morals have shifted since the 1920s. When Douglas rose to fame, the rules governing sexual behavior lumped together a broad range of illicit sexual behaviors into one big grab bag of immorality. Pederasty may have been the worst of the worst, but it was still a part of the whole. The difference between pederasty and other sexual crimes like adultery and homosexuality was a matter of degree. Over the course of the twentieth century, rules around sexual morality shifted, and the "charmed circle" of acceptable sexuality expanded.[20] Premarital sex lost its taboo. Homosexuality became tolerated. But child-adult sex remained outside the charmed circle, and became more distinctively monstrous in consequence, making it almost impossible today to understand the charms that Douglas's pederasty once held.

As Douglas's public notoriety grew, his reputation attracted new friends. These friends included feminist and queer women. "The loyalty and affection he inspired, often in the most unlikely people about him, was astonishing," one critic put it.[21] After her first meeting with Douglas in 1923, Nancy Cunard became one of his most devoted and steadfast supporters. Cunard was a political radical and activist whose sexual promiscuity and interracial relationships bespoke her own rejection of conventional morality. She met many of Douglas's present and former boyfriends over the years, including Silvio, Emilio Papa, and Eric Wolton, and spoke warmly of them all.[22] She called Douglas's "feeling for children" a "most important" aspect of his persona. "I used to notice the way you spoke to them—as if they were on the same level as yourself," she wrote in a posthumous letter to Douglas.[23] Publicly, Cunard denied knowledge of the sexual aspect of Douglas's relationships with children, but privately she tolerated it.

The writer Bryher, whose friendship with Douglas began with a fan letter she wrote him in 1921, also treated his sex life with remarkable tolerance. Bryher was an avant-garde novelist, filmmaker, and poet, who is often described as a lesbian, although she understood herself to be "a boy sort of escaped into the wrong body."[24] According to Bryher, Douglas also saw her as a boy, identifying her with the impish character of Harré from his novel *They Went*.[25] She met him for lunch in Florence. In a draft of her memoir, *Heart to Artemis*, Bryher described how when they walked the streets of Florence together, Douglas would be flocked by "'crocodiles,' dark-haired, mischievous, urchins, with Renaissance names, whom he scolded and spoilt as if they were a team of puppies." She praised Douglas as having "an astounding capacity for romantic love."[26] Later she struck this paragraph, aware that it exceeded the boundaries of publishability.

Bryher was enchanted by Douglas's sexual difference, which she connected to her own sense of sexual difference. She often wrote to Douglas about sex and sexuality, asking his opinion on the writings of André Gide (another notorious pederast) or Magnus Hirschfeld. Douglas rewarded her tolerance by being entirely open about his sexual affairs. His letters frequently updated her on the well-being of his "crocodiles."[27] He brought boys with him on visits to her modernist villa on the shores of Lake Geneva, and he confided in her when his affairs got him into trouble. He even complained to Bryher about how the price of arranging with poor Italian families for sexual access to their children was going up.[28] Despite viewing Bryher as a boy, Douglas never attempted to seduce her. He was more interested in her great wealth (she was the daughter of shipping magnate John Ellerman) than in her sexual availability.

The feminist writer Rebecca West also tolerated Douglas's sexual interest in boys. West herself was a sexual radical, who had an illegitimate son from her adulterous relationship with H. G. Wells, just one of her many affairs with notable figures. She first met Douglas in Florence in 1919. She admired his scholarship and considered him a master of prose, but she said that his "heart, as far as innocence is concerned, is as the Gobi desert."[29] Douglas was a wicked man, but that didn't keep West from enjoying his company. She told the story of a hike she took in the hills above Florence in 1919 with Douglas and D. H. Lawrence. They stopped by a riverbank to watch some boys who were stripping down to swim. "The water will be icy," Douglas said, and began to chuckle at the thought of the shock the boys would have when they jumped in. Lawrence, on the other hand, "let his breath hiss out through his teeth at the thought of their agony; but he seemed to find pleasure in it, as he would in any intense feeling."[30] It's an odd but canny anecdote, which captured Douglas's conscienceless pleasure at the sight of the naked boys, and Lawrence's dualistic mix of attraction and repulsion.

Lawrence was less tolerant of Douglas's pederasty than were most of the writers in their circle. According to Douglas, Lawrence was horrified by the boys in Florence "for showing an inch or so of bare flesh above the knee." "I don't like it! I don't like it! Why can't they wear trousers?" Lawrence supposedly demanded. Douglas explained to Lawrence that Florentine parents kept their boys in shorts to keep them out of the city's brothels, which would only serve clients in long pants.[31] Lawrence was as offended by Douglas's explanation as he had been by the sight of the bare flesh itself. "My own improprieties of speech he ascribed to some perverse kink of nature," Douglas wrote, "whereas they were merely an indication of good health."[32] This disparity between the men's approaches to sexuality caused conflicts between them.

After Lawrence's 1919 visit to Florence, he wrote a novel satirizing many of the people he'd met in the city. *Aaron's Rod*, published in 1922, told the story of Aaron Sisson, a union official from the Midlands who abandoned his wife and children for the bohemian life in London and Florence. The London chapters of the book included caricatures of Richard Aldington, H.D., and Brigit Patmore. The Florence chapters made vicious fun of the queer Englishmen who flocked to the city, including Reggie Turner, Maurice Magnus, and Norman Douglas himself.

Lawrence's caricatures were transparent. He gave his Douglas character the very Scottish name "James Argyle." He described Argyle as possessed of "a certain wicked whimsicality that was very attractive." Once a handsome man, "his face was all red and softened and inflamed, his eyes had gone small and wicked under his bushy grey brows. Still, he had a presence."[33] The nature of Argyle's wickedness is made clear in Lawrence's rendition of the caffè table conversations over which the older man presides. Argyle preaches against chastity, which he terms sterility, and he shows off the roses growing on his deck by saying, "I made Pasquale wear a wreath of them on his hair." Later he explains, "I didn't foreswear love, when I foreswore marriage and women. Not by ANY means."[34]

No one who knew Douglas could mistake the character's inspiration. "Do you think Douglas will identify himself with Argyle and be offended?" Law-

rence wrote to his publisher, Martin Secker. "I should think not," Secker responded.[35] Likely he was just placating Lawrence. Douglas heard word of the
caricature straightaway, although he denied having read the book. "There is
a funny description of me under the name of Argyle in D. H. Lawrence's last
book: <u>Aaron's Rod</u>," Douglas wrote to Archie in July 1922. "Turner and other
Florentines also figure therein."[36] To Bryher, he wrote that the caricature
"is sure to be pretty rotten stuff, saturated with the wrong kind of sexuality
(the negative kind) and with out any humour or even humanity."[37] Douglas complained frequently that Lawrence's views of sexuality were puritan-
ical and censorious. He wrote to Hellé Flecker that *Aaron's Rod*, which he
called "Aaron's Rot," was "third-rate sex-slobber" intended "to catch the neurotic American public."[38] Despite these private objections, Douglas remained
friendly with Lawrence.

The breaking point came two years later, when Lawrence published the
memoirs of their mutual friend Maurice Magnus, who had committed suicide in 1920. Magnus was an eccentric character, the supposed by-blow of
royalty. Magnus's fortunes swung erratically between wealth and bankruptcy.
He had helped Douglas out in the summer of 1917, when Douglas was at his
lowest fortune, by putting him up in his apartment in Rome. Later Douglas
tried to repay Magnus's generosity by helping to get his memoir of service in
the French Foreign Legion published. The memoir, however, was so filled
with obscene accounts of sodomy in the ranks that the endeavor proved fruit-
less. "How are you going to make it printable," the publisher Grant Richardson wrote to Douglas. "When you have taken out the unprintable stuff there
won't be a great deal left."[39] Douglas was unable to answer this question.

Lawrence met Magnus through Douglas, and ill-advisedly loaned him
money. Lawrence, who had little to spare, was shocked to see Magnus spend
the money like water. Unsurprisingly, Magnus's debts caught up with him,
and fearing arrest he committed suicide by drinking prussic acid. Afterward,
Lawrence gained possession of Magnus's manuscripts and managed to publish the memoirs by adding a one-hundred-page introduction that cruelly
caricaturized Magnus and took fierce aim at his relationship with Douglas
(referred to as "N____ D_____" in the text). Lawrence described Magnus as
a "mincing" and "common little bounder," and a "rabid woman-hater" who
was smitten with Douglas. He depicted Douglas in even more hateful terms,
accusing him of financially exploiting Magnus, whom he actually "despised"
as "a little busybody and an inferior." Lawrence finished with an account of

Magnus's suicide, concluding, "Well, poor devil, he is dead: which is all the better."[40] The line was hurtful to anyone who cared for Magnus, which Douglas claimed he did, whatever Lawrence thought.

Douglas was enraged by Lawrence's edition of Magnus's memoirs. When the book came out in 1924, he wrote a stinging rebuke, *D. H. Lawrence and Maurice Magnus: A Plea for Better Manners* (1925). Douglas denied being upset on his own behalf. "I have no fault to find with this travesty of myself; no fault whatever; it is perfectly legitimate fooling and my young friend might have presented me in far less engaging fashion, since I gave him permission to 'put me in as you please.'" No, Douglas insisted that what he found objectionable about the introduction was Lawrence's portrayal of Magnus, who could not defend himself from beyond the grave. Far from being a "scamp and a treacherous little devil," as described by Lawrence, Magnus was "not only a brave man, but one who was witty and amusing and most likeable."[41] By calling Magnus brave, Douglas pushed back against the queer stereotyping of Lawrence's portrait. He argued it was Lawrence who deserved censure for vulgarly feeding off the lives of his friends. But some of Douglas's friends were not entirely convinced by his protestations of indifference to Lawrence's acid portraits of himself. Compton Mackenzie, who had also extended a generous hand to Lawrence only to see himself satirized by Lawrence's pen, said that Douglas was insulted by Lawrence's anecdote about how he insisted on measuring out the exact amount of wine he had drunk in a restaurant before paying the bill.[42]

Lawrence's attack and Douglas's rejoinder captured the attention of the literary world in 1925. Everyone loves a good feud. Some took Douglas's side, agreeing that Lawrence had slandered Magnus.[43] Lawrence defended himself behind the scenes. He wrote to one friend, "Norman Douglas is really terrible. He despised Magnus and used him badly: wouldn't give him a *sou*: said most scandalous things of him: and Magnus was very bitter about it."[44] When Lawrence and Douglas crossed paths in a Florence caffè in the summer of 1926, they did not speak to each other. But soon they renewed their tenuous friendship. By Christmas 1926, Lawrence was back in Florence and meeting Douglas regularly for meals and drinks.[45] Douglas remained persuaded that Lawrence was "a sexual adolescent who never recovered from the shock of puberty."[46] Lawrence remained persuaded that Douglas was the devil. But they smoothed over their differences.

When the publisher Bennett Cerf traveled to Florence in 1928, he sought out both Douglas and Lawrence, who were his literary heroes. He met Douglas first. Over dinner at a trattoria, Douglas scoffed at Cerf's plan to visit Lawrence, asking why wanted to waste his time with the writer. But the next day, when Cerf couldn't find his way to Lawrence's villa for their scheduled lunch, Douglas offered to guide him. When they arrived at the villa, Lawrence and Douglas embraced with "tears of joy in their eyes." Cerf may as well have been invisible. Lawrence seemed ecstatic and invited Douglas inside. The men talked for an hour. Finally Douglas went for a walk, leaving Lawrence alone with Cerf. As soon as Douglas left the house, Lawrence wheeled on Cerf and said, "How dare you bring that man into my house!" He regaled Cerf with damning tales of Douglas's behavior. But when Douglas returned, the men embraced again. At last Cerf and Douglas bid their farewells. As soon as they were in the car together, Douglas launched into a series of damning tales about Lawrence's wife, Frieda. For Cerf, the day offered an instructive lesson on the lives of famous authors.[47]

Lawrence's early death from tuberculosis seemed to give Douglas the last laugh. When a friend exclaimed, "Would that I could have held L. in my arms when he died," Douglas replied "Gor'blime . . . I shouldn't at all care to have held L. in my arms."[48] After Lawrence's death, Douglas included a score-settling ten-page portrait of him in *Looking Back*. But if Douglas got the last word during their lifetimes, Lawrence has outshone Douglas in the afterlife of their literary reputations. He is the subject of countless biographies, an endeavor that Douglas once dismissed as "a waste of time."[49] There are multiple literary journals devoted to the study of Lawrence's work—not just in English, but in French as well. He is taught in university courses. His novels have been repeatedly adapted to film. And Douglas is almost entirely forgotten, erased from literary history, in no small part because of growing revulsion for his sexual behavior in the years following his death. Lawrence's judgment of Douglas stuck.

CHAPTER FOURTEEN

Epicurus

In the shade of a pine grove on a spring afternoon, at the end of a month's travel together in Greece, Norman Douglas explained his personal philosophy to Edward Hutton:

> D. I too am an Epicurean animal.
> H. Vous dites?
> D. Pleasure is the end of life.
> H. I don't altogether wish to deny it, especially at this hour . . . in such a shade. . . . Listen to the pine.
> D. Pleasure is the end: liberty the means.[1]

Hutton, a convert to Catholicism and somewhat of a moralist when it came to sex, believed there was more to life than pleasure, and that personal liberty should have bounds, but he could not deny the allure of Douglas's philosophy. Douglas made the life of pleasure sound too good.

Hutton and Douglas planned their trip to Greece with the intention of writing a travel book together on their return. It didn't work out that way. Hutton, who authored over forty books during his lifetime, was a much quicker writer. Douglas worked on a series of dialogues intended to punctuate the text, but he could not produce them quickly enough for Hutton's liking. "He thinks I can shake dialogues out of my sleeve, à la Plato," Douglas complained to John Mavrogordato.[2] Douglas withdrew after completing fifteen dialogues on subjects ranging from cooking to polytheism.[3] Hutton finished *A Glimpse of Greece* alone, but he knew that Douglas's original musings would be one of the book's main draws.

During the 1920s and '30s, Douglas was as noted for his philosophy as for his wickedness. His most famous bit of advice was "Always do as you please, and send everybody to Hell, and take the consequences. Damned good Rule of Life," which he scribbled on the back page of a copy of *Old Calabria* that he gave to Elizabeth David.[4] This defense of pleasure-seeking without regard for the consequences to anyone else was what made him so appealing to the disaffected generation who came of age after the Great War. The social world of pederasty during the interwar period took shape within a context of widespread disenchantment with traditional values like self-sacrifice and rectitude. Even Christian moralists like Hutton could not resist the appeal of Douglas's hedonism. In his *Glimpse of Greece* dialogues, Douglas decried monotheism, nationalism, and democracy, while expressing support for polygamy, the art of cooking, and slavery. Occasionally Hutton raised halfhearted objections, but he allowed himself to be swept along by the tide of his friend's arguments.

Many of Douglas's friends were seduced by his musings. Mavrogordato liked to pass evenings sipping Marsala, listening to Douglas philosophize until the morning light.[5] Muriel Draper called Douglas her "guide, philosopher, and friend."[6] When she met him as a young woman, he gave her classics to read and held forth on the world during long walks. "What an education you are to me," she wrote to him years later. He had taught her that there were things in life worth salvaging, "like friendship, and a well constructed sentence (like this one!!), and wine that isn't piss and dead violets, and good architecture and food and fucking."[7]

Douglas was a philosopher of the good life who dealt entirely in the concrete, never the metaphysical. He expressed his philosophy in epigrams, rather than treatises. "We live but once; we owe nothing to posterity; and a man's happiness counts before that of any one else," he wrote in *Together*.[8] Some men had tastes that met with the approbation of the world; some men's tastes ran afoul of the world's judgment—it made no difference to Douglas. Another of his epigrams was "Why prolong life save to prolong pleasure?" He first posed this question in his book of aphrodisiacs, *Paneros*, then included it later in his *Almanac*.[9] The *Almanac* also included another succinct formulation of his philosophy: "The business of life is to enjoy oneself; everything else is a mockery."[10] Faith Mackenzie took this advice to heart when she first met him, and it helped liberate her to pursue a wildly unconventional life devoted to love affairs, literature, travel, and friendship.[11] Douglas's philosophy might appear to be little more than the sexual prerogative of an entitled man dressed up in the raiment of classicism, but many of the friends who took his words to heart were women seeking to carve original lives for themselves in the new century.

Friends and readers debated the best label for Douglas's philosophy. His friend Richard MacGillivray Dawkins, an Oxford classicist, called him a "sceptical pagan." The British journalist Iain Hamilton described him as an "intransigent Apollonian." Brigit Patmore called him "Rabelaisian," a reference to the sixteenth-century French humanist renowned for his bawdy humor. Faith Mackenzie described him as a "materialist; rationalist; Platonist; hedonist; [and] sentimentalist," which is a long list of -ists for a man who more than once declared himself opposed to all -isms. For his part, Douglas said he "should prefer to be labelled Epicurean rather than hedonist," because his definition of pleasure extended beyond the body.[12]

He first made his reputation as a pagan, with his evocations of the Hellenic past in *Siren Land* and *Old Calabria*. Cecile Walton Robertson, a young painter from Edinburgh, discovered Douglas's books in 1921 in the attic of an ancient manor house in Dumfries, owned by an old lady directly descended from Edward III. Robertson was a bohemian free spirit, part of a circle of bisexual artists living in the city who were connected to John Gray, one of Oscar Wilde's former lovers.[13] She immediately fell in love with Douglas's books and wrote him a series of flirtatious letters, with rather improvisational spelling and punctuation.

"Dear Norman Douglas," she opened the first letter, "I instinctively want to attack your philosophy perhaps because all bulwarks + bastions invite assault." Such an opening was bound to attract Douglas's attention. She continued her attack. "Aren't you just pagan when it suits you to be," she asked. "What I want is to meet some one who realy is pagan when it comes to the fundamental things of life—you mustn't just call yourself a pagan because you love natural scenery, good food + being a little naughty," she wrote. "I don't think pagans were ever naughty, they were frankly bestial, some times cruelly depraved but never anything as trivial as naughty." Fans like Robertson were drawn to the "frankly bestial" spirit of Douglas's paganism. They didn't admire him in spite of his sexual amorality: they saw him as a philosophical model because of his greedy willingness to pursue pleasures of the flesh whatever their consequences. Riffing off the title of his 1921 book *Alone*, Robertson questioned whether a man who was "alone" could truly be a pagan. "If you had been truly pagan you would have children," she wrote. She sensed that he "failed to appreciate women" and hoped he wasn't a "bachelor" like the writer Henry James. For Robertson, the problem with James wasn't his queerness. She didn't object to queer men; she was married to a bisexual man. The problem with James was his sterility. James was the anti-pagan, the embodiment of restraint, repression, and asexuality.[14]

Douglas agreed with Robertson about James. There are differing accounts of whether the two authors knew each other. Draper claimed that they met several times at her Edith Grove house, but their conversation was always of "the most desultory character" because they "were too fundamentally divergent in their approach to life."[15] On the other hand, Douglas told Elizabeth David that he "never met Henry James," who was "quite a pleasant old lady, I'm told."[16] Either way, Douglas was well enough acquainted with James's persona and his books to develop an express dislike for the writer. James lacked the bestial element. It wasn't just that he was effeminate. Douglas had many effeminate queer male friends, like Maurice Magnus and Harold Acton. It was the denial of human appetite that made James's "approach to life" so radically divergent from Douglas's. Magnus wrote a book about sodomy in the French Foreign Legion that was so filthy it couldn't be published. Acton talked enthusiastically to Douglas about his "fuckings."[17] No one to this day knows if James died a virgin.

Cecile Robertson's fan letter made it clear that she was a woman of appetite. Douglas wrote back, as he often did to letters that held out the possibility for sexual or monetary reward. His letter was filled with sexual innuendo, some of which had to be explained to Robertson by her husband. She replied, "There all sorts of stories that go about regarding you—that people who love naughtiness and aren't really pagan enjoy + spread. I don't believe them— all. I suppose some must be true. But as regards my own reputation people usualy know the things that arent true + never dream of the things that are."[18] What sort of stories had Robertson heard of Douglas? Did she understand the erotic innuendoes that he made about boys in the pages of *Alone*? She wrote to Douglas, "I think you dear for you love children (you would certainly like mine)."[19] Did she know in what way Douglas loved children? When Robertson celebrated the frankly bestial sexuality of the true pagan, did she mean to include pederasty in the mix?

Perhaps she did. Robertson's best-known painting, *Romance* (1920), is a self-portrait depicting her holding her newborn son Edward while her older son Gavril looks on. She is posed as an odalisque, à la *Olympia* by Edouard

Manet. The painting suggests that Walton understood mother love to include an erotic element.

Although friends and readers frequently threw around the word *pagan* to describe Douglas, not everyone agreed. Rebecca West pointed out that Douglas only believed in material reality.[20] He had no patience for gods or abstract moral laws. He regarded all religion as "Mumbo-Jumbo."[21] He was especially damning of Christianity. There was no part of Christianity that appealed to Douglas, not even the holidays. "As for merry Christmas—fuck the whole bloody institution," he wrote once to Draper.[22] It was a typical Christmas greeting from Douglas. He despised Christianity's disdain for the appetites of human body, "that exquisite engine of delights." According to Douglas, the Christian dogma of "the antagonism of flesh and spirit" was "the most pernicious piece of crooked thinking which has ever oozed out of our poor deluded brain."[23] Foundational to Douglas's defense of pederasty was his rejection of sex as an evil. Pederasty was not bad for children, according to Douglas, because sex was a positive good for all human beings.

Douglas's rejection of Christianity ran as an undercurrent through his early books and grew fiercer as he aged. His hatred for the religion of his childhood took center stage in 1930, when he published a book-length screed against the West, titled *How about Europe?* The book came as a response to Katherine Mayo's 1927 bestseller *Mother India*, which castigated Hinduism for its sexual mistreatment of girls and women. Douglas had traveled to India several times in his life, and he abhorred Mayo's parochialism and Eurocentrism. According to Douglas, it was Christianity, not Hinduism, that was most "incompatible with decent sex-relations."[24]

The mischief had begun with the apostle Paul, who taught that the flesh was sinful. Since then Christianity had spawned a "pathological fear and loathing of the female sex." Christianity's history of witch burnings was case in point. The infamous witch hunters' guide, *Malleus Maleficarum*, was a "misogynist's handbook," according to Douglas. Christianity could stand to learn a great deal from Hinduism. "I venture to recommend the Kama Sutra as a counter-irritant," he suggested. To those like Mayo who condemned the practice of child prostitution in India (no doubt one of the factors that drew Douglas for his repeat visits), he responded by castigating the brutality of children's penal institutions in Europe. He had met boys who had survived these prisons. "Such children, whether boys or girls, would be happier and better cared for in Indian brothels," he argued.[25] Douglas believed that sex did no harm to a child, but he utterly rejected physical brutality against children. Moreover, Christian prudery, he alleged, led to sexual assaults. Society would be improved by a more relaxed attitude toward fucking.

Anti-Christianity was central to Douglas's philosophy, and a significant aspect of his appeal to readers. Some readers, however, found Douglas's apparent anti-Semitism less appealing. Douglas denied that he was an anti-Semite. His main complaint with Judaism, he claimed, was its responsibility for spawning Christianity. In his words, "It is my chief grievance against the Jews that they produced Jesus Christ."[26] Sometimes Douglas made anti-Semitic remarks of the more banal variety, typical to his social class.[27] Nonetheless, Douglas had many intimate Jewish friends throughout his life, including Maurice Magnus, Oscar Levy, and Walter Lowenfels. Douglas's anti-Semitism was more reflexive than programmatic. It wasn't key to his philosophy in the way that anti-Christianity was. The same might be said for Douglas's dislike of Islam. "Monotheism is sheer laziness," Douglas remarked to Hutton in one of their *Glimpse of Greece* dialogues. "Are you referring to Jehova?" Hutton asked. "Allah will do just as well," Douglas answered.[28] He was an equal opportunity anti-theist.

Douglas rejected morality with the same totality that he rejected God. Any regard for morality that he may have carried forward from early childhood was utterly destroyed by the Great War. "What's morality, damn it, nowadays," he wrote to Hutton in 1920.[29] After the war, Douglas took the position that a person's actions should be guided solely by self-interest. He didn't substitute an ethical code, like the Golden Rule, in place of morality. In his view, a person had no responsibility except to himself. He preached this perspective to anyone who would listen. "Take care of your belly, and your morals will take care of themselves," he advised Archie. He told Robin "not to cultivate a conscience—it is the most pestilential attribute of man." Never regret anything, he said, and send everybody else to Hell.[30] Morality, according to Douglas, was a blight that had destroyed the human spirit.

Through the remarkable power of his charisma, Douglas persuaded his friends to accept his refusal of all moral restraints. Martha Gordon Crotch reasoned, "You can't make laws and restrictions for people like [Douglas]—he is a law unto himself." Nancy Cunard defended him in similar terms.[31] Both women justified Douglas's amorality despite their understanding that his philosophy served as a rationale for having sexual encounters with children. They relaxed their own moral codes for Douglas because his extraordinary charisma made them believe that the children were lucky to know him. Some of Douglas's male friends even entertained fantasies about how lucky it would have been to meet him when they were boys. Harold Acton remarked in his memoir that Douglas would have been an ideal schoolmaster and lamented, "I regret that I met him too late, when I was more or less crystallized." Pino Orioli was more explicit, writing in his diary that if he had met Douglas when he was a boy: "I am sure he would have handled me beautifully. . . ."[32] Neither Acton nor Orioli were sexually inclined toward young boys, but both saw Douglas's pederasty in positive terms. The moral rules against intergenerational sex were not absolute. Context mattered. Sex between an adult and a child might not be that bad if the adult was Norman Douglas, his friends believed.

The writer Aldous Huxley was fascinated by Douglas's rejection of morality. Huxley himself was a sexual free-thinker, and the two corresponded on the subject.[33] Huxley drew on Douglas for characters in three of his novels: *Crome Yellow* (1921), *Those Barren Leaves* (1925), and *Time Must Have a Stop* (1944).[34] His caricatures of Douglas ranged from eccentric to sinister to flawed. The portraits weren't admiring, but neither were they censorious. Huxley was less sexually judgmental than Lawrence, which Douglas appreciated, raising no objection to the writer's depictions of himself. Huxley's caricatures helped create Douglas's widespread reputation as a wicked philosopher. More readers probably encountered Douglas's ideas filtered through Huxley's mouthpieces than through Douglas's own words. Characterizations of Douglas contributed to the social world of pederasty during the interwar era in equal measure to Douglas's own writings.

The first of Huxley's characters to integrate aspects of Douglas is Mr. Scogan, from *Crome Yellow*. Huxley did not yet really know Douglas, except by rumor, when he based Scogan on him.[35] As a consequence, Scogan is a one-dimensional character, a "slightly sinister" old man given to ribald remarks. Scogan admits to being an "obscene old man," and he speaks longingly about the "jovial frankness" of the past.[36] He is a voice of sexual libertinism and little more.

The second of Huxley's Douglas characters, Mr. Cardan from *Those Barren Leaves*, written after the two authors became friends, is more sinister. The novel takes place at the Italian palazzo of a wealthy Englishwoman who plays hostess to an assortment of young writers and old friends, including Cardan, an impoverished, decrepit hedonist who loves the ancient Greeks and

Rabelais. Cardan is "one of the obscure Great: potentially anything he chose to be, but actually, through indolence, unknown." Early in the novel, Cardan explains his amoral philosophy: "It's obvious there are no moral laws. There are social customs on the one hand, and there are individuals with their individual feelings and moral reactions on the other. What's immoral in one man may not matter in another. Almost nothing, for example, is immoral to me. Positively, you know, I can do anything and yet remain respectable in my own eyes, and in the eyes of others not merely wonderfully decent, but even noble."[37] One can imagine Huxley returning to his villa after a night of listening to Douglas hold forth over the wine bottle, and scribbling out the monologue before the words vanished. Cardan's declaration that he could do anything and yet remain respectable captured Douglas perfectly. Demonstrating his philosophy, Cardan abducts a mentally disabled heiress so that he can marry her for her money, but she dies from food poisoning before the marriage can be executed. The plot might be ripe for a tragedy, but in Huxley's hand it's satirical, and Cardan, while villainous, is also seductive. Another character laughingly refers to Cardan as "Satan," but everyone loves him nonetheless.

As Huxley engaged more seriously with philosophy later during his own life, he returned to the subject of Douglas's hedonism. In his 1944 novel, *Time Must Have a Stop*, Huxley incorporated aspects of Douglas into the character of Eustace Barnack, who is a flawed but sympathetic character. Barnack once had a promising career but threw it over to marry a wealthy Florentine widow. He spouts dirty limericks and indulges indecently in food, wine, and sex. His rigidly moralist brother-in-law dismisses him as "just a hedonist," but the novel reveals Barnack also to be generous, a good friend, and a loving uncle to his pure young nephew, Sebastian, who has come to visit him in Florence. Over an indulgent dinner of filleted sole, creamed chicken, and chocolate soufflé, washed down with vintage champagne, Barnack explains to Sebastian his philosophy of life: "Never put off till tomorrow the pleasure you can enjoy today." He talks to Sebastian of Epicurus and Rabelais and Boccaccio. Then at the evening's end, he dies from a massive coronary, proving the wisdom of his own philosophy.[38]

As Douglas aged, many expected him to meet the same end as Eustace Barnack. Surely a lifetime of never putting off pleasure would have ill effects. Instead he remained robust, "the best advertisement for the evil life." When a young fan went to meet Douglas in 1948, he worried that the "ageing hedonist" would be in bad form. Instead, he found Douglas to be "as blithe and carefree as a child of ten: his zest and appetite for life were apparently inexhaustible." The reason, he explained, was that Douglas's hedonism was not "the oysters and champagne of vulgar good-timers," but instead took the classical form of Epicurean *eudaimonia*.[39]

The ancient Greek term *eudaimonia* could be translated as flourishing, which was one of Douglas's favorite words. In his letters, he often reported on the well-being of his friends by saying that they were flourishing.[40] According to Aristotle, *eudaimonia* meant doing well and living well, defined as "virtuous activity in accordance with reason." Aristotle claimed that the standard of right conduct was defined by the virtuous person, by which he meant that a virtuous person chose right actions, not that his actions were made right because he chose them.[41]

Douglas scoffed at Aristotle's notion of virtue. In *Siren Land*, he sang the praises of local boys whose filthy language disregarded all taboos. "If this be not virtue, according to Aristotle's definition, what is?" Douglas asked mischievously. Later in the book, Douglas defined virtue as "the conduct which conduces to the actor's welfare; the line of least resistance along which the sage walks."[42] This definition owed more to Epicurus than Aristotle. Epicurus was a favorite philosopher of nineteenth-century British pederasts like Walter Pater.[43] Through Douglas's writings, Epicurus gained purchase in the social world of interwar pederasty as well. According to the ancient philosopher, pleasure, both physical and mental, was the only intrinsic good. Virtue played a utilitarian role in the good life, when it delayed immediate appetites causing the avoidance of future pain, "for what produces the pleasant life is not continuous drinking and parties or pederasty or womanizing or the enjoyment of fish and the other dishes of an expensive table."[44] Not continuous, perhaps, but frequent was fine, Douglas thought. He was wary of those who took Epicurean philosophy to the extreme, "rebuilding the old striving under the title of 'virtue.'"[45] His own philosophy remained fixed on self-interest as a guiding principle.

Self-interest could lead to the moderation of appetites. Douglas loved both food and drink, and yet he was neither a glutton nor a drunk, at least most of the time. Theodora FitzGibbon claimed that "he ate heartily, [and] drank everything available, yet I never saw him even remotely drunk."[46] By Douglas's own admission, sometimes he did get drunk. But it wasn't his typical mode. He loved wine and whisky, extolling the pleasures of the bottle in his writings, while those same writings required rising early and having a clear head, which he could not have done if he spent every evening drunk. Since he got pleasure from writing, he drank robustly but not to the point of drunkenness, for the most part. (Of course, only a heavy drinker could achieve such a balance in the first place.) Later in life, when alcohol threatened his health, he went through periods of abstinence.[47] Douglas embraced Epicurus's teaching that the business of life was pleasure, but he also lived by the other half of Epicurus's philosophy: the business of life was the avoidance of pain.

He tried to pass on this philosophy of moderation to Archie, whose gargantuan appetite for alcohol knew no bounds. Over the years, Douglas repeatedly implored Archie to cut back on his drinking for the sake of his present and future health. "These things revenge themselves in middle age, and very unpleasantly: especially alcohol like whiskey," he advised Archie.[48] His advice fell on deaf ears. Archie destroyed his health with heavy drinking. Perhaps he just lacked his father's robust constitution. Years of drinking, feasting, rough travel, and bouts of syphilis, malaria, and rheumatism barely withered Douglas.

As he grew old, he remained extremely robust. Many friends used this word to describe him. The adjective extended both to his philosophy and his bearing. Ian Greenlees, who didn't meet Douglas until the writer was in his sixties, admired the "robust sanity of his outlook" and his hardy fortitude. Greenlees joined Douglas on several of the walking tours he took throughout Italy during his Florentine years. Greenlees, who was forty-five years younger than Douglas, was impressed by the older man's ability to pass long days on the road followed by long evenings at the table. "He thought nothing of walking 20 miles a day into his sixties," Greenlees recalled, and yet he still had the energy for "talking and drinking far into the night."[49]

No wonder Douglas's philosophy seemed so appealing to a young man like Greenlees. Decades later, Greenlees's much younger lover Robin Chanter would write a barely disguised philosophical roman à clef, titled "Conversations with a Retired Gentleman," in which Greenlees appeared as the sage philosopher, passing on Douglas's Epicurean philosophy to a new generation. "I am afraid you are too old to go through all Douglas's programme," the Greenlees character tells the Chanter character, but "you could come to Italy with me. Every year I go to stay with a friend who owns an island not far from Nepenthe."[50] Douglas's Epicurean philosophy, informed by the Oxbridge pederasts of the late nineteenth century, had become a key ingredient of a certain rarified queer cultural milieu of the mid-twentieth century. In fact, Douglas as a character had become a reference point within that culture. Not only was he never a man outside society—he became, at the peak of his influence, the creator of a social world.

CHAPTER FIFTEEN

Moving Along

To outward appearances, Norman Douglas was the picture of robust manhood well into his sixties. He complained to friends and family that he was "getting impotent."[1] Yet he showed no evidence of this incapacity. Not only did he have the vigor to walk for twenty miles a day on rural roads, but he also maintained the capacity to get an erection for the boys he met along the way. In the summer of 1932, on a trip to Vorarlberg, Douglas and Pino Orioli hiked to a local waterfall to watch boys frolic naked. Orioli, who was two decades younger than Douglas, complained in his diary that the sight of the boys did not get him excited. He worried that he was "getting impotent" for real, unlike Douglas, "who says he is so but goes on like a bull."[2] Orioli's diaries from their trip to Vorarlberg, and from the many other trips the men took together in the 1930s, include explicit accounts of Douglas's sexual behavior that prove his enduring sexual appetite and virility. Orioli's diaries also reveal the everyday nature of child sex tourism, especially in Italy, before World War II. As Ian Littlewood, a historian of sex tourism, argues: "Indignation at Douglas's behaviour, if that is what we feel, should not blind us to the ordinariness of what he describes. He merely recalls the facilities that were available to any traveler with the relatively small amount of money required to pay for them."[3]

Douglas traveled frequently during the 1930s, whenever his finances and his work schedule would allow—and even sometimes when work and finances wouldn't permit but extenuating circumstances demanded it. Year after year he returned to Capri, Ischia, Sant'Agata, Calabria, and Menton. He traveled a couple times to Sicily and made a handful of visits to Tunisia and Lebanon, all locations within Sir Richard Burton's pederastic "Sotadic Zone."[4] Douglas also traveled to places not associated with pederasty. He visited

Bryher and Kenneth Macpherson's home on Lake Geneva and his own family home in Vorarlberg. He went repeatedly to Paris, although he claimed to dislike France. He visited Eric Wolton in East Africa, stopping in Djibouti, Arusha, Dodoma, and Mombasa. In 1934 he went with Orioli to India and Ceylon. And he longed to make a trip to China, but that never panned out.

Douglas took many of his trips in the company of Orioli. Sometimes they traveled with a handful of mutual friends like Charles Prentice, Kenneth Macpherson, Ian Greenlees, and Richard Aldington. Most often, Douglas and Orioli traveled just the two of them, which allowed the men the greatest freedom to pursue sexual encounters with boys and the older male youth whom Orioli preferred and Douglas sometimes resorted to. Those sexual encounters were a primary inspiration for their journeys, not a secondary benefit. Over the years, Douglas returned again and again to what he called "sacred" spots, where he'd had enjoyable sexual encounters in the past. He paid visits to old lovers and hunted for new lovers to take their place. At Douglas's urging, Orioli kept diaries of their journeys together, much as Wolton and Mari had done. Douglas told Orioli "it would be delightful reading in my old age."[5] It depends on one's definition of delightful.

Orioli's diaries describe, in far greater detail than Douglas's published writings, the innkeepers happy to procure children for the men, the boys eager to solicit the attention of the men in exchange for money or gifts, the families willing to engage their children in the sex trade. Orioli's travel diaries stretch the boundaries of the historicist approach to sexuality, by showing that something viewed as an absolute moral wrong in the present might have been viewed as commonplace by people in the recent past. The copies of the diaries archived at the New York Public Library are typed transcriptions prepared by Douglas, who took care to preserve Orioli's erratic spelling and grammar. "At first I thought of correcting Orioli's mis-spellings but the things seems to read more amusingly intimate if they remain unaltered," Douglas explained to Harold Acton.[6] Ever the scholar, Douglas faithfully reproduced the original source material, only making occasional pencil marks on the page where he was unable to discern Orioli's handwriting or where he wanted to comment on the text.

Despite Orioli's professional expertise as a publisher, he was not a confident English writer. His first travel diary, recording the men's trip together to Vorarlberg in the summer of 1930, was written primarily in Italian and only veered into English a handful of times. For example, he wrote a long English passage about visiting a swimming hole with two boys, Fifo and

26. Pino Orioli frolicking along a road in Thüringen, 1932. Private collection of Deirdre Sholto Douglas. Photograph by author.

Rody, the latter of whom was an Italian immigrant from the Tyrol. The passage captures Orioli's idiosyncratic voice:

"Ecce! Ecce! Look what a beauty. Look" says N. And on the wooden bridge, which separate the bath from the land, a little stretch of wood on a miserable drop of lake water, there, stand a real sculpterial creature, holding a cord, just a piece of cord, meant to be a leash for a dog. A handsome dog. . . . You will never see such an hansom creature as the boy that was holding the dog.

Orioli continued his ecstatic account of watching the boy with the dog, observing that N. was also enthusiastic—prompting a pencil notation from Douglas: "not about the dog." Orioli's reveries, however, were interrupted when Rody noticed his wandering attention. Orioli told Rody he was simply admiring the boy's beauty:

> It is a very good excuse not to make them jealous. They are so stupid, and you can take them in so easy, with art, sentimentality, romanticism, pretend to talk them seriously, never make any funn, never any jock, only be artistic, sentimental, then the Italian boys are with you. Easy to have them, but what do you get, false affection, false sentimentality, false romanticism, false all over, except in bed. In bed they are good. Frightfully good, but leave them alone after. They only pretend to understand you.

Later when the boys and men prepared to leave the swimming hole, Orioli offered a long silent goodbye to the boy with the dog:

> We love you. But we have to go. I would give willingly Rody and Fifo for you. Never dress. For me, you will never be dress. You are too beautiful to be dress. You are too beautiful to be dress and after all, I have seen you first undress and I would never be with you when clothed.[7]

A subsequent English passage in this first diary describes another encounter with a boy, which raises the possibility that Orioli shifted to English when he wanted to describe episodes that Anglophone friends might like to read about later. The passage described how Douglas introduced Orioli to a "little boy" named Gabriello, whom he told Orioli was his "old friend." Orioli answered, "Old friend, are you mad, he is only twelve, and down from the mountain." Douglas explained, "We shall have to eat five kilos of raspery for lunch, I have bought them from him. You don't mind it do you?" Douglas then effused about "darling" Gabriello, who had "no one looking after him, such an angel, and he lieves up in the mountain, so far, I have not been there.

We must go. Oh! But Fifo must not know about him."[8] Douglas often complained that Orioli couldn't keep a secret. He didn't want his friend to ruin his affair with Fifo.

Orioli didn't share Douglas's sexual interest in "little boys." His tastes ran more toward strapping youths of seventeen or eighteen. On yet another trip to the swimming hole, Orioli admired the naked body of a youth named Gerald, whom he called a "blonde siren." Douglas commented that Gerald was "un poco troppo peloso sotto le braccia per essere sireno"[9] (a little too hairy under the arms to be a siren). Douglas liked to enthuse about the smell of children's armpits.[10] Orioli responded that he found hairy armpits to be an aphrodisiac. He noted their differing sexual tastes but assigned no moral distinction between them, writing in his diary, "de gustibus, etc. etc.," a reference to the Latin phrase "de gustibus non est disputandum" (in matters of taste, there can be no dispute).[11] In short, to each his own.

Orioli's travel diaries appealed to those in their circle of friends who took a similarly non-judgmental attitude toward Douglas's erotic appetite for boys. John Mavrogordato, who was straight, read the 1930 diary one afternoon during a trip to Paris and later that evening took Douglas out to dinner at Prunier's, in the company of Harold Acton and Peter Pitt-Millward, another English pederast.[12] Richard Aldington was less sympathetic to the diaries, which he said were filled with "unsavoury adventures with curly-pated rascals and Greek genii."[13] But Aldington may have just been trying to escape attack for accompanying Orioli and Douglas on some of their trips, by implying they reserved their misbehavior for when he was not around.

Orioli's diaries grew more explicit over time. His account of the men's trip to Vorarlberg in 1932 was far more graphic than the 1930 diary. According to Orioli, soon after the men returned to Austria, Fifo tracked them down and attached himself to Douglas. The boy, who had turned sixteen, had become "a man now, not a pretty one, he was a pretty boy two years ago. Now he is rather an ugly man." At first Douglas tried to avoid Fifo, but Fifo was persistent and eventually Douglas renewed their sexual relationship. One of Orioli's most explicit passages in all the diaries recounted a sexual encounter between Fifo and Douglas during the 1932 trip. Following an afternoon's hike, Douglas and Orioli debated whether to stop in the woods or press on to the hotel. Orioli wrote, "N. is undecided if to sleep in the wood and toss off F. or go to our pub in a proper bed (he calls it a proper bed and be fucked by F)." After discussion, they "end on sleeping a bit in the wood—I tossing off—and then struggling over a kind of flaby cocks and lookworm coming (spunk) as N. said."[14] Orioli's account of this sexual interlude was unglossed. All the "art, sentimentality, [and] romanticism," as Orioli put it, were stripped away, leaving only the grotesque sexual calculus that operated within Douglas's affairs.

When Orioli and Douglas got the idea to turn one of the travel diaries into a book, Orioli had to rein in his writing. His next diary, of a trip they took to Calabria in spring 1933, left out the dirty words. Douglas sent an early bound copy to Mavrogordato, explaining that it was "not like the Austrian one, because it is intended for publication." The trip, which Douglas and Orioli had taken along with their friend Charles Prentice, had been sexually busy. As Douglas explained, "One could have done a lovely and authentic Calabrian journal, but who would have printed it?"[15] Certainly not Prentice, manager of Chatto & Windus, which in 1934 released the Calabria journal as *Moving Along: Just a Diary*. Only Orioli's name appeared on the spine. The book was written in first person, with Orioli as narrator, but friends knew that Douglas was largely responsible for the writing.[16]

After he published *Looking Back* in 1933, Douglas had declared himself bereft of further inspiration. His writing career, he informed his friends, was over: "I have definitely dropped all writing, and shut up my shop."[17] However, his need for money was ongoing. Orioli's need was just as profound, considering how the Depression cut into the profits at his bookshop. The men's collaboration on *Moving Along*, as well as on Orioli's subsequent memoir, *Adventures of a Bookseller*, which came out two years later, served both their interests. Douglas could earn money from his pen without originating new ideas. Orioli was able to profit off selling his life story to English readers, despite his inadequacies as a writer. Whatever the exact division of responsibilities, *Moving Along* bore the imprint of both its authors. Douglas's editing preserved much of the whimsy of Orioli's voice. Yet, as Elizabeth David put it, "the style certainly does smack strongly of Douglas."[18] Orioli may have left out the sex from his Calabria journal, but Douglas made sure that the pages of *Moving Along* were imbued with pederastic desire.

Moving Along was filled with rosy portraits of boys and youths the men met along the way. The book opened with a scene of Orioli and Douglas trailing a group of sailors through Pompeii and eavesdropping as the young men giggled over the fresco of Priapus weighing his enormous penis, which was painted in the vestibule of the Casa dei Vetti.[19] Any readers attentive to homoerotic themes would instantly have become attuned to the sexual orien-

27. Douglas amusing Marcello, Volterra, Italy. From *Moving Along* (1934), 154.

tation of the book's narrator. In subsequent scenes, Orioli admired handsome youths they met on the road, and Douglas befriended boys by giving them chocolates. Calabria, Douglas announced at one point in the narrative, "is a lovely country and her children are the prettiest on earth."[20] *Moving Along* may have offered a cleaned-up version of the men's travels in Italy, but only just barely.

In the diaries he wrote after *Moving Along*, Orioli resumed including explicit accounts of the men's sexual encounters. His November 1933 Sant'Agata diary referred several times to Douglas "fucking" boys. Other diaries avoided the word *fuck* but were still direct. The diaries described Douglas's sexual interests as flexible. He could stretch older when the opportunity presented itself. On a trip to Scanno, Orioli noted that Douglas "made friend with a youth but too old to call him youth." He "must have forgotten what a youth look." Douglas could also stretch much younger. Later on the same trip, Douglas had a sexual encounter in his room with a seven-year-old.[21] It's impossible to know what sexual acts he committed with the boy. Some of Douglas's defenders insisted that he "only" fondled young children. In public, Douglas would seat boys on his lap and make funny faces to amuse them, allowing the children to pull on his nose, ruffle his hair, or play with his glasses.[22] For example, Orioli described Douglas's flirtation with an eight-year-old boy named Herbert at a hotel. Herbert was the son of the proprietor and the encounter took place under the family's watchful eye, so it's unlikely that Douglas had any intimate contact with the child. When they returned to the hotel a second time, Herbert played with Douglas again, while Orioli took photos.[23] Douglas collected several photos of small children he met during his travels. Although not sexually explicit, a few were suggestive enough that he worried about the photos being seen by unfriendly eyes. The photos were clearly intended as sexual mementos.

In addition to men and boys, a number of women and girls attracted Douglas's attentions during his travels. When Douglas flirted with a serving girl at a restaurant in Sant'Agata, Orioli wrote, "Norman took a great fancie to her, and during lunch he plays with her as if she was a boy of thirteen. She is nineteen."[24] On a trip to Ischia, Douglas flirted with the thirteen-year-old daughter of the restaurant's *padrona*, feeding her "with sweets and caresses," causing Orioli to complain that Douglas "was in his womanizer mood."[25] He was happier when Douglas was in his anti-woman mood, such as when he got angry at the women readers who approached him in restaurants to tell him how much they loved his books. Orioli had no sexual interest in females, young or old. He didn't much like women as people. In his diaries, Orioli often referred to women as "quims," a slang for women's genitalia.[26]

Orioli's diaries described Douglas's sexual interests as being so flexible that they allegedly extended beyond the human realm. At one point Douglas took a dog with him to his bedroom at night. "My dear when the devil is hungry he eats flies," he announced. The next morning Douglas told Pino that "the dog was very satisfactory with a real volcanic lust."[27] Another time, while they sat drinking at a caffè in Abbadia San Salvatore, Douglas saw "a crétin" and "wanted to take him to his room."[28] Douglas never entirely abandoned his

28. Photograph of Douglas holding a small child, while Orioli holds a dog in the background. Norman Douglas Collection, Beinecke Rare Book and Manuscript Library, Yale University.

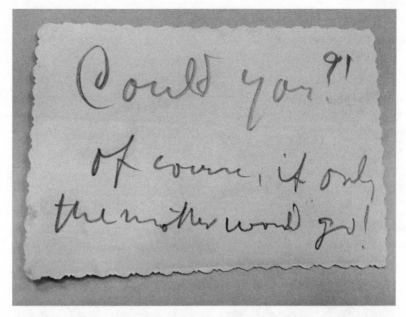

29. On the back of the photograph, Douglas has written: "Could you? Of course, if only the mother would go!" This photo remained within Douglas's private collection. Norman Douglas Collection, Beinecke Rare Book and Manuscript Library, Yale University.

pose as a nineteenth-century libertine sexual adventurer. As Martha Gordon Crotch put it, Douglas saw "beauty in curious intercourse."[29] Less forgivingly, one might say that he was attracted to vulnerable people, children and otherwise. But, for the most part, Orioli's diaries detailed Douglas's participation in an everyday world of child sex tourism that involved the active participation of hotelkeepers, parents, and the youths themselves.

Child sex work was common in southern Italy during the interwar era because the nation was impoverished, families were large, and many adult males had either died in the war or emigrated, leaving children desperate to earn money for food and school supplies. In a context where children performed all sorts of dangerous and backbreaking labor, sex work did not stand out as unreasonable. The countless poor boys who hawked food on the streets of Italian villages, like Gabriello the raspberry seller, were frequent targets of Douglas's sexual advances. In Scanno, Douglas "stopped under the chestnut trees" with a child named Pietro who was selling filberts. Orioli, for his part, stopped "under some tree along the Aniene and got a lot of pleasure out of dear Albino," who sold wine, beer, and sandwiches along the train platform.[30]

In Ischia, the men befriended "two milk boys." The boys came to the men's rooms, and one later made a return visit to Orioli, claiming to have lost 150 lire. This was probably an attempt at extortion, and it signaled that sex work, while relatively common, involved risks. The Fascists' moralization campaign put pressure on the men to keep their encounters secret. Orioli gave the boy two francs and sent him packing.[31]

Boys who worked as guides, waiters, and bellhops were also frequent targets of Douglas's and Orioli's advances. In Sant'Agata, a local innkeeper named Fattuta repeatedly procured children for Douglas under the guise of hiring them as guides. Not that Douglas needed guides, after four decades of visiting the village. Fattuta set the men up with a "charming" thirteen-year-old boy named Bebé, who was "slim and tall and rather refined for the place; dark eyes a regular straight nose and olive compaction," to lead them up Mount San Constanzo. Douglas commented that Bebé was "just adolescent" and "his voice most aphrodisiacal, not yet broken." Orioli opined that Bebé's balls were "still up." On the way up the mountain, Douglas and Bebé retired among the rocks. Orioli observed that the area was "more than a sacred spot" for Douglas—it was "full of indimenticable memoires," *dimenticare* being the Italian verb "to forget." After their return from the hike, the bookseller felt his hand "caressed by a warm soft little hand." It was Salvatore, a friend of Bebé, and "a darling of a boy who insisted to accompany us half way to Termini and also insisted to have fifty centesimi to buy an exercise school book."[32] The low price that Salvatore fixed for his sexual company suggests the high degree of need driving poor Italian boys into sex commerce. The need was so intense that poor boys competed over access to Douglas and Orioli. When Salvatore accompanied the men on a hike from Nerano to Termini, a couple of *scugnizzi*, or street boys, began to follow them down the path. Salvatore stoned the smaller boy, who turned back, but the men had to promise the older boy that they would come back another time before he agreed to stop following.[33] Likewise, during a visit to Genazzano, a boy named Angelino monopolized Douglas's company and drove "his own brothers and sisters away from him."[34]

Even children who weren't in desperate financial straits often responded positively to Douglas's gifts and attention. Dining at an osteria in Sant'Agata, Douglas tried to seduce the twelve-year-old son of the proprietor. Orioli observed that the boy was "rather a shy creature," but "Norman started with a few sweets and in a few minutes he had the child sitting next to him."[35] Plying children with sweets was one of Douglas's favorite tactics. He used it on Bebé during a hiking trip when the weather conditions got in the way of sex. "Norman wanted his fuck with Bebé," Orioli explained, "but he could not find a place suitable. The ground was wet from rain of last night, the wood was too thin and transparent, so he had to be pleased to feed him with Giandula all the time saying: mangia! Mangia! Vuoi un altro? Si o no? si o no?" The chocolate had its intended effect, according to Orioli, who described Bebé as "in a golden mood and just ripe for a fuck." But they never did find a place to consummate the encounter. The party returned to the restaurant in Sant'Agata, where "Norman managed to give a cockstand to Bebé who had to stand up finding the sitting down to unconfortable." Orioli remarked that it was a "pity there was no place to toss him off." The day was a comedy of errors in Orioli's retelling. It reads as disturbing today, but Bebé didn't raise any objections. The following day he brought his little brother Manizza to meet the men.[36]

As Orioli explained, the places where the men stopped to have sexual encounters with boys became "sacred" spots to Douglas. In Genazzano in 1933, Douglas made friends with a boy named Francesco and his brother Adamo. "And now leave me alone with the boys," Douglas instructed Orioli, who complained that Douglas was creating "another sacred spot, which I shall be obliged to visit if I go back to Genazzano with N."[37] Two years later, Douglas and Orioli returned to Genazzano, as Orioli predicted they would.[38] Francesco was "old and full of pimples—a pity." The men were even more disappointed to discover that Adamo was away at school.[39] But Douglas and Orioli soon turned their attention to other boys and young men who were visiting the village for a fireworks display.

Douglas didn't just return to sacred spots—he liked to pay return visits to the boys who had made the spots sacred. After meeting Fifo in 1930 and reconnecting with him in 1932, the men visited him again in 1936, at which point, according to Orioli, he was "no more the sweet boy of six years ago" but "big and lumpy, heavy and empty and rather ugly."[40] After meeting Francesco and Adamo in 1933, Douglas and Orioli met up with the boys again in 1935 and in 1937, when they hired Francesco as a servant. Again, the bloom was off the rose. Orioli remarked that Francesco was "a nice boy, but he does not appeal to me particularly," and Adamo was "not so pretty as he used to be."[41] Nonetheless, the men and the boys treated each other as old friends. This habit of making repeat visits to the same boys sometimes served in Orioli's favor, when a boy had matured from Douglas's ideal age range to his own. In Castrovillari, Douglas and Orioli paid a visit to Battistino. "He used to be thirteen or fourteen years old, and in those days Norman smothered him in chocolates. Now he is eighteen or nineteen, and I smother him in cigarettes," Orioli wrote.[42] The fact that the boys, now grown into men, welcomed return visits from Orioli and Douglas suggests that they did not view their earlier sexual encounters as monstrous. Whatever regrets Fifo or Francesco may have had, they were still open to seeing Douglas and Orioli, and sharing meals with them or working for them.

Some of the places where the men traveled Douglas had been visiting for so long that his former boyfriends had grown into old men. Near Termini, Douglas and Orioli encountered "old Costanzo," who had once been "a fine boy and rather appetizing for Norman."[43] These old lovers didn't seem to resent Douglas. In fact, Orioli observed, in Vorarlberg, the Sorrentine Peninsula, Calabria, and the Sabine Hills, "everyone seem to know Norman," and they all acted happy to see him.[44] On a trip to Scanno, Douglas and Orioli visited the home of Quirino, a twenty-nine-year-old blacksmith with a name fit for an emperor, as Orioli put it. "Once he has been a blond beautiful boy with light magnificent blue eyes. Than he was a real Emperour for N."[45] Whatever passed between them when he was a child, the fact that Quirino welcomed Douglas to his home suggests that the memories were not an active source of grief.

The poor boys and youth who willingly traded sex with Douglas and Orioli may, or may not, have been traumatized by their encounters with the men, but that doesn't mean they were eager participants. For the most part, they likely tried to get what they could while providing the least possible in return. Douglas and Orioli called the boys who tried to extract gifts or money without providing sex in return "shits." Mauro was a "real shit," Orioli wrote, because he "gets money from me and N. but doesn't do anything."[46] On a visit to Ischia, they decided that "every one seems a shit here. The land of shits we call the place." This was a grave disappointment to Orioli, who rhapsodized over the figures of the Ischian youths: "I don't thing I have ever seen such well shaped buttocks, the Ischian bum, as we call it, is some thing worth having. It is not a fat bum, or a big bum, what makes it so remarkable and beautifully shaped is that the people are sleem with a thin west and perfect curves."[47] Unfortunately for Orioli and Douglas, the Ischians did not seem to take the same accommodating attitude that the villagers in nearby Sant'Agata did. One time when Orioli and Douglas were sharing drinks in a bar, a couple of boys kept peeking in at them. When Douglas went to chat with the boys, "of course at once two or three men sprang from God knows where to interfere. Always like that, does not matter where you are!" Orioli complained.[48] Douglas also complained about the unavailability of Ischian boys in letters to Archie. "The only drawback of Ischia is that one can't have any love-affairs of any kind," Douglas noted during a two-month stay on the island. "Wine here is delicious, but Florentine pleasures are out of the question."[49] Attitudes toward child prostitution varied within Italy, within regions, and even from village to village. Douglas made a point of going back to places where the communities were tolerant.

Which isn't to say that Douglas and Orioli didn't have the occasional sexual encounter in places that were less tolerant. In Ischia, Orioli had one with a cabdriver named Ninuccio. He was worried it wouldn't come off: "While driving to Lacco I was so frighten he would turned into a shit, thank God when we arrived to the chapel he came up to the scratch, and now in a corner of that little path which goes to Punta Cornacchia I have got a sacred place." Orioli expressed the same relief following a sexual encounter with an Ischian youth named Milazzo: "I had a lovely and succesful moment with Milazzo whom by miracle was not in a shitting mood, he came up to the scratch."[50] Douglas had success with an "ugly servant boy" who brought his morning coffee at their pension. The boy, Douglas told Orioli, "was not altogether a shit."[51] What degree of coercion Orioli or Douglas exercised in these sexual encounters is impossible to know.

India and Ceylon proved even more difficult than Ischia for picking up boys. Douglas and Orioli traveled there hoping to write another book in Orioli's name. The typed manuscript of Orioli's travel diary includes no explicit references to sexual encounters between the men and the boys and youths they met along the way. Orioli may have left the encounters out, the way he did in the diary that became *Moving Along*, but Douglas's letters to Archie indicate it was also for lack of opportunity. "As to fucking—very difficult in India if you don't know the language," Douglas reported when he returned home.[52]

Orioli and Douglas met plenty of people they would have liked to fuck. At their first port of call, Colombo, the men admired the servant boys and "half-naked Sinhalese men" who worked as waiters, bath attendants, and street vendors. Following his usual routine, Douglas bought all the bananas and nuts in one boy's basket and told him to feed the monkeys. The gesture won him the affection of the boy, but no more.[53] When they asked a rickshaw driver to take them to a place where they could see dancing boys, the driver informed them that the establishment had been closed for immorality. Things did not improve when the men arrived in India. Finally in Bombay a driver did take them to a place with dancing boys, but Douglas and Orioli were disappointed to discover the boys were dressed in women's clothes, "both ugly and not at all young." Moreover their mouths were red from chewing betel. Douglas and Orioli threw money at the pair and fled. "They were two repulsive wizard cat-amites," Orioli wrote, showing a lack of familiarity with the Hindi and Urdu word *hijra*, used for the distinctive sex and gender caste to which the individuals Douglas and Orioli met likely belonged.[54]

The contrast between Douglas and Orioli's experiences in Sant'Agata and in India illustrates the importance of context for understanding the men's sex tourism. In places where the sex trade flourished, Douglas and Orioli took full advantage of customary practices. In places where the sex trade was limited or inaccessible to the men because of their lack of familiarity with local practices, the men had few encounters. As upsetting as the endless litany of sexual encounters in Orioli's diaries may be, they took place within established norms. Douglas and Orioli participated in a widespread sexual culture found at many of the places they visited.

Orioli commented several times in his diaries on other men they met during their travels who shared their taste in boys and youths. In Syracuse, Orioli watched the proprietor of a restaurant approach a family with a boy "about fourteen not bad looking rather plump. The proprietor went to their table, sat next to the boy and started caressing him in such a way that we decided he must be of that nature."[55] In Guarcino, Douglas and Orioli watched a "fat young priest with two boy students in a collège uniform. The priest went on caressing the boys all the time with a little too much affection. Sure he was a —."[56] The blank may have stood for *pederasta*, the most common Italian word used to describe homosexuality during the 1930s.[57] Or it may have stood for *finnochio* (fennel), a common slang word for queer men that Orioli used in a subsequent diary entry.[58] Whichever word Orioli left out, in early twentieth-century Italy, men like the restaurant proprietor, the priests, and Douglas and Orioli were familiar types.

As the Fascists tightened their grip on Italy during the mid-1930s, however, toleration for *pederasti* or *finnochi* declined. Orioli and Douglas complained about the impact of this shift on their travels. Once the men had reveled in encounters with the *scugnizzi* who crowded Naples.[59] But after 1935, the country changed. There were "no more scugnizzi." The street kids had vanished. "Naples has been disinfected, cleaned, the boys have been dressed up, the noise does not exist any more," Orioli wrote mournfully.[60] Men in the Fascist movement continued to have same-sex encounters with boys, but they became more secretive.[61]

Fascist Austria, unsurprisingly, was no better. By 1934, Douglas was complaining to W. H. D. Rouse that he couldn't stand returning to Vorarlberg any longer because of how the area had become swept up by Fascism. "That particular region is now completely Hitlerized (shitlerized) and I can't face it," Douglas wrote.[62] Despite his distaste for the political situation, Douglas kept going back. In July 1936, on a visit with Orioli, he met a boy named Louis and became so enamored that he returned to see the boy on his own a month later. "I don't know how long I remain in this neighbourhood. Possibly a week or even more. It all depends. Sap sat," he wrote to Archie, using their long-established code.[63] "Sap. sat." was short for *sapienti sat*, or "enough for the wise." Douglas wrote even more explicitly to Orioli about the progress of his love affair. "Had a glorious afternoon and evening with L.," Douglas updated Orioli in late August.[64] Louis "likes stamps and soldiers," he informed his friend. "We are going away today again and I don't know where to, nor for how long. To some place, I hope, where the beds don't creak, as they do everywhere except at Löwden in Bregenz."[65]

Wherever Douglas went, something else gave him away. His pocket diary stops abruptly on September 11, 1936.[66] He had been arrested, again. He was held for a week, then released on the condition that he leave Austria within twelve hours and never return. It was a lucky break. The Austrofascist regime could have sent him to an internment camp. Instead, he was back in Florence by September 20, telling everyone that he had experienced "heart trouble" in Vorarlberg and was giving up mountain climbing.[67] The truth was that Douglas's vigor had outlasted his homeland's tolerance for its sexual expression. The year 1936 was Douglas's final visit to the land of his birth. His traveling days were coming to an end.[68] Unfortunately for Douglas, life in Fascist Florence was getting just as dangerous.

Reflection III

Between his first arrest in 1916 and his second arrest in 1936, Douglas constantly kept one eye over his shoulder, looking out for the police. They nearly came for him in Capri, but Faith Mackenzie intervened. There were several times when the atmosphere in Florence grew so tense that Douglas felt compelled to flee. In Ischia, he faced extortion threats and the hostile stares of local men who tried to stop him from mixing with the local boys. Child prostitution may have been common in interwar Italy, but it functioned beyond the bounds of social acceptability. It was clearly outside the charmed circle, as Gayle Rubin put it.

Were attitudes toward pederasty really any different in the 1920s and 1930s than they are a century later? The word has changed. *Pederasty* has become archaic in the twenty-first century. It sounds contrived, a weak attempt at gussying-up *pedophilia*. Does this shift in terminology indicate a real change in beliefs over time? Or has language just become more honest today, stripping away the neoclassical gilding from what was always known to be a base practice? This is another iteration of the question that always haunts the history of sexuality. Does sexuality have a history?[1] Was the transition from the *sodomite* to the *homosexual* a matter of style or substance? Old wine in new skins? Or a fresh invention? Historians of sexuality, by definition, answer this question affirmatively: sexuality has a history, and shifts in language speak to transformations in beliefs and practices. Popular memory, on the other hand, inclines toward continualism, seeing homosexuals and pedophiles in the past, long before the letter.

The Douglas archive contains both continuities and disjunctures. It includes evidence that authorities, families, and communities could be just as hostile to adult men having sex with boys as they are today. And it includes evidence that authorities, families, and communities could be far more accommodating to sex between men and boys than they are today. The authorities didn't arrest Douglas in Capri; instead they scolded the local magistrate, Signor Capolozzi, for harassing him. Luciano's mother caused trouble with the police when Douglas started pursuing her son, but Luciano's father conspired with Douglas to get the boy out of Florence and enable the relationship. The Ischians tried to interfere with Douglas's pursuit of local boys, but the villagers in Sant'Agata, on the other side of the Sorrentine Peninsula, welcomed Douglas, and the local innkeeper Fattuta procured boys for him. The evidence reveals ambiguities in social attitudes to intergenerational sex, which is the most striking difference between then and now, when there is no ambiguity.

During the heyday of Douglas's literary life, he was notorious for his sexual affairs with boys, but his notoriety was not simply negative. He capitalized on his reputation, cultivating a "scandalous celebrity" that attracted more admirers than antagonists.[2] He was widely considered a good advertisement for the evil life. That construct made sense in a historical context when so many sexual behaviors fell outside the pale of respectability. It was easier to be admirably bad in the early twentieth century than it is a century later. It's still possible to become a scandalous celebrity today, maybe via the leak of a sex tape or an arrest for misdemeanor drug possession, but getting arrested for indecent assault on a minor is a career incinerator. There's no scandalous glamour for pedophiles.

Celebrities who are accused of pedophilia yet manage to cling to fame retain their reputations despite their sexual wrongdoing, not because of it. The overwhelming popularity of Michael Jackson's pop songs allowed him to rise above long-circulating rumors about his sexual relationships with boys. It wasn't *because* he was a purported pedophile that people liked him. Although, as the comedian Dave Chappelle joked in a 2019 stand-up special, "It's Michael Jackson!" His celebrity lessened the impact of the accusations. "I know more than half the people in this room have been molested in their lives, but it wasn't no goddamn Michael Jackson, was it?" Chappelle demanded. "This kid got his dick sucked by the king of pop. All we get is awkward Thanksgivings for the rest of our lives."[3] You can see a similar logic operating in the defenses of Douglas offered by some of his friends. Sex between men and children might be wrong, but it was less wrong when Douglas did it, because *it's Norman Douglas!*

The moral rule against pederasty had exceptions in the early twentieth century. Context mattered more than it matters today, when Chappelle's joke has put critics up in arms.[4] The Douglas archive illuminates the difference between a relativistic moral proscription and an absolute moral taboo. The taboo on intergenerational sex no longer permits exceptions. Pedophilia has become monstrous. Most would see this transition as evidence of moral progress. Douglas, of course, would not. He thought that the modern aversion to pederasty stemmed from a false and pernicious Christian belief that sex was sinful. Christianity's negative attitudes to the pleasures of the flesh underlay moralizing attitudes to sex with young people. Few people today are willing to address the question of whether sex by definition is harmful to children. Few people are willing to speak the words *sex* and *children* together.

To question whether any sexualized pleasure that children experience in connection with adults is constitutive of abuse strays into the unspeakable. The cultural critic Kathryn Bond Stockton has asked why American society is so "much less troubled by children's pain (for example, their economic suffering) than we are troubled by their sexualized pleasure, even though we cite their possible pain as our rationale for delaying their pleasure?"[5] Some might be offended by Stockton's comparison. The contemporary taboo particularizes child sexual abuse as a unique horror. A pedophile is a moral monster in a way that a person who employs child labor is not. We don't have an epithet for someone who profits from the economic exploitation of children. (At least, few people use *capitalist* as an epithet.) One could answer Stockton's question by saying that we need to be more troubled by children's economic suffering, rather than less troubled by their sexualized pleasure. I think that answer is incomplete. We can't ignore the question she asks about children's pleasure.

Has elevating intergenerational sex to the status of monstrosity led to the stigmatization of sexualized pleasure for children? Does the hardening of our modern taboo lead to the denial of children's sexual autonomy? In sum, are there effects to the hardened taboo that extend beyond adults to children? The history of sexuality as an academic field began with Michel Foucault's refutation of the "repressive hypothesis," in which he argued that Victorian restrictions on sexual speech did not stifle sexuality but rather produced it by creating an incitement to discourse. Building from Foucault, who saw "the case of children's sex" as a subject of great contention within modern sexuality, it follows that the hardening taboos against pedophilia in the second half of the twentieth century produced new sexual orderings for children as well as for adults.[6]

Douglas did not live long enough to witness the significant transformation of attitudes toward children's sexuality in the second half of the twentieth century. But he did live long enough to experience the declining salience of pederasty as a meaningful social category. The frequency of the word's usage in the corpus of English-language books fell precipitately after 1933, the year that *Looking Back* was published. At the same time, the word *homosexuality* was sharply inclining.[7] The old model of age-differentiated sex that had dominated male same-sex practices for centuries of western European history was on its way out, to be replaced by a new more egalitarian model of relations between adults of roughly equal age. Pederasty became unspeakable, a forgotten anachronism. This rapid and complete discrediting of the sexual practices that had defined Douglas's life left him struggling to survive during his final years, and left his fans and friends struggling to find the language to defend him.

PART IV

Heraclitus

CHAPTER SIXTEEN

On the Run

On June 1, 1937, Norman Douglas showed up unexpectedly at the door of his friend Martha Gordon Crotch in Vence, France. He had fled Florence to escape being arrested for raping a child. It wasn't the first time he had skipped town just ahead of the police, but this time was different. He wouldn't be returning to Italy when the danger passed. He would not return to Italy as long as the Fascists held power. Douglas's Florentine pleasures had come to their bitter end.

Benito Mussolini, Il Duce or leader of the National Fascist Party, ascended to the position of prime minister of Italy in 1922 following years of street violence. Throughout the 1920s, he consolidated power and violently suppressed dissenters until by the 1930s the Fascists dominated all aspects of Italian daily life. In 1935, when Mussolini invaded Ethiopia, the United Kingdom imposed sanctions against Italy. The Fascists plastered anti-British posters around Florence, but Douglas and quite a few other Britons remained.[1] Many Anglo-Florentines felt a righteous entitlement to stay. Others, like Douglas, didn't have anywhere else to go. "If I don't live here, where the Hell am I to live?" he asked.[2]

Archie, who was getting anxious, suggested that Douglas come back to England. But Douglas pooh-poohed the suggestion as "rather doubtful, to put it mildly."[3] In September 1935, Douglas fled Florence temporarily. He told Archie that he wasn't sure when he'd be returning to Italy, "possibly never." Then a reassuring telegram arrived from Orioli, and Douglas went back. It wasn't a happy homecoming. "The atmosphere is becoming decidedly unpleasant, owing to the sanctions," Douglas reported.[4] He raised the possibility of moving to Athens, where he had a handful of friends, but he had forgotten his

Greek. Douglas's 1936 arrest eliminated Austria from the list of possible refuges. He floated the idea of returning to India, but his health was starting to break down. He had developed a condition he referred to as *giddiness*, a dizzy sensation that overtook him whenever he was standing. He tried cutting out alcohol and cigars, but the abstinence had no effect. His old life in Florence was collapsing around him. Betti's and Picciolo's, his favorite restaurants, both closed. "I am itching to be out of this place. But where?" Douglas bemoaned.[5] In February 1937, Fascist authorities cracked down on the city's pederasts and homosexuals.[6] Douglas announced with relief that the scandal "did not come my way."[7] But his luck could only hold out so long.

Unexpectedly, the last straw that drove Douglas from Florence was not a sexual relationship with a boy. In January 1937, Douglas told Archie that he was "taking to girls again."[8] Trying to avoid trouble with the authorities, Douglas had turned his attention to the ten-and-a-half-year-old daughter of his laundress, a girl named Renata. Douglas described Renata as an "extraordinarily live little person." Harold Acton described her a "precocious little lass" who "loved lipstick and liqueurs as well as Norman's company."[9] Some of his old friends were surprised to see Douglas with a girl, but he dismissed their doubts. "Why not?" he wrote to John Mavrogordato, "I hope you don't take me for one of those damned sods (as I believe that they are called)? Vive la femme! That has always been my war-cry, and may I die with it on my lips."[10] In early April, Douglas went to Capri, planning to rent a small villa for a couple months, but he reported to Archie that the island "was impossible." Richard Aldington later claimed that Douglas was ordered off the island by Capri's Fascist mayor. Whatever happened in Capri so alarmed Douglas that he briefly left the Continent, traveling by boat to Tunis, until he got word from Orioli that it was safe to return to Italy.[11] He was "sick to death of Florence," he wrote to Robin, but he was happy to see Renata and take her out for ice creams. In May the girl added her signature to a letter Douglas sent to Archie.[12]

Two weeks later, Douglas was at Martha Gordon Crotch's door. She asked him what had happened. She wasn't seeking vicarious thrills, like the friends who read Orioli's journals. A woman of the world who was friends with sexual radicals, including the anarchist Emma Goldman and the pornographer Frank Harris, Crotch had an open mind. "I will ever try to be tolerant—to realise that it takes all kinds to make a world—to try to understand the point of view of others towards this sex business," Crotch declared in her diary. But she wasn't aroused by Douglas's pederastic encounters. She wrote, "It sickens and revolts me—the lust after youth—I can't get used to it. It's against my nature—the mother in me—the instinct to protect the child to shield it is outraged by what I hear."[13] She didn't ask what happened for prurient reasons; she wanted to know the truth.

Crotch thought she got what she asked for. "So far as these affairs are concerned he is ultra truthful," she wrote. He was truthful enough to shock her, although what Crotch found shocking may have fallen far shy of what Douglas did. The story Douglas gave Crotch was as follows: Renata's mother was a deaf seamstress and her father was a waiter. The family had little money. Because of their poverty, the parents did not object to Douglas's relationship with their sons Fausto and Marcello, Renata's older brothers. "His intimacy with them was of a varied kind," a fact known to the boys' parents. Douglas helped with the boys' schooling and work, presumably in exchange for sexual encounters. At some point, Renata began coming round to Douglas's apartment to pick up his washing. She liked to linger in the warm apartment. Douglas claimed "he was in love with the child—she inspired him. Her vitality character-fascination was wonderful." Crotch wrote, "When he was telling me the story I asked him point blank what he did to the child." Douglas told Crotch that he had kissed and fondled Renata. He claimed, "The child seduced me," and he "could not keep her away from the house." One time when Marcello came to remove her, Renata screamed in protest. Douglas maintained it was this incident that led a witness to report the relationship to the police.

English newspapers reported that Renata's mother had pressed charges against Douglas, but according to Douglas the police had pressed charges against Renata's mother, accusing her of prostituting her daughter. Marcello came to Douglas's apartment early in the morning of May 31, 1937, to report that his mother and father had been taken to the lockup the night before. Douglas panicked, "knowing of the hatred in Italy at the time for the English & the general political feeling that was making things very tense." So he packed his rucksack and fled for France. He spent one night with his friend Oscar Levy in Monte Carlo then traveled to Vence the next day. Orioli reported that the police arrived an hour after Douglas's departure. In his absence, they subjected Renata to an interrogation and examination, and determined that Renata remained "intacta" and uninjured. At least that is the story that Douglas told Crotch. It was a self-serving narrative. "For some time past there had been a wave of 'purity' passing over Italy—many men—well known got scared & ran—others had to leave," Crotch wrote. Douglas claimed he had been caught up by the *epurazione* campaign.[14]

Harold Acton, who lived in Florence at the time and witnessed the events firsthand, supported Douglas's political account of the scandal. Acton claimed that Renata's parents had no objection to her relationship with Douglas, but "the sight of him strolling through the streets, a *Toscano* between his lips and the girl pattering beside him, was noted by the Fascist authorities at a time when the English were in bad odour." On top of that, Renata's father had been heard making rude remarks about Mussolini. Douglas's lawyer warned that trouble was brewing, but the writer insisted on taking Renata out to a caffè, where he "proceeded to cram her with chocolate éclairs, wiping her chin when the cream overflowed." Soon afterward, Douglas received a call from an Italian Fascist with an English wife, warning him that Rome had issued directions to make an arrest. Douglas's protests that he was old and impotent fell on deaf ears. He had eight hours to cross the frontier. So he bolted.[15]

Archie took his father's age and decrepitude seriously, blaming the affair on Douglas's growing senility. According to Archie, Douglas made a fool of himself with Renata. He used to place a carnation in the keyhole of Renata's door every time he passed the child's house. Archie's explanation fit into emerging diagnostic categories that were refashioning pederasty into pedophilia, a mental illness. The sexologist Richard von Krafft-Ebing, who first introduced the term *pedophile* in his 1886 book *Psychopathia Sexualis*, attributed the perversion to mental weakness resulting from senile dementia, chronic alcoholism, and other mental disabilities. In the twentieth century, the pioneering child psychologist William Healy reaffirmed Krafft-Ebing's claim that senility was a primary cause of pedophilia.[16] But Archie's belief in Douglas's senility appears to have been wishful thinking. Crotch uncharitably observed that Archie was eager for his father to die so he could inherit the estate.

Several of Douglas's friends saw his advanced age in an exculpatory light. Viva King argued that Douglas could not have damaged Renata because he was too feeble. "Norman by then was far too old for any practical corruption," she explained. She claimed that Douglas "loved children, perhaps not wisely but too well," echoing Faith Mackenzie's defense of the pederast poet William Cory. According to King, Douglas was taking the child back to her home when she started screaming. "The neighbours thought that this was caused by the fear that Norman would after all keep her, but actually it was because she had no desire to return to the poverty of her home, where she would be parted from her sugar-daddy." King laid blame for the scandal squarely on Renata, who used Douglas as a "sugar-daddy," then threw a tantrum when separated from him.[17] She drew this account from Douglas himself, having never met the child.

Crotch also tried to shift some of the responsibility from Douglas to Renata. "If one brings cold reason to bear on facts ones realises the bairn was a Latin—abnormally sexual," Crotch wrote.[18] Despite Crotch's descriptions of herself as a defender of children, her moral antipathy to adult-child sex did not turn out to be absolute. Context mattered. Sex between an adult and a child was less problematic when the child was from an abnormally sexual ethnicity, or when the adult in question was Norman Douglas.

The Nietzschean philosopher Oscar Levy thought that Douglas's extraordinariness justified his sexual encounters with children entirely. "The Italians ought to have sent you yearly 12 boys and 12 girls as did the Athenians to the Minotaurus of Crete. On account of your literary merits. And because you are _not_ a minotaurus, but a nice gentleman, who does the children good," Levy wrote to Douglas immediately after the scandal erupted.[19] Douglas, who always justified his affairs as benefiting the children, appreciated this letter from Levy so much that he wrote "keep" across the top, when he sorted through his correspondence. But Levy's attitude was growing rare. Douglas could not expect widespread toleration of pederasty by the late 1930s.

Douglas would have liked to keep the cause for his flight from Florence secret, as he had done when he was forced from Austria, but he couldn't because England's scandal rags had caught wind of his troubles. Stories appeared in the *News of the World* (a Douglas favorite), as well as the *Referee* and the *Dispatch*. Once people found out what happened, Douglas had to come up with some response. He did his best to explain away his legal troubles as political. Douglas wrote to Faith Mackenzie, "I daresay you know there was some trouble in Florence—with a girl, for a change. Anyhow, I cleared out. The English papers got it all wrong, and made it much worse and more sensational than it was. That can't be helped. I am told there was a political background to the whole business."[20] He made the same excuse to Archie: "I am told there was a political background to the affair—English being very unpopular in Italy just now."[21] Archie and Mackenzie were both loyal to Douglas and could be relied on to pass his story along.

If there was a political dimension to Douglas's threatened arrest, it had nothing to do with any activism on his part. He considered himself non-political, completely averse to all -*isms*, no matter where they fell on the partisan spectrum. "Everything that ends in 'ism' is just bullshit, so far as I am concerned," he wrote to Nancy Cunard, an avowed radical.[22] When Cunard asked Douglas to contribute an essay to *Authors Take Sides*, her volume on the Spanish Civil War, he responded "Nobody is going to compel me to 'take sides'. To hell with sides."[23] His philosophy was to live for himself and damn everyone else to hell. "Politics are no concern of scholars, my dear," he told Bryher.[24]

But Douglas was also constitutionally averse to rules and rule-makers, which made him despise Fascism in particular among all the -*isms*. He complained vociferously to Crotch about "Mussolini's effort to clean up everything," calling it "hygiene gone mad."[25] Later, after the 1939 Munich Agreement, he called Mussolini and Hitler "gangsters" who deserved to be put to death "on the spot."[26] He despised the English expatriates who sided with the Fascists, like Oscar Wilde's old friend Reggie Turner, and the poet Ezra Pound, who met with Mussolini and produced pro-Fascist anti-Semitic propaganda during World War II.[27] Douglas wrote a four-line clerihew excoriating Pound:

> Ezra Pound
> Covers a good deal of ground
> Would—I begin to wonder—it
> Be better if he were under it?[28]

In short, never one to hide his opinions, Douglas made himself obnoxious to the Fascist authorities in Florence by his aversion to their politics as well as by his sexual behavior. At least that's what Orioli heard, in the weeks following Douglas's flight from Florence. Within an hour of Douglas's departure, Orioli had begun to busy himself with looking after his friend's interests. He soon met with Renata's brother Fausto, reporting to Douglas that "no one in the family is against you and all of them refuse to believe what they have accused you and the girl."[29] It may have helped that Douglas had offered Fausto a suit of clothes and two hundred lire, as well as school fees for Renata.[30] Orioli also met with Douglas's lawyer, a Mr. Carrozza, who began the legal process of clearing the path for Douglas's return by persuading the legal authorities to drop the threatened prosecution.

Throughout June, Douglas remained hopeful that he would soon be able to return home. But the situation grew bleaker in July, and Douglas asked Orioli, who had the keys to his apartment, to go through his belongings and destroy any incriminating evidence. Orioli took care to eliminate suspicious photos of children that Douglas had held on to, and he hid others in his own secret cupboard.[31] The case dragged on through the fall. Carrozza continued to work on appeals well into 1938.[32] At the end of January, Douglas heard from Carrozza that "everything is definitely finished," but he was still distrustful and declared, "Of course I shan't go there—not likely."[33] Douglas wasn't willing to take the chance of being arrested on his return.

During this period of limbo, Douglas remained in Vence. Crotch installed him in an empty apartment owned by friends. In July, Archie arrived in Vence after first making a stop in Florence to collect documents from his father's apartment. (Douglas later alleged that Archie stole valuable items from the apartment during that visit.)[34] Archie liked the bohemian town, which he had first visited in 1933, and he liked Crotch, whom he called "Auntie." He decided to lease a house in Vence for a year, along with his girlfriend of the moment, Eve, and her six-year-old daughter, Jacquie.[35]

"Vence is the funniest place," Crotch wrote, "& I seem to be the centre of something that draws people here—then they usually find some lost or discarded part of their lives hanging on to me."[36] Archie was one of those lost souls, hoping to find himself through meals shared with his father at Auntie's table. But it was not so easy. Father and son had not lived in the same place since Douglas sent Archie to school in England. Though they kept up a frequent and honest correspondence, the men saw each other only rarely. When they were reunited in Vence, Douglas found Archie unpleasant company.

"Queer development with Archie!" Douglas wrote to Orioli. "Archie has eczema all over, drinks too much."[37] Crotch described the situation in even more damning detail. Archie, she said, was "a mass of exema—but he drinks all day long & eats like an ogre." Every night he and Eve would go out, locking Jacquie in her room, and they would get terribly drunk, then return to their house and get in fights, throwing things at each other until they woke the child, who would scream loud enough for the neighbors to hear. When Archie and Eve weren't arguing, they were fucking. Archie liked to brag about his need to have sex three times a day, once after each meal. Crotch found his boast revolting. Douglas told Crotch that Archie's problems stemmed from being "badly knocked about" in the war. He had never recovered from being "shelled shocked [and] buried in a shell hole."[38] Douglas was less eager to admit his own culpability for his son's problems. Douglas's possible sexual abuse of Archie, his cruelty in permanently separating Archie from his mother, and his farming out of Archie to be raised by other people all must have contributed to his son's deep unhappiness.

Any hopes of a happy father-son reunion were interrupted by the reality of Archie's dysfunction. Soon Douglas was desperate to escape his son. "I am frightfully sick of Vence," he wrote to Orioli in late July.[39] Ever faithful, Orioli came to the rescue, spiriting Douglas away for a trip together to Corsica. Douglas sent Archie frequent and friendly postcards while they were away, advising him not to drink too much and asking after his health. The two were closer in absentia than when inhabiting the same town.

Eventually, Douglas and Orioli had to return. In October Douglas was back in Vence, and the situation with Archie was no better. While Douglas was gone, Eve had gotten pregnant and attempted suicide. She survived and contrived to miscarry the baby, which she told Auntie she had done dozens of times before.[40] The landlord wanted to kick Archie, Eve, and Jacquie out of their lodgings. Crotch pressured Douglas to speak with Archie about the untenability of his domestic life. She was worried that Archie encouraged Douglas into bouts of heavy drinking that his fragile constitution could no longer endure. Douglas told Crotch, "A. will down me unless I down him."[41] Finally the situation reached a breaking point, and Eve decided to return to England and place Jacquie with a relative. Archie followed soon after, leaving Douglas alone in Vence. The two men got along best when separated by a body of water.

Douglas moved into Archie's rooms only to discover that Archie hoped to stick him with the overdue rent bill.[42] His troubles didn't end there. Maybe Douglas was growing senile. He seemed unable to stop himself from repeating his past mistakes, despite the tenuousness of his situation. In November 1937, he befriended a ten-year-old boy named Chico Cramer, whose mother was a Dutch artist, recently returned to Europe after spending time in the United States. Chico's parents liked Douglas and expressed no concern about the hikes that Douglas began to take with their son through the hilly Provençal terrain. Crotch struggled to rationalize the affair. She argued to herself that Douglas would be "a delightful companion for the lad," as long as he remained sober.[43] However, villagers who knew Douglas's reputation began to gossip. Disaster was narrowly avoided when Chico and his family left Vence. They sent Douglas affectionate letters from their travels. "He misses you very much times and all at once can get a longing to be with you. Especially when he comes to a new place he longs for you to explore it with you together, I guess. He realizes even more now what a marvelous friend you were for him. We all miss you so often," Chico's mother wrote to Douglas. "I wish you war here," Chico wrote.[44]

By then, Douglas had transferred his affections. In spring 1938, Douglas made friends with a Corsican boy named Gabrielle, or Gaby for short. The boy was the adopted son of a dissolute family, one of three siblings who according to Crotch were "badly neglected" and "lived in squalor and dirt." Douglas met the children in a bar run by their father and befriended them by giving them cakes and money. Soon Gaby, who was particularly neglected, began visiting Douglas's apartment, so he could eat home-cooked meals prepared by the housekeeper. Douglas took Gaby on long walks through the hills. His attentions to the boy soon caught the eye of a group of local Catholic women who were hoping to remove Gaby from his adopted parents and place him with a French scout mistress. One of the Catholic women complained to Crotch about the "old Englishman" who gave Gaby cakes and money and taught him "all kinds of wickedness." The police, the woman claimed, were keeping Gaby under surveillance. Crotch was struck by the gravity of the situation. "The whole seriousness of what I had been told hit me like a blow. N.D. was in danger of having another incident added to his record."[45]

When Crotch saw Douglas the next day, she told him what she had heard, and he took flight. He was running out of countries where he could flee, but he had not yet burned his bridges in Switzerland. On June 8, he wrote to Archie from Lausanne, asking for news of the situation in Vence. Archie had returned to the French village in the spring and renewed his disastrous relationship with Eve (Jacquie remained in England with her father). Over the next couple weeks, Douglas sent a series of anxious letters to Archie, signing his name "Richard" in a lame attempt to disguise his identity.[46] Nothing seemed to have come of the Catholic women's threats to go to the police, and Douglas at last judged it safe to return to France. In late June, he joined his friend Oscar Levy in Étretat, a resort town on the Normandy coast.

Crotch felt betrayed by this turn of events. Douglas had broken his promise to her that he would "never do anything in this little place that cd. be criticised." She was beginning to entertain Archie's assessment that Douglas was going senile. "He just can't help it," she wrote in her diary. "A child of either sex has such a fascination for him it is uncanny—He can't keep his hands off them & from what he has told me—he never could."[47] Perhaps Douglas had never been able to resist his erotic desire for children, but he had been able to act on those desires with less trouble in the past. Between 1936 and 1938, Douglas fled arrest in three different countries on at least four different occasions. The increased frequency of his troubles with the law raises the question: Was Douglas changing or was it the world around him? Had senility made Douglas less capable of disguising his behavior, or was a world in the grips of Fascism less willing to tolerate the long-standing sex trade between needy children and wealthy adults? The answer to each of these questions probably was both at once.

Ironically, as Fascism sought to "purify" European sexual culture, the wars provoked by the rise of Fascism created an upsurge in the numbers of needy children who might be drawn into the sex trade. When civil war broke out in Spain in fall 1937, Douglas told Cunard that he would be happy to adopt a Spanish refugee child if she found a likely candidate during her frequent reporting missions to the country.[48] Nothing came of Douglas's initial offer. In August 1938, however, when Douglas visited Cunard at her house in Réanville, a Normandy town halfway between Paris and Étretat, he became enamored of a fourteen-year-old refugee named Gervasito who was living with his mother, Narcisa, in Cunard's house. Gervasito won Douglas's affections with his renditions of Republican marching songs. Narcisa was impressed by Douglas as a "great man," but not so impressed that she was willing to agree to his request to carry Gervasito away with him for a trip to Goa, India.[49]

Soon Cunard returned to Spain to report on the war and its refugees. In early September 1938, Douglas traveled to Paris to meet Cunard on her return. Douglas was happy to discover Narcisa and Gervasito living in the city. On September 8, he sent Martin Secker a postcard from the famous Left Bank watering hole Café de Flore, which bore a note from Gervasito: "Je suis espagnol, j'ai 14 ans et je vous remercier de tout mon coeur ça que vous avez voulu faire pour mes compatriotes."[50] Orioli, who came to see Douglas in Paris, was not impressed with Gervasito, calling him "an uncouth youth with tiresome habits." Orioli wrote to Crotch promising that Douglas wouldn't bring Gervasito with him down to Vence, since the boy would be sure to "make an awful lot of talk if he did."[51] As it turned out, Douglas never had the chance. One day at the Café de Flore, Douglas pointed Picasso out to Gervasito, and soon the boy attached himself to the famous Spanish painter instead.[52]

Douglas's interest in Spanish refugee children was not extinguished by

Gervasito's defection. The following year, he asked Cunard to find another Spanish refugee boy whom he could take in. In June 1939, Cunard introduced Douglas to a ten-year-old Basque refugee named Gustavo. But Douglas found the boy too dull.[53] After the failed meeting, Cunard told Douglas not to bother trying to adopt a Spanish child. "The fact of the Spanish character which is entirely different to the Italian character . . . will always be too much of a bar," she explained.[54] She may have been trying to warn Douglas that the sexual expectations he had developed from his long residence in Florence would not be welcomed by the refugees pouring out of Spain.

By then, Douglas had moved to the port town of Antibes, where there were new distractions. He made friends with Marcel, the nine-year-old son of his landlady, Jeanne Mercier. They went on walks together, and Douglas took the boy swimming every afternoon.[55] Despite his recent experiences in Vence, Douglas took no efforts to conceal his infatuation with children. For example, when Crotch had lunch with Douglas in Antibes in 1939, she was shocked to watch him fondle a little girl at the café, offering the child sips of his whisky and pinches of snuff. Crotch told Douglas that people were watching and tried to get him to leave the girl alone. "I don't care—let 'em look," Douglas retorted. Crotch finally got up and left the café.[56] The world was changing around him, but Douglas remained uncloseted, despite the obvious dangers.

Toward the end of his time in Antibes, Douglas also had one of his rare flirtations with an adult woman, a glamorous twenty-six-year-old named Elizabeth Gwynne, who had arrived in Antibes on a dinghy that she sailed through France's rivers and canals with her married lover Charles Gibson Cowan. Britain had declared war on Germany on September 3, and Cowan was hoping to escape the draft. By the time Gwynne and Cowan reached Antibes, their relationship was on the rocks. Gwynne fell in love with Douglas, who took her on his usual itinerary of hillside walks and meals at harborside restaurants. On May 2, 1940, Gwynne added her signature to a letter sent by Douglas to Archie, placing her in the company of a select number of the writer's favorite young lovers.[57] Eight days later, the German army marched into Belgium, the Netherlands, and Luxembourg. Gwynne and Cowan set off in their boat for Greece. By the next time Douglas saw her, after the war, Gwynne had a new married name, Elizabeth David, and was beginning her career as the most influential British food writer of the postwar era.

The German army marched into northern France, leading France to surrender on June 22. In the unoccupied south, where Douglas lived, the collaborationist Vichy government took power. Those in Douglas's circle were clearing out of the Continent. Orioli escaped to Portugal, hoping to reach the Azores. Bryher left her villa on Lake Geneva and returned to England (where she arranged to provide an annuity for the ever-broke Douglas).[58] Crotch went to the United States. Archie moved to Scotland. Levy went to Oxford.[59] The roads around Antibes were blockaded and food was scarce, as were coffee, tea, and soap. "This malnutrition is beginning to run me down," Douglas wrote on December 27.[60] Elizabeth David's cousin Neil Hogg, who worked for the British consulate in Lisbon, helped Douglas get a travel visa to neutral Portugal.

Douglas arrived in February 1941 and went to stay with Peter Pitt-Millward, an old friend from Capri. But Pitt-Millward left Portugal in May, dumping Douglas back in Lisbon. Stranded and broke, Douglas relied on the kindness of Hogg. He remained in Portugal for a year. During that time he reconciled with Orioli, who had distanced himself from Douglas after inheriting a fortune from Reggie Turner. Then Orioli died suddenly on January 2, 1942.[61] Hogg was recalled to England, leaving Douglas homeless. He couldn't stay in Portugal, which had only extended him a temporary residence permit.[62] He was left with only one choice. "It makes me quite sick to go to England and probably be buried there and never see certain friends again, but there is no help for it," he wrote.[63] At the end of January 1942, after twenty-five years' absence, Norman Douglas returned to Britain.

CHAPTER SEVENTEEN

England Is a Nightmare

The streets of Chelsea were black at night as Norman Douglas stumbled home from evenings spent at the Cross Keys Pub, across the Albert Bridge from his old lodgings in Battersea. His crowd from the *English Review* days were gone. Conrad, Lawrence, Ford, Galsworthy, Seccombe, and Hudson, all dead; and Belloc laid low by a stroke. But Douglas rarely drank alone. In the spring of 1944, Douglas spent many evenings at the Cross Keys in the company of a new generation of writers including Constantine FitzGibbon, Brian Howard, Desmond Ryan, and John Davenport. Amid the desolation of war, Douglas went on like an ox, his robust constitution unbowed by seven decades of hard living. One night Theodora FitzGibbon, who was married to Constantine, overheard Douglas get into a spat with Brian Howard after the Cross Keys closed. Howard, concerned for the old man's safety in the blackout, had reached for Douglas's arm to guide him down the narrow sidewalk of Upper Cheyne Row. "Do stop holding my arm, please," Douglas insisted. The steps are very difficult to see, Howard protested. "I had to live on nothing but carrots in Estoril for two weeks, and my eyesight is much better than yours, duckums, I'm sure," Douglas snapped.[1]

The drama of the war years left Douglas as unaffected as his years of heavy drinking. In spring 1944, as London was being bombarded by the Luftwaffe, Douglas wrote to Levy, "I have now been two years and more than two months in this country; they have been the most uneventful and also the most unhappy of my life."[2] He dismissed the V-1 and V-2 missiles as minor irritations. When the air-raid sirens went off, he told Archie, "I take no notice of them; just turn around in bed." He was "quite fatalistic" about the danger.[3] Harold Acton said Douglas "took the buzz-bombs in his stride." He was far more concerned about the lack of good food and drink in wartime London than he was about getting blown up by the Nazis.[4]

As soon as he had arrived in England, he began to complain about the rations. The food, after Lisbon, left much to be desired. "Wine and tobacco and whisky and other necessities of life are hard to come by," he wrote to Hellé Flecker.[5] He couldn't readjust to the poor fare available at the city's pubs, where the choices were shepherd's pie, fish pie, and so-called sausages. He tried to revisit Genarro's, an Italian restaurant in Soho that had once been his favorite, but the cooking was terrible. He was reduced to eating a "filthy sandwich" for dinner many nights.[6] Douglas grieved for the lack of pederastic sexual opportunities in London as much as he grieved for the lack of good food. World War II London wasn't the best place to pick up boys, since so many of the city's children had been evacuated. But as with whisky, he longed for what he could not have. The writer Maurice Richardson had lunch with Douglas in 1943 at the Author's Club. By the end of the meal, "Norman was enthusing about the smell of children's armpits and I got faintly embarrassed," Richardson recalled.[7]

Douglas befriended at least one boy during his London years, Prince Rupert zu Löwenstein-Wertheim-Freudenberg, or Rupie, as he was known for short. Later famous as the financial manager for the Rolling Stones, Rupie was nine in 1942. As he recalled, "My family knew Norman Douglas quite well and he was very kind to me. He became a sort of god-father and took me to exhibitions and the odd film and gave me books which he though suitable for educating a child. They were mainly Greek myths and legends."[8] Their friendship also included quotidian pleasures, like trips to the fun fair. Rupie didn't say whether Douglas attempted any sexual contact with him. It's possible that Douglas settled for mere proximity to Rupie and sagely avoided any grounds for arrest. It's just as likely that Douglas did pursue sexual encounters with Rupie and got away with it. Reflecting on this childhood relationship many years later, Rupie either didn't remember the encounters as abusive, or he didn't care to discuss his abuse in public.

Douglas distracted himself from the general absence of boys in his wartime life by spending a lot of time with women friends. His wartime diaries include frequent use of sexual symbols, both the Venus mark and the Mars mark, placed after the last names of friends, including King and Mackenzie. He may have been keeping track of letters or meetings, using the sexual symbols to distinguish between husbands and wives who shared a last name. Or he may have been following earlier patterns of marking sexual encounters in his diaries, in which case these years suggest an uptick in encounters with women. He certainly spent a lot of his time with women during the war.[9]

His first stop after arriving in England was at the home of his friend Faith Mackenzie, who was living in a small cottage on the far western edge of Hampstead Heath. The house was too remote and too cold for Douglas, who had never appreciated the English countryside.[10] He went next to Susan Palmer, an aspiring painter he'd known for years. Like many of Douglas's women friends, Palmer had the advantage of a wealthy family.[11] Her father, Arnold Palmer, was a writer and book reviewer, and a fan of Douglas's writing. He owned an apartment in London at Apsley House, on Finchley Road, where he was happy to host Douglas for a spell. Susan Palmer did her part by hiring Douglas as an Italian tutor, providing him with a small income.

When the Palmers needed the room again, Douglas went to stay with Nancy Cunard at her hotel, Cliffords Inn, on Chancery Lane. Despite Cunard's willing hospitality, Douglas decided he needed his own rooms, and he found lodgings at the charmless Symonds House in Mayfair, across the street from the five-star Claridge's Hotel, where he had stayed during his younger and wealthier days.[12] A few months later, he moved to a flat on Half Moon Street, near Cunard's new lodgings on Queen Street.

Douglas and Cunard spent a lot of time together during the war years, drinking and eating in London's pubs. At least, Douglas ate. Cunard notoriously lived off alcohol and cigarettes. They patronized Verreys, Shellys, the Ladder Club, Ye Grapes, and the King's Arms in Shepherd Market.[13] Sometimes Cunard took Douglas to the Café Royal brasserie, which managed to serve reasonable food throughout the war years, if at exorbitant prices. There was rarely whisky to be found, but Douglas made the best of the Reid's Stout and other British beers on tap. He may have shaken off Brian Howard's advances, but he was happy to cling closely to Cunard as they made their way home at night in the dark. There were eighty-nine steps, Douglas told Cunard, between his rooms and hers.[14]

At the time, Cunard was in the midst of a passionate affair with the American journalist Morris Gilbert. But perhaps when Gilbert wasn't around, she and Douglas had a sexual relationship. On Christmas night, 1943, Cunard hosted a little party at her bedsit. At the evening's end, Cunard and Douglas were alone together. "Come sit by me on the sofa," he said to her. They lay down together on the narrow sofa, "playing at being in the *Wagon Lits*," as

Cunard put it, imagining they were crossing France toward Italy, "and as romantic about it as could be! *And why not?*" Cunard hadn't known Douglas
when he was young, "but, damn it," she wrote, "the charm you had then in
1943, at the age of seventy-five. . . ."[15]

Although he complained of rheumatism and giddiness, Douglas looked
hale and healthy. Cunard said he arrived in London appearing "strong, rosy,
well-fed, [and] ready to cope with everything!"[16] He still commanded a tremendous charisma that drew friends and admirers beyond what he could
tolerate. In Florence, he had kept his address private to avoid enthusiastic
fans seeking out his company. In London, someone gave away his Half Moon
Street address, and Douglas was bombarded by visitors. "I am overrun with a
pack of fools of both sexes who waste my time and get my address," he wrote
to Archie. "I have implored everybody not to give it [but] they tell each other,
and then all their friends, and that begins the mischief."[17] Pederasty was becoming increasingly intolerable in the mid-twentieth century, but Douglas's
scandalous celebrity continued to attract admirers. In April 1943, Douglas
tried to escape his fans by moving into a spare bedroom in the flat of an old
Capri friend, Nigel Richards, in Hereford Square, South Kensington. Then
Richards enlisted as a rear gunner with the RAF and was shot down over Germany in 1944. Douglas moved on to another Kensington address, Southwell
Gardens.

Wherever he moved, Douglas continued to attract new friends. He met
Constantine and Theodora FitzGibbon at the Cross Keys Pub, which he frequented while living in Southwell Gardens. Theodora was the first of the pair
to attract his attention. A beautiful actress in her late twenties, she was a former lover of the surrealist painter Peter Rose Pulham, and an acquaintance
of artists including Balthus, Cocteau, and Dalí. She had married Constantine
FitzGibbon, an aspiring writer, during the war. The couple often went drinking at the Cross Keys. One night a white-haired stranger asked Theodora her
name. "Theo FitzGibbon," she answered. "Nonsense . . . that was my wife's
name," Norman Douglas said. As it turned out, Constantine FitzGibbon was
a cousin of Douglas's wife, on her father's side. In a letter to Archie, Douglas
described Constantine as "very pleasant."[18] In fact, Constantine was a hard-
drinking womanizer, given to knock-down fights with his wife. But Theodora
truly was exceedingly pleasant.

When Constantine's military service sent him away from London, Douglas began to spend increasing time alone with Theodora.[19] She called him

"Uncle Norman," like many of his younger friends did.[20] It sounded unthreatening, but Theodora was well aware of Douglas's predatory sexuality. Once Douglas took Theodora for a long walk across Hampstead Heath, remarking on the looks of the girls they passed. She recalled, "Having heard a little about his unusual sex life I remarked on this interest, to get the sharp answer: 'Pretty girls are my business!'"[21] In short, Theodora had heard about Douglas's sexual relations with boys and was surprised to see him pay attention to the girls they passed. Theodora, who was born in 1916, had come of age during an era in which a new model of homosexuality was replacing older ideas about pederasty.[22] Homosexuality as Theodora understood it was part of a binary system of sexual orientation, in which people were either attracted to their own sex or the opposite sex. Age mattered less in this construction of sexual identity. But Douglas never identified as a homosexual. As a category, adult men likely held the least sexual appeal to Douglas, coming after boys, girls, and adult women. Douglas elaborated on his sexual tastes to Theodora during their years of friendship, and she admired him for his forthrightness. "He loved to shock," she wrote, "and it was this mixture of immense and diverse knowledge, classicism, lucidity and bluntness to the point of bawdiness which made him perhaps the most interesting person I have ever met."[23]

Another female friend Douglas made during the war, Viva King, who was a generation older than Theodora FitzGibbon, had a better understanding of Douglas's sexual self-conception. Once known as the "queen of Bohemia," King was a central figure in London's artistic circles during the interwar years. She and her husband, Willie King, a curator at the British Museum, were both sexually attracted to young men. The Kings met Douglas at a dinner party in 1943, and afterward Viva sought out Douglas's friendship, inviting him for meals at her flat in Thurloe Square. Douglas's resistance to dining in other people's homes had been worn down by years of empty pockets and poor food. In 1945 Douglas moved close to the Kings in Thurloe Square.

Over drinks in Viva's parlor, they often discussed sex. "Norman was not, as most people think, a homosexual but rather a pan-sexual, if there is such a word," Viva King claimed.[24] There was such a word, and it seemed especially fitting for Douglas, who had often been likened to Pan. King described him as an "old pagan." Once she asked him to admit that "sex with a woman is better." According to King, he answered, "You're damn right, my dear, it's far better and more mysterious." King was not a reliable reporter, and it's likely that she invented this remark. Or perhaps Douglas was telling King what she wanted to hear. It's possible they had a sexual affair. They were intimate enough to plan a getaway to Somerset in the summer of 1943.[25] King also claimed, unreliably, that after Douglas and his wife were separated, he often went to visit her on the Continent "because she was such a good fuck." In short, she depicted Douglas as heartily enthusiastic about sex with women.

At the same time, King was clear-eyed about Douglas's sexual interest in children. One evening she and Douglas got onto the subject of whether sex should be taught in schools. "Norman was asked his opinion as to whether ten years old was too young for such knowledge. 'Nonsense,' he replied, 'children can't learn early enough what fun it is.'"[26] Douglas refused to disavow children's entitlement to sexualized pleasure. King found Douglas's outré comments more funny than shocking: "In the matter of humour, Norman and I were as one and I have laughed with him more than anyone I knew." Another time when she was shocked by the sight of a "deformed" man, Douglas made her laugh by saying, "I have just been having a little affair with him, my dear."[27] King admired Douglas's "devilish" sexual amorality.

Willie King admired Douglas as much as his wife did. He hired Douglas to tutor him in Italian, supposedly to help with his wartime cipher work at Bletchley Park. The arrangement was probably more for Douglas's benefit than his own. King had inherited enough wealth from his aristocratic family to be generous with his friends.[28] He also volunteered to serve as Douglas's literary agent and executor, hoping to generate revenue for Douglas through book sales. Douglas's royalties amounted to only a meager eighteen pounds in 1942. That is "what it is to be a distinguished writer," Douglas complained in a letter to Archie.[29] The lack of royalties was especially galling in light of the enormous popularity of pirated editions of Douglas's *Some Limericks* among American soldiers, a popularity that pointed to at least some ongoing popular appreciation for pederastic humor.[30]

If Douglas had the inspiration to write new books, he may not have felt so grieved by the lack of royalties for *Some Limericks* and *South Wind*, which was considered out of copyright in the United States. But Douglas was in a reflective, rather than creative, mind-set. "I have shut up my little writing shop for good," he told Theodora FitzGibbon.[31] The absence of access to boys in wartime London deprived him of inspiration. He did his best to make money from old works. In 1941 he put together his almanac of aphorisms, dedicating it to Neil Hogg in gratitude for hosting him in Lisbon. But he printed only fifty initial editions, which he distributed to friends.[32] Then in 1943 he wrote a series of reflections on his books for Bryher's wartime literary magazine, *Life and Letters*. Bryher's personal generosity, however, likely yielded Douglas more income than this small writing job. Eventually, Douglas collected the pieces he wrote for Bryher in a book titled *Late Harvest*, published after the war.

Douglas also sat down with Willie King and reviewed his previous works, line by line, filling in salacious details, adding commentary, and correcting pseudonyms. The men fastidiously worked their way through *Looking Back*, *Alone*, *In the Beginning*, *Birds and Beasts of the Greek Anthology*, *Paneros*, and *South Wind*. Douglas treated his own writing with his customary scholarly care. He noted each of the obscene words and sentences that had been cut from *In the Beginning*. He supplied citation information for references to books within the texts. He even corrected a handful of minor mistakes he had made (for example, in *South Wind* he once erred in describing the moon cycle).

Maybe the whistling bombs had more effect on Douglas than he was willing to admit. The war had put him in a fatalistic mood. He was beginning to consider his legacy. He wanted to be remembered for his books, but the personal notoriety that had once improved his book sales now threatened to swamp the memory of the texts themselves. This possibility upset Douglas, who despite the scoffing humor of his narrative voice had approached his writing with great seriousness. He wanted to be remembered more as a writer than as a character.

He liked a biographical essay that had been written about him by his friend Richard Dawkins in 1933. Dawkins put the books before the man. He wrote that Douglas "has let us see a great deal of himself in his books, and what he has shown us is, I think, well worth looking at; and what is more, if we do not look at this picture with some care, we are apt to miss not a little of what he has to give us." Dawkins emphasized that knowledge of Douglas's biography served to amplify appreciation of his books.[33] However, Douglas was enraged by an article about him that appeared in the winter of 1941, which flipped the ordering of the personal and the literary.

Richard Aldington's "Errant Knight of Capri" first appeared in the American magazine *Esquire* in December 1941, and then was reprinted in the English magazine the *Queen*, in April 1942. Aldington and Douglas had met in Florence during the 1930s, and Aldington accompanied Douglas and Pino Orioli on more than one of their tours of the Italian countryside, witnessing firsthand the men's sexual encounters with boys. No sexual innocent him-self, Aldington had lived for years with his married older lover, Brigit Pat-more, before unceremoniously dropping her for her younger son's new wife, Netta Patmore. Douglas called the situation "a ridiculous and degrading tangle," and wrote to Bryher, "Thank God I don't get messed up with other people's wives."[34] As it turned out, Aldington was equally disapproving of Douglas's sexual proclivities and was willing to broach the subject in public.

Aldington opened his 1941 article with the sentence, "Every notorious per-son acquires a legend which is repeated round the world by word of mouth until it is solidly established among all the other popular fallacies which people 'know as fact.'" The lede left no doubt that Aldington's focus in "Er-rant Knight of Capri" would be on the man, not his books. The article fol-lowed with a summary of Douglas's life. Although Aldington did not refer directly to Douglas's pederasty, he did write of Douglas's insistence on "com-plete personal freedom."[35] This disclosure would not have upset Douglas on its own. What bothered him was that Aldington's article only attended to his personal notoriety and hardly even mentioned his books, besides a dismis-sive reference to *South Wind* as a "potboiler." On top of that, Aldington had gotten several biographical details wrong. Douglas marked up both copies of the article, correcting errors such as Aldington's claim that he was half Scot, half Austrian. "3/4 Scot, 1/4 German," Douglas scribbled in the margins.[36]

In a letter to the *Spectator*, Douglas laid out his objections to Aldington's article. Rather than enumerate the twenty-three factual errors, as he had in his private notes, Douglas simply described the piece as inaccurate and raised a broader objection to its personal tone. "Why not a few literary criticisms instead of all these tiresome personal details?" he asked. "What astonishes me is that English readers are supposed to relish this kind of empty twaddle about—not about a duchess, but about an ordinary writer." He also noted, to his great distress, that Aldington had announced his intention to tackle Douglas as a biographical subject more thoroughly in the future. "Disquieting news," Douglas remarked. *Caveat lector*: reader beware.[37]

The *Spectator* gave Aldington the chance to respond. "I had not the slight-est idea that I had written anything he would disapprove of, especially as my article in general was laudatory," Aldington protested. What Douglas was ac-tually upset by, Aldington suggested, was the fact that he had sided with Law-rence in the two men's quarrel over the memoirs of Maurice Magnus.[38] Ald-ington was not entirely off-base. In a private letter to Nancy Cunard, Douglas did complain about Aldington's telling of the Lawrence affair. But he insisted that he didn't care on his own behalf, simply for the sake of Magnus, whose character Lawrence had "maliciously distorted."

Douglas told Cunard that he didn't care what anyone said about him in print: "I am far too tough to care a tuppence."[39] Still, there was no denying that Douglas was upset to see his personal life overtake his books in the construction of his legacy. Unfortunately, picking a fight with Aldington only worsened things. Aldington was a spiteful man. When he finally got around to writing his book about Douglas, it would not be as laudatory as "Errant Knight." He would tell everyone what he really thought of Douglas's behavior.

The publication of Aldington's article in winter 1941 forced Douglas to confront the question of his legacy. The desolation of the war made it impossible to ignore the looming possibility of his own imminent death. Douglas's worst fear was that he would die in England without ever again seeing Italy. No matter how long he spent in Britain, he could not adjust to the cold gloom and poor food. "Entre nous, I am slowly eating my heart out," he wrote to Elizabeth David. "I have lived too long on the Mediterranean, and this uprooting is bad for me at my age."[40] This was a frequent refrain in his letters.

He was unhappy in London. Trips out of London into the countryside made him no happier. He made a quick pilgrimage to the family estate in Banchory, where he visited his older brother, but he fled Scotland as soon as possible. Despite frequent invitations, he refused to visit Archie and his new wife Marion and their children, who spent the war in Ayr, south of Glasgow. He took a few getaways to the English coast—Lyme Regis in Dorset, and Mousehole in Cornwall—but they were no substitute for the Bay of Naples or the Côte d'Azur. A trip to the Roman ruins in Chester didn't compare to Taormina or Syracuse. After more than two years in Britain, Douglas wrote to his younger son, Robin, that he was still finding it "difficult to de-Mediterraneanize."[41] He regretted having left Antibes, despite everything he heard about the starvation endured by his friends who remained.[42]

Soon after the Allied invasion of Normandy in June 1944, Douglas began to strategize ways to return to the Continent. "I have applied to go to France for work of any kind," he wrote to Archie in September. He was hoping to return to Antibes, where his former landlady Jeanne Mercier was holding a room for him, but his "ideal" was "to get to Italy as soon as ever possible, sell the place in Florence, and end my days on Capri."[43] Unfortunately, Douglas's advanced age and questionable past made him as unattractive to the War

Office in 1944 as he had been in 1915. No one would hire him. "I get more homesick every day," Douglas told Cunard in June 1945.[44] When the war ended, there were massive celebrations in the streets of London, but Douglas barely took notice. "Nothing interests me," he wrote to Edward Hutton in August 1945, a week after Japan's surrender. "I have been feeling like that ever since I arrived 3½ years ago."[45] All he cared about was getting back to Italy.

By summer 1945, his friends Nancy Cunard, Basil Leng, and Ian Greenlees had all returned to the Continent. They wrote to Douglas telling him that the conditions in France and Italy were awful, but that didn't weaken his desire to return.[46] He was living in a constant state of semi-starvation in England, he said.[47] At last, when Douglas's friend David Jeffreys was appointed British vice consul in Naples, his dream came within reach. In the spring of 1946, he overcame a mountain of obstacles to get his passport renewed, secure a visa to enter Italy, buy tickets for his travel, and make arrangements with his bank to have access to funds when he arrived. On June 21, 1946, Douglas arrived at Victoria Station to catch the train to Dover. A small crowd of friends gathered to see him off: Willie and Viva King, Ian Parsons and Norah Smallwood from Chatto & Windus, Neil Hogg, John Davenport, David Low and his wife. Douglas was in great spirits.[48] After two days and nights on the train, he wasn't in quite as good shape when he arrived in Rome. It was a "bloody journey," but it was worth it. "Have been 3/4 drunk since my arrival," he wrote. "Everything in abundance here. . . . Wine in torrents."[49]

CHAPTER EIGHTEEN

Footnote on Capri

More bombs fell on Naples than on any other Italian city during World War II. When Norman Douglas arrived there in September 1946, after a couple restorative months in Positano, he found a shell of the city he used to know. Buildings were reduced to rubble. But in one regard the city seemed restored rather than ruined, as far as Douglas was concerned. The ragged *scugnizzi*, or street urchins, whom Il Duce once chased away, had returned in great numbers. They walked about shirtless, scrawny ribs poking through their skin, smoking cigarettes, pissing in the streets, and begging for food or money from the Allied servicemen who occupied the city. Depending on perspective, they were a blight or an opportunity. After his arrival in Naples, Douglas lost no time in making the acquaintance of one such boy. His name was Ettore Masciandaro, and Douglas saw him as his last great love. Others saw the relationship in a more sinister light.

Masciandaro was nine years old when Douglas met him. He looked even younger owing to starvation. Masciandaro's home had been blown up in the bombings, and he'd been living in the streets with his mother and two little brothers ever since. His father was a prisoner in Germany. "When I found him in Naples he was a mere skeleton, and so pale that he seemed to be transparent, or at least translucent," Douglas told Bryher.[1] Douglas told different stories of exactly how they met. According to Nancy Cunard, Douglas had saved Masciandaro from a street fight with other Neapolitan toughs.[2] But Harold Acton said that Douglas met Masciandaro in the Galleria Umberto I, a glass-domed structure that was a popular postwar pickup spot for boy prostitutes.[3] Viva King had drinks with Douglas in the Galleria in the summer of 1946 and witnessed the "gangs of small boys scrounging for cigarette ends" who were "much patronized by Norman." Occasionally, King noted, "one saw a boy leading an American soldier—where, one wondered?"[4] This was King's coy way of describing the rampant sex work at the Galleria. One of the boys who Douglas "patronized" was Masciandaro.

Douglas became attached to Masciandaro. When he left Naples for Capri in October, he sought the permission of Masciandaro's mother, Antoinetta, to bring her son with him as his errand boy. He promised Antoinetta he would send Masciandaro to school in Capri. This promise to take care of his education placed Masciandaro in the select company of Douglas's favorite boys, like Eric Wolton and René Mari. Douglas saw Masciandaro as his beloved, or *eromenos*, in a classical pederastic relationship. But everyone else who knew them saw Masciandaro as a scheming delinquent who had gotten his hooks into Douglas and wouldn't let go until he'd shaken the last penny from the deluded old man's pockets. It was postwar Italy, not ancient Greece. The days of *erastes* and *eromenos* were long passed.

Douglas had to admit that educating Masciandaro was a challenge. With Douglas feeding him and clothing him, Masciandaro soon regained his physical health, but he couldn't just shake off the traumas of the war. His ongoing sexual exploitation by Douglas surely compounded his suffering. When they first arrived in Capri, Masciandaro was too "dislocated and restless" to go to school.[5] After a month or so, he agreed to return to the classroom, but more often he could be found passing time with Douglas at the island's caffès. Douglas made no effort to hide the sexual nature of their relationship from public view. Photographs taken on the piazza show Masciandaro touching Douglas or leaning into him. This was one of the main reasons that Douglas had returned to Italy: for the freedom to spend his final years having sex with boys. Douglas wrote to Richard Dawkins, "I am glad to have left England with its filthy food and filthy climate and ten thousand unnecessary restrictions (none here!)."[6] The social world of pederasty that Douglas had known since childhood was fading into history, but postwar poverty and dislocation in Italy ensured that child prostitution remained rampant.

In Capri, Douglas lived under the protection of Edwin Cerio, the former mayor, who loaned him a small apartment on the Unghia Marina, where he moved with Masciandaro.[7] Old ties preserved Douglas from the condemnation of a changing world. Eventually Cerio needed the apartment back, at which point another wealthy patron stepped in to protect Douglas.[8] Bryher

30. Norman Douglas with Ettore Masciandaro on the piazza in Capri, 1947. Norman Douglas Forschungsstelle, Bregenz.

31. Norman Douglas with Ettore Masciandaro, Caterola, 1947. Norman Douglas Forschungsstelle, Bregenz.

agreed to buy a villa in Capri for her former husband, Kenneth Macpherson, and his lover, the Welsh photographer Islay Lyons, on the condition that they provide Douglas a home in its downstairs suite. Douglas and Masciandaro moved into Macpherson's Villa Tuoro in midsummer 1947.[9]

The apartment was only a few small rooms, but the villa had wonderful views of the Faraglioni rocks and Monte Solario. Douglas frequently lunched upstairs, enjoying meals prepared by Macpherson's excellent cook, Tonino. For Douglas's seventy-ninth birthday, Macpherson reported, "Wine and champagne flowed like the fountains of Rome."[10] Macpherson even hired Douglas's old lover Emilio Papa, who had spent much of the war in a concentration camp, to serve as the household's factotum. The reunion between Douglas and Papa was cut short by tragedy, however, when Papa traveled back to Florence to arrange for the sale of Douglas's apartment and was fatally injured in a plane crash during his return to Capri. Papa lingered for six days in the hospital before dying from his burns. Douglas was devastated by the death. He wrote to tell Archie the news three separate times, seemingly incapable of processing the tragedy. "There will never be anybody who can replace him," Douglas wrote, "we shall never find another Emilio."[11] He had lost the companionship of his most loyal former lover, but Douglas remained protected by his many wealthy and powerful friends. He appeared poised to end his days feted as a great man.

But his patrons could not protect Douglas from the impact of changing times. The social norms that had restricted speech around sex and sexuality were loosening. Coy evasions no longer satisfied postwar audiences. There was a lot of curiosity about Douglas, some of it stoked by the influx of tourists to Capri following the end of the war. In September 1949, Douglas even appeared in a pictorial article in *Life* magazine about "pagan" Capri and the "frank lovemaking" of its "bizarre" international set.[12] Douglas warned his friends that "a regular rash of nonsense will come out about me as soon as I am dead."[13] In particular, he worried over rumors that Richard Aldington was working on a very nasty full-length biography of him.

Throughout his life, Douglas had always professed an aversion to what he described as "social curiosity."[14] In his very first book, *Siren Land*, he wrote about a man whom he once befriended whose profession he did not know: "I never had the curiosity to inquire; I like to taste my friends, but not to eat them."[15] The remark carried more than a whiff of aristocratic snobbery. Douglas was raised in a cultural milieu that regarded personal interrogations

32. Norman Douglas (*second from left*) and Emilio Papa (*second from right*) with friends at Positano, 1946. Private collection of Deirdre Sholto Douglas. Photograph by author.

as vulgar. He repeated this sentiment in his 1925 critique of D. H. Lawrence's portrait of Maurice Magnus, writing, "I like to taste my friends but not to eat them; in other words, I hold the old-fashioned view that all interrogation, all social curiosity, is vulgar and therefore to be avoided."[16] Douglas looked down on the lower-middle-class Lawrence for exposing Magnus's personal foibles to the glare of public opinion. Friends of Douglas also recalled him using this line in conversation.[17] It was part of his stable of wisdom to be dispensed to younger friends.

Maybe these protestations were just a defensive mechanism to deter others from looking too closely at his own life. Although Douglas made an art of self-disclosure in his books, he walked a fine line, offering up just enough salacious detail to interest readers while still preserving sufficient discretion to avoid trouble. The problem was that the morsels Douglas offered up made people hungry for more. Victor Cunard, who first met Douglas in 1922, remembered that "at that time, his private life about which he was neither communicative nor secretive, aroused an almost morbid curiosity amongst the inquisitive." According to Cunard, Douglas was "utterly unconcerned about what was said of him."[18] But the truth was more complicated. When the reference volume *Who's Who* wrote to Douglas in 1922 seeking biographical information, he answered by writing crosswise on the preprinted reply form: "The only item in my biography fit for publication is the date of my birth, and that can be revealed at a price which the Who's Who crowd would consider excessive. They will be at liberty, in due course, to print the year of my death, and to stuff it up their backsides."[19]

To Douglas's distress, the queries kept coming. There was no holding back the deluge of interest in his notorious life. Frightened to imagine what nosy journalists, or Aldington, might write about him, Douglas reluctantly agreed to cooperate with Constantine FitzGibbon on an authorized biography. Fitz-Gibbon arrived in Capri in January 1949, armed with two advance contracts, one from the British publisher Cassell and the other from the American publisher Knopf. He and Theodora moved into the Villa Solatia, where Douglas's friend, the Russian writer Maksim Gorky, had lived at the beginning of the century. Each afternoon, FitzGibbon and Douglas would meet at the Arco Naturale, a tavern set in a stone cave, overseen by an old proprietress named Peppinella.[20] FitzGibbon would interview Douglas as the two men drank wine made by Peppinella's husband. Then the following morning FitzGibbon would write up his research before returning to the Arco Naturale with a fresh set of questions. All did not go smoothly. At times Douglas bristled under this regime of questioning. Macpherson remembered one time that Douglas came home from a session with FitzGibbon "in a flap, muttering: Damned bad manners writing about a man in his lifetime."[21] For his part, FitzGibbon grew frustrated by Douglas's "reticence" on key subjects, like Elsa.

Aldington had once called Douglas "infernally reticent about himself."[22] His reputation for privacy on certain subjects was so well known that when several of Douglas's friends agreed to be interviewed for a BBC radio broadcast celebrating his eightieth birthday, they prefaced their remarks with apologies. "On the brink of this intended tribute, I tremble," Roger Senhouse said. "I do not intend to trespass. He has himself marked out the boundaries of our knowledge of his life, and in the light of what he has chosen to tell us—and all that he has left unsaid—I would have to be blind to overstep them—blind and faithless."[23] Senhouse, who had his own secrets to protect, could empathize with Douglas. Senhouse likely would have been mortified to know that after his death an edited collection of letters would be published that revealed the intimate details of his sadomasochistic sexual relationship with Lytton Strachey, including the night they role-played a crucifixion scene.[24]

If Douglas had lived to hear that story, he would have laughed. But he objected to any invasion of his own privacy. He told Macpherson "over and over" that "there were to be no letters published after his passing."[25] When Douglas learned in the 1920s that Robin was selling off letters he'd sent him, he didn't speak to his son again for years. "A peculiarly offensive proceeding—this sale of the private letters of living people as though they were so much cheese or bacon," Douglas huffed. "It testifies to a bestial lack of refinement."[26] Yet he engaged in the business himself when he was hard up for cash, selling letters that Joseph Conrad had written to him. He waited until after Conrad's death, but he still made the sale over the objections of Conrad's literary executor.[27] Douglas was inconsistent and self-serving when it came to his supposedly "cardinal principle" of respecting personal privacy.

He loved gossip. He wrote letters to friends begging for their news of recent scandals in Florence or Vence.[28] But he liked to hold himself above the vulgarity of passing along gossip. As Theodora FitzGibbon explained, "Norman was always a bit miserly about revealing scandal, telling you only so much."[29] For the most part, Douglas's principled objection to social curiosity was about protecting himself from the consequences of his own sexual behavior. This put Constantine FitzGibbon in a difficult position. Douglas agreed to cooperate with FitzGibbon's biography because he thought it would spike other books (particularly Aldington's), but he did so with the expectation that FitzGibbon would present a friendly portrait of himself, and the more questions that FitzGibbon asked, the more unlikely that outcome became.

Biographers of living subjects often have to accommodate their subjects' desires to shape their own legacies.[30] Douglas placed no restrictions on what FitzGibbon wrote. He told the young author, "You can say anything you like about me, provided it is the truth."[31] He had extended this carte blanche to friends before. When Faith Mackenzie was working on her three-volume series of memoirs, Douglas told her, "Say anything you like about me. Say that my real name is Schmidt, that I was a corpse-washer by profession till the Gestapo discovered in me such unusual abilities for intrigue that I am now in secret negotiations with the Portuguese government about Madeira . . . say anything you like, in print, and put it on thick: I don't give a damn; I'm fireproof."[32] Mackenzie didn't take him up on the offer. She wasn't fireproof. She included affectionate portraits of Douglas's wickedness in each volume, but left out the gory details. For example, telling the story of how she gave Douglas an alibi that allowed him to flee England after being charged with sexual assault, Mackenzie left both Douglas's name and the specific charges out of the anecdote.[33]

Constantine FitzGibbon was no more able to take Douglas up on his offer to "write anything" than Faith Mackenzie had been. In the year 1949, he could not write a sympathetic book about Douglas that included information about his relationships with boys, but, on the other hand, he couldn't write truthfully about Douglas's life without centering the boys. After nearly a year on the island, FitzGibbon had only completed four chapters of the biography, ending with Douglas's marriage.[34] He stopped before he reached Eric Wolton.

Douglas had anticipated this problem. His complete advice, as FitzGibbon recalled it in a 1974 essay, was "say anything . . . but I don't know how you're going to get around *Alec*."[35] Long after both Douglas's and Wolton's deaths, FitzGibbon still felt the need to disguise Eric Wolton's identity by calling him Alec in print. The stakes had been much higher twenty-five years earlier, in 1949, when Douglas and Wolton were both very much alive, as were Douglas's sons, whom FitzGibbon considered friends. There was no way to write about Wolton, or the boys who followed, FitzGibbon realized. And if he couldn't write about the boys, then he couldn't write about Douglas as a writer. The books were inspired by his sexual infatuations. They simply could not be left out of an accurate literary biography.

Once FitzGibbon realized the impossibility of completing his book, he became "despondent" according to Theodora.[36] His alcoholism worsened. He abused Theodora. Theodora suggested he turn the material he'd collected into a novel, but FitzGibbon wasn't game. Instead he tendered his resignation to his publishers and turned over the materials to another writer, John Davenport, who was hired by Cassell and by Knopf to complete the book in his place. As much as FitzGibbon experienced the collapse of the book project as a personal failure, Davenport's experiences reveal that it was the subject, not the writer, who was to blame.

Davenport's efforts to produce a book about Douglas were a comedy of errors. Or maybe a tragedy of errors. He had first befriended Douglas in London during World War II and gotten the idea then to write about him. FitzGibbon pipped him to the post, but Davenport gladly took over the contract after FitzGibbon gave up. Nancy Cunard hoped that Davenport would know how to treat "certain aspects" of Douglas's life.[37] Douglas was more dubious. When Cunard asked him how initial interviews in Capri were going, Douglas said simply, "Let 'em write what they like, my dear—let 'em, let 'em."[38]

After Davenport's visit to Capri, he and the radio producer Douglas Cleverdon set out to interview former friends of Douglas in Italy and France. Asking pointed questions, Davenport elicited a fair number of indiscreet answers. But when the two men returned to London, they discovered that the recording machine had malfunctioned. The tape was blank. "Norman's spirit must have chuckled," Harold Acton said.[39] Nothing improved after this inauspicious beginning. Ultimately, Davenport stumbled over the same insuperable difficulty that tripped up FitzGibbon: Douglas's sexual affairs with boys.[40] Davenport died in 1966 without ever having completed the biography. Compton Mackenzie suggested that Davenport's failure was part of a bigger picture: "He had a first-class brain but instead of getting down to the books he was going to write he wrote reviews." And, Mackenzie said, "the unwritten book I regret most was the life of Norman Douglas."[41]

These failed biographers of Douglas set the model for many who followed. Brian Howard, who like FitzGibbon and Davenport got to know Douglas in London during the war, tried his hand at writing a biography of the old man and failed. (Perhaps not so surprising for an author whose own biography is subtitled *Portrait of a Failure*.)[42] D. M. Low, who first met Douglas back during the Florence years, began working on a book about him before the writer died but hadn't completed it by the time of his own death, twenty years later.[43] Allan Massie got the idea to write a biography of Douglas in the 1960s but was talked out of it by John Davenport.[44] And there were other would-be aspirants in the sixties whose names appear in the sources but whose books never reached print: Robert Sandell, Claudine Etienne. All that each left behind was a pile of wrecked dreams. Robin Douglas thought that "no one could write" his father's biography, "because of its complexities."[45]

Douglas's sexual history made it hard for biographers to write about him, but it didn't stop his fans and friends from adoring him. Many admirers came to see Douglas in Capri during his final years and spent long afternoons and evenings drinking with him on the piazza: Elizabeth David, Sybille Bedford, Willie and Viva King, Eric Wolton with his family, Nancy Cunard, Harold Acton. As a new wave of cosmopolitan expatriates settled into the island's villas, Douglas gathered around himself a final circle of friends. In addition to Macpherson and Lyons, there was the writer Graham Greene; the musicologist Cecil Gray; the singer Gracie Fields; the lawyer Arthur Johnson and his wife, Viola; and the English vice consul in Naples, David Jeffreys.

Many of these friends commented how the Capriotes treasured Douglas during his final years. Edwin Cerio engineered an honorary citizenship for Douglas, only the second ever to be granted by the island. Cunard said she had never "come across ONE single person" on the island who didn't know him and love him.[46] Bedford remembered how the "Capresi innkeepers gave him of their best." When they went to dinner, "for the rest of us it was too often stringy *melanzane*, thick macaroni, undistinguished fish," but Douglas got the choicest bites.[47] Some of the restaurateurs on the island he had known for more than fifty years, like Carmela Cerrotta—"La Bella Carmelina"—who had been a famous tarantella dancer at the turn of the century and later ran a caffè near the Villa Jovis. In 1950 she jumped to her death from the upstairs window of her home on Via Tiberio, with her tambourine in hand. The loss cut Douglas, who wrote about her death to Elizabeth David.[48]

Occasionally, Douglas could even be spied on the piazza working on his writing. Although he had exhausted his inspiration and had trouble writing, he helped shepherd two projects to publication at the end of his life. The first was an introductory essay for a collection of Islay Lyons's evocative black-and-white photographs of the island, published in a slim volume titled *Footnote on Capri*. "Not long ago I thought to have closed up my little writing-shop for good and all," Douglas wrote, but "a glance at these admirable photographs has made me change my mind."[49] As accomplished as the photographs were, it's more likely that Douglas wrote the essay out of gratitude to Lyons for providing him a home.

The other project Douglas worked on during his final days was the long-lost proofs for *Venus in the Kitchen*, a set of aphrodisiac recipes that had originated with the proposal Pino Orioli made to Faith Mackenzie in 1928 to translate an Italian cookbook. This humorous little volume filled with impossible recipes for dishes like stuffed sow's vulva and leopard's marrow was the product of many hands, including not just Mackenzie but also Bedford (who would later become famous for her food writing). Silly as the project was, Douglas paid the proofs his customary level of scrutiny, even making small corrections to adjust the recipes.[50]

To his admirers, Douglas appeared vital to the very end. Journalist Michael Davidson and Robin Maugham, the nephew of W. Somerset Maugham, made a pilgrimage together to see Douglas in 1951 and found him drinking

Negronis at the Caffè Victoria, behind the piazza. Shaky on his legs, Douglas was attended by a curly-haired twelve-year-old in orange velvet shorts named Paolo, whose job it was to usher him safely along the steep streets between the piazza and the Villa Tuoro. When Douglas caught Maugham and Davidson checking out Paolo (both men had a taste for boys), he remarked, "I've always loved a very large possession attached to a very small boy." It was another of his signature lines.

The men went to dinner together at Douglas's favorite trattoria. During the meal, a grizzled sailor came by and kissed Douglas's hand. "Thirty years ago he was the prettiest creature on the Piazza," Douglas remarked. Despite his debility, Davidson and Maugham found Douglas still "youthful in mind" and "brimming with fun and wit." The next day Robin Douglas arrived in Capri. He warned Davidson and Maugham that another drunken night like the one before might kill his father. Maugham apologized that they had already made plans to meet again. "Go," Robin told them, "it's on a happy evening with friends like you that he wants to die."[51]

Another pilgrim who sought out Douglas in these final days left with a less positive impression. The young American poet David Louis Posner met Douglas in the piazza and was asked by Macpherson to walk the old man home at the end of the night. Posner captured the deflating experience in verse:

> The tiresome fact is, a man never knows
> he's tuckered out,
> obscene without being funny;

Douglas's witticisms about small boys with big possessions had apparently fallen flat with Posner. Eventually Posner and Douglas reached the Villa Tuoro. They sat out on the terrace and looked at the stars while Douglas waxed on about his favorite themes: his disdain for Christianity, his sexual affairs with local children, and his love for the ancient Greeks. Posner's poem ends on an ambivalent note. Douglas's advice is not meritless. Perhaps the obscene old man isn't funny anymore, but neither is he without wisdom.[52]

As far as Robin Douglas was concerned, his father had become totally senile by then. His carryings-on with Masciandaro and Paolo in the piazza were proof in point. Robin's final visit to Capri was a disaster. Father and son had always been at odds. Years passed in which they didn't speak. Douglas was a neglectful father. Robin had bouts of depression and psychosis that estranged him from many people—he and Archie spent most of their adult lives not speaking to each other. But Robin tried to make up with Douglas at the end.

In the late 1940s, he was living in Chicago with his third or fourth wife, earning decent money working for an advertising company, but suffering from various health woes. He came to visit Capri in fall 1947 and had a great time, writing afterward to his father that he felt "more at home" on the island "than I have felt any place at all, during the past 20 years."[53] Robin had lived in Capri as a toddler, after his parents' divorce, before Elsa tried to get custody. Perhaps he still had memories from those years. When he returned to the United States in November 1947, he began making plans for a return visit. He came three more times, in 1948, 1949, and in September 1951. But his final visit was a disaster.

The fly in the ointment was Masciandaro. Douglas's relationship with Masciandaro was far more combative than his earlier relationships with Wolton, Mari, and Papa had been. There were whispers of trouble in early 1948, when Antoinetta came to Capri to collect her son and bring him back to the mainland. Robin believed that Masciandaro had been evicted from Capri by the local police "allegedly to protect him from N."[54] But where Robin got this information is uncertain, and he certainly wasn't a reliable witness. Some of Douglas's friends thought Antoinetta retrieved the boy as part of a plan to extort money from the old man, although a handful of friendly letters sent by Masciandaro and Antoinetta after his departure suggest the family remained on affectionate terms with Douglas.[55] Indeed, Masciandaro periodically returned to Capri for visits, which became increasingly volatile over time.

Robin's 1951 visit had coincided with one of Masciandaro's return trips. The relationship between the eighty-two-year-old man and the now fourteen-year-old boy had degenerated into violence. Masciandaro, according to Robin, was not just a thief, but a "homicidal neurotic," especially when he was under the influence of alcohol. Macpherson claimed that Masciandaro was institutionalized in a "loony bin" before his visit in fall 1951.[56] But Douglas was completely dependent on the boy, and when Masciandaro left the house, Douglas would fall into "a state of gloom and sulks and hysterics." When Masciandaro was around, Douglas behaved even worse, sometimes acting with such public indecency that Robin was ashamed to be seen in his company. Robin objected equally to Douglas's public sexual attentions to Paolo and to a "grubby little urchin" boy who worked at the caffè in the Arco Naturale.

During a visit there, Robin "saw molestation of that one which filled me with loathing and disgust," he wrote to Macpherson. "What is this peculiar erotic complex of N's for wanting to consort with the scum of humanity?" He had no sympathy or concern for the boys Douglas molested. He hated them with passion.[57]

Robin reserved a special hatred for Masciandaro. "E. is definitely of the scum, that we have known all along and you cannot make a silk purse out of a sow's ear," he wrote to Macpherson, who shared Robin's opinion, calling the boy "a foul little waif."[58] However, Macpherson wasn't willing to go along with Robin's suggestion that they resolve the degrading situation by having Masciandaro murdered. "Personally I think that an accident could be engineered insofar as E. is concerned," Douglas advised Macpherson. "After all, the Mafia is still most exceedingly active and powerful."[59] Robin's advice to Macpherson about what to do with his senile father was equally coldhearted. "N. threatens to commit suicide. Why try to stop him? I maintain that everyone has the right to end his/her life if the means are to hand and the desire is strong enough. If N. has some pills . . . then why try to stop N. from using them?"[60] There was only so much contemptuous and ill treatment a son could put up with, Robin complained. He had reached his limit.

So, it turned out, had Douglas.

CHAPTER NINETEEN

Omnes Eodem Cogimur

The situation in Capri deteriorated rapidly after Robin left. Douglas's health collapsed. He was crippled by arthritis. Erysipelas, a bacterial skin infection he had suffered from since the early 1920s, raged across his face. Arterio-sclerosis cut off the blood supply to his brain. He began to lose his memory.[1] He became hysterical. He hallucinated. The Villa Tuoro was plunged into chaos by the fights that broke out between Douglas and Masciandaro.[2]

On Christmas Day, 1951, in the midst of a luncheon party, Kenneth Macpherson heard screaming from Douglas's apartment. When he was drunk, Masciandaro would scream that he was going to knife all the dirty Englishmen and Germans. Worried that the boy was murdering Douglas, Macpherson burst through the door and punched Masciandaro in the face. He demanded that the boy leave the house. "How DARE you behave like this to your great friend and benefactor," he yelled at Masciandaro. "How DARE you allow our peaceful home to become this Witches' Sabbath," he berated Douglas. Douglas fell down on his knees weeping and begging Macpherson to allow Masciandaro to stay.

Macpherson relented, and over the next several days, Masciandaro came and went at will. On January 1, Douglas came upstairs "blubbering and mewling for his awful crocodile." The boy had left the house in a rage. Douglas threatened to kill himself. "What are you waiting for?" Macpherson wanted to ask. He was desperate to evict Douglas, but the old man was "completely off his rocker." Macpherson felt that his hands were tied. Instead of evicting Douglas, he hired a male nurse to watch him, then took off with Islay Lyons to Anticoli, a bohemian hilltop village fifty kilometers from Rome.[3]

They weren't gone for long when a friend named Jean Vandeleur showed up unexpectedly in Anticoli with a message for them to return to Capri at once. Vandeleur, who lived in Rome, had called the Villa Tuoro to ask Macpherson a question. Douglas took the call instead and insisted that Vandeleur track down Macpherson in Anticoli because he was dying. Vandeleur rented a car and drove through the night with her husband to find Macpherson and Lyons. The next morning, Macpherson called Douglas's nurse, who told him that Masciandaro had left to go to the movies and Douglas had become hysterical, insisting he would be dead in an hour. In fact, he lived through the night and woke up the next morning without any memory of the previous evening's hysterics. The nurse assured Macpherson that Douglas wasn't quite on death's door. "Why isn't euthanasia legally essential?" Macpherson asked Bryher. "Why can't that unfortunate old man just decently kick the bucket?"[4]

Macpherson and Lyons returned to Capri on January 21. Douglas had written a suicide note earlier that day, but he tucked it aside when his friends returned. Two weeks later, on the evening of February 5, he brought it out again and placed it on his desk. He said good night to Macpherson and Lyons. (Lyons's version: "God be with you, my dears. You keep the old bugger. I shan't need him"; or Macpherson's version: "Ta-ta dearie. God be with you. *You* take him. *I* don't want him.") Then he called Lyons back and asked him to bring out the locked suitcase he kept under the spare bed. Lyons knew it contained his pills and offered to get him what he wanted, but Douglas dismissed him with a chuckle. Maybe he didn't want Lyons to feel culpable for what happened next.

That evening Douglas took a fatal dose of painkillers. The next morning Lyons and Macpherson found him unconscious, surrounded by empty glass pill bottles, more pills scattered on the carpet. It took two days for him to die. Douglas's regular doctor, a Capri character known as Dotoressa Moor, tried to resuscitate him, aided by a couple Sisters of S. Elisabetta, but he slipped deeper and deeper into unconsciousness. No one could make out his final incoherent groanings and mutterings. Macpherson claimed he died repeating the word *love*. Lyons joked it was probably "Get those fucking nuns away from me," but later conceded it may have been "love to so-&-so." Douglas died late on the evening of February 7. But his witnesses faked the death certificate to say he had died on the morning of the eighth, so they could have another day to plan the funeral.[5]

In his suicide note, Douglas had asked Macpherson to "make out heart trouble as the cause, for the sake of the reputation of Capri." Macpherson announced that Douglas had fallen into a coma and died peacefully. Rumors spread nonetheless. On the piazza, some people said that Douglas died of leprosy.[6] Others guessed correctly that it had been suicide. Constantine Fitz-Gibbon valiantly denied this in a brief 1953 celebration of his relation's life. "He talked frequently of suicide," but, FitzGibbon insisted, "he did not commit suicide."[7] He probably believed what he wrote. Macpherson and Lyons hid the suicide note from everyone. Only long after Macpherson died did Lyons share the true story. And even then, many of Douglas's surviving friends refused to admit the truth, at least in public.

Before Douglas died, he told Macpherson to "just throw my corpse into the Piazza."[8] He had no money left to his name, and in fact had been giving away items of value to Masciandaro for years, to the resentment of his sons. But his friends and admirers on Capri came together to make his funeral an event. After his corpse lay in state at the Villa Tuoro, his coffin was carried through the streets of Capri to the Protestant cemetery. The procession was led by the island's police, bringing Bryher much amusement.[9] The coffin was followed by his friends on the island. Elena and Nella Papa, Emilio's widow and daughter, came down from Florence. And behind them flowed dozens of Capriotes. Edwin Cerio gave a moving oration. Then the coffin was lowered into a grave between two young cypress trees, facing out across the Bay of Naples toward Vesuvius.

Macpherson had a headstone and tomb carved of verde serpentine marble erected in the cemetery. Inscribed in the stone were the words *Omnes Eodem Cogimur*: Where we all must gather. Douglas had quoted this line from Horace's odes in his first sole-authored book, *Siren Land*. The sirens, Douglas wrote, were "once earth-powers, they have now retired into the dim purple depths of ocean." And so, he observed, "gods and demi-gods go the way of men—*eodem cogimur*."[10] Douglas, Macpherson insisted, belonged among the ranks of gods.

Not everyone agreed. Conflict over Douglas's legacy began straightaway. The first blast across the bow came on February 22, when Harold Nicolson criticized the general tenor of the obituaries of Douglas that had flooded the English press. In his regular "Marginal Comment" column for the *Spectator*, Nicolson wrote that Douglas's obituaries had covered up his shocking behavior by using the rhetorical device of the denial of opposites—for example, *it cannot be said that he was a puritan*. But however much Nicolson might have wished to speak more directly about Douglas's misdeeds, he was no more able to publish the truth than were other obituarists. The words *sex with children* were still unprintable in 1952. Instead, Nicolson settled for declaring himself to be "shocked by people who, when past the age of 70, openly avow indulgences which they ought to conceal," seeming to excoriate Douglas for his refusal to hide his misdeeds. Nicolson admitted that his marginal comment reflected a "very confused state of mind." He criticized hypocrisy in one breath while demanding it in the next.[11]

To Douglas's friends, there was nothing "confusing" about Nicolson's comment. It was a clear attack. The *Spectator* received fifty or sixty letters over the next couple of weeks complaining about Nicolson's article.[12] The magazine published protests from Constantine FitzGibbon, Desmond Harmsworth, Edward Hutton, and Graham Greene. Hutton and Greene appeared as the staunchest defenders of Douglas's character. He was, in Greene's words, "a man more loved by more people than is usually the lot of any of us."[13]

This exchange between Nicolson and his critics established the basic poles of the extended argument over Douglas's legacy that would stretch into the future, even into the composition of this book. Douglas behaved shockingly by having sex with children, but countless people, including many of those children, loved him devotedly. Neither aspect can be left out of an honest rendering of Douglas's life, but neither can they easily be fit together. In Douglas's time, it was easier to tell the story of his greatness and let the mores of the era censor the truth about his wrongdoing. Today we can only see his wrongdoing, and the mores of our era won't permit us to take seriously any claims to his greatness.

Other friends of Douglas complained privately about Nicolson's treatment. The writer Neil Bell wrote to thank Greene for his defense of Douglas, saying that when he read Nicolson's comment, "I thought of writing + saying he lied but I did not think they would print my letter." Willie King also complained about Nicolson to Greene, but didn't write to the *Spectator* because "I have known him for thirty years + cannot squabble with him in print." Peter Hutton wrote to his father that Nicolson's piece was "like a dirty schoolboy telling jokes in some cupboard." Even Robin Douglas, who had wished his father dead at the end, rose quickly to his defense and decried Nicolson's article.[14]

Macpherson underwent a similar rapid reversal in his feelings. Three weeks before Douglas's death, Macpherson had written to Bryher, "I begin to see that the only kind of memoir I can write about N. will be a howling farce!" After Douglas's suicide freed him from the burden of caring for the old man, Macpherson grew to love him once again. He joined the collective outrage against "that dreary Harold Nicolson's attack on the maestro," and began to compile his own appreciation of Douglas in response.[15]

Macpherson's slim volume, *Omnes Eodem Cogimur*, was privately printed in 1953. Illustrated with photographs taken by Islay Lyons, the memoir celebrated Douglas's greatness and minimized his sexual history by treating it as mere naughtiness. Douglas was exhilarating and capable of "flights of brilliance, of wit and erudition, that could sweep one before him as a sapling before a flood." He was a philosopher of pleasure, the last of the ancient Greeks. His penchant for obscenity, in Macpherson's retelling, was an ornament to his brilliance, revealing his lack of pretension. Macpherson included a few of Douglas's witticisms in the book, like the time Douglas sat dozing on the terrace at the Villa Tuoro and a friend tried to wake him up:

"Come on, Norman," says David loudly, "time is short!"
N.D.'s eyes pop open. "Tiny shorts?"

Since Macpherson distributed *Omnes Eodem Cogimur* only to select friends, his readers can be expected to have understood the joke. Of course Douglas's eyes would pop open at the mention of tiny shorts, and the small bodies presumably snuggly encased within them.[16]

Once Douglas died, Macpherson hagiographized him. But other friends felt uncertain about how to memorialize him. Martha Gordon Crotch wrote about the dilemma in her diaries. After spending the war years in the United States, Crotch returned to France in the late 1940s. She and Douglas exchanged occasional letters, but they never resumed their old intimacy. For a long time, Crotch was angry about Douglas's scandalous public attentions to boys in Vence and Antibes, and the effects his behavior had on her own reputation. Later she forgave him. When she heard the news of his death, she was cooking breakfast and thinking about how Douglas would object to her crisping the bacon. Memories of their times together came flooding back. She could hear his voice, and she recalled the shocking stories he used to tell her. She felt his old charm sweeping over her. "Norman D is so much on my mind," she wrote a month after his death. "I must try to write something that gives an idea of him as I knew him. Not easy to do about a man so complex & bewildering as he was." Crotch recognized her own limitations as a writer. "To write truthfully about Norman one would have to use much unprintable language—Heminway [*sic*] perhaps could get away with it—but I'm not Hemingway." To write about Douglas without including the obscene stories he had once told her, however, would diminish his greatness. Some of the stories "must be erased I tell myself. . . . But again, would it not I think be like interfering—altering some great work of art—a wonderful picture— All men of genius depict life in its pristine state—Who would put a vest on Venus—as it were?" Even though Crotch condemned Douglas's sexual history, she saw his greatness as inseparable from his terribleness. That's why she called him the "world's best bad man." To capture Douglas's genius required acknowledging his infamous behavior.[17]

But Crotch wouldn't be the one to write that honest portrait. She published a short essay titled "Some Memories of Norman Douglas" later that year. Like Macpherson's *Omnes Eodem Cogimur*, Crotch's memoir focused solely on Douglas's greatness. She described "the sterling qualities of the man, his deep sense of human freedom, his great love of beauty, his generous heart." She told a few stories of his humor. She recalled the time they first met, when she was on a visit to Florence and she mistook the door to a laundry chute for the door to a bathroom. She tumbled down headfirst and had to be dragged out ignominiously. As friends and strangers gathered round to speculate about what had happened, Douglas appeared and joked she had "gone sightseeing-mad and was trying to locate Dante's Inferno" (Dante being Florence's most famous writer). Crotch's anecdotes captured Douglas's irreverence, but she said not a word about his erotic fixations. She didn't just erase some of those stories—she erased all of them.[18]

Bryher, on the other hand, sought to collect new stories of Douglas after his death. To prepare her own memorial to her friend of thirty years, Bryher interviewed the friends who knew him best. She spoke to Crotch, who described Douglas's knowledge of every little flower, and to Edwin Cerio, who remembered Douglas's devotion to the forests of Capri. She talked to Edward Hutton, who praised Douglas's linguistic skills, and to Louis Golding, who spoke about his impact on a younger generation of writers. Faith Mackenzie opened up about Douglas's ribaldry; Michael Swan described Douglas as naughty. Constantine FitzGibbon repeated Douglas's advice to write anything; Ian Parsons said Douglas "never opened his heart to anyone."[19] The result of all this research was a twenty-four-page transcript that Bryher never published separately, but later shaped into a chapter of her 1963 memoir, *Heart to Artemis*.

Bryher focused her portrait on Douglas's boundless erotic energy. She admired him as a writer and first wrote to him to praise his novel *They Went*. But once they met, what she learned from their friendship had more to do with sex than literature. "He brought me up, like a puppy, by hand," Bryher recalled. He encouraged her "to have a will of my own," or, in other words, to embrace her sexual desire for women, even as he advised her to abide by the public etiquette that would protect her from gossip. He made no attempt to hide his own sexual tastes from her. "And then there were the crocodiles," Bryher recalled, "the dark-haired, mischievous urchins with Renaissance names who ran errands and ate, as reward, plates of pasta like miniature mountains." In Bryher's original draft, she followed this sentence with the explanation: "Actually, what Douglas had was an astounding capacity for romantic love." But she cut this remark from the published chapter, leaving his pederasty implied, rather than directly stated.

In *Heart to Artemis*, Bryher captured Douglas as a man in love with humanity, and loved by humanity in return. She accompanied him to Capri in 1924 and watched as "men offered him wine, women with babies in their arms rushed up so that he might touch them, [and] the children brought him flowers." When she rejoined him for dinner later that evening, he was "wildly, gloriously drunk." She walked him back to the hotel, turning down his offers to spend the night together on Monte Solaro. When Bryher sighted three English schoolmistresses ahead, she tried to steer him away, but it was too late. "He broke away from my grasp, pranced towards them, taking off his hat, and said courteously but in a voice that could have been heard on the other side of the Piazza, 'Well, my dears, and whom are you tucking in with tonight.'"

Bryher's recitation of Douglas's sexual overtures to women may have been intended to counterbalance the allusion to his pederasty. In the unpublished typescript, Bryher described Douglas's erotic energies as infinite and indeterminate. "It might have been a boy, an old woman with a glass of wine, or a child" who attracted Douglas's gaze; he would find the beauty in them all. "He did not need to touch them; some power rose in him and transformed whoever was there into what they had dreamed of being." Again, these sentences did not make it to the published chapter, perhaps because Bryher was uncertain whether people would believe her disclaimer that Douglas looked but didn't touch. In her typescript, Bryher echoed Crotch's complaints about the impossibility of capturing Douglas in words. "What can any sentence make of him but a pale shade?" she asked. In *Heart to Artemis*, Bryher concluded, "Nothing that I can write will make you feel the forces of his love for the visible world."[20]

CHAPTER TWENTY

Pinorman versus Grand Man

"Please do not read this book as an attempted biography of Norman Douglas," Richard Aldington warned on the opening page of his 1954 biography of
Norman Douglas, *Pinorman*.[1] His warning, perhaps a feeble attempt to stave
off lawsuits, did nothing to assuage the anger of Douglas's friends. They may
have struggled internally with the question of how to write an honest account
of the writer after his death, but they were united in their agreement that
Aldington's vicious portrait went beyond the pale. Aldington didn't just allude to Douglas's immorality—he straight out called Douglas a "pederast."
He wasn't interested in balancing the fact of Douglas's genius with the truth
of his sexuality. In the future, Aldington wrote, some "biographer will have
to put in some uphill work trying to explain on psychological grounds how a
man in many ways so distinguished, in appearance so dignified, with accomplishments and all kinds of out-of-the-way learning seldom brought together
in one mind, cultivated a vice which seems so odious and degrading."[2] But he
wasn't that biographer. Aldington was content to reveal the truth about Douglas's sexual relationships with children and leave it at that.

Douglas had expected as much from Aldington. To begin with, he had a
low opinion of biographies written by novelists such as Aldington. "The novelist's touch in biography . . . consists, I should say, in a failure to realize the pro-
fundities and complexities of the ordinary human mind," Douglas wrote after
Lawrence published his introduction to Maurice Magnus's memoirs.[3] Aldington had taken Lawrence's side, calling the introduction "superbly written,"
and claiming that Douglas had really been angry at Lawrence for caricaturiz-
ing him in his 1922 novel *Aaron's Rod*.[4] It's true that Douglas disliked *Aaron's
Rod*. He was almost as antagonistic to novelists' renditions of real people

within their fiction as he was to their attempts at biography. "No authentic child of man will fit into a novel. History is the place for such people; history or oblivion," Douglas wrote.[5] He had a personal stake in this claim, having been caricaturized, with varying degrees of sympathy, not only by Lawrence but by Aldous Huxley, Compton Mackenzie, and Hans Fischer as well.

Aldington joined the lists four years later, in his 1937 novel *Seven against Reeves*. His caricature of Douglas was the crudest of the bunch. Aldington named his Douglas character Mr. Philboy. He may as well have called him Mr. Buggerer. Aldington's Philboy was a literary man who shared Douglas's mannerisms of reveling in sensationalist stories of terrible accidents and calling food he disliked "muck." And if Aldington's choice of pseudonym weren't enough to signal Douglas's pederasty to readers, Aldington also included a portrait of Pino Orioli under the name of "Erasto Paederini." The humor was not exactly subtle.[6]

Douglas thought even less of *Seven against Reeves* than he had of *Aaron's Rod*. Aldington, he wrote to Nancy Cunard, "pictures me and another person, a particular friend of his own, as engaged (under the thinnest of disguises) in so disgusting a transaction that this old and intimate friend, more sensitive than myself, promptly broke off relations with him and never resumed them." In his typical bluff fashion, Douglas claimed that he was "too tough to care a tuppence" about the caricature.[7] But the novel confirmed his long simmering dislike of Aldington and made him wary when Aldington announced that he intended to write a biography of him.[8] Douglas never had to see his worries come to fruition, since Aldington waited until after Douglas died to publish the manuscript—most likely to avoid being sued for libel.

Aldington claimed that *Pinorman* was a group portrait of Norman Douglas, Pino Orioli, and Charles Prentice, but everyone who read the book recognized it for what it was: a sustained attack on Douglas alone. He pilloried Douglas as a terrible person, with terrible taste in food, and a bad writer to boot. Aldington's repeated descriptions of Douglas's sexual relations with children made up the white-hot core of this blistering portrait. He tore away the veil of discretion that had covered previous allusions to Douglas's immorality. "He was quite literally *paiderastes*, a lover of boys, and it is falsifying his whole existence to ignore it," Aldington wrote. Douglas embraced the sexual mores of the ancient Greeks. "The *Musa Puerilis* of Strato was entirely in his line." But Douglas lived nearly two thousand years after Strato, when pederasty was no longer acceptable. His encounters with children led to repeated conflicts with "outraged parents," and his path was "strewn with broken boys and empty bottles."[9]

Aldington's critique was not wholly humanitarian. His anger at Douglas's sexual behavior stemmed as much from his own offended pride as from concern for the well-being of the children. As Aldington explained, he had "never presumed to criticise" Douglas until the writer showed up to a lunch date bringing along "a depraved-looking slum child whose behaviour during the day left absolutely no doubt as to the nature of their relationship." Like Robin, Aldington was enraged about being forced to socialize with one of Douglas's boys. "I had always kept wholly aloof from these conquests of his," Aldington explained. He resented spending time with "this 'pestilential' young companion." The boy was not even good-looking, Aldington complained, and neither were Douglas's other boyfriends whom Aldington had the misfortune to meet. "The two or three specimens of Norman's conquests I happened to see were peculiarly detestable-looking children," but Aldington admitted in a rare show of generosity, "that may not have been their fault." Aldington bemoaned that these encounters ruined the *Greek Anthology* for him. He used to enjoy those "beautifully formed little poems," but he "never for a moment imagined them as guttersnipes from the back streets of Naples, Florence and London." Douglas had spoiled the mystique.[10]

Not content with this attack on Douglas's pederasty, Aldington larded *Pinorman* with criticisms of Douglas's aesthetics and writing as well. He repeatedly attacked Douglas's taste in food, which was much admired but, according to Aldington, mostly undistinguished. (Aldington considered himself to be a true gourmand.) He was equally iffy about Douglas's writing. He devoted an entire chapter of *Pinorman* to dismissing *South Wind*. Aldington claimed the critique was not his own but that of an unnamed French friend. Nobody believed the ruse. According to Aldington, *South Wind* was derivative of Oscar Wilde and George Moore, and Douglas even plagiarized Wyndham Lewis in one line. His books only went downhill from there.

"I think no writer of his status and reputation has so much duplicated and padded his later books as Norman," Aldington wrote. Douglas had been remarkably unproductive.[11] (This is unsurprising criticism from an author who boasted of writing the 85,000-word *Seven against Reeves* in 85 days. Aldington was nothing if not productive.)[12] At the end, Aldington summed up Douglas's life in a list of derogatory labels: "he was a bum, a sponge, a cadger, a borrower, even a swindler." He would "surely be a fascinatingly difficult study for that biographer" who dared to take him on.[13]

But it was Richard Aldington, not Norman Douglas, who got taken on after *Pinorman* was published. The reaction to the book was violent. It began
early, before the official release. Douglas's old friend D. M. Low had learned
about the contents of the book shortly before publication and relayed the information to Nancy Cunard. "How angry we are going to be—no doubt, no
doubt—with many of the things in the book," she wrote to Low after their
conversation. She blamed the book on Aldington's spiteful character. "I suppose you know what his great once-love says," Cunard told Low. "He is just
dreadful about <u>everybody</u>!"[14] She would know. Aldington had viciously lam-
pooned her in his short story "Now She Lies There," published in his 1932 collection *Soft Answers*.[15] When Cunard finally had the chance to read *Pinorman*,
she almost cried.[16] She wrote to Aldington's publisher, accusing him of libel
and threatening to wage a "collective protest" against the book.[17] Once the reviews of *Pinorman* started coming out, it appeared to Aldington that Cunard
had made good on her promise.

Cunard reviewed the book for *Time and Tide*, in the April 17, 1954, issue.
She titled her review "'Bonbons' of Gall." Cunard's tone was as unforgiving
as the book itself. "What a mess of consistent, consecutive and almost un-
adulteratedly nasty, misrepresentative, derogatory and preposterous *nattering*
against the man *and his writing*!" Cunard wrote. The book was a "wry abom-
ination" that "evokes the image of a splattering of mud bullets all over a great
piece of granite." Cunard took issue with every aspect of the book, down to its
title, denying ever having heard anyone refer to Douglas and Orioli as Pinorman.[18] This absurd refusal to acknowledge a nickname that the two men did,
in fact, use signified Cunard's unwillingness to give any ground. If Aldington
painted Douglas black as the devil, then Cunard would pin a pair of wings
on him.

Cunard rallied Douglas's friends to join her attack on *Pinorman*. D. M.
Low published a review in the *Listener* that described Aldington's book as
a "clumsy caricature" and the result of an "unrelenting personal grudge."
Aldington's animus, according to Low, stemmed from his belief that Douglas
had suppressed any mention of Aldington in Orioli's two memoirs. Aldington
seemed to be suffering from a "persecution mania." Low wasn't quite willing
to beatify Douglas, whom he conceded "was not a saint." But he had no problem insulting Aldington.[19]

V. S. Pritchett's review in the *New Statesman and Nation* alleged that
Aldington's hatchet job stemmed from professional jealousy. "Mr. Aldington
is setting up as the blistering and hanging judge of writers whose chief sins

are that they are Mr. Aldington's superiors and seem to have been negligent of him," Pritchett wrote.[20] Compton Mackenzie's review for the *Spectator* likened Aldington to a hyena nosing in the entrails of a dead lion—except that the hyena laughs. "Mr. Aldington's self-centered emotion shuns laughter," Mackenzie observed acidly. The book was a "farrago" and "atrabilious hotchpotch," that deserved to be thrown in the trash.[21] Constantine FitzGibbon reviewed the book for the *Times Literary Supplement*. "No sneer, no insinuation, is omitted," he wrote. "Stories which even Mr. Aldington does not believe are dragged in to disfigure the carnival balloons that the novelist has here blown up." Aldington's portraits of Douglas, Orioli, and Prentice were so distorted, according to FitzGibbon, that the book's only value was to a biographer of Aldington himself, who might gain some insight into the author's low morals.[22]

None took their attack on *Pinorman* as far as the best-selling author Graham Greene, who in 1954 was at the height of his career. He told Kenneth Macpherson that he intended to "kill" the book. He wrote to Edward Hutton that he was reading *Pinorman* for the *London Magazine*, and "I intend to review it in terms as libelous as those used by Aldington of Norman."[23] He achieved what he set out to do. After receiving Greene's review, the editor of the *London Magazine*, John Lehmann, wrote back apologetically that the piece was too libelous to publish. "I am terribly sorry about this," he apologized, and enclosed Greene's check.[24]

Unwilling to let it drop, Greene decided to send his review to Aldington—ostensibly to seek his permission to publish it. "There is little doubt that legal objections will be taken to this review from the point of libel," he wrote, "however I do hope that as you have seen fit to write in this way of Norman Douglas you will have no objection to my replying with this degree of force."[25] Aldington did not agree. He did draft a long angry response to Greene, telling him, "If you don't know what Norman's relations with those endless children were than you know nothing about him." But he never sent the letter.[26] That wasn't the end of it. After Aldington died in 1962, Greene finally published his review in the *London Magazine*.[27] The dead can't sue for libel.

The blowback against *Pinorman* so outraged Aldington that he wanted to sue Nancy Cunard. The lawyer for his publisher persuaded Aldington that Cunard's threat to wage a "collective protest" didn't rise to the standard of conspiracy.[28] Nonetheless, Aldington refused to take the abuse of *Pinorman* lying down. He and a handful of allies wrote letters to the editor of *Time and Tide* protesting the bad reviews that came pouring in. D. H. Lawrence's widow, Frieda, related the story of a time Douglas casually offered her a boy of fourteen, saying that he preferred them younger. "Anybody who knows about Douglas know[s] that he was no little Lord Fauntleroy," Frieda Lawrence wrote.[29]

Aldington privately boasted that "Frieda has written a wonderful letter to Nancy, pulling her back hair down."[30] Aldington also quoted Frieda Lawrence in a protest he sent to the *Listener*. He said Frieda had written that he was more than fair to Douglas, when he "could have presented an ogre feeding on small boys." Aldington complained that "the spectacle of Saint Norman Douglas, Martyr, is too ridiculous."[31] But Low, who had specified in his review of *Pinorman* that Douglas was *not* a saint, responded to Aldington's protest by calling the beatification of Douglas a figment of Aldington's imagination.[32]

Responding to his critics in letters to the editor did not satisfy Aldington. He put together a pamphlet responding to his critics and toyed with calling it "Herpetology of Literary London" or "Black Douglas and White Ladyship."[33] He planned to begin with Cunard's letter threatening "collective action" (the famously pale Cunard was the white lady), then follow with letters from friends supporting his allegations that Douglas sexually abused children. Frieda Lawrence, Rob Lyle, and Roy Campbell would all be contributors. He hoped for something from W. Somerset Maugham, who had privately affirmed Aldington's portrait of Douglas, but Maugham declined. Maugham had visited Douglas during his final days in Villa Tuoro, laughing over wine like two old friends. Plus he shared Douglas's proclivity for male youths. It seems unlikely that Maugham would have enlisted in Aldington's assault.[34] Aldington also planned to include a photograph of Douglas seated with a child on his lap that had been printed in Orioli's *Moving Along*. He thought the picture was revealing.[35]

Aldington's correspondence planning the pamphlet was also revealing, in its own way. It betrayed the hatred for homosexuality that impassioned his attack on Douglas. Aldington called Douglas's supporters "Nancy boys" and complained that it was "strange how many sods there are. I don't understand it."[36] His fervid ally in the battle, Frieda Lawrence, shared his aversion, writing to Aldington that "it scares me a little that there are so many flourishing pansies around."[37] Aldington's former lover Brigit Patmore believed that Aldington's homophobia played a big role in his "malicious" book. She thought that Douglas did little more than caress the boys who flocked around him, but Aldington "was always aggressively anti-homosexual and, like so many Englishmen of his type, gloried in his supposed manhood."[38] At one point, Aldington floated the idea of calling his pamphlet "Sods in Clover," but a lawyer shot down the idea, warning that Aldington's blatant bias would lead to "a wealth of mistaken sentiment over Oscar Wilde and John Gielgud which would be revived in favour of Douglas."[39] In 1954 his critics saw Douglas's sexual relationships with boys in the light of homosexuality, a sexual category that had become more recognizable in the mid-twentieth century than the archaic sexual category of pederasty, which was swiftly descending into meaninglessness. For Douglas, age trumped sex. For Aldington, sex trumped age.

Aldington's pamphlet made it to proofs, before the printers' lawyer advised against proceeding any further with something so libelous. "I think that by the time all offending references are removed there will, as you say, be nothing left to publish," the lawyer warned.[40] The pamphlet had to be abandoned. It later ended up in the hands of a collector of Douglasana, who declared himself definitively on Douglas's side. "The really striking thing about your pamphlet is that no-one seems to be able to see Norman Douglas as anything but black or white," the lawyer had noted in his assessment of the pamphlet. As he recognized, the rage of Douglas's critics was more than matched by the devotion of his friends.

Cunard did not stop at rallying Douglas's friends against *Pinorman*. Since shortly after Douglas's death, she had been working on her own biography of the writer. From the outset, Cunard envisioned the project as a counterpoint to Aldington's forthcoming attack. She never had the intention to present a balanced portrait. Take, for example, Cunard's adaptation of Martha Gordon Crotch's diary entries about Douglas. Cunard traveled to Vence in October 1952 to look through Crotch's papers. The two women didn't get along. Crotch thought Cunard was cheap, and privately she grumbled that Douglas had never really liked the heiress.[41] Cunard found Crotch annoying, and she was irritated that Crotch hadn't put her diaries and letters into any order, despite Cunard's advance requests.[42] Nonetheless, Cunard managed to take extensive notes on Crotch's material, preparing pages of transcripts from the diaries and then covering them with red-penciled annotations reading "use" and "No" and "NO."

The annotations make her intentions clear. Cunard wanted to celebrate Douglas's character. She selected excerpts from Crotch's diaries that recorded evidence of his anti-Fascist grumblings, his good taste, and his independent-mindedness. She cut sections that recorded his sexual liaisons with children. From a diary entry dated November 9, 1936, Cunard chose to include Crotch's observation that Douglas "loves to eat and drink, but he does both in the most epicurean manner." She cut Crotch's assessment that Douglas was "a very bad man really. Judging by the standards one has been taught and exhorted to uphold, he is really a wicked debauchee, steeped in vice." From diary entries dated October 1937, Cunard kept Crotch's record of Douglas's recriminations against Mussolini. She cut Crotch's account of Douglas's assault on Renata. From diary entries in September 1938, Cunard kept evidence of Douglas's disdain for Neville Chamberlain's Munich Agreement, but she cut Crotch's mentions of Douglas's relationship with a fifteen-year-old Spanish refugee and the gossip it provoked.[43] In sum, Cunard curated the evidence to produce a one-dimensional portrait of Douglas as a "Grand Man," to quote the title of her book.

Cunard raced *Grand Man* through production. It was in proofs by the time *Pinorman* was published, and it reached reviewers' desks months later.[44] Ironically, *Grand Man* began on an identical note to *Pinorman*, with Cunard denying that her book was a biography. "This is no baron of beef on the score of Norman Douglas, no attempt at any kind of biography," she declared in the opening sentence. Rather, she hoped the pages would evoke Douglas's "radiant humanism."[45] She also hoped it would reestablish his masculinity, which she thought had been impugned by Aldington. Cunard described Douglas as a paragon of masculinity. "His walk was straight and his bearing was manly," she wrote. He was "definitely one of the most masculine beings ever met with." He was such a "strong, masculine being" that he was disgusted by everything mawkish. Cunard made her point again and again.[46] Favorable reviewers picked up on the theme. "She fully realizes his essential masculinity, which has been too often obscured by some of those who shared certain of his sexual proclivities, and for whom he reserved opprobrious terms in several languages," John Davenport explained. In short, he may have been a pederast, but he was no homosexual.[47]

Grand Man made no pretensions at neutrality. It was a highly personalized portrait, anchored by a 169-page posthumous "Letter to Norman," written by Cunard, recalling the times they had spent together. This was followed by a section titled "Appreciation by Several Friends," which compiled letters from Victor Cunard, Harold Acton, Charles Duff, Arthur Johnson, and Kenneth Macpherson. The combined portrait skated lightly over any mention of Douglas's sexual life. Cunard wrote warmly of several of Douglas's boy-friends, including Wolton and Mari and Papa, but she purposefully obscured the erotic nature of those relationships. Her Douglas could do no wrong.

Reviewers found Cunard's portrait as unsatisfyingly imbalanced as Aldington's had been. Davenport called Cunard "over-rhapsodic" and said she refused to recognize any blemishes in Douglas whatsoever. Her portrait was a "welcome antidote" to Aldington's "grotesque Pinorman" but it was not an objective study. Raymond Mortimer wrote that while *Pinorman* "seemed grumpy and little else," *Grand Man* "passes too lightly over everything." He called the book a slapdash "hotch-potch"—only a slightly milder criticism than Compton Mackenzie's description of *Pinorman* as an "atrabilious hotch-potch." Malcolm Elwin made the same comparison in his review: "Mr. Richard Aldington's unsympathetic portrait in *Pinorman* was generally deplored; now the balance is redressed by Miss Nancy Cunard's fervent adulation in *Grand Man*." Cunard's book was marred by a "want of critical detachment." There was so much more to Douglas, Elwin complained. Derek Hudson's review was explicit about the "more" that Cunard left out. *Grand Man* offered the "other side of the picture," an affectionate biography to redress Aldington's unsympathetic book, but "reverse the image, and even the most appealing touches—that always alert interest in the young for instance—will receive an unfriendly interpretation."[48]

Allusions to Douglas's pederasty popped up in a few other reviews of *Grand Man*. John Connell acknowledged that Douglas "liked few people after they were 14." The reviewer for the *Times Literary Supplement* described Douglas as "boyish," having the "hearty appetites and the objective curiosity of a healthy schoolboy," as well as a "very naughty old boy." Davenport, who had been working on his own biography, criticized Cunard for overlooking the importance of Douglas's "change in sexual directive" after his divorce. And a reviewer for *Desiderata* acknowledged that Douglas's public sexual misdeeds were blemishes on his personality, as Aldington had alleged. But the *Desiderata* reviewer also made another important point. It was, he argued, Douglas's very willingness to make himself vulnerable to attacks by acknowledging his sexual relationships with boys that "should surely make us appreciate not less, but more, his frankness."[49] This seems, to me, the most salient point. I appreciate Douglas's frankness for what it reveals about the social world of pederasty during his lifetime.

CHAPTER TWENTY-ONE

Looking Back

By looking at the ongoing conversation about Norman Douglas in the decades since his death, it becomes apparent just how dramatically attitudes toward sex between adults and children have shifted over time. In 1954, when Aldington and Cunard went toe to toe, it was hardly possible to publish words like *pederasty*. But the edifice of old-fashioned restraint began to crumble in the late 1950s. Revisions of the Obscene Publications Act in 1959 and 1964 allowed for more open speech about sexuality.[1] These legal shifts were mirrored by changes in social norms that made writers more willing to state the facts directly. Although Douglas's friends continued trying to safeguard his reputation, it became impossible for them to stifle the truth.

In the age of *La Dolce Vita*, Capri flourished as a celebrity hot spot, inspiring fluff pieces about the island that increasingly made unguarded references to Douglas's sexual history. A January 1959 article in the glossy magazine *Holiday* included a story about Douglas having been asked by local police to leave the island because he went too far in his Tiberian debaucheries.[2] Robin Douglas wrote to the editor, complaining about the "slanderous, libellous, scurrilous, and scandalous" reference to his father.[3] And Kenneth Macpherson, Douglas's literary executor and guardian of his legacy, wrote his own letter complaining that the article was "wrong in every detail." The author fought back, responding that Douglas was "unscrupulous" about his "strange amours, which from a legal point of view were criminal, and resulted from time to time in his being 'considerably fussed' by the attentions of the police."[4] Months later, a similar article in *Time* magazine made the same claim that Douglas had been asked to leave Capri by the police. Again, Macpherson and Robin Douglas wrote to the editor defending Douglas's legacy.[5] But they were no more effective than King Canute trying to hold back the tide.

In 1966 Douglas's authorized biographer, John Davenport, died without having completed the work he had inherited from Constantine FitzGibbon. Davenport had been stymied by the same reluctance to name Douglas's pederasty in print that earlier had silenced FitzGibbon. But by 1966 times had changed, and Davenport's death opened the way for a new biographer who was unafraid to write openly about adult-child sex. Mark Holloway, like Fitz-Gibbon and Davenport, had met Douglas in London during World War II. As a young writer, he admired the old literary lion. He first floated the possibility of doing Douglas's biography in 1956 but was put off by Davenport's prior claim. A decade later, when Holloway read the news of Davenport's death, he wrote at once to the publisher Secker & Warburg to volunteer for the job.[6]

Macpherson initially welcomed Holloway's proposed biography. He had been disappointed by FitzGibbon's and Davenport's failures, and he told Holloway he had always wanted a "responsible and good biography" of his friend.[7] His meaning was clear. Macpherson did not want a biography that would expose Douglas's sexual history. Holloway, who idolized Douglas, appeared to be the man for the job. He told Macpherson that he thought Richard Aldington "must surely have been mentally or physically diseased." He made the same approach to Douglas's surviving old friends, asking for interviews. He wrote to eighty-four-year-old Compton Mackenzie that he had "no desire to expose Douglas's innards on a dissecting table for the gratification of scandalmongering sensationalists," and he hoped to "refute scurrility of the Aldington kind." He told Roger Senhouse that he had to ask some uncomfortable questions, but he did so with the intention "only to possess sufficient knowledge of my subject to enable me to refute scurrility of the Aldington type."[8]

Holloway's initial interviews, however, had unexpected consequences. A couple months into the project, he realized that Aldington's allegations were not scurrilous. In spring 1967, he wrote to the publisher A. S. Frere that "Aldington's book—whatever one may think of the way it was written or the author's attitude of mind—seems to me to contain much that rings true." Holloway began to shift his approach to Douglas. Instead of refuting scurrility, he now pledged to deal with "the homosexual aspects" of Douglas's life "as frankly and fairly as any other."[9] Like Aldington, Holloway thought of Douglas's sexuality as "homosexual" by definition, because of the sex of the boys.

In this line of thought, pederasts were a subset of homosexuals, who, in Holloway's liberal outlook, were worthy of compassionate understanding.

Holloway's outlook fit into popular discourse in mid-1960s Britain, which closely associated male homosexuality and pederasty. As acceptance of homosexuality accelerated in Britain, some activists believed that pederasty would soon become accepted as well. The period from the early 1960s through the late 1970s represented a high point in the relaxation of stigmas against adult-child sex. The Pedophile Information Exchange (PIE) was established in 1974 as an advocacy group that lobbied for lowering the age of consent for male homosexual relations, which had been set higher than the age of consent for heterosexual relations following the passage of the Sexual Offenses Act legalizing homosexuality in 1967.[10]

PIE was later driven underground and repudiated by British homosexual rights advocates, but not until after the publication of Holloway's biography. Holloway's attempt to understand Douglas's sexual history took place at a critical moment when the relaxation of censorship laws allowed for writing about adult-child sex, and the relaxation of social stigmas allowed for a limited sympathy to be extended to the men who pursued such liaisons. Holloway's pledge to treat Douglas's sexual history frankly and fairly did not entirely appease Macpherson and others. When Holloway sought to read Pino Orioli's travel diaries at the New York Public Library, Macpherson wrote a letter to the archivist Lola Szaldits asking that she only allow him access providing "these diaries contain nothing of a scandalous nature."[11] Szaldits, who had a friendly correspondence with Holloway, gave him a heads-up about Macpherson's back-channel communication. Holloway laughed off Macpherson's fustiness: "When did Macpherson say Douglas was going to be beatified? Or was it, canonized?" Macpherson knew as well as anyone that "no one can write a book worth reading about Douglas's life without including in it 'something of a scandalous nature,'" Holloway wrote to Szaldits. He felt certain that Douglas, if he were alive, would approve of his book, and that, he said, was good enough for him.[12]

Kenneth Macpherson never had the chance to cast his own judgment on Holloway's biography. He died in the summer of 1971, years before the completed biography was finally published. Holloway encountered so many problems ushering his book to print that he once admitted to believing that Douglas had put the evil eye on him. By the time the biography came out in 1976, nobody read Douglas anymore. All his books were out of print in Britain (though Holloway remained hopeful there would be a revival).[13] A handful of Douglas's friends remained alive, and they still read everything concerning the great man. They were not pleased with Holloway's frankness about Douglas's sexual history, or about his revelation that Douglas had committed suicide. Harold Acton and Ian Greenlees both wrote hostile reviews.[14]

Ironically, Holloway conceived of his biography as a defense of Douglas. He included extensive evidence of Douglas's sexual relationships with children, as well as of his arrests and legal problems in England, Italy, and Austria. But he gave credence to Douglas's claims to have been a benefactor to his boys. "Whatever his sins," Holloway reflected, "I was convinced in the end that he had done far more good than harm."[15] In short, by the mid-1970s it was no longer possible for a biographer to hide the evidence of Douglas's sexual history; the only question was how to judge it. Holloway judged Douglas's legacy to have been more positive than harmful. Some critics disliked the book for being too generous to Douglas. The writer Geoffrey Grigson questioned whether it was appropriate to write such an "uncensorious" account of Douglas's life, when the biography revealed that "he was everything that every moralist has to condemn."[16]

Many agreed with Grigson that Douglas deserved censoring. Constantine FitzGibbon returned to the subject of Douglas in a 1974 article in *Encounter*. He recalled his own failed attempts at a biography in the late 1940s, but instead of using the mealymouthed formulations that he had clung to back then (references to Douglas's "recklessness towards the more generally accepted social conventions"), FitzGibbon now baldly stated that Douglas had pursued sexual encounters with children. As far as he could tell, "Norman's sexual relationships with boys were sexual play, not a perversion of the sexual act." Even so, FitzGibbon "was not capable of empathy," as he put it. "In no circumstances could I imagine myself wishing to have a physical sexual relationship with a pre-adolescent child, male or female." As a result, he had needed to abandon the project. He explained his decision to return to the topic in his 1974 article as owing to the drastic change in the "general climate of opinion."[17] Holloway, however, suspected that FitzGibbon was just trying to beat him to the punch. Holloway found the article's tone overly critical and wrote a letter to the editor calling the essay "scandalmongering." FitzGibbon retaliated by calling Holloway a bore.[18]

Elizabeth David also wrote to *Encounter* to correct errors in FitzGibbon's article, but she didn't dispute any of his disclosures about Douglas's sexual history.[19] David admitted to having admired her friend's sexual iconoclasm. She praised his wisdom about "the importance of the relationship between the enjoyment of food and wine and the conduct of love affairs."[20] His advice to "always do as you please, and send everybody to Hell" had guided her life.[21] Like Holloway, David saw Douglas's legacy in positive terms. She was grateful that he had enlarged her understanding of the world. Two essays she wrote about their friendship during the 1960s constructed a new legacy for Douglas, by representing him as an embodiment of authentic Epicureanism. He wasn't a gourmet obsessed with rich meals in fine restaurants. He liked "genuine *maccheroni*," "wine properly made," and "fruit from the trees he knew to have been well tended and grown."[22] David's essays gave Douglas a new afterlife as a patron saint of authentic food.

She was joined in her celebration of Douglas as an Epicurean by several other women food writers who had known him well. Theodora FitzGibbon, Constantine's wife, became a prominent cookbook writer and food historian in the 1950s. In her memoirs, she wrote about Douglas's early influence on her development as a cook. FitzGibbon freely admitted to Douglas's pederasty, which she defended as typical at the time.[23] Untroubled by this facet of Douglas's history, FitzGibbon's memoirs focused instead on their times together in the kitchen in wartime London and later at caffè tables in Capri.

The novelist and essayist Sybille Bedford also contributed to the cult of Douglas the Epicure. Bedford was born into the German petty aristocracy and spent her adolescence among the Bohemian exiles of Sanary-sur-Mer, where she was befriended by Aldous Huxley and the children of Thomas Mann. She likely first got to know Douglas in the 1930s, after his exile from Florence, although their acquaintance may have dated back earlier. The two resumed their friendship in Capri after the war, and she helped him write the recipes for *Venus in the Kitchen*. At the time, she was working on her own cookbook, which never found a publisher. Later she became a noted food writer, in addition to a journalist of serious subjects such as the 1964 trial of former Auschwitz officers. In her 1990 essay collection *As It Was: Pleasures, Landscapes and Justice*, Bedford recalled a meal she had shared with Douglas in Capri in 1948. The essay forthrightly acknowledged his pederasty, but chose to remember Douglas for his devotion to the pleasures of the table. Like Elizabeth David and Theodora FitzGibbon, Bedford took the balance of Douglas's life, and her gratitude for what he'd taught her about food outweighed her disregard for his sexual history.[24]

Douglas's reputation as a great Epicurean hero reached its peak in Roger Williams's 1999 novel, *Lunch with Elizabeth David*. Williams's treatment of Douglas exceeded all who came before him in praising the forgotten author. In the novel, Williams described Douglas's love for food and for boys as twinned expressions of his joie de vivre. Williams writes at length about the initial sexual encounter between twelve-year-old Eric Wolton and Douglas, when "the two talked and experimented, trying to find what gave pleasure, which games were fun."[25] This account does not fit into the trauma model of child sexual abuse. In the novel, Wolton is not damaged by the encounter, although his later unhappy marriage might suggest a lingering injury. Reviews of the book were mostly appreciative. *Publishers Weekly* praised Williams for "delicately handling the boy's innocent sexual explorations with his mentor."[26]

Another school of admiration for Douglas came, perhaps surprisingly, out of Italy. Douglas was not translated into Italian until after his death, but beginning in the mid-1950s, he was rediscovered by Italian historians and folklorists. *Old Calabria*, for example, is seen as a valuable historical source about a region of the country that, during Douglas's era, was often regarded both by fellow Italians and by travelers as bleak and backward.[27] Douglas captured this region without either overt bias or excessive romanticism. Claudio Gargano has argued that "in him, the only one among the many writers who nourish the myth of an archaic and sensual Italy, there is no trace of exoticism or local color."[28] Ciro Sandomenico, author of a 1996 biography of Douglas subtitled *Una Vita Indecente*, praises Douglas's writings for creating a "multichromatic map" of the Italian countryside.[29] Italian translations of Douglas are sold today in bookstores in Ischia and elsewhere in his beloved Siren Land. Local historian Vincenzo Astarita leads Norman Douglas walking tours through the Sorrentine Peninsula and organizes a "Happy Birthday Norman" event every year to keep the writer's memory alive.[30] And the only publisher I ever met who expressed unadulterated enthusiasm for my own work on Douglas was a Neapolitan.

Contemporary English-language treatments of Douglas, however, are overwhelmingly negative. During the late 1980s and 1990s, the figure of the monstrous pedophile took center stage in the cultural imagination of English-speaking countries, entirely replacing the earlier ambivalent figure of the pederast. The pedophile, or child sexual predator, was the subject of sex crime panics on both sides of the Atlantic.[31] People who wrote or spoke about adult-child sex in non-condemnatory terms risked public attack. The rhetoric of molestation became "so powerful that those who do not join in its *danse macabre* are often accused of participating (either literally or figuratively) in the abuse."[32]

As the archetype of the pedophile solidified, the treatment of Douglas in both fiction and nonfiction grew increasingly negative. In literary biographies where Douglas made an appearance, he was dismissed offhand as a "notorious pedophile."[33] He fared no better in fiction. Francis King's 1992 novel *The Ant Colony*, about postwar Florence, depicted Douglas as a dirty old bugger who paid boys to jack off in front of him.[34] Alex Preston's 2014 novel, *In Love and War*, set in Florence during the 1930s, portrayed Douglas as a heartless monster. In one scene invented by Preston, Douglas cruelly insults a middle-aged Eric Wolton, who has come to visit, then throws him out of his apartment. Later, in another invented scene, Douglas makes a perilous flight from Florence that leads to the tragic death of the hero's love interest.[35] Despite Preston's dark portrayal of Douglas, a few critics complained that he had gone too far in humanizing him, and Preston himself worried that he had gone easy on the writer.[36]

There are still ardent defenders of Douglas who acknowledge Douglas's pederasty but share Holloway's opinion that the good outweighed the bad. This is the generalized opinion of the scholars who have worked on the nine-volume series of Douglas's correspondence published by the Vorarlberg state library in Bregenz. Michael Allan, a lead editor, has repeatedly argued for a positive reading of Douglas's relationships with boys. In a 2006 talk introducing the second volume, which collected letters from Douglas's most significant boy lovers, Allan observed that "these writings are affectionate, mundane, factual and nostalgic by turn. Nowhere, however, is there any mention made of sex; not once. Rather is it love and a deep respect which emerge from and between the lines of these many pages. These four boys, these four young men, revered and loved Norman and he—I quote his biographer, Mark Holloway: '... he loved them; he loved them truly, for their own sakes.'"[37]

To preserve his rosy take on Douglas's pederastic relationships, Allan has made editorial decisions that obscure the crude sexual aspects of Douglas's pederasty. For example, in a 2014 volume, Allan chose to include a Latin passage from John Mavrogordato's journal that described Douglas's sexual encounters with two brothers named Italo and Marcello, but to leave it untranslated "in best British public-school tradition."[38] As a responsible editor, Allan has been faithful to the sources, but he has simultaneously sought to soften their impact. The Bregenz editorial team has not yet published the most sexually explicit materials from Douglas's life: the travel diaries written by his partner in crime, Pino Orioli. These sources do more than any others to disrupt the pederastic ideal that Douglas sheltered behind. I am aware that my own work, by focusing on Douglas's sexual history rather than his writing, upsets some of the Bregenz team. Even as they acknowledge his sexual history, they still seek to shield his reputation from censure.

For me, the diaries were the inspiration for starting down the path to writing this book. Reading them made me believe that this project was not just possible but necessary. It was the dissonance between the two sets of sources—the crude record of Douglas's sexual life and the loving letters from the boys—which demanded consideration. In the absence of the diaries, the vulgar realities of his sexual relationships could be finessed away. And in the absence of the voices of the children, the normalcy of adult-child sex in the past could be overlooked. Brought together, the two sets of sources forced a reckoning with the complexities of the past.

Reflection IV

How do I weigh the balance of Douglas's life? Throughout the writing of this book, my fear has been that people will judge me for being too sympathetic. Any treatment of Douglas that sees him as other than a monster is probably too sympathetic for most readers. But I don't think the archetype of the monstrous pedophile is helpful for making sense of the history of adult-child sex. Monsters stand outside society. Douglas, despite his frequent claims to stand apart and above society, was very much a man of his times. He took part in thriving markets in child sex. He supported himself by writing for an audience who were seduced by his erotic accounts of curly-haired boys. He moved in a circle of friends who either shared his sexual tastes or accepted them with little judgment. He was desired, admired, and even loved by many of the boys he seduced. By not dismissing Douglas as a monster, we are forced to acknowledge a historical moment not too long ago when adult-child sex was part of a norm of unequal and exploitative sexual relations that empowered privileged men to do as they pleased, and left women, children, and the poor to make the best of it.

It would be easy to see nothing but black in the life of Norman Douglas, since he was so public about having sex with young people that he left behind heaps of evidence to condemn him. Many of his contemporaries, well-esteemed figures among them, had sex with young people too, but they were concerned enough about their reputations to be discreet. Douglas had the gall to be open. He was an independent thinker who didn't care what other people thought, or thought of him. He hated Christianity, and said so. He loved boys, and said so. The first of these perversions has become less shocking since his death, the second more so.

Douglas's openness about his sexual life makes it impossible for me to view him so starkly, however. It is the very richness of the evidence—the letters, the photographs, the books, the diaries—that compels me to render him in shades of gray. How can I cast aside the words of the children who said they loved him? I worry that this sentence will lead to accusations that I have fallen too far on the white side. I have been too sympathetic to a man who deserves no sympathy. This is the peril of writing about a life. When you try to understand a person and contextualize their life within their own times, it's easy to succumb to their point of view. I feel a misplaced sympathy for Douglas. I can sense myself rooting for Cunard in her fight with Aldington, even though I know that Aldington's book is more honest.

There are undoubtedly some readers who will feel I have fallen too far on the black side. I have focused too much on Douglas's sexual misdeeds and given too short shrift to the genius of his writing. I have succumbed to presentism and been too judgmental about Douglas's life, instead of preserving a proper historicist distance from past norms and practices. I have wanted to understand the social history of pederasty, but I have been reluctant to accept the possibility that sex between adults and children could be okay in any context. I want to historicize my moral norms and cling to them all the same. Wishing to avoid the judgment of right-minded readers, I have been too insistent on my distaste for Douglas. This is also a peril of writing about a life. As Janet Malcolm remarks in a review of a biography of Susan Sontag: "Biographers often get fed up with their subjects, with whom they have become grotesquely overfamiliar. We know no one in life the way biographers know their subjects. It is an unholy practice, the telling of a life story that isn't one's own."[1]

It's possible that I'm guilty of both flaws: too white in some passages, too black in others.

I have been seduced by Douglas, and I have lashed out at him in resentment. How do I weigh the balance of Douglas's life? He was a brilliant linguist. He wrote masterful prose. He had a curious mind. He was charming. He could be a loyal and generous friend. He was charismatic. He had a tremendous spirit of fun. He was an independent thinker. He despised cant. He despised tyranny. He did terrible things. He had sexual encounters with countless pubescent and prepubescent children, mostly boys, also girls. He cruelly separated his wife from their children and laughed at her tragic death. He neglected his sons and possibly abused them. He used rich friends for their money. He cared only about himself and his own pleasure. His accomplishments don't outweigh his deficits enough to justify commemoration through biography, except for the fact that the specific nature of his deficits offers a clear window onto a historical reality that has been too little studied. It is Douglas's wrongs that make his life worth studying. I weigh the balance of his life and find him useful. For a historian, that is the judgment that matters.

Despite my misplaced sympathies, I think this book falls into Aldington's camp, rather than Cunard's. In my order of priorities, Douglas's personal life comes before his books. I would never have written about Douglas for the sake of his books alone. But if this book is not a literary biography, as the handful of remaining Douglas fans might have wished, neither is it an exposé. It's not, as Aldington titled his memoir, a "life-for-life's sake." It's a "life for the sake of history," driven by questions about changing sexual mores, seeking answers both in the evidence of Douglas's life and in the evidence of his writing.

Mores about sex between adults and children continued to change after Douglas's death. Attitudes became more censorious in the 1950s, when a moral panic erupted tarring homosexuals as child abusers. Attitudes softened in the late 1960s and 1970s, as the sexual revolution discredited many moral regulations of erotic behavior. When I was a child in the 1980s, panic over pedophiles surged. At the same time, I experienced adult male sexual interest in myself and my friends as a routine aspect of daily life. By the time I reached thirteen, men often approached me in public spaces including schools, subways, parks, and movie theaters. I regarded the men who expressed their interest in a range of ways: as threatening, annoying, or even attractive, depending on context. Today there is consensus about the iniquity of pedophilia. And yet that consensus has not eliminated widespread erotic fixation on children, judging from the market for child pornography. According to law enforcement agencies, the issue has magnified during the first decades of the twenty-first century, both in quantity and in violence.[2] This inconsistency suggests that our present sexual mores are less stable than we imagine. Attitudes are likely to change again. The first decades of the twenty-first century will not be the final word.

Acknowledgments

For this book, more than most, it feels vital to begin the acknowledgments by stressing that all missteps are the fault of the author and should not be held against the countless generous people who offered assistance and support along the way.

For most of the journey from research through writing, rewriting, and editing, I remained unconvinced that the book would ever be published. It is astonishing to me to have finally reached the point in the process where I can thank the people who helped me get here. There is one person who believed in the project from the beginning, and kept telling me, through my most profound moments of doubt, that the book would be published and that it would be great! That true believer is my father, Jonathan Sinnreich. If I weren't my father's daughter, I don't think I would ever have imagined writing this book in the first place. It takes some unconventional family dinner-table conversations to mature into the sort of person who thinks that writing a book that flies in the face of taboo is a good idea.

On the other end of the spectrum, I must thank my husband, Timothy Cleves, who has never liked the idea of this book or its subject, but who has always loved me and supported me in the endeavor regardless. He's suffered through a lot of uncomfortable conversations sparked by people innocently asking me about my latest research. Only occasionally has he asked me to pipe down in public places. I appreciate his patience, and I promise to work on a more palatable project now that Douglas is finished. My kids, Eli and Maya, also deserve a shout-out for putting up with a mother who talks about pederasty all the time.

A few people with personal connections to the subject of this book have gone out of their way to help my research. I am grateful to Deirdre Sholto Douglas, Norman Douglas's granddaughter through his son Robin, who shared her personal archive of Douglas materials with me, including many photographs. Deirdre spent a full day with me, telling me stories she had received through the family, and giving me an intimate glance into one of the least-recorded aspects of Douglas's life: his family. Thank you also to Dr. John Coyne and Mrs. Kay Coyne, who welcomed me to their home, Tilquhillie Castle, in Banchory, Scotland. They allowed me to see Douglas's family estate with my own eyes and brought me to the cemetery where members of the family were once buried. They also shared their own research into the Douglas family, as well as stories learned from Douglas family members. I am also grateful to Willi Meusburger and the team in Bregenz, who made it possible for me to visit Douglas's childhood home, Falkenhorst, and his grandparents' home, Babenwohl.

Because of the tricky nature of this book, it was important to me to get feedback from trusted readers before I sent the manuscript out to publishers. Several people read the entire manuscript and gave helpful criticism. Gabriela Hirt has been second only to my father as the book's staunchest supporter. She commented on the first draft of the manuscript and helped me out with German translations to boot. *Danke.* Thanks also to Greg Blue, Masha Zager, Yorick Smaal, and Aram Sinnreich, who's also been a great believer. Jean Moorcroft Wilson was in the Berg Collection room at the New York Public Library as I first read the Orioli diaries, and when I asked her whether I should risk writing a book about Douglas, she told me that I must. I told her that I would direct all complaints her way! I thank her for her continuing encouragement since our first fateful meeting, including her feedback on a draft. Thanks also to Gillian Frank, Timothy Stewart-Winter, John Kaag, Jason Colby, Jennie Goloboy, Kari Jones, and everyone else who read chapters and responded. Thanks to Amanda Littauer who has been my interlocutor in a twenty-plus-year dialogue about history and sexuality. Working on this project while she was working on her own scholarship about queer youth has been a delight. Last but not least, big thanks to my editor, Timothy Mennel, who liked the book enough to publish it!

I've been very encouraged (surprised?) by the positive feedback that I've received following talks I've given about Douglas. At the biennial Norman Douglas symposium in Bregenz, Austria, I profited enormously from the conversations that I had with fellow speakers, including Cecil Woolf, Jerry

Wensinger, and Michael Allan. Thank you also to my fellow panelists and audience members at the Queer History Conference at San Francisco State in 2019; the annual meeting of the Organization of American Historians in 2019; the "Thinking Sex After the Great War" conference in Brussels in 2018; and the Queer Localities conference at Birkbeck, University of London, in 2017; and to my colleagues at the University of Victoria, who turned out for my "Works in Progress" talk on Douglas and asked great questions. UVic also provided a summer research grant that funded an early visit to the Beinecke Library, which helped launch the project. Additional support from the Social Sciences and Humanities Research Council (SSHRC) has been invaluable.

I've relied on several research assistants during the past few years. Thanks to Alexie Glover and Amy Glemann, especially, who each accompanied me to the Beinecke Library and helped me to research both Douglas and the best places to eat pizza and lobster rolls in the New Haven area. Thanks also to Christina Fabiani, Monique Ulysses, and Ryan T. Wyett. I am likewise grateful to the archivists and librarians who facilitated my research at institutions throughout the United States, Canada, and Europe. Many people have generously shared their knowledge about Douglas and his circle with me, including Lorenzo Benadusi, Alyson Price, Mark Roberts, David Deiss, Lucia Annicelli, Kristin Mahoney, and Vincenzo Astarita. Every anecdote, tip, and suggestion along the way has helped me finally reach this point: the end.

Abbreviations

NDCB   Norman Douglas Collection, Beinecke Library, Yale University

NDHR   Norman Douglas Papers, Harry Ransom Center, University of Texas at Austin

NNPB   Nikolai Nadezhin Papers, Beinecke Library, Yale University

NYPL   Berg Collection, New York Public Library

PMLM   Pierpont Morgan Library & Museum, New York City

SNDV   Sammlung Norman Douglas Brief, Nachlass Archibald Douglas, NDS-A-141, Vorarlberger Landesbibliotek, Bregenz, Austria

UCDH   D. H. Lawrence Papers, UCLA Library, Department of Special Collections Manuscripts Division

UCLA   Miscellaneous Ephemera Collection, UCLA Library, Department of Special Collections Manuscripts Division

UCND   Norman Douglas Papers, 1879–1952, UCLA Library, Department of Special Collections Manuscripts Division

Books

William King, Norman Douglas's onetime literary executor, reviewed and annotated several of Douglas's books with the author in his last decade of life. Those books, archived at the Berg Collection of the New York Public Library, have been an important source.

WKA   William King annotated copy of *Alone*, Berg Collection, New York Public Library

WKBB   William King annotated copy of *Birds and Beasts of the Greek Anthology*, Berg Collection, New York Public Library

WKIB   William King annotated copy of *In the Beginning*, Berg Collection, New York Public Library

WKLB   William King annotated copy of *Looking Back*, Berg Collection, New York Public Library

WKP   William King annotated copy of *Paneros*, Berg Room, New York Public Library

Notes

Introduction

1. Bryher, *The Heart to Artemis: A Writer's Memoirs* (London: Collins, 1963), 228.
2. Algernon Islay de Courcy Lyons to his mother, August 25, 1948, box 48, "personal correspondence" folder, NDCB.
3. James Money, *Capri: Island of Pleasure* (1986; repr., London: Faber Finds, 2012); Shirley Hazzard, *Greene on Capri: A Memoir* (New York: Farrar, Straus and Giroux, 2000). A new celebratory account of the island has recently been published: Jamie James, *Pagan Light: Dreams of Freedom and Beauty in Capri* (New York: Farrar, Straus and Giroux, 2019).
4. Norman Douglas, *Looking Back: An Autobiographical Excursion* (New York: Harcourt, Brace, 1933), 11. Albums containing the original calling cards are archived at Yale's Beinecke Library: box 46, NDCB.
5. Joseph J. Fischel, *Sex and Harm in the Age of Consent* (Minneapolis: University of Minnesota Press, 2016).
6. Estelle B. Freedman, *Redefining Rape: Sexual Violence in the Era of Suffrage and Segregation* (Cambridge, MA: Harvard University Press, 2013), 3.
7. Helmut Graupner, "Sexual Consent: The Criminal Law in Europe and Overseas," *Archives of Sexual Behavior* 29, no. 5 (2000).
8. Stephen Mintz, *Huck's Raft: A History of American Childhood* (Cambridge, MA: Harvard University Press, 2006), 252.
9. Steven Angelides, *The Fear of Child Sexuality: Young People, Sex, and Agency* (Chicago: University of Chicago Press, 2019).
10. Yorick Smaal and Mark Finnane, "Some Questions of History: Prosecuting and Punishing Child Sexual Assault," in *The Sexual Abuse of Children*, ed. Yorick Smaal, Andy Kaladelfos, and Mark Finnane (Clayton, Australia: Monash University Publishing, 2016).
11. The rarity of such sources is noted in Michael Matthew Kaylor, "Romantic Appropriations," in *A Companion to Greek and Roman Sexualities*, ed. Thomas K. Hubbard (Hoboken, NJ: John Wiley & Sons, 2014), 600.

12. Kadji Amin, *Disturbing Attachments: Genet, Modern Pederasty, and Queer History* (Durham, NC: Duke University Press, 2017), 34.

13. Amin, 25. Gert Hekma and D. H. Mader make a similar argument: "The history of pederasty is to a large extent the history of homosexuality, and vice versa; one cuts off a part of their history only at a risk to themselves." Thomas K. Hubbard, Beert Verstraete, and Daniel C. Tsang, eds., *Censoring Sex Research: The Debate over Male Intergenerational Relations* (Walnut Creek, CA: Left Coast Press, 2013), 187.

14. Gillian Frank, "'The Civil Rights of Parents': Race and Conservative Politics in Anita Bryant's Campaign against Gay Rights in 1970s Florida," *Journal of the History of Sexuality* 22, no. 1 (2013); Lillian Faderman, *The Gay Revolution: The Story of the Struggle* (New York: Simon & Schuster, 2015), 334–39, 412, 58.

15. Joshua Gamson, "Messages of Exclusion: Gender, Movements, and Symbolic Boundaries," *Gender & Society* 11, no. 2 (1997); Hubbard, Verstraete, and Tsang, *Censoring Sex Research*, xiii; Chris Ashford, "Queering Consent: (Re)Evolving Constructions of the Age of Consent and the Law," in *Legal Perspectives on State Power: Consent and Control*, ed. Chris Ashford, Alan Reed, and Nicola Wake (Newcastle upon Tyne, UK: Cambridge Scholars Publishing, 2016); Jim Downs, *Stand by Me: The Forgotten History of Gay Liberation* (New York: Basic Books, 2016), 130–36.

16. Richard Yuill and Dean Durber, "'Querying' the Limits of Queering Boys through the Contested Discourses on Sexuality," *Sexuality & Culture* 12, no. 4 (2008): 258.

17. For a discussion of the role that viscerality plays in archival practice and historiography, see Zeb Tortorici, *Sins against Nature: Sex and Archives in Colonial New Spain* (Durham, NC: Duke University Press, 2018), 25–45.

18. Elise Chenier, "The Natural Order of Disorder: Pedophilia, Stranger Danger and the Normalising Family," *Sexuality & Culture* 16, no. 2 (2012): 173; Catharine A. MacKinnon, "Does Sexuality Have a History?," *Michigan Quarterly Review* 30 (1991): 1; Steven Angelides, "Feminism, Child Sexual Abuse, and the Erasure of Child Sexuality," *GLQ: A Journal of Lesbian and Gay Studies* 10, no. 2 (2004).

19. Yuill and Durber, "'Querying' the Limits," 262. See also George Rousseau, ed., *Children and Sexuality: The Greeks to the Great War* (London: Palgrave Macmillan, 2007), xiii.

20. Judith Levine, *Harmful to Minors: The Perils of Protecting Children from Sex* (Minneapolis: University of Minnesota Press, 2002); Patrick McCreery, "Innocent Pleasures? Children and Sexual Politics," *GLQ: A Journal of Lesbian and Gay Studies* 10, no. 4 (2004); Yuill and Durber, "'Querying' the Limits"; Susan Clancy, *The Trauma Myth: The Truth about the Sexual Abuse of Children—and Its Aftermath* (New York: Basic Books, 2009), 77–110; Hubbard, Verstraete, and Tsang, *Censoring Sex Research*.

21. Steven Maynard, "'Horrible Temptations': Sex, Men, and Working-Class Male Youth in Urban Ontario, 1890–1935," *Canadian Historical Review* 78, no. 2 (1997);

Louise Jackson, *Child Sexual Abuse in Victorian England* (New York: Routledge, 2000), 96–106; Matt Houlbrook, *Queer London: Perils and Pleasures in the Sexual Metropolis, 1918–1957* (Chicago: University of Chicago Press, 2005); Stephen Robertson, "'Boys, of Course, Cannot Be Raped': Age, Homosexuality and the Redefinition of Sexual Violence in New York City, 1880–1955," *Gender & History* 18, no. 2 (2006); Don Romesburg, "'Wouldn't a Boy Do?' Placing Early-Twentieth-Century Male Youth Sex Work into Histories of Sexuality," *Journal of the History of Sexuality* 18, no. 3 (2009); Chris Brickell, "'Waiting for Uncle Ben': Age-Structured Homosexuality in New Zealand, 1920–1950," *Journal of the History of Sexuality* 21 (2012); Yorick Smaal, "Boys and Homosex: Danger and Possibility in Queensland, 1890–1914," in *Children, Childhood and Youth in the British World*, ed. Shirleene Robinson and Simon Sleight (London: Palgrave Macmillan, 2016); Yorick Smaal and Mark Finnane, "Flappers and Felons: Rethinking the Criminal and Homosex in Interwar Australia, 1920–1939," in *From Sodomy Laws to Same-Sex Marriage: International Perspectives since 1789*, ed. Sean Brady and Mark Seymour (London: Bloomsbury Academic, 2019).

22. Matt Cook, *London and the Culture of Homosexuality, 1885–1914* (Cambridge: Cambridge University Press, 2003).

23. Linda C. Dowling, *Hellenism and Homosexuality in Victorian Oxford* (Ithaca, NY: Cornell University Press, 1994); Cook, *London and the Culture of Homosexuality*; Rousseau, *Children and Sexuality*, 173–230; Jana Funke, "'We Cannot Be Greek Now': Age Difference, Corruption of Youth and the Making of *Sexual Inversion*," *English Studies: A Journal of English Language and Literature* 94, no. 2 (2013). Foucault also wrote about Greek pederasty: Michel Foucault, *The History of Sexuality*, trans. Robert Hurley, vol. 2, *The Use of Pleasure* (New York: Vintage, 1990).

24. Timothy d'Arch Smith, *Love in Earnest: Some Notes on the Lives and Writings of English 'Uranian' Poets from 1889 to 1930* (London: Routledge & Kegan Paul, 1970); Kaylor, "Romantic Appropriations"; Donald Rosenthal, *The Photographs of Frederick Rolfe* (North Pomfret, VT: Asphodel Editions, 2008).

25. Google Books Ngram Viewer.

26. Toto Roccuzzo, *Taormina, l'isola nel cielo: Come Taormina divenne Taormina* (Catania, Sicilia: Giuseppe Maimone, 1992); Claudio Gargano, *Capri pagana: Uranisti e amazzoni tra Ottocento e Novecento* (Capri: Edizioni la Conchiglia, 2007); and the following chapters in *Homosexuality in Italian Literature, Society, and Culture, 1789–1919*, ed. Lorenzo Benadusi, Paolo L. Bernardini, Elisa Bianco, and Paolo Guazzo (Newcastle upon Tyne, UK: Cambridge Scholars Press, 2017): Lorenzo Benadusi, Paolo Bernardini, and Paola Guazzo, "In the Shadow of J. J. Winckelmann: Homosexuality in Italy during the Long Nineteenth Century"; Mario Bolognari, "Taormina and the Strange Case of Baron Von Gloeden"; Barbara Pozzo, "Male Homosexuality in Nineteenth-Century Italy: A Juridical View"; Eugenio Zito,

"'Amori et Dolori Sacrum': Canons, Differences and Figures of Gender Identity in the Cultural Panorama of Travellers in Capri between the Nineteenth and Twentieth Century." Michael Rocke's foundational work on pederasty in Renaissance Florence has also been very helpful: *Forbidden Friendships: Homosexuality and Male Culture in Renaissance Florence* (New York: Oxford University Press, 1996).

27. Stefania Arcara, "Hellenic Transgressions, Homosexual Politics: Wilde, Symonds and Sicily," *Studies in Travel Writing* 16, no. 2 (2012). Also see Paul Fussell, *Abroad: British Literary Traveling between the Wars* (New York: Oxford University Press, 1980), 119–30; Ian Littlewood, *Sultry Climates: Travel and Sex* (Cambridge, MA: Da Capo Press, 2001); and *Norman Douglas: 2. Symposium, Bregenz und Thüringen, Vlbg., 18./19.10.2002*, ed. Wilhelm Meusburger (Bregenz: Norman Douglas Forschungsstelle, Vorarlberger Landesbibliothek, 2002).

28. Joseph Allen Boone, *The Homoerotics of Orientalism* (New York: Columbia University Press, 2014), 51–110.

29. James R. Kincaid, *Child-Loving: The Erotic Child and Victorian Culture* (New York: Routledge, 1992).

30. Kathryn Bond Stockton, *The Queer Child, or Growing Sideways in the Twentieth Century* (Chapel Hill, NC: Duke University Press, 2009), 12.

31. Estelle Freedman, "'Uncontrolled Desires': The Response to the Sexual Psychopath, 1920–1960," *Journal of American History* 74, no. 1 (1987); Philip Jenkins, *Moral Panic: Changing Concepts of the Child Molester in Modern America* (New Haven, CT: Yale University Press, 1998); Steven Angelides, "The Emergence of the Paedophile in the Late Twentieth Century," *Australian Historical Studies* 36, no. 126 (2005); Chrysanthi S. Leon, *Sex Fiends, Perverts, and Pedophiles: Understanding Sex Crime Policy in America* (New York: New York University Press, 2011); Gillian Harkins, "Foucault, the Family and the Cold Monster of Neoliberalism," in *Foucault, the Family and Politics*, ed. Robbie Duschinsky and Leon Antonio Rocha (Hampshire, UK: Palgrave Macmillan, 2012); Chenier, "The Natural Order of Disorder"; Fischel, *Sex and Harm in the Age of Consent*. On a parallel note, see Nicholas Syrett's observation that before the late twentieth century, adult husbands of child brides were rarely considered sexually perverse: *American Child Bride: A History of Minors and Marriage in the United States* (Durham: University of North Carolina Press, 2016).

32. Rose Corrigan, "Making Meaning of Megan's Law," *Law & Social Inquiry* 31, no. 2 (2006). Also see Nadia Wager, "Michael Jackson: As an Expert in Child Sexual Abuse Here's What I Thought When I Watched *Leaving Neverland*," *The Conversation*, March 8, 2019, http://theconversation.com/michael-jackson-as-an-expert -in-child-sexual-abuse-heres-what-i-thought-when-i-watched-leaving-neverland -113160.

33. Thomas Carlyle, *On Heroes, Hero-Worship, and the Heroic in History* (London: James Fraser, 1841), 47.

34. Algernon Islay de Courcy Lyons to his mother, August 25, 1948, box 48, "personal correspondence" folder, NDCB.

35. Richard MacGillivray, *Norman Douglas* (Florence: G. Orioli, 1933); Kenneth Macpherson, *Omnes Eodem Cogimur* (Torino: privately printed, 1953); Nancy Cunard, *Grand Man: Memories of Norman Douglas* (London: Secker & Warburg, 1954); Mark Holloway, *Norman Douglas: A Biography* (London: Secker & Warburg, 1976).

36. For a complete list of publications, see https://vlb.vorarlberg.at/was-haben-wir /bibliotheksshop/publikationen/norman-douglas/.

37. A.P., "Old Calabria," *Punch*, February 1, 1956, 185.

38. A. J. A. Symons, "Tradition in Biography," in *Tradition and Experiment in Present-Day Literature* (New York: Haskell House, 1929), 152.

39. A. J. A. Symons, *The Quest for Corvo: An Experiment in Biography* (London: Cassell, 1934). The letters were later published: Fr. Rolfe [Baron Corvo], *The Venice Letters*, ed. Cecil Woolf (London: Cecil & Amelia Woolf, 1974).

40. Douglas to A. J. A. Symons, January 24, 1934, PMLM.

41. Douglas, *Looking Back*, 255. Also, Douglas to Edward Hutton, February 26 and March 8, 1934, box 3, UCND.

42. *The Quest for Corvo* became the model for a new genre of first-person biographies that still feels fresh today. Among my favorites are Janet Malcolm, *The Silent Woman: Sylvia Plath and Ted Hughes* (New York: Knopf, 1994); Richard Holmes, *Footsteps: Adventures of a Romantic Biographer* (New York: Vintage, 1996); Geoff Dyer, *Out of Sheer Rage: In the Shadow of D. H. Lawrence* (London: Little, Brown, 1997); and John Kaag, *American Philosophy: A Love Story* (New York: Farrar, Straus and Giroux, 2016).

43. For a particularly good recent essay in this vein, see Claire Dederer, "What Do We Do with the Art of Monstrous Men?," *Paris Review*, November 20, 2017. For information on Symons, see Robert Scoble, *The Corvo Cult: The History of an Obsession* (London: Strange Attractor Press, 2014), 231–47.

44. *Norman Douglas Selected Correspondence*, ed. Arthur S. Wensinger and Michael Allan, vol. 2, *Dear Doug! Letters to Norman Douglas from Eric Wolton, René Mari, Marcel Mercier and Ettore Masciandaro and a Selection of Letters from Emilio Papa* (Graz/Feldkirch, Austria: W. Neugebauer Verlag, 2008), 24.

45. Elizabeth David, *An Omelette and a Glass of Wine*, ed. Jill Norman (Guildford, CT: Lyons Press, 1987), 120, 130.

46. Gayle Rubin, "Thinking Sex: Notes for a Radical Theory of the Politics of Sexuality," in *Culture, Society and Sexuality: A Reader*, ed. Richard Parker and Peter Aggleton (New York: Routledge, 1984).

47. Rubin, 154.

48. "Norman Douglas: A Tribute by Compton Mackenzie, Moray McLaren, C. M.

Grieve and Others," November 11, 1948, box 40, folder 623, NDCB; Graham Greene, introduction to *Venus in the Kitchen: Or Love's Cookery Book*, by Pilaff Bey [Norman Douglas] (New York: William Heinemann, 1952), 5.

Chapter One

1. Norman Douglas, *An Almanac* (London: Chatto & Windus, 1945), 82, 78. *Hic iacet* translates to "here lies" and is a common phrase found on old headstones.
2. Norman Douglas, *Alone* (London: Chapman & Hall, 1921), 48.
3. Lytton Strachey to Douglas, October 29, 1923, box 19, folder 315, NDCB.
4. *Norman Douglas Selected Correspondence*, ed. Arthur S. Wensinger and Michael Allan, vol. 6, *Dear Sir (or Madam): Letters of Norman Douglas to Bryher and Two Letters from Bryher to Douglas* (Graz/Feldkirch, Austria: W. Neugebauer Verlag, 2013), 222.
5. Norman Douglas, *Together* (New York: Robert M. McBride, 1923), 83. This passage appeared first in a 1910 essay by Douglas, "Uplands of Sorrento," *English Review* 7 (1910): 125.
6. Norman Douglas, *Siren Land* (London: J. M. Dent & Sons, 1911), 34; Douglas, *London Street Games* (London: Chatto & Windus, 1931), xi.
7. Douglas, *Together*, 55–56, 62–64; E. M. Forster to Douglas, November 6, 1927, box 17, folder 246, NDCB; Lytton Strachey to Douglas, October 29, 1923, box 19, folder 315, NDCB.
8. Douglas, *Together*, 143–46.
9. *Together*, 237–38.
10. *Together*, 56.
11. Douglas used variants of this line at least twice in his writings; Normyx [Norman Douglas and Elsa FitzGibbon], *Unprofessional Tales* (London: T. Fisher Unwin, 1901); Douglas, *Siren Land*, 248.
12. Douglas, *An Almanac*, 52.
13. Mark Holloway notes for Martha Gordon Crotch biography, chap. 6, box 4, folder 2, MHGC.
14. Douglas to Elizabeth David, May 31, 1940, box 18, folder 7, EDS.
15. Douglas, *Together*, 213–25.
16. A couple rare exceptions that discuss sibling incest are C. Dallett Hemphill, *Siblings: Brothers and Sisters in American History* (New York: Oxford University Press, 2011), 41–46; and Brian Connolly, *Domestic Intimacies: Incest and the Liberal Subject in Nineteenth-Century America* (Philadelphia: University of Pennsylvania Press, 2014). For histories of father-daughter incest, see Linda Gordon, "Incest as a Form of Family Violence: Evidence from Historical Case Records," *Journal of Marriage and Family* 46, no. 1 (1984); Rachel Devlin, "'Acting Out the Oedipal Wish': Father-Daughter Incest and the Sexuality of Adolescent Girls in the United States, 1941–1965," *Journal*

of Social History 38, no. 3 (2005); and Lynn Sacco, *Unspeakable: Father-Daughter Incest in American History* (Baltimore: Johns Hopkins University Press, 2009).

17. Catharine A. MacKinnon, "Does Sexuality Have a History?," *Michigan Quarterly Review* 30 (1991): 1–2.

18. Steven Angelides, "Feminism, Child Sexual Abuse, and the Erasure of Child Sexuality," *GLQ: A Journal of Lesbian and Gay Studies* 10, no. 2 (2004): 142.

19. Valerie Sanders, "'Lifelong Soulmates?': The Sibling Bond in Nineteenth-Century Fiction," *Victorian Review* 39, no. 2 (2013).

20. Mark Holloway, *Norman Douglas: A Biography* (London: Secker & Warburg, 1976), 3–28. Holloway derived information about the family from a memoir by Douglas's half-sister, Grete Gulbransson, the daughter of Vanda and Jakob Jehly: *Geliebte Schatten: Eine Chronik Der Heimat* (Berlin: Grote, 1934).

21. Douglas to Archie Douglas, January 24, 1930, box 24, folder 372, NDCB.

22. Norman Douglas, *Looking Back: An Autobiographical Excursion* (New York: Harcourt, Brace, 1933), 388–92.

23. Douglas, *An Almanac*, 51. The line appeared originally in *Looking Back*, 68.

24. Constantine FitzGibbon, "Norman Douglas: A Biography" typescript (carbon) with "notes" for "Norman Douglas," 21, NYPL.

25. Ellen Bayuk Rosenman, *Unauthorized Pleasures: Accounts of Victorian Erotic Experience* (Ithaca, NY: Cornell University Press, 2004), 46.

26. John Chandos, *Boys Together: English Public Schools, 1800–1864* (New Haven, CT: Yale University Press, 1984). Relationships between older and younger girls at boarding schools have also received scholarly attention. See, for example, Martha Vicinus, "Distance and Desire: English Boarding-School Friendships," in *The Lesbian Issue: Essays from Signs*, ed. Estelle B. Freedman, Barbara C. Gelpi, Susan L. Johnson, and Kathleen M. Weston (Chicago: University of Chicago Press, 1985).

27. Douglas, *Looking Back*, 52–56. Douglas changes Collier's name to Cellier in *Looking Back*. Collier's correct name is given in WKLB. Douglas makes many arch comments about Collier's constipation and the state of his bowels in *Looking Back*, which implies physical familiarity at the very least.

28. Charles Upchurch, *Before Wilde: Sex between Men in Britain's Age of Reform* (Berkeley: University of California Press, 2009), 55–60.

29. Frank Harris's memoirs, for example, describe mutual masturbation at his boarding school during the 1870s as routine, and anal sex as a rare exception: *My Life and Loves* (Paris: privately printed, 1922), 26–27.

30. "Friday, Feb. 18th. 1949," box 7, folder 94, NDCB.

31. Jack Saul, *The Sins of the Cities of the Plain* (London: privately printed, 1881), 32–34; Morris B. Kaplan, "Who's Afraid of John Saul: Urban Culture and the Politics of Desire in Late Victorian London," *GLQ: A Journal of Lesbian and Gay Studies* 5, no. 3 (1999). Another pornographic text including boarding school scenes from the

late 1890s is the *Paidikion,* a privately circulated manuscript now in the Cornell Human Sexuality Collection; Toby Hammond, "*Paidikion*: A Paiderastic Manuscript," *International Journal of Greek Love* 1, no. 2 (1966).

32. Drewey Wayne Gunn, *Gay Novels of Britain, Ireland and the Commonwealth, 1881–1981: A Reader's Guide* (Jefferson, NC: McFarland, 2014), 12–13.

33. Holloway, *Norman Douglas,* 43.

34. Kim M. Phillips and Barry Reay, *Sex Before Sexuality: A Premodern History* (Cambridge: Polity, 2011), 60–65.

35. Oliver S. Buckton, *Secret Selves: Confession and Same-Sex Desire in Victorian Autobiography* (Chapel Hill: University of North Carolina Press, 1998), 87–91.

36. Upchurch, *Before Wilde,* 55–60; Dean Pavlakis, "Reputation and the Sexual Abuse of Boys: Changing Norms in Late-Nineteenth-Century Britain," *Men and Masculinities* 17, no. 3 (2014).

37. FitzGibbon, "Norman Douglas: A Biography" typescript, 17, NYPL.

38. George Rousseau, ed., *Children and Sexuality: The Greeks to the Great War* (London: Palgrave Macmillan, 2007), 173–230; Linda C. Dowling, *Hellenism and Homosexuality in Victorian Oxford* (Ithaca, NY: Cornell University Press, 1994), 110–53.

39. Faith Compton Mackenzie, *William Cory: A Biography* (London: Constable, 1950), 18, 44, 61.

40. Timothy d'Arch Smith, *Love in Earnest: Some Notes on the Lives and Writings of English 'Uranian' Poets from 1889 to 1930* (London: Routledge & Kegan Paul, 1970).

41. Leo McKinstry, *Rosebery: Statesman in Turmoil* (London: John Murray, 2005); *Norman Douglas Selected Correspondence,* ed. Arthur S. Wensinger and Michael Allan, vol. 4, *Italiam Petimus: Letters of Edward Hutton to Norman Douglas and a Selection of Letters from Douglas to Hutton* (Graz/Feldkirch, Austria: W. Neugebauer Verlag, 2011), 10; Simon Goldhill, *A Very Queer Family Indeed: Sex, Religion, and the Bensons in Victorian Britain* (Chicago: University of Chicago Press, 2016).

42. The line is "They told me, Heraclitus, they told me you were dead." See Compton Mackenzie, *My Life and Times: Octave 9, 1946–1953* (London: Chatto & Windus, 1970), 266; and Richard Aldington, *Pinorman: Personal Recollections of Norman Douglas, Pino Orioli and Charles Prentice* (London: William Heinemann, 1954). Douglas admired Cory's translation; Norman Douglas, *Three of Them* (London: Chatto & Windus, 1930), 47.

43. Harris, *My Life and Loves.*

44. Douglas, *Looking Back,* 333.

45. *Looking Back,* 334.

46. Douglas refers to Sherbrooke as Miriam in *Looking Back,* but he gives her correct name in WKLB.

47. Graham Ovenden and Robert Melville's art history book about Victorian child photography is now seen as problematic and quasi-pornographic: *Victorian Children*

(London: Academy Editions, 1972). See Catharine Lumby, "Ambiguity, Children, Representation, and Sexuality," *CLCWeb: Comparative Literature and Culture* 12, no. 4 (2010).

48. Harold March, *Romain Rolland* (New York: Twayne, 1971), 64. Sofia was also admired by the portraitist Franz von Lenbach, then in his late fifties, who painted her picture.

49. In *Looking Back*, 123, Douglas refers to Luigi Guerrieri Gonzaga by the pseudonym Luigi Sforza. Sforza's true family name and the dates of Douglas's engagement are in WKLB. Douglas specifies that Sofia was the sister he was engaged to in WKA.

50. *Looking Back*, 41.

51. *Looking Back*, 39.

52. Richard J. Evans, *Tales from the German Underworld: Crime and Punishment in the Nineteenth Century* (New Haven, CT: Yale University Press, 1998), 175.

53. Douglas, *Looking Back*, 42.

54. *Looking Back*, 113. Douglas thought Wohlgemut may have been a descendant of Albrecht Dürer's painting teacher Michael Wohlgemuth.

55. Cecil Woolf, *A Bibliography of Norman Douglas* (London: Rupert Hart-Davis, 1954), 146.

56. Douglas, *Looking Back*, 68, 367, 309.

57. *Looking Back*, 11. This is the second calling card included, but Douglas wrote only a single sentence after the first card. There is an earlier memory presented in the book's introduction, before the first calling card.

58. Ludwig became an important figure in early gay history and was included by Edward Prime-Stevenson in his book *The Intersexes* (1908), which the author gifted to Douglas. Xavier Mayne [Edward Irenaeus Prime-Stevenson], *The Intersexes: A History of Similsexualism* (privately printed, 1910), 241–42, 452. A description of Norman Douglas's copy of *The Intersexes*, with his penciled notes, can be found in a catalog of the rare books dealer Elysium Press, https://www.elysiumpress.com/images/upload/cat389_3.pdf.

59. Douglas, *Looking Back*, 232.

60. This interpretation of Douglas's sexual history contrasts with the interpretation of Holloway, who argues that Douglas turned his erotic attention to children later, in his thirties. Holloway, *Norman Douglas*, 115, 69.

61. For example, see Aldous Huxley, *Those Barren Leaves* (London: Chatto & Windus, 1928), 33.

62. Douglas, *Looking Back*, 333–36.

63. Mabel [Ninds] to Douglas, February 6, 1938, box 18, folder 286, NDCB.

64. Jana Funke, "'We Cannot Be Greek Now': Age Difference, Corruption of Youth and the Making of *Sexual Inversion*," *English Studies: A Journal of English Language and Literature* 94, no. 2 (2013).

Chapter Two

1. Keith Moore, "Mediterranean Blue," *The Repository*, Royal Society, March 19, 2013, https://blogs.royalsociety.org/history-of-science/2013/03/19/mediterranean -blue/.

2. Norman Douglas, *Looking Back: An Autobiographical Excursion* (New York: Harcourt, Brace, 1933), 209.

3. Douglas to Jane Douglass, March 12, 1888, box 17, folder 242, NDCB.

4. Eric G. E. Zuelow, *A History of Modern Tourism* (London: Palgrave Macmillan, 2016), 76–90.

5. Douglas, *Looking Back*, 206.

6. Gustave Heinrich Theodor Eimer, *Organic Evolution as the Result of the Inheritance of Acquired Characters According to the Laws of Organic Growth* (London: Macmillan, 1890), 241–43.

7. Norman Douglas, *Birds and Beasts of the Greek Anthology* (London: Chapman & Hall, 1928), 132–35.

8. Norman Douglas, *Late Harvest* (London: Lindsay Drummond, 1946), 28.

9. Hans Licht [Paul Brandt], *Sexual Life in Ancient Greece*, trans. J. H. Freese (London: Routledge & Kegan Paul, 1956), 193–94.

10. Douglas, *Looking Back*, 206.

11. Robert Aldrich, *The Seduction of the Mediterranean: Writing, Art and Homosexual Fantasy* (London: Routledge, 1993), 125.

12. Douglas, *Looking Back*, 117.

13. *Paris and Its Environs* (Leipzig: K. Baedeker, 1881), 109, 227. Douglas mentions the Louvre's copy of the statue in *Birds and Beasts*. For Parisian morgue tourism, see Harvey Levenstein, *Seductive Journey: American Tourists in France from Jefferson to the Jazz Age* (Chicago: University of Chicago Press, 1998), 110.

14. G. N. Douglass, "Variations of Plumage in the Corvidae," *The Zoologist: A Monthly Journal of Natural Science* 10, 3rd ser. (February 1886): 73; Douglass, "Variations of Colour in the European Squirrel," *The Zoologist: A Monthly Journal of Natural Science* 10, 3rd ser. (November 1886): 456. There was also a third note, Douglass, "Present Distribution of the Beaver in Europe," *The Zoologist: A Monthly Journal of Natural Science* 10, 3rd ser. (December 1886): 484. The full run of *The Zoologist* is digitized at the Biodiversity Heritage Library, http://www.biodiversitylibrary.org /bibliography/40487#/summary.

15. G. N. Douglass, "On the Herpetology of the Grand Duchy of Baden," *The Zoologist: A Monthly Journal of Natural Science* 15, no. 179, 3rd ser. (September 1891): 381.

16. G. N. Douglass, "On the Herpetology of the Grand Duchy of Baden," *The Zoologist: A Monthly Journal of Natural Science* 15, no. 172, 3rd ser. (April 1891): 143.

17. Greta LaFleur, *The Natural History of Sexuality in Early America* (Baltimore: Johns Hopkins University Press, 2018).

18. Norman Douglas, pocket diary, 1890, box 34, folder 570, NDCB.

19. Douglas, *Looking Back*, 197.

20. Judith R. Walkowitz, *City of Dreadful Delight: Narratives of Sexual Danger in Late-Victorian London* (Chicago: University of Chicago Press, 1992), 45–46.

21. Lise Shapiro Sanders, *Consuming Fantasies: Labor, Leisure, and the London Shopgirl, 1880–1920* (Columbus: Ohio State University Press, 2006).

22. Emma Liggins, *George Gissing, the Working Woman, and Urban Culture* (Burlington, VT: Ashgate, 2006), 125.

23. Douglas, *Three of Them*, 12–15.

24. Deborah Lutz, "Dandies, Libertines, and Byronic Lovers: Pornography and Erotic Decadence in Nineteenth-Century England," in *Decadences: Morality and Aesthetics in British Literature*, ed. Paul Fox (Stuttgart: ibidem-Verlag, 2006).

25. Constantine FitzGibbon, *Norman Douglas: A Pictorial Record* (London: Richards Press, 1953), 22.

26. Douglas, *Looking Back*, 239. Douglas gives the date for this flirtation as 1892 in WKLB.

27. *Looking Back*, 211. Incest also recurs as a theme in Decadent literature: Ray Furness, "Decadence and Fin de Siècle," in *The Cambridge History of Literary Criticism*, vol. 6, *The Nineteenth Century, c. 1830–1914*, ed. M. A. R. Habib (Cambridge: Cambridge University Press, 2013).

28. WKLB, 1.

29. Constantine FitzGibbon, "Norman Douglas: Memoir of an Unwritten Biography," *Encounter*, September 1974, 27.

30. Mark Holloway, *Norman Douglas: A Biography* (London: Secker & Warburg, 1976), 82.

31. Douglas, *Looking Back*, 191.

32. *Looking Back*, 167.

33. For example, see George Grote, *History of Greece*, vol. 3 (New York: Harper & Brothers, 1858), 223.

34. Joseph Allen Boone, *The Homoerotics of Orientalism* (New York: Columbia University Press, 2014), 51–110.

35. Richard Phillips, "Writing Travel and Mapping Sexuality: Richard Burton's Sotadic Zone," in *Writes of Passage: Reading Travel Writing*, ed. James Duncan and Derek Gregory (New York: Routledge, 1999).

36. Douglas, *Looking Back*, 329.

37. G. Norman Douglass, "On the Darwinian Hypothesis of Sexual Selection," *Natural Science: A Monthly Review of Scientific Progress* 7, no. 45 (1895); Douglass, "On the

Darwinian Hypothesis of Sexual Selection. Ii—the Case of the Wall-Lizard," *Natural Science: A Monthly Review of Scientific Progress* 7, no. 46 (1895).

38. Holloway, *Norman Douglas*, 98.

39. WKLB, 234.

40. Douglas, *Looking Back*, 196.

41. Laurie Bernstein, *Sonia's Daughters: Prostitutes and Their Regulation in Imperial Russia* (Berkeley: University of California Press, 1995), 98; Julie A. Cassiday and Leyla Rouhi, "From Nevskii Prospekt to Zoia's Apartment: Trials of the Russian Procuress," *Russian Review* 58, no. 3 (1999).

42. Douglas gives Anyuta's last name as Ponomareff in WKLB, 236. I spell her surname Ponomareva, as she signed her own letters, referenced below. Douglas later used the last name Ponomareff for a character in one of the short stories he co-wrote with his wife, Elsa FitzGibbon; see Normyx [Norman Douglas and Elsa FitzGibbon], *Unprofessional Tales* (London: T. Fisher Unwin, 1901), 2.

43. Douglas to Archie Douglas, November 4, 1921, box 21, folder 346, NDCB.

44. Bernstein, *Sonia's Daughters*, 42, 98.

45. A translator I consulted, Irina Gavrilova, offered the definition of Pusin'ka as "little daddy." The translator that Mark Holloway consulted, on the other hand, thought that Pomomareva was calling Douglas "Pussinka," a Russian version of the English word *pussy*. See MHRH, vol. 4.

46. Mark Holloway, "The Norman Douglas Collection at Yale," *Yale University Library Gazette* 50, no. 1 (1975): 12. In the biography, Holloway calls the letters "charming, but rather sad"; *Norman Douglas*, 119. Douglas claimed to have burned all but one of Ponomareva's letters in a fit of housekeeping conducted shortly before writing his memoirs. In fact, two letters survived the purge, and one includes a fragment that might have belonged to a third letter.

47. Sarah M. S. Pearsall, *Atlantic Families: Lives and Letters in the Later Eighteenth Century* (New York: Oxford University Press, 2008), 9.

48. Anyuta Ponomareva to Douglas, August 7 [n.d.], September 27 [n.d.], box 27, folder 252, NDCB. Translated by Irina Gavrilova.

49. Douglas, *Looking Back*, 197. Douglas's friend Brigit Patmore claimed that the cane was a gift from Douglas's aristocratic Russian girlfriend, but she was mistaken; Brigit Patmore, *My Friends When Young: The Memoirs of Brigit Patmore* (London: William Heinemann, 1968), 121. Douglas wrote to Archie in 1921 that the cane had been a gift from Ponomareva; Douglas to Archie Douglas, November 4, 1921, box 21, folder 346, NDCB.

50. Anyuta Ponomareva to Douglas, fragment [n.d.], box 27, folder 252, NDCB. Translated by Irina Gavrilova. The value of 200 rubles calculated according to https://www.historicalstatistics.org/Currencyconverter.html.

51. Anyuta Ponomareva to Douglas, August 7, September 27, [n.d.], box 27, folder 252, NDCB. Translated by Irina Gavrilova.

52. Douglas, *Looking Back*, 162.

53. WKLB, 236. The Demidov family is detailed in https://en.wikipedia.org/wiki /Pavel_Pavlovich_Demidov,_2nd_Prince_of_San_Donato. The entry includes a John Singer Sargent portrait, from 1895–96, of a woman labeled Princess Helene Petrovna Demidova, but Sargent scholars identify the subject as Sophie Ilarinovna Demidoff. https://www.johnsingersargent.org/Princess-Demidoff-Sophie -Ilarinovna.html Coincidentally, Princess Aurore Karageorgevitch and her husband lived in Florence during World War I, before Douglas settled in that city; see Harold Acton, *Memoirs of an Aesthete* (1948; repr., London: Methuen, 1970), 53.

54. Holloway, *Norman Douglas*, 119.

55. Richard Aldington, *Pinorman: Personal Recollections of Norman Douglas, Pino Orioli and Charles Prentice* (London: William Heinemann, 1954), 61.

56. Douglas, *Looking Back*, 224.

Chapter Three

1. Norman Douglas, *Siren Land and Fountains in the Sand* (London: Secker & Warburg, 1957), 95.

2. Percy Bysshe Shelley, "Letter XV," in *Essays, Letters from Abroad, Translations and Fragments, by Percy Bysshe Shelley*, ed. Mary Shelley (1840), vol. 2, *Letters from Italy*, http://terpconnect.umd.edu/~djb/shelley/lettersfromitaly.html. Douglas quotes Shelley at *Looking Back*, 303.

3. Douglas calls Foley "Nathaniel Filson" in *Looking Back: An Autobiographical Excursion* (New York: Harcourt, Brace, 1933), and gives his true name, Nelson Foley, in WKLB, 370. For Foley's umbrella patent, see https://www.google.com/patents /US660248.

4. For literature on the history of sex tourism, see Paul Fussell, *Abroad: British Literary Traveling between the Wars* (New York: Oxford University Press, 1980), 113–30; Robert Aldrich, *The Seduction of the Mediterranean: Writing, Art and Homosexual Fantasy* (London: Routledge, 1993); Ian Littlewood, *Sultry Climates: Travel and Sex* (Cambridge, MA: Da Capo Press, 2001), 24; Chiara Beccalossi, "The 'Italian Vice': Male Homosexuality and British Tourism in Southern Italy," in *Italian Sexualities Uncovered, 1789–1914*, ed. John H. Arnold, Joanna Bourke, and Sean Brady (London: Macmillan Palgrave, 2015); and Mario Bolognari, "Taormina and the Strange Case of Baron Von Gloeden," in *Homosexuality in Italian Literature, Society, and Culture, 1789–1919*, ed. Lorenzo Benadusi, Paolo L. Bernardini, Elisa Bianco, and Paolo Guazzo (Newcastle upon Tyne, UK: Cambridge Scholars Press, 2017).

5. Barbara Pozzo, "Male Homosexuality in Nineteenth-Century Italy: A Juridicial View," in *Homosexuality in Italian Literature, Society, and Culture, 1789–1919*, ed. Lorenzo Benadusi, Paolo L. Bernardini, Elisa Bianco, and Paolo Guazzo (Newcastle upon Tyne, UK: Cambridge Scholars Press, 2017).

6. Pozzo quotes from Giovanni Dall'Orto, who writes, "Per tale regione è considerata un male minore (a patto che sia condotta in segreto) una fase di 'omosessualità di compensazione' dei giovani (fra loro o con gli 'omosezzuali,' questi ultimi rigorosamente nel ruolo 'passivo') fino a quando non abbiano un reddito sufficiente per pagare le prostitute"; Pozzo, 120–25.

7. Bolognari, "Taormina and the Strange Case of Baron Von Gloeden," 160.

8. Frank Harris, *Oscar Wilde: His Life and Confessions*, vol. 1 (New York: Brentano's, 1916), 250–51.

9. Littlewood, *Sultry Climates*, 107.

10. Lord Rosebery was widely reputed to have sexual relationships with men, but his biographer disputes this; Leo McKinstry, *Rosebery: Statesman in Turmoil* (London: John Murray, 2005).

11. Eugenio Zito, "'Amori Et Dolori Sacrum': Canons, Differences and Figures of Gender Identity in the Cultural Panorama of Travellers in Capri between the Nineteenth and Twentieth Century," in *Homosexuality in Italian Literature, Society, and Culture, 1789–1919*, ed. Lorenzo Benadusi, Paolo L. Bernardini, Elisa Bianco, and Paolo Guazzo (Newcastle upon Tyne, UK: Cambridge Scholars Press, 2017).

12. Douglas, *Looking Back*, 377.

13. Beccalossi, "The 'Italian Vice.'" *Femminielli* are part of the trans past and present, but were not understood as trans in the late nineteenth century. On the challenge of defining historic archetypes as "trans," see Genny Beemyn, "A Presence in the Past: A Transgender Historiography," *Journal of Women's History* 25, no. 4 (2013).

14. Norman Douglas to Oscar Levy, February 2, 1914, in *Norman Douglas Selected Correspondence*, ed. Arthur S. Wensinger and Michael Allan, vol. 3, *Goût de l'espace: Letters of Oscar Levy to Norman Douglas and a Selection of Letters from Douglas to Levy* (Graz/Feldkirch, Austria: W. Neugebauer Verlag, 2010), 22–23.

15. Naples continued to have high numbers of boy prostitutes well into the twentieth century; see Wardell Baxter Pomeroy, *Dr. Kinsey and the Institute for Sex Research* (New York: Harper & Row, 1972), 421–26.

16. Douglas, *Looking Back*, 216.

17. Monica Konrad, *Nameless Relations: Anonymity, Melanesia and Reproductive Gift Exchange between British Ova Donors and Recipients* (New York: Berghahn Books, 2005), 161.

18. WKLB.

19. Julie Peakman, *Amatory Pleasures: Explorations in Eighteenth-Century Sexual Culture* (London: Bloomsbury Academic, 2016), 101–12.

20. Deborah Gorham, "The 'Maiden Tribute of Modern Babylon' Re-Examined: Child

Prostitution and the Idea of Childhood in Late-Victorian England," *Victorian Studies* 21, no. 3 (1978); Judith R. Walkowitz, *City of Dreadful Delight: Narratives of Sexual Danger in Late-Victorian London* (Chicago: University of Chicago Press, 1992), 81–134.

21. Douglas to Archie Douglas, July 28, 1925, box 22, folder 352, NDCB.

22. All quotations from Douglas about the affair are taken from Douglas, *Looking Back*, 199–202. Douglas used a single *n* for her name in *Looking Back*, but added a second *n* in WKLB.

23. Carl Ipsen, *Italy in the Age of Pinocchio: Children and Danger in the Liberal Era* (New York: Palgrave Macmillan, 2006), 183.

24. Brigit Patmore, *My Friends When Young: The Memoirs of Brigit Patmore* (London: William Heinemann, 1968), 125–28.

25. H. M. Tomlinson, review of *Looking Back*, by Norman Douglas, *Spectator*, May 5, 1933, 645.

26. Raymond Mortimer, "The Story of a Friendship," *Sunday Times*, box 40, folder 638, NDCB.

27. Theodora FitzGibbon, *Love Lies a Loss: An Autobiography, 1946–1959* (London: Century, 1985), 92.

28. Bolognari, "Taormina and the Strange Case of Baron Von Gloeden." Dall'Orto is quoted in Bolognari, 182.

29. Beccalossi, "The 'Italian Vice,'" 193.

30. Ipsen, *Italy in the Age of Pinocchio.*

31. Norman Douglas, *Reports of Subjects of General and Commercial Interest. Italy. Report on the Pumice Stone Industry of the Lipari Islands* (London: H. M. Stationery Office, 1895).

32. Beccalossi, "The 'Italian Vice,'" 203.

33. See, for example, Mark Holloway, *Norman Douglas: A Biography* (London: Secker & Warburg, 1976), 116; and Gary Simes, "Douglas, Norman," in *Who's Who in Gay and Lesbian History: From Antiquity to the Mid-Twentieth Century*, ed. Robert Aldrich and Gary Wotherspoon (London: Routledge, 2001).

34. Douglas describes his relationship with Carpenter in *Looking Back*, 1–7. For information about Wallace Carpenter, see Kurt Gänzl, *Victorian Vocalists* (New York: Routledge, 2017). Euphemia Wallace Carpenter's birth date is given in a genealogy of her second husband, the Austrian antiquarian Baron von Siebold: *Nederland's Adelsboek* (Gravenhage: W. P. van Stockum & Zoon, 1917), 177.

Chapter Four

1. E. F. Douglas, diary (1901–1902), May 24, 1902, 236, box 38, folder 603, NDCB.

2. Kurt Aram [Hans Fischer], *Violet: Der Roman einer Mutter* (Berlin: Ullstein, 1913), 1.

3. Norman Douglas, *Looking Back: An Autobiographical Excursion* (New York: Harcourt, Brace, 1933), 304–6.

4. Aram, *Violet*, 6.
5. Simon Goldhill, *A Very Queer Family Indeed: Sex, Religion, and the Bensons in Victorian Britain* (Chicago: University of Chicago Press, 2016), 22.
6. Constantine FitzGibbon, [Norman Douglas: an unfinished biography], box 34, folders 2–5, CFHR.
7. Vanda Douglass Jehly, Armatin diary, January 20, January 23, and March 10, 1894, DSD. Translations by Gabriela Hirt.
8. Aram, *Violet*, 6–10.
9. Aram, 11.
10. Mark Holloway, *Norman Douglas: A Biography* (London: Secker & Warburg, 1976), 96.
11. FitzGibbon, [Norman Douglas], 71.
12. FitzGibbon, 85.
13. Douglas to Archie Douglas, May 30, 1927, box 22, folder 353, NDCB. See also Douglas to Archie Douglas, August 12, 1925, box 22, folder 351, NDCB.
14. Constantine FitzGibbon, "Norman Douglas: Memoir of an Unwritten Biography," *Encounter*, September 1974, 35.
15. Viola Johnson, letter to the editor, *Encounter*, February 1975, 94–95.
16. Constantine FitzGibbon, letter to the editor, *Encounter*, February 1975, 95–96.
17. Elsa FitzGibbon scrapbook, DSD.
18. Muriel Draper, "Buffetings in a South Wind: Some Memories of Norman Douglas," box 11, folder 355, MDPB.
19. FitzGibbon, "Norman Douglas: Memoir of an Unwritten Biography."
20. FitzGibbon, [Norman Douglas], 98.
21. Douglas, *Looking Back*, 82–83.
22. Douglas to Faith Mackenzie, July 14, 1951, in *Norman Douglas Selected Correspondence*, ed. Arthur S. Wensinger and Michael Allan, vol. 1, *Respectful Ribaldry: A Selection of Letters from Norman Douglas to Faith Compton Mackenzie* (Graz/Feldkirch, Austria: W. Neugebauer Verlag, 2008), 153. It's possible that this sexual encounter took place during a different trip to Delhi.
23. FitzGibbon, "Norman Douglas: Memoir of an Unwritten Biography," 35.
24. Johnson, letter to the editor, 94–95.
25. Robin Maugham, *Escape from the Shadows* (London: Hodder and Stoughton, 1972), 198.
26. E. F. Douglas, diary (1901–1902). Elsa's diary is archived in the Douglas Papers at the Beinecke Library, but it does not come from Douglas's personal collection. He surely would have destroyed the diary if he could have. The diary was in the possession of Elsa's sister Violet (Viva) Fairholme, who gave it to Archie Douglas after his father's death. Archie, who had little contact with his mother's side of the family when his father was living, sought to reconnect with these lost kin in 1952. After

Archie visited, Viva wrote to him that she had found a diary of his mother's that was "all about you as a tiny boy + very interesting, written in English." Archie later sold the diary to the Beinecke. See Viva Fairholme to Archie Douglas, October 10, 1953, SNDV.

27. E. F. Douglas, diary (1901–1902), 79.

28. Cecil Woolf, *A Bibliography of Norman Douglas* (London: Rupert Hart-Davis, 1954), 26.

29. E. F. Douglas, diary (1901–1902), 56.

30. E. F. Douglas, diary (1901–1902), 234–36.

31. Aram, *Violet*, 1.

32. E. F. Douglas, diary (1901–1902), 275.

33. FitzGibbon, [Norman Douglas], 104.

34. Douglas noted how his domicile came in handy in his divorce in *Looking Back*, 35. He later advised his own son Archie to get divorced in Scotland when his first marriage ended; Douglas to Archie Douglas, March 28, 1931, box 23, folder 358, NDCB.

35. Divorce. G. N. Douglass v. E. L. T. Fitzgibbon or Douglass, April 1904, CS46 Court of Sessions: warrants of the Register of Acts and Decreets, 5th Series, CS46/1904/4/27.

36. "Ex-Diplomat's Divorce: Secret Visits of a German Officer," *Star*, May 14, 1904. A Welsh newspaper also carried an account of the divorce: "In by the Window: Austrian Baron and Scotsman's Wife: Diplomatist's Action for Divorce," *Evening Express*, March 19, 1904.

37. FitzGibbon, [Norman Douglas], 90.

38. File 40899: Custody of children of George Norman Douglas, allegations of immorality by his former wife. Including: Paper 40899, folios 533–538; paper 41014, folios 539–543; paper 41445, folios 544–549, BNA; Norman Douglas, pocket diary, 1908, box 34, folder 572, NDCB.

39. Archie Douglas to Mark Holloway, January 1970, MHRH, vol. 4.

40. Douglas, *Looking Back*, 241–44. WKLB, 294, notes that the "events" were that Douglas had "won a lawsuit against his wife."

41. Archie Douglas to Mark Holloway, September 30, 1969, MHRH, vol. 4.

42. Martha Gordon Crotch, diary, book 8, October 3, 1937, box 3, MHGC.

43. Draper, "Buffetings in a South Wind." Another friend recalls Douglas being more disturbed than jubilant about the manner of Elsa's death. According to Walter Lowenfels, Douglas once fled a restaurant that smelled of burnt meat because it reminded him of Elsa. Walter Lowenfels, "Remembering Norman Douglas, 'a Letter,'" *Literary Review* 5, no. 3 (1962).

44. Letter to the editor from Mrs. F. Flydes, *Telegraph*, June 13, 1977, box 40, folder 638, NDCB.

45. Compton Mackenzie, *My Life and Times: Octave Five, 1915–1923* (London: Chatto & Windus, 1966), 52.

46. Archie Douglas to Mark Holloway, September 30, 1969, MHRH, vol. 4.

47. Gayle Rubin, "Thinking Sex: Notes for a Radical Theory of the Politics of Sexuality," in *Culture, Society and Sexuality: A Reader*, ed. Richard Parker and Peter Aggleton (New York: Routledge, 1984).

48. Richard Aldington, *Pinorman: Personal Recollections of Norman Douglas, Pino Orioli and Charles Prentice* (London: William Heinemann, 1954), 60.

49. William Grange, *Cultural Chronicle of the Weimar Republic* (Lanham, MD: Scarecrow Press, 2008), 101.

50. FitzGibbon, "Norman Douglas: Memoir of an Unwritten Biography," 34.

51. Mark Holloway, "The Norman Douglas Collection at Yale," *Yale University Library Gazette* 50, no. 1 (1975): 5.

Chapter Five

1. Ferdinand Gregorovius, *Island of Capri: A Mediterranean Idyll*, trans. M. Douglass Fairbairn (London: T. Fisher Unwin, 1896), 20.

2. "Current Literature: The Island of Capri," *The Academy and Literature*, October 24, 1896, 307.

3. La Capria is quoted in Claudio Gargano, *Capri pagana: Uranisti e amazzoni tra Ottocento e Novecento* (Capri: Edizioni la Conchiglia, 2007), 135. In the original Italian, "il più grande . . . di tutti gli scrittori che hanno scritto su Capri."

4. Constantine FitzGibbon, [Norman Douglas: an unfinished biography], box 34, folders 2–5, CFHR.

5. Mary Douglass Fairbairn to Douglas, April 9, 1903, box 17, folder 237, NDCB.

6. Fitzgibbon, [Norman Douglas: an unfinished biography], 98–103, CFHR.

7. Norman Douglas, *Late Harvest* (London: Lindsay Drummond, 1946), 21, viii.

8. Norman Douglas, *Looking Back: An Autobiographical Excursion* (New York: Harcourt, Brace, 1933), 374. Elsa records the news of Campo Alegre's death in a diary entry dated February 8, 1902, in E. F. Douglas, diary (1901–1902), box 38, folder 603, NDCB.

9. Natalie Barney to Mark Holloway, September 4, 1967, MHRH, vol. 2.

10. Douglas, *Late Harvest*, 19.

11. Douglas, *Looking Back*, 301–3. WKLB includes Douglas's nasty description of his would-be seductress, Laura Basile [Bessarion], as "lo Cunto dei Cunti."

12. For Draper's memories of meeting Douglas, see Muriel Draper, "Buffetings in a South Wind: Some Memories of Norman Douglas," box 11, folder 355, MDPB. For Webb's financial support of Douglas, see Martin Birnbaum, *The Last Romantic: The Story of More than a Half-Century in the World of Art* (New York: Twayne, 1960), 33; Douglas, *Looking Back*, 43–44.

13. Richard Aldington, *Pinorman: Personal Recollections of Norman Douglas, Pino Orioli and Charles Prentice* (London: William Heinemann, 1954), 151–54, 203–4.

14. Eugenio Zito, "'Amori Et Dolori Sacrum': Canons, Differences and Figures of Gender Identity in the Cultural Panorama of Travellers in Capri between the Nineteenth and Twentieth Century," in *Homosexuality in Italian Literature, Society, and Culture, 1789–1919*, ed. Lorenzo Benadusi, Paolo L. Bernardini, Elisa Bianco, and Paolo Guazzo (Newcastle upon Tyne, UK: Cambridge Scholars Press, 2017), 142.

15. Robert Aldrich, *The Seduction of the Mediterranean: Writing, Art and Homosexual Fantasy* (London: Routledge, 1993), 125–26.

16. Douglas, *Looking Back*, 152–61.

17. William Manchester, *The Arms of Krupp, 1587–1968* (New York: Little, Brown, 1968), 231.

18. Will H. L. Ogrinc, "Frère Jacques: A Shrine to Love and Sorrow: Jacques d'Adelswärd-Fersen (1880–1923)," 2006, http://semgai.free.fr/doc_et_pdf/Fersen-engels.pdf.

19. Douglas, *Looking Back*, 293–99.

20. Birnbaum, *Last Romantic*, 33.

21. The two novels are Compton Mackenzie, *Vestal Fire* (1927; repr., London: Chatto & Windus, 1964), and Roger Peyrefitte, *The Exile of Capri*, trans. Edward Hyams (London: Secker & Warburg, 1961).

22. Ted Morgan, *Somerset Maugham* (New York: Simon & Schuster, 1980), 23.

23. Robin Maugham, *Escape from the Shadows* (London: Hodder and Stoughton, 1972), 105.

24. Alan Searle to Mark Holloway, March 6, 1968, MHRH, vol. 2.

25. Simon Goldhill, *A Very Queer Family Indeed: Sex, Religion, and the Bensons in Victorian Britain* (Chicago: University of Chicago Press, 2016), 135.

26. Faith Compton Mackenzie, *Always Afternoon* (London: Collins, 1943), 90–91.

27. Norman Douglas, *Birds and Beasts of the Greek Anthology* (London: Chapman & Hall, 1928). Douglas also wrote to his friend the classicist John Mavrogordato that he preferred Brooks's translations to those of Humbert Wolfe, a far more well-respected poet. Douglas was likely alone in that opinion. *Norman Douglas Selected Correspondence*, ed. Arthur S. Wensinger and Michael Allan, vol. 7, *Straining Friendship to Breaking Point: Letters from John Mavrogordato to Norman Douglas and a Selection of Letters from Douglas to Mavrogordato* (Graz/Feldkirch, Austria: W. Neugebauer Verlag, 2014), 26.

28. Louis Golding, *Sunward* (London: Chatto & Windus, 1924). See also Aldous Huxley's novel *Crome Yellow* (London: Chatto & Windus, 1921), 161, where a character based on Douglas ruminates in ribald terms about Tiberius.

29. Douglas, *Looking Back*, 374.

30. Douglas, *Late Harvest*, viii.

31. Norman Douglas, Notebooks A, B, C, & D, box 44, NDCB.

32. Birnbaum, *Last Romantic*, 33.

33. Norman Douglas, *The Blue Grotto and Its Literature* (London: Adams Bros., 1904), 5.

34. Douglas, Notebook A, 13, 8, box 44, folder B1 + B2, NDCB.

35. Norman Douglas, *Three Monographs* (Napoli: Luici Pierro, 1906), 102.

36. *Three Monographs*, 108.

37. Joseph Cavorse, ed., *The Lives of the Twelve Caesars by Suetonius* (New York: Modern Library, 1931), 145.

38. Tiberius appears in the pornographic book *Monumens de la vie privée des douze Césars*, which Douglas consulted during his research. See Douglas, Notebook C, 141, box 44, folder B2, NDCB.

39. Normyx [Norman Douglas and Elsa FitzGibbon], *Unprofessional Tales* (London: T. Fisher Unwin, 1901), 42.

40. Douglas, *The Blue Grotto and Its Literature*, 13.

41. Douglas, *Three Monographs*, 121–35.

42. Lytton Strachey to Douglas, November 15, 1923, box 19, folder 315, NDCB.

43. For comparisons between Douglas and Lucian, see Pino Orioli, "To India with Norman," NYPL; "England's Lucians," *Times Literary Supplement*, February 15, 1952, Clippings folder, HUT: I: C: 6: H1–6, BIF; and John Davenport, "A Man of Boundless Tolerance," box 122, folder 4275, BPB. For "Erotes" as pederastic swan song, see James Jope, "Interpretation and Authenticity of the Lucianic Erotes," *Helios* 38, no. 1 (2011). It's possible that "Erotes" has been wrongly ascribed to Lucian, but this dialogue was included with his writings during Douglas's era.

44. Edward Hutton, *A Glimpse of Greece* (London: Medici Society, 1928), 266.

45. Norman Douglas, *Siren Land and Fountains in the Sand* (London: Secker & Warburg, 1957), 116, 29. Douglas's 1915 book *Old Calabria*, about his travels through southern Italy, included a similar treatment of the life of the flying monk Joseph of Copertino, whom Douglas called "a seventeenth-century pioneer of aviation." *Old Calabria* (London: Martin Secker, 1915), 68–76.

46. Mackenzie, *Vestal Fire*.

47. Faith Compton Mackenzie, *As Much as I Dare: The Autobiography of Faith Compton Mackenzie* (London: Collins, 1938), 241. Faith's husband, Compton Mackenzie, also likened Douglas to Silenus in "Norman Douglas: A Tribute," aired on the Scottish Home Service, November 11, 1948, box 40, folder 623, NDCB.

48. Theodora FitzGibbon, *A Taste of Love: The Memoirs of Bohemian Irish Food Writer Theodora FitzGibbon* (Dublin: Gill & Macmillan, 2015), chap. 25.

49. "Love and Mr.—: Postscript to a Happy Pagan . . . Who helped make Capri the Most Notorious Island," Clippings folder, HUT: I: C: 6: H1–6, BIF.

50. Nancy Cunard, *Grand Man: Memories of Norman Douglas* (London: Secker & Warburg, 1954), 52.

51. Oscar Levy to Douglas, December 14, 1924, box 18, folder 269, NDCB. Levy wasn't

the only critic to observe this parallel between Douglas and Petronius. See also Hannah Pierce, "How Well Have They Worn?—17. *South Wind*," April 28, 1966, box 40, folder 638, NDCB.

52. *Norman Douglas Selected Correspondence*, ed. Arthur S. Wensinger and Michael Allan, vol. 3, *Goût de l'espace: Letters of Oscar Levy to Norman Douglas and a Selection of Letters from Douglas to Levy* (Graz/Feldkirch, Austria: W. Neugebauer Verlag, 2010).

53. Linda C. Dowling, *Hellenism and Homosexuality in Victorian Oxford* (Ithaca, NY: Cornell University Press, 1994).

Reflection I

1. Islay Lyons notebook, box 61, NDCB.

2. Emma Renold, Jessica Ringrose, and R. Danielle Egan, eds., *Children, Sexuality and Sexualization* (London: Palgrave Macmillan, 2015), 1–8.

3. Steven Angelides, *The Fear of Child Sexuality: Young People, Sex, and Agency* (Chicago: University of Chicago Press, 2019).

Chapter Six

1. Joseph Conrad to Douglas, February 2, 1908, box 17, folder 233, NDCB.

2. "An Unnatural Feud," *The Cavalier*, December 1908, 540–47.

3. Ovid, box 12, UCND.

4. Cecil Woolf, *A Bibliography of Norman Douglas* (London: Rupert Hart-Davis, 1954).

5. Norman Douglas, *Looking Back: An Autobiographical Excursion* (New York: Harcourt, Brace, 1933), 44.

6. Frederick R. Karl, "Joseph Conrad, Norman Douglas, and the *English Review*," *Journal of Modern Literature* 2, no. 3 (1971/72).

7. *The Collected Letters of Joseph Conrad*, ed. Frederick R. Karl and Laurence Davies, vol. 3, *1903–1907* (Cambridge: Cambridge University Press, 1988), 235.

8. See, for example, Joseph Conrad, "The Secret Sharer," in *'Twixt Land and Sea* (New York: Hodder & Stoughton, 1912), 113–75.

9. J. H. Stape, "'Intimate Friends': Norman Douglas and Joseph Conrad," *The Conradian* 34, no. 1 (2009): 158.

10. *Collected Letters of Joseph Conrad*, 3:230–31.

11. *Collected Letters*, 3:230–31.

12. *Collected Letters*, 3:238. Douglas provided different, but similarly low, estimates of total sales, at other points.

13. *Collected Letters*, 3:277.

14. *The Collected Letters of Joseph Conrad*, ed. Frederick R. Karl and Laurence Davies, vol. 4, *1908–1911* (Cambridge: Cambridge University Press, 1990), 68.

15. Woolf, *A Bibliography of Norman Douglas*, 167–68.

16. William Kingdon Clifford, *Lectures and Essays, by the late William Kingdon Clifford* (New York: Macmillan, 1886), 346.

17. The play is *A Provincial Lady*. See Conrad's preface to Edward Garnett, *Turgenev: A Study* (London: W. Collins, 1917).

18. Walter Leuba and Ernest Dilworth, *Two Dialogues: George Santayana, Norman Douglas* (Pittsburgh: privately printed, 1974), 30.

19. Cecil Woolf to Douglas, March 31, 1951; Douglas to Woolf, April 7, 1951, box 20, folder 326, NDCB. Gershon Legman repeated this rumor in his *Rationale of the Dirty Joke: An Analysis of Sexual Humor* (New York: Grove Press, 1968).

20. "Thomas Andrew Hall," *Dictionary of Irish Architects, 1720–1940*, Irish Architectural Archive (2019), http://www.dia.ie/architects/view/2327/HALL -THOMASANDREW.

21. *The Letters of D. H. Lawrence*, vol. 3, part 1, *October 1916–June 1921*, ed. James T. Boulton and Andrew Robertson (Cambridge: Cambridge University Press, 1984), 28–29.

22. *Collected Letters of Joseph Conrad*, 4:244.

23. Woolf, *A Bibliography of Norman Douglas*, 149.

24. Norman Douglas, "Land of Chaos," *Cornhill Magazine*, July–December 1910, 381.

25. "Land of Chaos," 389.

26. "Land of Chaos," 381.

27. Claire Dederer, "What Do We Do with the Art of Monstrous Men?," *Paris Review*, November 20, 2017.

28. Toto Roccuzzo, *Taormina, l'isola del cielo: Come Taorminao divenne "Taormina"* (Catania, Sicilia: Giuseppe Maimone, 1992), 56–63; Mario Bolognari, "Taormina and the Strange Case of Baron Von Gloeden," in *Homosexuality in Italian Literature, Society, and Culture, 1789–1919*, ed. Lorenzo Benadusi, Paolo L. Bernardini, Elisa Bianco, and Paolo Guazzo (Newcastle upon Tyne, UK: Cambridge Scholars Press, 2017).

29. Stefania Arcara, "Hellenic Transgressions, Homosexual Politics: Wilde, Symonds and Sicily," *Studies in Travel Writing* 16, no. 2 (2012).

30. Douglas, "Land of Chaos," 390.

31. Pino Orioli, "Sant'Agata, 1933," 6, NYPL.

32. Norman Douglas, *Late Harvest* (London: Lindsay Drummond, 1946), 74–75.

33. Norman Douglas, *Siren Land and Fountains in the Sand* (London: Secker & Warburg, 1957), 75.

34. Lytton Strachey to Douglas, November 15, 1923, box 19, folder 315, NDCB.

35. Norman Douglas, *Alone* (London: Chapman & Hall, 1921), 182.

36. Douglas, *Late Harvest*, 76.

37. Compton Mackenzie, *My Life and Times: Octave Four, 1907–1915* (London: Chatto & Windus, 1965), 179.

38. Joseph Conrad to Douglas, December 16, 1912, in *The Collected Letters of Joseph Conrad*, ed. Frederick R. Karl and Laurence Davies, vol. 5, *1912–1916* (Cambridge: Cambridge University Press, 1996), 148.

39. Joseph Allen Boone, *The Homoerotics of Orientalism* (New York: Columbia University Press, 2014), 51, 271–75.

40. Douglas, *Siren Land and Fountains in the Sand*, 212, 52.

41. Boone, *The Homoerotics of Orientalism*, 51.

42. Joseph Conrad to Douglas, August 16, 1912, in *Collected Letters of Joseph Conrad*, 5:98.

43. Norman Douglas, pocket diary, October 21, 1912, box 34, folder 374, NDCB.

Chapter Seven

1. Eric Wolton to Douglas, August 1911, in *Norman Douglas Selected Correspondence*, ed. Arthur S. Wensinger and Michael Allan, vol. 2, *Dear Doug! Letters to Norman Douglas from Eric Wolton, René Mari, Marcel Mercier and Ettore Masciandaro and a Selection of Letters from Emilio Papa* (Graz/Feldkirch, Austria: W. Neugebauer Verlag, 2008), 14.

2. Peter N. Stearns, "Challenges in the History of Childhood," *Journal of the History of Childhood and Youth* 1, no. 1 (2008): 35, 39–40.

3. Shirley Jülich and Eileen B. Oak, "Does Grooming by Child Abusers Lead to Stockholm Syndrome? The Social Work Practice Implications," *Aotearoa New Zealand Social Work* 28, no. 3 (2016): 47–56.

4. Norman Douglas, pocket diary, November 5, 1910, box 35, folder 573, NDCB.

5. John Davidson, *Fleet Street and Other Poems* (London: Grant Richards, 1909), 27–28.

6. Martha Gordon Crotch, typescript autobiography, 463, box 2, MHGC.

7. Louise Jackson, *Child Sexual Abuse in Victorian England* (New York: Routledge, 2000), 96–106; Matt Houlbrook, *Queer London: Perils and Pleasures in the Sexual Metropolis, 1918–1957* (Chicago: University of Chicago Press, 2005), 232–36.

8. Douglas, pocket diary, 1910, box 35, folder 573, NDCB.

9. Douglas, pocket diary, 1914, box 35, folder 575, NDCB.

10. Douglas, pocket diary, 1911, box 35, folder 574, NDCB.

11. "Fisher Boy, 1841–44," in *American Sculpture in the Metropolitan Museum of Art*, vol. 1, ed. Thayer Tolles (New York: Metropolitan Museum of Art, 1999), 14–15. Coincidentally, one of the purchasers for *Fisher Boy* was Prince Anatole Demidoff, a relative of Douglas's Russian lover, Helen Demidoff.

12. Eric Wolton, "Italian Diary 1911," 58, MHRH.

13. Eric Wolton, [Cotrone letter], MHRH.

14. Leslie Gardiner, *South to Calabria* (London: William Blackwood, 1968), 151.

15. Norman Douglas, "Uplands of Sorrento," *English Review* 7 (1910): 125.

16. Kadji Amin, *Disturbing Attachments: Genet, Modern Pederasty, and Queer History* (Durham, NC: Duke University Press, 2017), 117–18; Norman Douglas, *Late Harvest* (London: Lindsay Drummond, 1946), 8–9.

17. Norman Douglas, *Old Calabria* (London: Martin Secker, 1915), 1, 10, 18, 65.

18. *Old Calabria*, 318–22.

19. Norman Douglas, *Looking Back: An Autobiographical Excursion* (New York: Harcourt, Brace, 1933), 30.

20. *The Collected Letters of Joseph Conrad*, ed. Frederick R. Karl and Laurence Davies, vol. 4, *1908–1911* (Cambridge: Cambridge University Press, 1990), 446.

21. Robin Douglas, "My Boyhood with Conrad," *Cornhill Magazine*, January 1929.

22. *Collected Letters of Joseph Conrad*, 4:472–73.

23. Eric Wolton, [Malaria letter], MHRH.

24. Douglas, *Looking Back*, 31.

25. Douglas, *Late Harvest*, 48.

26. Douglas, *Looking Back*, 45.

27. *Collected Letters of Joseph Conrad*, 4:495–96.

28. Mark Holloway, *Norman Douglas: A Biography* (London: Secker & Warburg, 1976), 196.

29. Norman Douglas, *London Street Games* (London: Chatto & Windus, 1931), ix.

30. *London Street Games* research material, box 2, folders 23, 24, 25; box 42, folder 646, NDCB.

31. Douglas, *London Street Games*, ix.

32. Robin Douglas, "Ah! There You Are!," *Virginia Quarterly Review* 16, no. 4 (1940): 582.

33. Holloway, *Norman Douglas*, 224.

34. Norman Douglas, "In Our Alley," *English Review*, November 1913.

35. Grace Eckley, *Children's Lore in Finnegans Wake* (Syracuse, NY: Syracuse University Press, 1985).

36. Douglas, "In Our Alley," 540.

37. "In Our Alley," 541.

38. Mark Morton, *The Lover's Tongue: A Merry Romp through the Language of Love and Sex* (Toronto: Insomniac Press, 2003), 121–23.

39. Douglas, *London Street Games*, 12.

40. *London Street Games*, ix–xi.

41. Douglas, *Looking Back*, 331. Also see Philip Waller, *Writers, Readers, and Reputations: Literary Life in Britain 1870–1918* (Oxford: Oxford University Press, 2006)

42. Helen Smith, "'I am glad you have nailed our colours to the mast': Norman Douglas and Edward Garnett," in *Norman Douglas: 7. Symposium, Bregenz und Thüringen, Vlbg., 12./13. 10. 2012*, ed. Wilhelm Meusburger (Bregenz, Austria: Norman Douglas Forschungsstelle, Vorarlberger Landesbibliothek, 2013), 69–76.

43. James Y. Dayananda, "(Mary) Adelaide Eden Phillpotts," in *Dictionary of Literary Biography*, vol. 191, *British Novelists Between the Wars*, ed. George M. Johnson (Farmington Hills, MI: Gale, 1998).

44. Passage quoted in letter from Rupert Hart-Davis to Mark Holloway, February 24, 1970, MHRH, vol. 4.

45. Hugh Walpole to Douglas, 1913, box 19, folder 323, NDCB.

46. "Norman Douglas: A Tribute by Compton Mackenzie, Moray McLaren, C. M. Grieve and Others," November 11, 1948, box 40, folder 623, NDCB.

47. J. H. Stape, "'Intimate Friends': Norman Douglas and Joseph Conrad," *The Conradian* 34, no. 1 (2009): 159.

48. Douglas, pocket diary, 1913, box 35, folder 575, NDCB.

49. See, for example, Douglas to Richard Curle, January 9, 1913, box 1, UCND.

50. Neil Bell to Graham Greene, March 16, 1952, box 17, folder 7, GGPB.

51. Douglas, *Looking Back*, 326–27. Harrison's biographer argues that he was more supportive of Flecker and others than Douglas claimed; Martha S. Vogeler, *Austin Harrison and the* English Review (Columbia: University of Missouri Press, 2008), 134–35.

52. Douglas moved to Albany Mansions on March 7, 1913. Douglas, pocket diary, 1913, box 35, folder 575, NDCB.

53. Douglas, "Ah! There You Are!"

54. Douglas, *Looking Back*.

55. Wolton to Douglas, November 6, 1921, in *Norman Douglas Selected Correspondence*, 2:18–19.

56. Wolton to Douglas, November 6, November 24, and December 25, 1921, in *Norman Douglas Selected Correspondence*, 2:21–24.

57. Thomas K. Hubbard, Beert Verstraete, and Daniel C. Tsang, eds., *Censoring Sex Research: The Debate over Male Intergenerational Relations* (Walnut Creek, CA: Left Coast Press, 2013), 15–20.

58. Joseph J. Fischel, *Sex and Harm in the Age of Consent* (Minneapolis: University of Minnesota Press, 2016), 125; Kathryn Bond Stockton, *The Queer Child, or Growing Sideways in the Twentieth Century* (Chapel Hill, NC: Duke University Press, 2009), 68.

59. There are critiques of Rind's work included within the edited book where his essay appears; Hubbard, Verstraete, and Tsang, *Censoring Sex Research*, 139–44. Susan Clancy discusses critiques of her work in *The Trauma Myth: The Truth about the Sexual Abuse of Children—and Its Aftermath* (New York: Basic Books, 2009), 77–107.

60. Nicholas Syrett argues for historians taking children at their word in his book on child marriage; Syrett, *American Child Bride: A History of Minors and Marriage in the United States* (Durham: University of North Carolina Press, 2016). In a historical parallel, many of the boys who had sexual affairs with the infamous Australian pedophile Clarence Henry Howard-Osborne "stoutly defended his integrity and

righteousness" long after; Paul R. Wilson, *The Man They Called a Monster: Sexual Experiences between Men and Boys* (North Ryde, New South Wales: Cassell Australia, 1981). Some historians view Wilson's book as problematic; personal correspondence with Yorick Smaal, September 30, 2019.

Chapter Eight

1. Faith Compton Mackenzie, *As Much as I Dare: The Autobiography of Faith Compton Mackenzie* (London: Collins, 1938), 276, 62.
2. *Norman Douglas Selected Correspondence*, ed. Arthur S. Wensinger and Michael Allan, vol. 1, *Respectful Ribaldry: A Selection of Letters from Norman Douglas to Faith Compton Mackenzie* (Graz/Feldkirch, Austria: W. Neugebauer Verlag, 2008), 18.
3. Joseph Conrad to J. B. Pinker, December 4, 1916, in *The Collected Letters of Joseph Conrad*, ed. Frederick R. Karl and Laurence Davies, vol. 5, *1912–1916* (Cambridge: Cambridge University Press, 1996), 683–84.
4. Norman Douglas, *Looking Back: An Autobiographical Excursion* (New York: Harcourt, Brace, 1933), 338–40.
5. Joseph Conrad to J. B. Pinker, December 4, 1916, in *Collected Letters of Joseph Conrad*, 5:683–84.
6. WKLB, 454.
7. Norman Douglas, pocket diary, 1915, box 35, folder 576, NDCB.
8. Douglas to Archie Douglas, March 14, 1916, box 21, folder 344, NDCB.
9. Norman Douglas, *Alone* (London: Chapman & Hall, 1921), 4.
10. *Alone*, 15.
11. Humbert Wolfe, *Portraits by Inference* (London: Methuen, 1934), 159–61.
12. Richard Aldington to Rob Lyle, September 16, 1954, NYPL.
13. Harford Montgomery Hyde, *The Love That Dared Not Speak Its Name: A Candid History of Homosexuality in Britain* (New York: Little, Brown, 1970), 191.
14. "News in Brief," *Times*, October 13, 1916, 5.
15. Compton Mackenzie, *My Life and Times: Octave Five, 1915–1923* (London: Chatto & Windus, 1966), 52.
16. Fr. Rolfe [Baron Corvo], *The Venice Letters*, ed. Cecil Woolf (London: Cecil & Amelia Woolf, 1974), 37.
17. Douglas to Archie Douglas, June 13 and July 16, 1916, box 21, folder 345, NDCB.
18. Arnold Smith to Douglas, February 12, 1917, box 19, folder 312, NDCB. This letter appears to come from a boy Douglas met before fleeing London.
19. Entry dated November 27, 1916, in Register of the Court of Summary Jurisdiction sitting at Westminster Police Court. PS/WES/A1/87, MET. For South Kensington Station as a popular pickup spot, see Matt Houlbrook, *Queer London: Perils and Pleasures in the Sexual Metropolis, 1918–1957* (Chicago: University of Chicago Press, 2005), 36.

20. "Alleged Grave Offence: Battersea Author and Schoolboy. Sequel to Meeting at South Kensington Museum," *Fulham Chronicle*, December 8, 1916. See also "Remanded in Custody," *Times*, November 28, 1916; "A Grave Charge: Battersea Author's Visit to South Kensington Museum," *Chelsea News and General Advertiser*, December 1, 1916.

21. Louise Jackson, *Child Sexual Abuse in Victorian England* (New York: Routledge, 2000), 12.

22. Michel Foucault, *Power/Knowledge: Selected Interviews and Other Writings, 1972–1977*, trans. Colin Gordon et al. (New York: Pantheon Books, 1980), 119.

23. Entry dated January 11, 1917, in Register of the Court of Summary Jurisdiction sitting at Westminster Police Court. PS/WES/A1/89, MET. Knightsbridge was another common cruising spot.

24. Entry dated December 5, 1916, in Register of the Court of Summary Jurisdiction sitting at Westminster Police Court. PS/WES/A1/88, MET. British historians of sexuality have argued that "loitering with intent to commit a felony" was coded language for homosexuality in the courts. See, for example, H. G. Cocks, *Nameless Offences: Homosexual Desire in the 19th Century* (London: I. B. Tauris, 2003), 56; Alison Oram, *Her Husband Was a Woman! Women's Gender-Crossing in Modern British Popular Culture* (London: Routledge, 2007), 82.

25. Register of the Court of Summary Jurisdiction sitting at Westminster Police Court. PS/WES/A1/88, MET. Prior to 1971, there were twenty shillings in a pound, and twelve pence in a shilling.

26. Joseph Conrad to J. B. Pinker, December 4, 1916, in *Collected Letters of Joseph Conrad*, 5:638–84.

27. Douglas to Mr. Partridge, September 29, 1939, folder 1, PMLM.

28. Joseph Conrad to J. B. Pinker, December 9, 1916, in *Collected Letters of Joseph Conrad*, 5:685.

29. Douglas, *Looking Back*, 340.

30. Compton Mackenzie mentions the friends who provided bail, but not by name, in Mackenzie, *My Life and Times*, 5:92.

31. Mackenzie, *As Much as I Dare*, 273–74.

32. Mark Holloway, *Norman Douglas: A Biography* (London: Secker & Warburg, 1976), 230.

33. Entry dated January 2, 1917, in Register of the Court of Summary Jurisdiction sitting at Westminster Police Court. PS/WES/A1/89, MET.

34. "The Museum Charge: Battersea Author Establishes an Alibi in Grave Case," *Chelsea News and General Advertiser*, January 12, 1917.

35. Mackenzie, *As Much as I Dare*, 273–74.

36. Esmond Knight, *Seeking the Bubble* (London: Hutchinson, 1943). Knight's cousin, Robert Duncan Knight, drowned off Madeira in 1922.

37. Holloway, *Norman Douglas*, 232.

38. "Apprehensions Sought," *Police Gazette*, January 30, 1917.

39. Mackenzie, *As Much as I Dare*, 273–74.

40. Mackenzie, *My Life and Times*, 5:92.

41. Robin Maugham, *Escape from the Shadows* (London: Hodder and Stoughton, 1972), 197.

Chapter Nine

1. Derek Patmore, "Norman Douglas: Exiled Grand Seigneur," *Everyman*, September 10, 1931, box 40, folder 633, NDCB.

2. Joseph Conrad to Douglas, February 2, 1908, box 17, folder 233, NDCB.

3. Norman Douglas, "Uplands of Sorrento," *English Review* 7 (1910): 127.

4. Norman Douglas, *Together* (New York: Robert M. McBride, 1923), 236.

5. Douglas, "Uplands of Sorrento," 128.

6. Douglas to Archie Douglas, June 27, 1916, box 21, folder 344, NDCB.

7. Douglas to Martin Secker, January 26, 1917, HLH.

8. Douglas to Secker, February 24, 1917, HLH.

9. Douglas to Secker, March 13, 1917, HLH.

10. Norman Douglas, *Alone* (London: Chapman & Hall, 1921), 168.

11. Norman Douglas, *South Wind* (New York: Modern Library, 1925), 223.

12. Douglas, *Alone*, 168.

13. Douglas, *South Wind*, 198, 64, 322, 268, 247.

14. *South Wind*, 211.

15. Eden Philpotts to Douglas, May 16, 1918, box 19, folder 309, NDCB.

16. Douglas to Muriel Draper, February 27, 1918, box 2, folder 67, MDPB.

17. William King, "Introductory Letter," *South Wind* (London: Secker and Warburg, 1947), vii.

18. Mark Holloway, "Norman Douglas," in *The Craft of Literary Biography*, ed. Jeffrey Meyers (London: Macmillan Press, 1985), 238.

19. Edwin Cerio calls Douglas the "prince of modern visitors to Capri" in Cerio, *The Masque of Capri* (London: Nelson, 1957), 128. Douglas also served as one of the translators for Cerio's earlier work, *That Capri Air* (London: William Heinemann, 1929).

20. "New Books and Reprints," *Times Literary Supplement*, June 7, 1917, 274.

21. *Times Literary Supplement*, June 20, 1918, 286.

22. Virginia Woolf, "*South Wind* by Douglas, Norman," *Times Literary Supplement*, June 14, 1917, 283.

23. Raymond Mortimer, "The Story of a Friendship," *Sunday Times*, box 40, folder 638, NDCB.

24. E. M. Forster to Douglas, November 10, 1917, box 17, folder 246, NDCB.

25. Michael Holyroyd, "Norman Douglas and Lytton Strachey Together: Two Portraits in Miniature," in *Norman Douglas: 7 Symposium, Bregenz und Thüringen, Vlbg., 12./13. 10. 2012*, ed. Wilhelm Meusburger (Bregenz, Austria: Norman Douglas Forschungsstelle, Vorarlberger Landesbibliothek, 2013), 110–15.

26. H. T. Webster, "Norman Douglas: A Reconsideration," *South Atlantic Quarterly* 49, no. 2 (April 1950): 226.

27. Humbert Wolfe, *Portraits by Inference* (London: Methuen, 1934), 161.

28. Martin Green, *Children of the Sun: A Narrative of "Decadence" in England after 1918* (New York: Basic Books, 1976), 75.

29. Lewis Leary, *Norman Douglas* (New York: Columbia University Press, 1968), 29.

30. Cecile Walton Robertson to Douglas, June 13, 1922, box 19, folder 311, NDCB.

31. Norman Douglas, *D. H. Lawrence and Maurice Magnus: A Plea for Better Manners* (privately printed, 1925); Maurice Magnus to Douglas, October 5, 1917, box 18, folder 272, NDCB.

32. Peter Hutton to Mark Holloway, March 4, 1976, MHRH, vol. 8. This attitude is recapitulated by scholar Neil Ritchie, who describes Hutton as a "prim, orthodox, conformist family man." Quoted in *Norman Douglas Selected Correspondence*, ed. Arthur S. Wensinger and Michael Allan, vol. 4, *Italiam Petimus: Letters of Edward Hutton to Norman Douglas and a Selection of Letters from Douglas to Hutton* (Graz/ Feldkirch, Austria: W. Neugebauer Verlag, 2011), xiii.

33. Douglas to Edward Hutton, n.d., HUT: I: B:14, BIF.

34. Viva King, *The Weeping and the Laughter* (London: MacDonald and Jane's, 1976), 24.

35. Douglas to Hutton, June 19, 1930, box 3, UCND.

36. Douglas to Hutton, March 8 and April 2, 1934, box 3, UCND.

37. *Norman Douglas Selected Correspondence*, 4:10.

38. Quoted in Ian Littlewood, *Sultry Climates: Travel and Sex* (Cambridge, MA: Da Capo Press, 2001), 132.

39. Douglas, postcard to Hutton, 1920, box 3, UCND.

40. Hutton to Douglas, March 19, 1918, in *Norman Douglas Selected Correspondence*, 4:35.

41. Douglas to W. H. D. Rouse, December 6, 1917 (1918?), CCOL.

42. Norman Douglas, "A Traveller of the 'Twenties," *Anglo-Italian Review* 2 (1918): 79.

43. Norman Douglas, "To Valmontone," *Anglo-Italian Review* 6 (1920): 315.

44. Douglas, *Alone*, 48.

45. This explanation comes from the expanded version of the essay in *Alone*, 46.

46. Norman Douglas, "At Levanto," *Anglo-Italian Review*, nos. 3–4 (1919): 170–73.

47. "At Levanto."

48. Douglas to Rouse, December 6, 1918, CCOL.

49. John Addington Symonds, *A Problem in Greek Ethics: Being an Inquiry into the Phenomenon of Sexual Inversion* (London: private circulation, 1901), 8.

50. Douglas to Hutton, October 14, 1921, HUT: I: B:14, BIF.
51. Douglas, *Alone*, 16.
52. John Addington Symonds, *Sketches in Italy and Greece* (London: Smith, Elder, 1874), 114–42; Douglas, *Alone*, 213.
53. Stefania Arcara, "Hellenic Transgressions, Homosexual Politics: Wilde, Symonds and Sicily," *Studies in Travel Writing* 16, no. 2 (2012): 142.
54. Douglas, *Alone*, 74–75.
55. *Alone*, 182, 25, 261, 99–102.
56. *Alone*, 274.

Chapter Ten

1. René Mari, journal, July 22, 1922, DSD.
2. Norman Douglas, *Together* (New York: Robert M. McBride, 1923), 71–83.
3. Mari's description reads: "C'était très joli dedans; nous étions presque entourés d'une enceinte de murs dentellé, le sol était couvert de mousse, et il y avait quatre ou 5 arbres de sapins." René Mari, journal, September 15, 1921, DSD.
4. Norman Douglas, *Looking Back: An Autobiographical Excursion* (New York: Harcourt, Brace, 1933), 351–52.
5. René Mari, journal, August 3, 1922, DSD. Mari also mentions a visit to "un tres vieux chateau, il n'y a que des ruines," on August 28, 1921, which may have been their very first visit to Blumenegg.
6. Oscar Wilde, *The Portrait of Mr. W. H.* (New York: Mitchell Kennerley, 1921). The story was originally published in *Blackwood's Magazine* in 1889.
7. Norman Douglas, pocket diary, 1918, box 35, folder 577, NDCB.
8. Douglas to Muriel Draper, February 12, 1918, box 2, folder 67, MDPB.
9. Douglas, *Looking Back*, 78.
10. Norman Douglas, *Late Harvest* (London: Lindsay Drummond, 1946), 43.
11. Douglas, *Looking Back*, 254–60.
12. WKLB, 316.
13. Douglas, *Looking Back*, 261.
14. Edmond et Jules de Goncourt, *La Lorette* (Paris: G. Charpentier, 1883). There's mention of a male sex worker strolling from the Notre-Dame-de-Lorette in William A. Peniston, *Pederasts and Others: Urban Culture and Sexual Identity in Nineteenth-Century Paris* (New York: Harrington Park Press, 2004), 59.
15. Alexandre-Jean-Baptiste Parent-Duchâtelet, *Prostitution in Paris* (Boston: Charles H. Brainard, 1845), 164.
16. Douglas, *Looking Back*, 264.
17. *Looking Back*, 346–47.

18. Norman Douglas, *Alone* (London: Chapman & Hall, 1921), 17–18; Douglas, *Looking Back*, 346.
19. Douglas, *Late Harvest*, 34.
20. Douglas, *Together*, 14.
21. Douglas, *Looking Back*, 130, 350.
22. Douglas to John Mavrogordato, September 23, 1921, in *Norman Douglas Selected Correspondence*, ed. Arthur S. Wensinger and Michael Allan, vol. 7, *Straining Friendship to Breaking Point: Letters from John Mavrogordato to Norman Douglas and a Selection of Letters from Douglas to Mavrogordato* (Graz/Feldkirch, Austria: W. Neugebauer Verlag, 2014), 109.
23. Hans Licht [Paul Brandt], *Sexual Life in Ancient Greece*, trans. J. H. Freese (London: Routledge & Kegan Paul, 1956), 415.
24. Douglas, *Looking Back*, 348.
25. Norman Douglas, *They Went* (London: Chapman & Hall, 1930).
26. René Mari, journal, July 29, 1922, DSD.
27. Mari, journal, August 2, 1922, DSD.
28. Mari, journal, August 21, 1922, DSD.
29. Douglas to Archie Douglas, July 29, 1922, box 21, folder 347, NDCB.
30. Douglas, *Together*, 4.
31. *Together*, 108.
32. *Together*, 43–44.
33. *Together*, 242–43.
34. Douglas to Mavrogordato, January 4, 1923, in *Norman Douglas Selected Correspondence*, 7:157.
35. Douglas to Archie Douglas, January 6 and April 3, 1921, box 21, folder 349, NDCB.
36. Robin Douglas, *16 to 21* (London: A. M. Philpot, 1925), 132–33. Robin uses the pseudonym Devonshire Smythe for Somerset Maugham.
37. Douglas to Archie Douglas, May 25, 1925, box 22, folder 351, NDCB.
38. Rosana E. Norman et al., "The Long-Term Health Consequence of Child Physical Abuse, Emotional Abuse, and Neglect: A Systematic Review and Meta-Analysis," *PLoS Medicine* 9, no. 11 (2012).
39. G. Orioli, *Adventures of a Bookseller* (New York: Robert M. McBride, 1938), 217.
40. Douglas to Hellé Flecker, July 2, 1924, NYPL.
41. René Mari to Pino Orioli, June 10, 1924, in *Norman Douglas Selected Correspondence*, ed. Arthur S. Wensinger and Michael Allan, vol. 2, *Dear Doug! Letters to Norman Douglas from Eric Wolton, René Mari, Marcel Mercier and Ettore Masciandaro and a Selection of Letters from Emilio Papa* (Graz/Feldkirch, Austria: W. Neugebauer Verlag, 2008), 35.
42. Mari to Douglas, June 12, 1933, box 18, folder 276, NDCB.

43. Mari to Douglas, February 7, 1934, in *Norman Douglas Selected Correspondence*, 2:47.
44. Orioli, *Adventures of a Bookseller*, 217.

Reflection II

1. Guenter Lewy, *False Consciousness: An Essay on Mystification* (1982; repr., New York: Routledge, 2017), 3–5.
2. Jordana Greenblatt, "The 'Yes' Which Is Not One," in *Beyond Gender: An Advanced Introduction to Futures of Feminist and Sexuality Studies*, ed. Greta Olson et al. (New York: Routledge, 2018).
3. Vern L. Bullogh, "Age of Consent," *Journal of Psychology and Human Sexuality* 16, nos. 2–3 (2005).
4. Joseph J. Fischel, *Screw Consent: A Better Politics of Sexual Justice* (Berkeley: University of California Press, 2019).
5. Janet Halley, "The Move to Affirmative Consent," *Signs: Journal of Women in Culture and Society* 42, no. 1 (2015).
6. Lara Karaian, "What Is Self-Exploitation? Rethinking the Relationship between Sexualization and 'Sexting' in Law and Order Times," in *Children, Sexuality and Sexualization*, ed. Emma Renold, Jessica Ringrose, and R. Danielle Egan (London: Palgrave Macmillan, 2015), 344–45.
7. Constantine FitzGibbon, "Norman Douglas: Memoir of an Unwritten Biography," *Encounter*, September 1974, 36.
8. Martha Gordon Crotch, diary, book 8, 1937, box 1, MHGC.

Chapter Eleven

1. Kenneth Macpherson quotes Douglas's epithet, in Macpherson to Edward Hutton, March 20, 1952, BIF.
2. Douglas to Martin Secker, February 24, 1917, HLH.
3. Giovanni Dall'Orto, "Florence," in *Encyclopedia of Homosexuality*, ed. Wayne R. Dynes, Warren Johansson, and William A. Percy (New York: Garland, 1990).
4. Michael Rocke, *Forbidden Friendships: Homosexuality and Male Culture in Renaissance Florence* (New York: Oxford University Press, 1996), 3, 87–111, 16.
5. Harold Acton, *The Last of the Medici Done into English by Harold Acton with Introduction by Norman Douglas* (Florence: privately printed for subscribers by G. Orioli, 1930).
6. G. Orioli, *Adventures of a Bookseller* (New York: Robert M. McBride, 1938), 236.
7. Chiara Beccalossi, "The 'Italian Vice': Male Homosexuality and British Tourism in Southern Italy," in *Italian Sexualities Uncovered, 1789–1914*, ed. John H. Arnold, Joanna Bourke, and Sean Brady (London: Macmillan Palgrave, 2015), 198.

8. *The Letters of Lytton Strachey*, ed. Paul Levy (New York: Farrar, Straus and Giroux, 2005), 130.

9. Ronald Firbank, *The Princess Zoubaroff* (London: G. Richards, 1920). For analysis of the play, see Richard Canning, "Penetrating (the) *Prancing Novelist*," in *Brigid Brophy: Avant-Garde Writer, Critic, Activist*, ed. Richard Canning and Gerri Kimber (Edinburgh: Edinburgh University Press, 2020).

10. Douglas to Muriel Draper, September 23, 1918, box 2, folder 67, MDPB.

11. Douglas to John Mavrogordato, October 25, 1921, in *Norman Douglas Selected Correspondence*, ed. Arthur S. Wensinger and Michael Allan, vol. 7, *Straining Friendship to Breaking Point: Letters from John Mavrogordato to Norman Douglas and a Selection of Letters from Douglas to Mavrogordato* (Graz/Feldkirch, Austria: W. Neugebauer Verlag, 2014), 128. Editor Michael Allan identifies the abbreviation as standing for coitus interruptus, or withdrawal, but this is unlikely.

12. Douglas to Archie Douglas, February 7, March 17, and April 3, 1921, box 21, folder 346, NDCB.

13. Matt Houlbrook, *Queer London: Perils and Pleasures in the Sexual Metropolis, 1918–1957* (Chicago: University of Chicago Press, 2005), 236.

14. Douglas to E. M. Forster, January 5, 1923, Forster Letter Book #1, EMFC.

15. Christopher Duggan, *A Concise History of Italy*, 2nd ed. (Cambridge: Cambridge University Pres, 2014), 202–20.

16. Douglas to Archie Douglas, March 29, 1923, box 21, folder 348, NDCB.

17. Douglas to Mavrogordato, March 4, 1924, in *Norman Douglas Selected Correspondence*, 7:173.

18. Douglas to Archie Douglas, April 3, 1921, box 21, folder 346, NDCB.

19. Kinta Beevor, *A Tuscan Childhood* (New York: Viking, 1993), 104.

20. Harold Acton, *Memoirs of an Aesthete* (1948; repr., London: Methuen, 1970), 107.

21. Orioli, *Adventures of a Bookseller*, 100, 15, 65–66, 76, 218. For a disparaging account of Oscar Browning, see Virginia Woolf, *A Room of One's Own* (London: Hogarth Press, 1929).

22. The date of their first meeting is sometimes given as 1922, but Douglas's papers at UCLA include a Christmas 1921 postcard from Douglas to Orioli. Box 4, UCLA.

23. Eric Linklater, *A Year of Space: A Chapter in Autobiography* (London: Macmillan, 1953), 270–72.

24. Charles Prentice, "Arcades Ambo" (1930), box 43, folder 14, NDCB; Brigit Patmore, *My Friends When Young: The Memoirs of Brigit Patmore* (London: William Heinemann, 1968), 26; Nancy Cunard, *Grand Man: Memories of Norman Douglas* (London: Secker & Warburg, 1954), 103.

25. Osbert Sitwell, *On the Continent: A Book of Inquillinics* (London: Macmillan, 1958), 61–62; Douglas to Draper, September 23, 1918, box 2, folder 67, MDPB.

26. Martin Birnbaum, *Last Romantic: The Story of More than a Half-Century in the World*

of Art (New York: Twayne, 1960), 33; D. H. Lawrence to Pino Orioli, January 30, 1930, box 2, UCDH.

27. Douglas to Pino Orioli, November 21, 1923(?), box 4, UCND.

28. For examples, see Douglas to Orioli, May 18 and June 9, 1924; June 8 and July 27, 1927, box 4, UCND.

29. *Norman Douglas Selected Correspondence*, 7:77.

30. Douglas to Archie Douglas, June 4, 1923, box 21, folder 348, NDCB.

31. Douglas to Archie Douglas, February 5, 1924, box 21, folder 349, NDCB.

32. Douglas to Orioli, June 9, 1924, box 4, UCND.

33. Douglas to Bryher, April 14, 1924, box 1, folder 335, NDCB.

34. Douglas to Mavrogordato, October 24, 1924, in *Norman Douglas Selected Correspondence*, 7:176.

35. Bryher to Brigit Patmore, July 1924, in *Norman Douglas Selected Correspondence*, ed. Arthur S. Wensinger and Michael Allan, vol. 6, *Dear Sir (or Madam): Letters of Norman Douglas to Bryher and Two Letters from Bryher to Douglas* (Graz/Feldkirch, Austria: W. Neugebauer Verlag, 2013), 153.

36. Cunard, *Grand Man*, 70. Cunard thought Silvio was charmingly original, but the phrase *asperge montée* (white asparagus) was French slang for a skinny woman. See Albert Rhodes, *Monsieur at Home* (London: Field & Tuer, 1886), 109.

37. Douglas to Mavrogordato, November 20, 1924, in *Norman Douglas Selected Correspondence*, 7:177. Douglas made the same complaint in a letter to Archie, November 3, 1924, box 21, folder 349, NDCB.

38. Norman Douglas, pocket diary, 1924, box 35, folder 580, NDCB.

39. *Norman Douglas Selected Correspondence*, ed. Arthur S. Wensinger and Michael Allan, vol. 2, *Dear Doug! Letters to Norman Douglas from Eric Wolton, René Mari, Marcel Mercier and Ettore Masciandaro and a Selection of Letters from Emilio Papa* (Graz/Feldkirch, Austria: W. Neugebauer Verlag, 2008), 52–55.

40. Douglas to Orioli, August 1, 1928, box 4, UCND.

41. Douglas to Bryher, July 6, 1937, in *Norman Douglas Selected Correspondence*, 6:338. Douglas also asked Orioli to cheer up Papa; Douglas to Orioli, June 2, 1937, box 4, UCND.

42. Emilio Papa to Douglas, December 26, 1938, in *Norman Douglas Selected Correspondence*, 2:71.

43. Papa to Douglas, June 25, 1939, in *Norman Douglas Selected Correspondence*, 2:98.

44. Cunard, *Grand Man*, 85.

45. Douglas to Archie Douglas, July 23 and August 1, 1925, box 22, folder 351, NDCB.

46. Douglas to Draper, June 4, 1924, box 2, folder 67, MDPB.

47. For further discussion of these paintings, see Rachel Hope Cleves, "Teddy's Illustrated Letter," in *Queer Objects*, ed. Chris Brickell and Judith Collard (New Brunswick, NJ: Rutgers University Press, 2019), 89–93.

48. Douglas to Archie Douglas, April 15, 1927, box 22, folder 353, NDCB.
49. Perry Wilson, *Women in Twentieth-Century Italy* (London: Palgrave Macmillan, 2010), 65.
50. Gabriella Romano, *The Pathologisation of Homosexuality in Fascist Italy: The Case of 'G'* (London: Palgrave Macmillan, 2019), 56.
51. Douglas to Archie Douglas, April 25 and May 17, 1927, box 22, folder 353, NDCB.
52. Douglas to Mavrogordato, August 1, 1927, in *Norman Douglas Selected Correspondence*, 7:217.
53. Douglas to Orioli, February 19, 1939, box 4, UCND.
54. Douglas to Archie Douglas, April 17, 1927, box 22, folder 353, NDCB.

Chapter Twelve

1. Brigit Patmore, *My Friends When Young: The Memoirs of Brigit Patmore* (London: William Heinemann, 1968), 124; "50 pp. leather notebook in hand of Islay Lyons," box 61, NDCB.
2. Douglas to Archie Douglas, March 29, 1930, box 22, folder 357, NDCB.
3. Douglas to Archie Douglas, March 14 and March 31, 1922, box 21, folder 347, NDCB.
4. Douglas to Archie Douglas, October 6, 1922, box 21, folder 347, NDCB.
5. *Norman Douglas Selected Correspondence*, ed. Arthur S. Wensinger and Michael Allan, vol. 7, *Straining Friendship to Breaking Point: Letters from John Mavrogordato to Norman Douglas and a Selection of Letters from Douglas to Mavrogordato* (Graz/Feldkirch, Austria: W. Neugebauer Verlag, 2014), 157.
6. Rachel Potter, *Obscene Modernism: Literary Censorship and Experiment, 1900–1940* (New York: Oxford University Press, 2013).
7. Norman Douglas, *Late Harvest* (London: Lindsay Drummond, 1946), 121. Cross was a pseudonym for Annie Sophie Cory.
8. Shoshana Milgram Knapp, "Revolutionary Androgyny in the Fiction of 'Victoria Cross,'" in *Seeing Double: Revisioning Edwardian and Modernist Literature*, ed. Carola M. Kaplan and Anne B. Simpson (New York: St. Martin's Press, 1996), 11.
9. Douglas to W. H. D. Rouse, December 6, 1917, CCOL.
10. Aleister Crowley to Douglas, 1922, box 17, folder 231, NDCB.
11. See *Norman Douglas Selected Correspondence*, 7:245.
12. Norman Douglas, *Siren Land and Fountains in the Sand* (London: Secker & Warburg, 1957), 129. Another example is his reference to Krafft-Ebing in his review of the novel *The Broken Halo* in *Late Harvest*, 122.
13. *Norman Douglas Selected Correspondence*, ed. Arthur S. Wensinger and Michael Allan, vol. 6, *Dear Sir (or Madam): Letters of Norman Douglas to Bryher and Two Letters from Bryher to Douglas* (Graz/Feldkirch, Austria: W. Neugebauer Verlag, 2013), 89.
14. *Norman Douglas Selected Correspondence*, ed. Arthur S. Wensinger and Michael Al-

lan, vol. 5, *Byzantine Talks: Letters of Norman Douglas to Richard Macgillivray Dawkins and a Single Letter from Dawkins to Douglas* (Graz/Feldkirch: W. Neugebauer Verlag, 2012), 165.

15. *Norman Douglas Selected Correspondence*, 6:222.

16. Douglas to Pino Orioli, February 23, 1928, UCND. See also Douglas to Archie Douglas, November 9, 1926, NDCB; Douglas to Elizabeth David, September 23, 1940, EDS.

17. Douglas to Hellé Flecker, April 16, 1919, NYPL.

18. Douglas to Richard Dawkins, May 6, 1940, in *Norman Douglas Selected Correspondence*, 5:149.

19. Douglas's tone was ironical, but his interest in naturalism was earnest. See the careful addenda he made to a presentation copy of the book that was given to his literary executor. WKBB.

20. Norman Douglas, *Birds and Beasts of the Greek Anthology* (London: Chapman & Hall, 1928), 15.

21. Sonya Lida Tarán, "Eisi Trixes: An Erotic Motif in the Greek Anthology," *Journal of Hellenic Studies* 105 (1985).

22. See, for example, George Chauncey, *Gay New York: Gender, Urban Culture, and the Making of the Gay World, 1890–1940* (New York City: Basic Books, 1995), 87–95; Peter Boag, *Same-Sex Affairs: Constructing and Controlling Homosexuality in the Pacific Northwest* (Berkeley: University of California Press, 2003), 25–36.

23. Douglas, *Birds and Beasts*, 29.

24. *Birds and Beasts*, 27, 40, 37.

25. Douglas to Archie Douglas, September 29 and October 8, 1927, box 22, folder 353, NDCB.

26. Douglas used this phrase many times. For example, *Norman Douglas Selected Correspondence*, 7:215; *Norman Douglas Selected Correspondence*, ed. Arthur S. Wensinger and Michael Allan, vol. 1, *Respectful Ribaldry: A Selection of Letters from Norman Douglas to Faith Compton Mackenzie* (Graz/Feldkirch, Austria: W. Neugebauer Verlag, 2008), 47.

27. Douglas to Archie Douglas, July 25, 1927, box 22, folder 353, NDCB.

28. *Norman Douglas Selected Correspondence*, 7:215.

29. Cecil Woolf, *A Bibliography of Norman Douglas* (London: Rupert Hart-Davis, 1954), 78.

30. Douglas to Orioli, May 1928, box 4, UCND. See also Douglas to John Mavrogordato, April 30, 1928, in *Norman Douglas Selected Correspondence*, 7:249.

31. Douglas, *Late Harvest*, 24.

32. Norman Douglas, *In the Beginning* (New York: John Day Company, 1928), 10–12.

33. *In the Beginning*, 4, in WKIB.

34. *In the Beginning*, 84–88.

35. *In the Beginning*, 70, in WKIB.

36. *In the Beginning*, 210–11.

37. *In the Beginning*, 247–48.

38. *In the Beginning*, 218, in WKIB.

39. *In the Beginning*, 258.

40. *In the Beginning*, 304.

41. Douglas, *Late Harvest*, 23.

42. Lord David Cecil, "'Obscene' Writing," *Spectator*, October 1, 1932, 9; Jack Lindsay, "Norman Douglas," *London Aphrodite: A Literary Periodical*, no. 5 (1929): 385; Robin Chanter, "Conversations with a Retired Gentleman" [unpublished manuscript], BIF.

43. D. H. Lawrence to Martin Secker, February 8 and March 8, 1927, in *The Letters of D. H. Lawrence*, vol. 5, *1924–27*, ed. James T. Boulton and Lindeth Vasey (Cambridge: Cambridge University Press, 1989), 638, 51.

44. D. H. Lawrence to Douglas, October 26, 1927, box 18, folder 267, NDCB. Douglas to Archie Douglas, November 28, 1927; January 19, 1928, box 22, folders 354, 355, NDCB.

45. Charles Prentice (?) to Douglas, November 19, 1928, box 7, folder 86, NDCB.

46. Douglas to Orioli, July 3, 1928, box 4, UCND; Douglas to Muriel Draper, June 6, 1928, box 2, folder 68, MDPB; Douglas to Mavrogordato, in *Norman Douglas Selected Correspondence*, 7:250.

47. Muriel Draper, "Buffetings in a South Wind: Some Memories of Norman Douglas," box 11, folder 355, MDPB; Douglas to Draper, July 24, 1925; April 7, 1929, box 11, folder 355, MDPB; Douglas to Archie Douglas, January 20, 1934, box 21, folder 349, NDCB; Douglas to Archie Douglas, October 29, 1927, box 22, folder 354, NDCB. See also Douglas to Archie Douglas, July 22, 1923, box 21, folder 348, NDCB.

48. Martha Gordon Crotch, diary, book 4, October 3, 1937, box 3, MHGC.

49. Nancy Cunard, *Grand Man: Memories of Norman Douglas* (London: Secker & Warburg, 1954), 70.

50. Douglas to Archie Douglas, January 12, 1921, box 20, folder 346, NDCB. See also Douglas to Reggie Turner, June 17, 1925, box 2, UCND.

51. Douglas to Robin Douglas, October 21, 1923, box 4, UCND.

52. Douglas to Edward Hutton, February 12, 1927, in *Norman Douglas Selected Correspondence*, ed. Arthur S. Wensinger and Michael Allan, vol. 4, *Italiam Petimus: Letters of Edward Hutton to Norman Douglas and a Selection of Letters from Douglas to Hutton* (Graz/Feldkirch, Austria: W. Neugebauer Verlag, 2011), 239.

53. D. H. Lawrence to Giuseppe Orioli, October 1928; January 14, 1929, collection 654, box 2, folder 27, UCDH.

54. Martin Birnbaum, *Last Romantic: The Story of More than a Half-Century in the World of Art* (New York: Twayne, 1960), 33.

55. Douglas to Muriel Draper, July 30, 1928, box 2, folder 68, MDPB.

56. Douglas to Draper, June 6, 1928, box 2, folder 68, MDPB.

57. Lytton Strachey to Douglas, February 4, 1928, box 19, folder 315, MDPB.

58. Michael Holyroyd, "Norman Douglas and Lytton Strachey Together: Two Portraits in Miniature," in *Norman Douglas: 7 Symposium, Bregenz und Thüringen, Vlbg., 12./13. 10. 2012*, ed. Wilhelm Meusburger (Bregenz, Austria: Norman Douglas Forschungsstelle, Vorarlberger Landesbibliothek, 2013), 110–15.

59. Norman Douglas, *Some Limericks: Collected for the Use of Students, & Ensplendour'd with Introduction, Geographical Index, and with Notes Explanatory and Critical* (privately printed, 1928), 77.

60. *Some Limericks.*

61. *Norman Douglas Selected Correspondence,* 6:240.

62. Harold Acton to Douglas, December 18, 1928, box 17, folder 225, NDCB.

63. Douglas to Somerset Maugham, May 15, 1929, PMLM.

64. Douglas to Draper, November 8, 1928, box 2, folder 68, MDPB; Douglas to Archie Douglas, November 27, 1928, box 22, folder 355, NDCB.

65. K to B, December 27, 1928, box 7, folder 93, NDCB; Richard Aldington, *Pinorman: Personal Recollections of Norman Douglas, Pino Orioli and Charles Prentice* (London: William Heinemann, 1954), 112.

66. Woolf, *A Bibliography of Norman Douglas,* 95.

67. Norman Douglas, *Some Limericks* (London: Atlas Press, 2009).

68. Douglas to Archie Douglas, March 28, 1931, box 23, folder 358, NDCB.

69. Douglas to W. H. D. Rouse, May 31, 1935, CCOL; Martha Gordon Crotch, diary, October 1952, MHGC.

70. Douglas had started researching aphrodisiacs even earlier; see Douglas to Edward Hutton, February 12, 1927, in *Norman Douglas Selected Correspondence,* 4:239.

71. *Norman Douglas Selected Correspondence,* 4:294.

72. *Norman Douglas Selected Correspondence,* 3:107.

73. *Norman Douglas Selected Correspondence,* 7:278.

74. Douglas, *Late Harvest,* 68.

75. Douglas made the correction on the presentation copy of *Paneros* that he prepared for his literary executor, William King, WKP.

76. Norman Douglas, *Paneros: Some Words on Aphrodisiacs and the Like* (London: Chatto & Windus, 1931), 14, 16, 21, 35, 45, 59, 60.

77. *Paneros,* 5, 85.

78. Edward A. Bunyard to Douglas, August 19, 1930, box 11, folder 140, NDCB.

79. Douglas, *Paneros,* 80.

Chapter Thirteen

1. Nancy Cunard, *Grand Man: Memories of Norman Douglas* (London: Secker & Warburg, 1954), 59–67.

2. Victor Cunard, "Norman Douglas, 1868–1952," *Time and Tide*, March 29, 1952.

3. Cunard, *Grand Man*, 252.

4. Derek Patmore, "Norman Douglas: Exiled Grand Seigneur," *Everyman*, September 10, 1931.

5. Arthur Lett-Haines to Elizabeth David, October 28, 1951, box 21, folder 10, EDS.

6. *Frieda Lawrence: The Memoirs and Correspondence*, ed. E. W. Tedlock (New York: Knopf, 1964), 335, 345.

7. Faith Compton Mackenzie, *As Much as I Dare: The Autobiography of Faith Compton Mackenzie* (London: Collins, 1938), 276.

8. Martha Gordon Crotch, diary, book 4, November 9, 1936, MHGC.

9. Martha Gordon Crotch, "Some Memories of Norman Douglas" (1952), box 4, folder 1, MHGC.

10. Theodora FitzGibbon, *A Taste of Love: The Memoirs of Bohemian Irish Food Writer Theodora FitzGibbon* (Dublin: Gill & Macmillan, 2015), chap. 25.

11. Cunard, *Grand Man*, 201.

12. Mark Holloway to Valerie Cuthbert, November 5, 1968, MHRH, vol. 3.

13. Constantine FitzGibbon, "Norman Douglas: Memoir of an Unwritten Biography," *Encounter*, September 1974, 26.

14. Roger Senhouse, "Norman Douglas: An Appreciation on His 80th Birthday," *Listener*, February 3, 1949.

15. Alan Massie, "A Hedonist of the Old School," *Spectator*, December 10, 2005, 37.

16. Lori Spencer to Elizabeth David, April 19, 1991, box 5, folder 15, EDS.

17. Michael Davidson, *The World, the Flesh and Myself* (London: Mayflower-Dell, 1962), 262.

18. Louis Golding, *Sunward* (London: Chatto & Windus, 1924), 188–99.

19. Eric Linklater, *A Year of Space: A Chapter in Autobiography* (London: Macmillan, 1953), 270. See also Douglas Goldring, *Odd Man Out: The Autobiography of a "Propaganda Novelist"* (London: Chapman & Hall, 1935), 285.

20. Gayle Rubin, "Thinking Sex: Notes for a Radical Theory of the Politics of Sexuality," in *Culture, Society and Sexuality: A Reader*, ed. Richard Parker and Peter Aggleton (New York: Routledge, 1984).

21. "Portrait of Norman Douglas," *Times Literary Supplement*, July 4, 1952, 429–30.

22. Cunard, *Grand Man*, 13, 185.

23. Cunard, 104.

24. *Analyzing Freud: Letters of H.D., Bryher, and Their Circle*, ed. Susan Stanford Friedman (New York: New Directions, 2002), 4.

25. Bryher, *The Heart to Artemis: A Writer's Memoirs* (London: Collins, 1963).

26. Bryher, "Heart to Artemis," 7, box 89, folder 3302, BPB.

27. See, for example, Douglas to Bryher, June 29 and July 18, 1923; June 28, 1924, in *Norman Douglas Selected Correspondence*, ed. Arthur S. Wensinger and Michael Allan,

vol. 6, *Dear Sir (or Madam): Letters of Norman Douglas to Bryher and Two Letters from Bryher to Douglas* (Graz/Feldkirch, Austria: W. Neugebauer Verlag, 2013), 104, 107, 50.

28. Bryher, "Heart to Artemis," 6, box 89, folder 3302, BPB.

29. Rebecca West, *D. H. Lawrence* (London: Martin Secker, 1930), 19.

30. West, 30.

31. Norman Douglas, *Late Harvest* (London: Lindsay Drummond, 1946), 53–54.

32. Norman Douglas, *Looking Back: An Autobiographical Excursion* (New York: Harcourt, Brace, 1933), 287.

33. D. H. Lawrence, *Aaron's Rod* (New York: Penguin Books, 1922), 268–74.

34. Lawrence, 274, 98, 306.

35. D. H. Lawrence to Martin Secker, November 23, 1921, in *Letters from D. H. Lawrence to Martin Secker, 1911–1930* (London: Martin Secker, 1970), 45.

36. Douglas to Archie Douglas, July 12, 1922, box 21, folder 347, NDCB.

37. *Norman Douglas Selected Correspondence*, 6:92.

38. Douglas to Hellé Flecker, July 5 and August 29, 1922, NYPL.

39. Grant Richardson to Douglas, January 26, 1922, box 17, folder 251, NDCB.

40. *Memoirs of the Foreign Legion by M. M.*, ed. D. H. Lawrence (London: Martin Secker, 1924), 19, 23, 88.

41. Norman Douglas, *D. H. Lawrence and Maurice Magnus: A Plea for Better Manners* (privately printed, 1925), 6–7.

42. Compton Mackenzie's recollections in "Norman Douglas: A Tribute," BBC, box 40, folder 623, NDCB. Faith Mackenzie agreed with her husband about the cause of Douglas's anger: Faith Compton Mackenzie, *More than I Should* (London: Collins, 1940), 162.

43. "The Owlglass," *Outlook*, November 1, 1924.

44. D. H. Lawrence to Edward McDonald, April 6, 1925, in *The Letters of D. H. Lawrence*, vol. 5, *1924–27*, ed. James T. Boulton and Lindeth Vasey (Cambridge: Cambridge University Press, 1989), 230–31.

45. *Letters of D. H. Lawrence*, 5:472.

46. Cunard, *Grand Man*, 247.

47. Bennett Cerf, *At Random: The Reminiscences of Bennett Cerf* (New York: Random House, 1977), 68–69.

48. David Low, "Arcades Ambo," n.d., box 43, folder 14, NDCB.

49. Douglas to Martha Gordon Crotch, April 23, 1936, box 1, folder 2, UCND.

Chapter Fourteen

1. Edward Hutton, *A Glimpse of Greece* (London: Medici Society, 1928), 293.

2. *Norman Douglas Selected Correspondence*, ed. Arthur S. Wensinger and Michael Al-

lan, vol. 7, *Straining Friendship to Breaking Point: Letters from John Mavrogordato to Norman Douglas and a Selection of Letters from Douglas to Mavrogordato* (Graz/ Feldkirch, Austria: W. Neugebauer Verlag, 2014), 213.

3. Douglas to Archie Douglas, March 23, 1927, box 22, folder 353, NDCB.

4. Elizabeth David, *An Omelette and a Glass of Wine*, ed. Jill Norman (Guildford, CT: Lyons Press, 1987), 123.

5. *Norman Douglas Selected Correspondence*, 7:38.

6. Muriel Draper, "Buffetings in a South Wind: Some Memories of Norman Douglas," 565, box 11, folder 355, MDPB.

7. Muriel Draper to Douglas, November 22, 1938, box 17, folder 235, NDCB. Draper may have been alluding to a reference to "dead violets" in Walter Pater's *Marius the Epicurean*, a foundational neo-Hellenic pederastic text; Walter Pater, *The Works of Walter Pater*, vol. 3, *Marius the Epicurean: His Sensation and Ideas*, vol. 2 (New York: Cambridge University Press, 2011), 101. See also Michael Matthew Kaylor, "Romantic Appropriations," in *A Companion to Greek and Roman Sexualities*, ed. Thomas K. Hubbard (Hoboken, NJ: John Wiley & Sons, 2014), 593.

8. Norman Douglas, *Together* (New York: Robert M. McBride, 1923), 67.

9. Norman Douglas, *Paneros: Some Words on Aphrodisiacs and the Like* (London: Chatto & Windus, 1931), 5; Douglas, *An Almanac* (London: Chatto & Windus, 1945), 9.

10. *An Almanac*, 1.

11. Faith Compton Mackenzie, *As Much as I Dare: The Autobiography of Faith Compton Mackenzie* (London: Collins, 1938).

12. Richard MacGillivray, *Norman Douglas* (Florence: G. Orioli, 1933), 57; Iain Hamilton, "Douglas con Amore," *Spectator*, September 10, 1954; Brigit Patmore, *My Friends When Young: The Memoirs of Brigit Patmore* (London: William Heinemann, 1968), 128; Mackenzie, *As Much as I Dare*, 276; Norman Douglas, *Late Harvest* (London: Lindsay Drummond, 1946), vii.

13. Emmanuel Cooper, *The Sexual Perspective: Homosexuality and Art in the Last 100 Years in the West* (1986; repr., London: Routledge, 2005), 143.

14. Cecile Walton Robertson to Douglas, December 10, 1921, box 19, folder 311, NDCB.

15. Draper, "Buffetings in a South Wind." See also Douglas's remark to Harold Acton that James was "a feline and gelatinous New Englander," which does suggest a personal acquaintance; Harold Acton, *More Memoirs of an Aesthete* (London: Methuen, 1970), 139.

16. Douglas to Elizabeth David, April 29, 1944, box 18, folder 7, EDS.

17. Harold Acton to Douglas and Pino Orioli, February 1937, box 5, UCND.

18. Cecile Walton Robertson to Douglas, June 13, 1922, box 19, folder 311, NDCB.

19. Robertson to Douglas, December 10, 1921, box 19, folder 311, NDCB.

20. Rebecca West, *D. H. Lawrence* (London: Martin Secker, 1930), 20.

21. Norman Douglas, *Looking Back: An Autobiographical Excursion* (New York: Harcourt, Brace, 1933), 56–57.

22. Douglas to Draper, December 9, 1938, box 2, folder 68, MDPB.

23. Norman Douglas, *Siren Land and Fountains in the Sand* (London: Secker & Warburg, 1957), 152.

24. Norman Douglas, *How About Europe? Some Footnotes on East and West* (London: Chatto & Windus, 1930), 46.

25. *How About Europe? Some Footnotes on East and West* (London: Chatto & Windus, 1930), 46–48, 105.

26. Douglas to John Mavrogordato, December 23, 1922, in *Norman Douglas Selected Correspondence*, 7:153. See also Douglas to Robin Douglas, December 24, 1923, box 5, UCND.

27. Norman Douglas, *Alone* (London: Chapman & Hall, 1921), 12; Douglas to Mavrogordato, September 27, 1927, in *Norman Douglas Selected Correspondence*, 7:226.

28. Hutton, *A Glimpse of Greece*, 148–51.

29. Douglas to Edward Hutton, April 2, 1920, box 3, UCND.

30. Douglas to Archie Douglas, January 24 and March 14, 1922, box 21, folder 347, NDCB.

31. Martha Gordon Crotch, diary, book 4, November 9, 1936, MHGC; Nancy Cunard, *Grand Man: Memories of Norman Douglas* (London: Secker & Warburg, 1954), 26.

32. Acton, *Memoirs of an Aesthete*, 386; Giuseppe [Pino] Orioli, Sant'Agata and Ischia diary, 1934, 31, NYPL.

33. Aldous Huxley to Douglas, January 7, 1930; October 13, 1934, box 17, folder 260, NDCB.

34. Peter Edgerly Firchow, "Norman Douglas as Seen through Aldous Huxley's Eyes," in *Norman Douglas: 4. Symposium, Bregenz und Thüringen, Vlbg., 20./21. 10. 2006*, ed. Wilhelm Meusburger (Bregenz, Austria: Norman Douglas Forschungsstelle, Vorarlberger Landesbibliothek, 2007).

35. M. C. Rintoul, *Dictionary of Real People and Places in Fiction* (London: Routledge, 1993), 372.

36. Aldous Huxley, *Crome Yellow* (London: Chatto & Windus, 1921), 31, 154, 61.

37. Aldous Huxley, *Those Barren Leaves* (London: Chatto & Windus, 1928), 24–25, 70.

38. Aldous Huxley, *Time Must Have a Stop* (London: Chatto & Windus, 1944), 49, 118–36.

39. John Fleming, "A Visit to Norman Douglas," box 40, folder 638, NDCB.

40. Douglas to Archie Douglas, May 25, 1925; July 14, 1926; November 23, 1934, NDCB.

41. Gabriel Richardson Lear, "Aristotle," in *International Encyclopedia of Ethics*, ed. Hugh LaFollette (London: Blackwell, 2013), 348–62.

42. Douglas, *Siren Land and Fountains in the Sand*, 75, 159.

43. Kaylor, "Romantic Appropriations," 593.

44. Epicurus, Letter to Menoiceus, Diogenes Laertius, X, 131–32, in *The Hellenistic Philosophers* vol. 1, trans. A. A. Long and D. N. Sedley (Cambridge: Cambridge University Press, 1987), 21.
45. Douglas, *Siren Land and Fountains in the Sand*, 152.
46. Theodora FitzGibbon, *A Taste of Love: The Memoirs of Bohemian Irish Food Writer Theodora FitzGibbon* (Dublin: Gill & Macmillan, 2015), chap. 25.
47. Douglas to Archie Douglas, October 15, 1936, box 23, folder 366, NDCB.
48. Douglas to Archie Douglas, March 29, 1930, box 22, folder 358, NDCB.
49. Ian Greenlees, *Norman Douglas* (London: published for the British Council and the National Book League by Longmans, Green, 1957), 17, 28.
50. Robin Chanter, "Conversations with a Retired Gentleman" [unpublished manuscript], 18–20, BIF.

Chapter Fifteen

1. Douglas to Archie Douglas, March 28, 1931, box 23, folder 358, NDCB.
2. Giuseppe [Pino] Orioli, Thüringen diary, 1932, 6, NYPL.
3. Ian Littlewood, *Sultry Climates: Travel and Sex* (Cambridge, MA: Da Capo Press, 2001), 133.
4. Richard Phillips, "Writing Travel and Mapping Sexuality: Richard Burton's Sotadic Zone," in *Writes of Passage: Reading Travel Writing*, ed. James Duncan and Derek Gregory (New York: Routledge, 1999).
5. G. Orioli, *Adventures of a Bookseller* (New York: Robert M. McBride, 1938), 260.
6. Douglas to Harold [Acton], n.d., box 20, folder 330, NDCB.
7. Giuseppe [Pino] Orioli, Vorarlberg diary, 1930, 101, NYPL.
8. Orioli, 115.
9. Orioli, 13.
10. Paul Fussell, *Abroad: British Literary Traveling between the Wars* (New York: Oxford University Press, 1980), 120.
11. Giuseppe [Pino] Orioli, Scanno diary, August 1933, 17, NYPL.
12. *Norman Douglas Selected Correspondence*, ed. Arthur S. Wensinger and Michael Allan, vol. 7, *Straining Friendship to Breaking Point: Letters from John Mavrogordato to Norman Douglas and a Selection of Letters from Douglas to Mavrogordato* (Graz/Feldkirch, Austria: W. Neugebauer Verlag, 2014), 75.
13. Richard Aldington, *Pinorman: Personal Recollections of Norman Douglas, Pino Orioli and Charles Prentice* (London: William Heinemann, 1954), 108.
14. Orioli, Thüringen diary, 1932, 8.
15. Douglas to John Mavrogordato, November 13, 1933, in *Norman Douglas Selected Correspondence*, 7:364–65.
16. Douglas to Edward Hutton, September 21, 1933, box 3, UCND; Douglas to Elizabeth

David, August 9, 1950, EDS; Douglas to Archie Douglas, June 2, 1934, box 23, folder 360, NDCB.

17. Douglas to W. H. D. Rouse, May 22, 1935, CCOL.

18. Elizabeth David, *Italian Food* (New York: Penguin Books, 1999), 319–20.

19. G. Orioli, *Moving Along: Just a Diary* (London: Chatto & Windus, 1934), 3.

20. Orioli, 131.

21. Orioli, Scanno diary, 1933, 7, 17.

22. Giuseppe [Pino] Orioli, Syracuse diary, January 16–February 11, 1936, 64, NYPL.

23. Orioli, Thüringen diary, 1932, 28.

24. Giuseppe Orioli, "A Week in Siren Land with Norman" (1933), NYPL.

25. Giuseppe [Pino] Orioli, Sant'Agata diary, 1934, 45–58, NYPL.

26. Orioli, Sant'Agata diary, 1934, 35, 156; Orioli, Thüringen diary, 1932, 7.

27. Orioli, Sant'Agata diary, 1934, 48.

28. Giuseppe [Pino] Orioli, Chianciano and Ischia diary, August 30–September 1935, 20, NYPL.

29. Martha Gordon Crotch, diary, 1937, 815–17, MHGC.

30. Orioli, Scanno diary, 1933, 12, 13.

31. Orioli, Chianciano diary, 1935, 32.

32. Orioli, "A Week in Siren Land," 8–8.

33. Orioli, "A Week in Siren Land," 21.

34. Orioli, *Moving Along*, 250.

35. Orioli, "A Week in Siren Land," 9.

36. Orioli, "A Week in Siren Land," 16, 26.

37. Orioli, Scanno diary, 1933, 17.

38. Douglas to Archie Douglas, September 7, 1934, box 23, folder 362, NDCB.

39. Orioli, Chianciano diary, 1935, 24–26.

40. Giuseppe Orioli, "Switzerland and Vorarlberg. July, 1936," 12, NYPL.

41. Giuseppe Orioli, "Pino's Diary. Sabine Mountains. December 1936–January 1937," 3–7, NYPL.

42. Orioli, *Moving Along*, 62.

43. Orioli, "A Week in Siren Land." 8.

44. Orioli, "A Week in Siren Land." 9.

45. Orioli, Scanno diary, August 1933, 11.

46. Orioli, Chianciano diary, 1935, 10.

47. Orioli, Sant'Agata diary, 1934, 75.

48. Orioli, Chianciano diary, 1935, 35.

49. Douglas to Archie Douglas, June 27 and June 30, 1934, box 23, folder 361, NDCB.

50. Orioli, Sant'Agata diary, 1934, 171, 184.

51. Orioli, Chianciano diary, 1935, 42.

52. Douglas to Archie Douglas, March 9, 1935, box 23, folder 362, NDCB.

53. Giuseppe Orioli, "To India with Norman" (December 21, 1934–March 3, 1935), 66, NYPL.

54. Orioli, "To India with Norman," 334. For hijras, see Aniruddha Dutta, "An Epistemology of Collusion: Hijras, Kothis and the Historical (Dis)Continuity of Gender/Sexual Identities in Eastern India," *Gender & History* 24, no. 3 (2012).

55. Orioli, Syracuse diary, 1936, 7.

56. Orioli, "Pino's Diary. Sabine Mountains," 35.

57. Lorenzo Benadusi, "Private Life and Public Morals: Fascism and the 'Problem' of Homosexuality," *Totalitarian Movements and Political Religions* 5, no. 2 (2004): 196n3.

58. Orioli, Chianciano diary, 1935, 12.

59. Orioli, "To India with Norman."

60. Orioli, Chianciano diary, 1935, 45.

61. Lorenzo Benadusi, *The Enemy of the New Man: Homosexuality in Fascist Italy* (Madison: University of Wisconsin Press, 2012).

62. Douglas to W. H. D. Rouse, April 19, 1934, CCOL.

63. Douglas to Archie Douglas, August 26, 1936, box 23, folder 365, NDCB.

64. Douglas to Pino Orioli, August 29, 1936, box 4, UCND.

65. Douglas to Orioli, September 2, 1936, box 4, UCND.

66. Douglas, pocket diary, 1936, box 36, folder 586, NDCB.

67. Douglas to Archie Douglas, September 20, 1936, box 23, folder 365, NDCB.

68. *Norman Douglas Selected Correspondence*, ed. Arthur S. Wensinger and Michael Allan, vol. 4, *Italiam Petimus: Letters of Edward Hutton to Norman Douglas and a Selection of Letters from Douglas to Hutton* (Graz/Feldkirch, Austria: W. Neugebauer Verlag, 2011), 346.

Reflection III

1. David Halperin, "Is There a History of Sexuality?," *History and Theory* 28, no. 3 (1989); Catharine A. MacKinnon, "Does Sexuality Have a History?," *Michigan Quarterly Review* 30 (1991).

2. Clara Tuite, *Lord Byron and Scandalous Celebrity* (Cambridge: Cambridge University Press, 2015), 34–46.

3. *Dave Chappelle: Sticks and Stones* (2019), dir. Stan Lathan, written by Dave Chappelle.

4. Aja Romano, "Dave Chappelle's Netflix Special Targets Michael Jackson's Accusers, #MeToo, and Cancel Culture," *Vox*, August 29, 2019, https://www.vox.com/2019/8/29/20835637/dave-chappelle-netflix-special-hidden-ending-cancel-culture.

5. Kathryn Bond Stockton, *The Queer Child, or Growing Sideways in the Twentieth Century* (Chapel Hill, NC: Duke University Press, 2009), 62.

6. Michel Foucault, *The History of Sexuality: An Introduction*, trans. Robert Hurley, 3 vols. (New York: Vintage Press, 1990), 1:30–43.

7. "Pederasty, homosexuality" search in Google Ngrams Book Viewer, English corpus, for the years 1868–1952.

Chapter Sixteen

1. Lorenzo Benadusi, *The Enemy of the New Man: Homosexuality in Fascist Italy* (Madison: University of Wisconsin Press, 2012). Douglas remarked on all the English people in Florence in the summer of 1935: Douglas to Archie Douglas, June 7, 1935, box 23, folder 362, NDCB.

2. Douglas to Archie Douglas, February 1, 1929, box 22, folder 356, NDCB. See also Douglas to Archie Douglas, August 30, 1929, box 22, folder 356, NDCB.

3. Douglas to Archie Douglas, June 25, 1935, box 23, folder 362, NDCB.

4. Douglas to Archie Douglas, September 26 and October 31, 1935, box 23, folders 362, 363, NDCB.

5. Douglas to Archie Douglas, December 6, 1936, box 23, folder 365; January 19, 1937, box 24, folder 366, NDCB.

6. For information, see Benadusi, *The Enemy of the New Man*, 156–61.

7. Mark Holloway, *Norman Douglas: A Biography* (London: Secker & Warburg, 1976), 424.

8. Douglas to Archie Douglas, January 5, 1937, box 24, folder 366, NDCB.

9. Martha Gordon Crotch, diary, October 24, 1937, box 1, vol. 8, MHGC; Harold Acton, *More Memoirs of an Aesthete* (London: Methuen, 1970), 141.

10. Douglas to John Mavrogordato, August 5, 1937, in *Norman Douglas Selected Correspondence*, ed. Arthur S. Wensinger and Michael Allan, vol. 7, *Straining Friendship to Breaking Point: Letters from John Mavrogordato to Norman Douglas and a Selection of Letters from Douglas to Mavrogordato* (Graz/Feldkirch, Austria: W. Neugebauer Verlag, 2014), 392.

11. Douglas to Pino Orioli, April 20 and April 26, 1937, box 4, UCND.

12. Douglas to Robin Douglas, May 20, 1937, box 5, UCND; Douglas to Archie Douglas, May 12, 1937, box 24, folder 366, NDCB.

13. Martha Gordon Crotch, diary, book 9, 26, MHGC.

14. Martha Gordon Crotch, diary, October 24, 1937, 0815–0817, MHGC.

15. Acton, *More Memoirs of an Aesthete*, 141–43.

16. Philip Jenkins, *Moral Panic: Changing Concepts of the Child Molester in Modern America* (New Haven, CT: Yale University Press, 1998), 100.

17. Viva King, *The Weeping and the Laughter* (London: MacDonald and Jane's, 1976), 197.

18. Martha Gordon Crotch, diary, October 24, 1937, 0816, MHGC.

19. Oscar Levy to Douglas, July 4, 1937, in *Norman Douglas Selected Correspondence*, ed. Arthur S. Wensinger and Michael Allan, vol. 3, *Goût de l'espace: Letters of Oscar Levy to Norman Douglas and a Selection of Letters from Douglas to Levy* (Graz/Feldkirch, Austria: W. Neugebauer Verlag, 2010), 153.

20. *Norman Douglas Selected Correspondence*, ed. Arthur S. Wensinger and Michael Allan, vol. 1, *Respectful Ribaldry: A Selection of Letters from Norman Douglas to Faith Compton Mackenzie* (Graz/Feldkirch, Austria: W. Neugebauer Verlag, 2008), 104.

21. Douglas to Archie Douglas, June 16, 1937, box 24, folder 367, NDCB.

22. *Norman Douglas Selected Correspondence*, ed. Arthur S. Wensinger and Michael Allan, vol. 6, *Dear Sir (or Madam): Letters of Norman Douglas to Bryher and Two Letters from Bryher to Douglas* (Graz/Feldkirch, Austria: W. Neugebauer Verlag, 2013), 108.

23. Nancy Cunard, *Grand Man: Memories of Norman Douglas* (London: Secker & Warburg, 1954), 108.

24. Bryher, excerpt from "Heart to Artemis," 3, box 89, folder 3302, BPB.

25. Martha Gordon Crotch, diary, October 10, 1937, 0812, MHGC.

26. Douglas is quoted in Holloway's unpublished biography of Martha Gordon Crotch, chap. 6, box 4, folder 2, MHGC.

27. Douglas to Edward Hutton, November 9, 1935, box 3, UCND.

28. Letters from Douglas to Nancy Cunard, box 13, folder 7, NCHR.

29. Pino Orioli to Douglas, July 19, 1937, box 18, folder 288, NDCB.

30. Douglas to Orioli, June 2, 1937, box 4, UCND.

31. Orioli to Douglas, July 27, 1937, box 18, folder 288, NDCB.

32. Douglas to Orioli, January 17, February 2, and February 5, 1938, box 4, UCLA.

33. Douglas to Archie Douglas, January 29, 1938, box 24, folder 368, NDCB.

34. Douglas to Levy, January 1, 1942, in *Norman Douglas Selected Correspondence*, 3:213.

35. Douglas to Hutton, December 15, 1937, box 3, UCND.

36. Martha Gordon Crotch, diary, 0803, MHGC.

37. Douglas to Orioli, July 19 and July 24, 1937, box 4, UCND.

38. Martha Gordon Crotch, diary, 0803, MHGC.

39. Douglas to Orioli, July 24, 1937, box 4, UCND.

40. Mark Holloway, unpublished biography of Martha Gordon Crotch, chap. 6, box 4, folder 2, MHGC.

41. Martha Gordon Crotch, diary, October 9, 1937, 0812, MHGC.

42. Douglas to Archie Douglas, December 31, 1937, box 24, folder 367, NDCB.

43. Martha Gordon Crotch, diary, November 14, 1937, 0910, MHGC.

44. Lise Cramer to Douglas, 1938; Chico Cramer to Douglas, 1938, box 17, folder 231, NDCB.

45. Martha Gordon Crotch, diary, 1938, 18–19, MHGC.

46. See, for example, letters dated June 10, June 13, and June 15, 1938, from "Richard" to Archie Douglas, box 24, folder 368, NDCB.

47. Martha Gordon Crotch, diary, 1938, 20, MHGC.

48. Cunard, *Grand Man*, 108–9.

49. Cunard, 153–55.

50. Douglas to Martin Secker, September 8, 1938, uncataloged material, box 104, NYPL.

51. Martha Gordon Crotch, diary, September 9, 1938, MHGC.

52. Douglas to Richard Dawkins, November 8, 1938, in *Norman Douglas Selected Correspondence*, ed. Arthur S. Wensinger and Michael Allan, vol. 5, *Byzantine Talks: Letters of Norman Douglas to Richard Macgillivray Dawkins and a Single Letter from Dawkins to Douglas* (Graz/Feldkirch: W. Neugebauer Verlag, 2012), 128–29.

53. Douglas to Bryher, June 10, 1939, box 21, folder 339, NDCB.

54. Nancy Cunard to F. W. Hutchinson, June 18, 1939, box 30, folder 497, NDCB.

55. Douglas to Elizabeth David, August 15, 1940, box 18, folder 7, EDS.

56. Martha Gordon Crotch, diary, 1939, 35–36, MHGC.

57. Douglas to Archie Douglas, May 2, 1940, box 24, folder 372, NDCB.

58. Trustee Department Coutts and Co. to Douglas, November 5, 1940, box 45, NDCB.

59. Douglas to Archie Douglas, December 3, 1940, box 24, folder 372, NDCB.

60. Douglas to Archie Douglas, December 27, 1940, box 24, folder 372, NDCB.

61. Douglas to Archie Douglas, January 4, 1942, box 25, folder 374, NDCB.

62. Douglas to Hellé Flecker, September 12, 1941, NYPL.

63. Douglas to Elizabeth David, December 19, 1941, box 18, folder 7, EDS.

Chapter Seventeen

1. Theodora FitzGibbon, *A Taste of Love: The Memoirs of Bohemian Irish Food Writer Theodora FitzGibbon* (Dublin: Gill & Macmillan, 2015), 471–72.

2. *Norman Douglas Selected Correspondence*, ed. Arthur S. Wensinger and Michael Allan, vol. 3, *Goût de l'espace: Letters of Oscar Levy to Norman Douglas and a Selection of Letters from Douglas to Levy* (Graz/Feldkirch, Austria: W. Neugebauer Verlag, 2010), 274.

3. Douglas to Archie Douglas, March 17, 1944, box 25, folder 376; December 18, 1943, box 25, folder 375; January 27, 1944, box 25, folder 376, NDCB.

4. Harold Acton, *More Memoirs of an Aesthete* (London: Methuen, 1970), 143.

5. Douglas to Hellé Flecker, January 31, 1942, NYPL.

6. Douglas to Archie Douglas, August 6, 1942, and December 18, 1943, box 25, folders 374, 375, NDCB.

7. Paul Fussell, *Abroad: British Literary Traveling between the Wars* (New York: Oxford University Press, 1980), 120.

8. *Norman Douglas Selected Correspondence*, 3:225–26.

9. Norman Douglas, diaries, 1942, 1943–1944, box 36, folders 590, 591, NDCB.

10. Douglas to Archie Douglas, January 19, 1942, box 24, folder 374, NDCB.

11. Martha Gordon Crotch, diary, October 24, 1937, 0815, MHGC.

12. Douglas to Archie Douglas, February 13 and February 24, 1942, box 24, folder 374, NDCB.

13. Nancy Cunard, *Grand Man: Memories of Norman Douglas* (London: Secker & Warburg, 1954), 173.

14. Cunard, 183.

15. Cunard, 191.

16. Cunard, 164.

17. Douglas to Archie Douglas, March 10, 1943, box 245, folder 375, NDCB. Douglas also complained about being "overrun with a pack of shits of both sexes" to his son Robin; Douglas to Robin Douglas, March 22, 1943, box 5, UCND.

18. Douglas to Archie Douglas, April 11, 1945, box 25, folder 378, NDCB.

19. Douglas to Archie Douglas, October 3, 1945, box 25, folder 378, NDCB.

20. See, for example, Sylvia Beach to Douglas, February 3, 1939, box 17, folder 227, NDCB; Dorothy Ireland to Douglas, 1937, box 20, folder 328, NDCB; Nigel Richards to Douglas, March 9, 1936, box 19, folder 310, NDCB.

21. FitzGibbon, *A Taste of Love*, 167.

22. David Halperin, *One Hundred Years of Homosexuality* (New York: Routledge, 1990); Annamarie Jagose, *Queer Theory* (Dunedin, New Zealand: Otago University Press, 1996).

23. FitzGibbon, *A Taste of Love*, 165.

24. Viva King, *The Weeping and the Laughter* (London: MacDonald and Jane's, 1976), 198.

25. Faith Compton Mackenzie to Bryher, June 29, 1943, folder 1270, BPB.

26. King, *The Weeping and the Laughter*, 198.

27. King, 205.

28. Aileen Dawson, "William King (1894–1958), Museum Curator and Friend of Norman Douglas," in *Norman Douglas: 9. Symposium, Bregenz und Thüringen, Vlbg., 7./8. 10. 2016*, ed. Wilhelm Meusburger (Bregenz, Austria: Norman Douglas Forschungsstelle, Vorarlberger Landesbibliothek, 2017).

29. Douglas to Archie Douglas, February 19, 1943, box 25, folder 375, NDCB.

30. FitzGibbon, *A Taste of Love*.

31. FitzGibbon, 169.

32. Cecil Woolf, *A Bibliography of Norman Douglas* (London: Rupert Hart-Davis, 1954), 125.

33. Richard MacGillivray [Dawkins], *Norman Douglas* (Florence: G. Orioli, 1933), 8.

34. Douglas to Bryher, March 16, 1937, box 21, folder 338, NDCB.

35. Richard Aldington, "Errant Knight of Capri," *Esquire*, December 1941.

36. Norman Douglas notes on "Errant Knight of Capri," box 39, folder 607, NDCB.

37. Norman Douglas, "Caveat Lector," *Spectator*, May 29, 1942, 509.

38. Richard Aldington, "Mr. Norman Douglas's Caveat," *Spectator*, August 6, 1942, 13.

39. Douglas to Nancy Cunard, March 11, 1942, box 3, folder 6, NCHR.

40. Douglas to Elizabeth David, February 10, 1942, EDS. See also Douglas to Hellé Flecker, September 12, 1941, NYPL.

41. Douglas to Robin Douglas, May 22, 1944, box 5, UCND.

42. Douglas to Archie Douglas, June 15, 1945, box 25, folder 378, NDCB.

43. Douglas to Archie Douglas, September 2, 1944, and June 15, 1945, box 25, folders 377, 378, NDCB.

44. Cunard, *Grand Man*, 209.

45. Douglas to Edward Hutton, August 21, 1945, HUT: 1: B: 14, BIF.

46. Douglas to Archie Douglas, October 3, 1945, box 25, folder 379, NDCB.

47. Cunard, *Grand Man*, 210.

48. David Low to Edward Hutton, June 28, 1946, HUT: I: C: 2: H1–15, BIF.

49. Douglas to Archie Douglas, June 26, 1946, box 25, folder 380, NDCB.

Chapter Eighteen

1. *Norman Douglas Selected Correspondence*, ed. Arthur S. Wensinger and Michael Allan, vol. 6, *Dear Sir (or Madam): Letters of Norman Douglas to Bryher and Two Letters from Bryher to Douglas* (Graz/Feldkirch, Austria: W. Neugebauer Verlag, 2013), 475.

2. Nancy Cunard, *Grand Man: Memories of Norman Douglas* (London: Secker & Warburg, 1954), 214, 25.

3. Harold Acton, *More Memoirs of an Aesthete* (London: Methuen, 1970), 331–33. The American sexologist Alfred Kinsey witnessed the child trade at the Galleria when he visited Naples in 1955; Wardell Baxter Pomeroy, *Dr. Kinsey and the Institute for Sex Research* (New York: Harper & Row, 1972), 421–26.

4. Viva King, *The Weeping and the Laughter* (London: MacDonald and Jane's, 1976), 205.

5. Douglas to Bryher, June 8, 1947, in *Norman Douglas Selected Correspondence*, ed. Arthur S. Wensinger and Michael Allan, vol. 2, *Dear Doug! Letters to Norman Douglas from Eric Wolton, René Mari, Marcel Mercier and Ettore Masciandaro and a Selection of Letters from Emilio Papa* (Graz/Feldkirch, Austria: W. Neugebauer Verlag, 2008), 135.

6. *Norman Douglas Selected Correspondence*, ed. Arthur S. Wensinger and Michael Allan, vol. 5, *Byzantine Talks: Letters of Norman Douglas to Richard Macgillivray Dawkins and a Single Letter from Dawkins to Douglas* (Graz/Feldkirch: W. Neugebauer Verlag, 2012), 177.

7. Douglas to Archie Douglas, November 19, 1946, box 25, folder 381, NDCB.

8. Douglas to Archie Douglas, December 31, 1946, and March 24, 1947, box 25, folders 381, 382, NDCB; Douglas to Robin Douglas, March 21 and May 27, 1947, box 6,

folder 1, NDHR. Douglas still owned an apartment in Florence, but it was occupied by a couple installed by the Fascists, forcing Douglas into a long legal battle to regain possession of the apartment so he could sell it.

9. Douglas to Archie Douglas, September 25, 1947, box 25, folder 382, NDCB.

10. Kenneth Macpherson to Robin Douglas, December 10, 1947, box 6, folder 1, NDHR.

11. Douglas to Archie Douglas, December 8, 1944, and February 29, 1948, box 25, folders 377, 383, NDCB. After Papa's death, Douglas allowed Papa's widow and daughter to live in the Florence apartment rent-free for three years, much to the upset of Archie, who struggled to support his own wife and three children, and wrote frequently to his father begging for handouts; Douglas to Archie Douglas, February 29, March 16, April 6, May 17, and June 4, 1948, box 25, folder 383, NDCB.

12. "Capri," *Life*, September 19, 1949, 74–80.

13. Nancy Cunard, "'Bonbons' of Gall," *Time and Tide* 35, no. 16 (April 17, 1954): 517.

14. Norman Douglas, *D. H. Lawrence and Maurice Magnus: A Plea for Better Manners* (privately printed, 1925), 8.

15. Norman Douglas, *Siren Land and Fountains in the Sand* (London: Secker & Warburg, 1957), 138.

16. Douglas, *D. H. Lawrence and Maurice Magnus*, 8.

17. Acton, *More Memoirs of an Aesthete*, 275; Cunard, *Grand Man*, ix.

18. Victor Cunard, "Norman Douglas, 1868–1952," *Time and Tide*, March 29, 1952.

19. Norman Douglas to *Who's Who*, April 8, 1922, SNDV.

20. Theodora FitzGibbon, *Love Lies a Loss: An Autobiography, 1946–1959* (London: Century Publishing, 1985), 67.

21. Kenneth Macpherson to Mark Holloway, August 17, 1967, MHRH, vol. 1.

22. Richard Aldington, "The Case of Norman Douglas," box 40, folder 640, NDCB.

23. Roger Senhouse, "Norman Douglas: An Appreciation on His 80th Birthday," *Listener*, box 40, folder 628, NDCB.

24. *The Letters of Lytton Strachey*, ed. Paul Levy (London: Telegraph Books, 2005).

25. Kenneth Macpherson to Archibald Douglas, February 21, 1957, box 47, NDCB.

26. Norman Douglas, *Looking Back: An Autobiographical Excursion* (New York: Harcourt, Brace, 1933), 223.

27. Norman Douglas to the Literary Executor of Joseph Conrad, October 23, 1925, box 21, folder 342, NDCB. The letters were subsequently printed in full in a San Francisco literary journal; "Letters of Joseph Conrad," *Argonaut*, October 3, 1925, 13.

28. See, for example, Douglas to Martha Gordon Crotch, August 5, 1939, box 1, UCND.

29. FitzGibbon, *Love Lies a Loss*, 77.

30. Meryle Secrest, *Shoot the Widow: Adventures of a Biographer in Search of Her Subject* (New York: Knopf, 2007).

31. Constantine FitzGibbon, "Norman Douglas: Memoir of an Unwritten Biography," *Encounter*, September 1974, 28–29.

32. Douglas to Faith Mackenzie, August 24, 1941, in *Norman Douglas Selected Correspondence*, ed. Arthur S. Wensinger and Michael Allan, vol. 1, *Respectful Ribaldry: A Selection of Letters from Norman Douglas to Faith Compton Mackenzie* (Graz/Feldkirch, Austria: W. Neugebauer Verlag, 2008), 123.

33. Faith Compton Mackenzie, *As Much as I Dare: The Autobiography of Faith Compton Mackenzie* (London: Collins, 1938), 273–74.

34. Douglas to Archie Douglas, January 29, 1950, box 26, folder 385, NDCB.

35. FitzGibbon, "Norman Douglas: Memoir of an Unwritten Biography," 28.

36. FitzGibbon, *Love Lies a Loss*, 92.

37. Cunard, *Grand Man*, 216.

38. Cunard, 220.

39. Acton, *More Memoirs of an Aesthete*, 333.

40. Allan Massie, "A Hedonist of the Old School," *Spectator*, December 10, 2005.

41. Compton Mackenzie, *My Life and Times: Octave Ten, 1953–1963* (London: Chatto & Windus, 1971), 15.

42. Marie-Jaqueline Lancaster, *Brian Howard: Portrait of a Failure* (London: Timewell Press, 2005); Martin Green, *Children of the Sun: A Narrative of "Decadence" in England after 1918* (New York: Basic Books, 1976).

43. D. M. Low to Mark Holloway, February 14, 1967, MHRH, vol. 1.

44. Massie, "A Hedonist of the Old School."

45. Filippi Amedeo to Phillips Temple, April 3, 1951, NYPL.

46. Nancy Cunard notes on *Grand Man*, box 3, folder 6, NCHR.

47. Sybille Bedford, *Quicksands: A Memoir* (New York: Counterpoint, 2005), 48.

48. Douglas to Elizabeth David, August 1, 1950, box 18, folder 7, EDS.

49. Norman Douglas, *Footnote on Capri* (London: Sidgwick and Jackson, 1952), 5.

50. Rachel Hope Cleves, "Philotes in the Kitchen: Norman Douglas' Friendships with Faith Compton Mackenzie, Elizabeth David, Sybille Bedford and Theodora Fitzgibbon," in *Norman Douglas: 9. Symposium, Bregenz und Thüringen, Vlbg., 7./8.10.2016*, ed. Wilhelm Meusburger (Bregenz, Austria: Norman Douglas Forschungsstelle, Vorarlberger Landesbibliothek, 2017).

51. Davidson and Maugham offer very similar descriptions of their weekend with Douglas in Michael Davidson, *The World, the Flesh and Myself* (London: Mayflower-Dell, 1962), 262–73; Robin Maugham, *Escape from the Shadows* (London: Hodder and Stoughton, 1972), 197.

52. David Posner, "Dialogue with Norman Douglas," *Poetry* 110, no. 6 (1967).

53. Robin Douglas to Douglas, July 23, 1948, box 6, folder 8, NDHR.

54. Archie Douglas to Kenneth Macpherson, January 11, 1952, box 47, NDCB.

55. Ettore and Antoinetta Masciandaro to Kenneth Macpherson, June 20 and November 5, 1948, box 18, folder 277, NDCB.

56. Kenneth Macpherson to Bryher, January 2, 1952, box 36, folder 1294, BPB.

57. Robin's accounts of Douglas's relationship with Masciandaro can be found in three letters to Kenneth Macpherson, dated September 26, 1951; January 11, 1952; and January 13, 1952; and one letter to Islay Lyons, dated January 13, 1952, box 47, NDCB.

58. Kenneth Macpherson to Mark Holloway, August 17, 1967, MHRH, vol. 2.

59. Robin Douglas to Kenneth Macpherson, January 11, 1952, box 47, NDCB.

60. Robin Douglas to Islay Lyons, January 13, 1952, box 47, NDCB.

Chapter Nineteen

1. Bryher to Nikolai Nadezhin, February 25, 1952, box 1, folder 9, NNPB.

2. Kenneth Macpherson to Bryher, January 2, 1952, box 36, folder 1294, BPB.

3. Macpherson to Bryher, January 2, 1952, box 36, folder 1294, BPB.

4. Macpherson to Bryher, January 18 and January 24, 1952, box 36, folder 1294, BPB.

5. Islay Lyons to Mark Holloway, August 9, 1975, MHRH, vol. 8.

6. Macpherson to Bryher, February 15, 1952, box 36, folder 1294, BPB.

7. Constantine FitzGibbon, *Norman Douglas: A Pictorial Record* (London: Richards Press, 1953), 34.

8. Macpherson to Bryher, January 2, 1952, box 36, folder 1294, BPB.

9. Bryher to Nikolai Nadezhin, February 25, 1952, box 1, folder 9, NNPB.

10. Norman Douglas, *Siren Land and Fountains in the Sand* (London: Secker & Warburg, 1957), 85.

11. Harold Nicolson, "Marginal Comment," *Spectator*, February 22, 1952, 11.

12. William King to Edward Hutton, March 12, 1952, HUT: I: C: 2: H1–15, BIF.

13. Edward Hutton, letter to the editor, *Spectator*, February 29, 1952, 16; Desmond Harmsworth, letter to the editor, *Spectator*, March 7, 1952, 18; Constantine FitzGibbon, letter to the editor, *Spectator*, March 7, 1952, 18; Graham Greene, letter to the editor, *Spectator*, March 14, 1952, 20.

14. Neil Bell to Graham Greene, March 16, 1952, box 17, folder 7, GGPB; William King to Edward Hutton, March 9, 1952, and Peter Hutton to Edward Hutton, December 3, 1952, HUT: I: C: 2: H1–15, BIF; Robin Douglas to Edward Hutton, March 7, 1952, HUT: I: C: I: 41–49, BIF.

15. Macpherson to Bryher, January 18 and April 8, 1952, box 36, folder 1294, BPB.

16. Kenneth Macpherson, *Omnes Eodem Cogimur* (Torino: privately printed, 1953).

17. Martha Gordon Crotch diary, February 9, March 8, and August 1952, MHGC.

18. Martha Gordon Crotch, "Some Memories of Norman Douglas" (1952), box 4, folder 1, MHGC.

19. Bryher, Notes, box 39, folder 609, BPB.

20. Bryher, "Norman Douglas," box 89, folder 3302, BPB; Bryher, *The Heart to Artemis: A Writer's Memoirs* (London: Collins, 1963), 227–38.

Chapter Twenty

1. Richard Aldington, *Pinorman: Personal Recollections of Norman Douglas, Pino Orioli and Charles Prentice* (London: William Heinemann, 1954), vii.
2. Aldington, 205, 118.
3. Norman Douglas, *D. H. Lawrence and Maurice Magnus: A Plea for Better Manners* (privately printed, 1925), 30, 7.
4. Richard Aldington, *Life for Life's Sake: A Book of Reminiscences* (New York: Viking Press, 1941), 375–76.
5. Norman Douglas, *Looking Back: An Autobiographical Excursion* (New York: Harcourt, Brace, 1933), 26.
6. Richard Aldington, *Seven against Reeves: A Comedy-Farce* (London: William Heinemann, 1937), 214–33.
7. Douglas to Nancy Cunard, March 11, 1942, box 3, folder 6, NCHR.
8. Douglas's dislike of Aldington dated back to 1933, when Aldington wrote an intrusive article about Bryher's father's funeral; see Douglas to Bryher, 1933, box 21, folder 337, NDCB.
9. Aldington, *Pinorman*, 82–83, 135.
10. Aldington, 118–20.
11. Aldington, 125–63.
12. Charles Doyle, *Richard Aldington: A Biography* (London: Macmillan, 1989), 183.
13. Aldington, *Pinorman*, 205.
14. Nancy Cunard to D. M. Low, March 13, 1954, box 43, folder 10, NDCB.
15. Doyle, *Richard Aldington*, 164.
16. Fred D. Crawford, *Richard Aldington and Lawrence of Arabia: A Cautionary Tale* (Carbondale: Southern Illinois University Press, 1998), 98–101.
17. Richard Aldington, 99 T.L.S., 3 telegrams to Rob Lyle, NYPL. Kenneth Macpherson also complained to the publisher; Macpherson to A. S. Frere, June 1, 1954, box 29, folder 509, NDCB.
18. Nancy Cunard, "'Bonbons' of Gall," *Time and Tide* 35, no. 16 (April 17, 1954): 517.
19. D. M. Low, "East Wind," *Listener* 51 (May 20, 1954): 891.
20. V. S. Pritchett, "And Friend," *New Statesman and Nation*, May 29, 1954. Pritchett grouped *Pinorman* with another recent biography by Aldington, of the writer T. E. Lawrence.
21. Compton Mackenzie, "Sidelight," *Spectator*, April 30, 1954, 518.
22. Constantine FitzGibbon, "Group Portrait," *Times Literary Supplement*, May 7, 1954, 300.
23. Graham Greene to Kenneth Macpherson, April 28, 1954; and Greene to Edward Hutton, April 26, 1954, box 17, folder 7, GGPB.
24. Greene to John Lehmann, April 20 and May 13, 1954, box 17, folder 7, GGPB.

25. Greene to Richard Aldington, May 18, 1954, NYPL.

26. Aldington to Greene, May 30, 1954, NYPL.

27. Graham Greene, "Poison Pen," *London Magazine*, March 1966.

28. Eugene Byrne to Richard Aldington, October 19, 1954, NYPL.

29. Frieda Lawrence, letter to the editor, *Time and Tide* 35, no. 22 (May 29, 1954): 724. Cunard responded by calling D. H. Lawrence a master of the "'nice-nasty' manner" and saying he had been unfair to Maurice Magnus; Nancy Cunard, *Time and Tide* 35, no. 23 (June 5, 1954): 752–54.

30. Richard Aldington to Netta Aldington, May 12, 1954, in *Richard Aldington: An Autobiography in Letters*, ed. Norman T. Gates (University Park: Pennsylvania State University Press, 1992), 272.

31. Richard Aldington, letter to the editor, *Listener* 51 (June 10, 1954): 1013.

32. D. M. Low, letter to the editor, *Listener* 51 (June 17, 1954): 1055.

33. H. Alan Clodd to Graham Greene, June 24, 1960, box 17, folder 8, GGCB.

34. Islay Lyons's photos of Somerset Maugham and Norman Douglas, box 48, NDCB.

35. Richard Aldington to Rob Lyle, September 12, 1954, NYPL.

36. Aldington to Lyle, September 13 and September 15, 1954, NYPL.

37. Frieda Lawrence to Richard Aldington, June 13, 1954, NYPL.

38. Brigit Patmore, *My Friends When Young: The Memoirs of Brigit Patmore* (London: Heinemann, 1968), 28–30.

39. Aldington to Lyle, September 16, 1954; Eugene Byrne to Aldington, October 19, 1954, NYPL.

40. Horne & Birkett letter to Rob Lyle, January 7, 1955, NYPL.

41. Martha Gordon Crotch to Betty, May 1, 1955, box 2, MHGC.

42. Nancy Cunard, notes on Martha Gordon Crotch diaries, box 3, folder 6, NCHR.

43. Cunard, notes on Crotch diaries, 3–6, box 3, folder 6, NCHR.

44. Nancy Cunard to D. M. Low, March 13, 1954, box 43, folder 10, NDCB.

45. Nancy Cunard, *Grand Man: Memories of Norman Douglas* (London: Secker & Warburg, 1954), ix.

46. Cunard, 5, 10, 67.

47. John Davenport, "Profile in Sunlight," *New Statesman and Nation*, August 7, 1954.

48. Davenport, "Profile"; Raymond Mortimer, "The Story of a Friendship," *Sunday Times*, August 8, 1954; Malcolm Elwin, "Norman Douglas Defended," *John O'London's Weekly*, August 27, 1954, 855; Derek Hudson, "Other Side of the Picture," *Daily Telegraph*, August 6, 1954.

49. John Connell, "The Grand Old Man of Capri," *Evening News*, August 4, 1954; S. Frazer, "Robust Epicurean," *Times Literary Supplement*, August 27, 1952; Davenport, "Profile"; C.W. "Norman Douglas and His Friends," *Desiderata* 7, no. 45 (November 12, 1954): 1–4.

Chapter Twenty-One

1. Stephen Keane, "Homosexual and Lesbian Expression," in *Censorship: A World Encyclopedia*, ed. Derek Jones (Abingdon, UK: Routledge, 2001).

2. Aubrey Menen, "The Bewitching Island of Capri," *Holiday*, January 1959, box 42, folder 648, NDCB.

3. Robin Douglas to James V. Sellend, December 15, 1958, box 29, folder 509, NDCB.

4. Kenneth Macpherson, "Stormy South Wind," *Holiday* [n.d.], box 42, folder 648, NDCB.

5. "Isle of Dreams," *Time* 74 (August 3, 1959): 26; Kenneth Macpherson to *Time*; Robin Douglas to *Time* magazine [n.d.], box 42, folder 648, NDCB.

6. Mark Holloway to David Farrer, September 21, 1966, MHRH, vol. 1.

7. Kenneth Macpherson to Mark Holloway, November 11 and December 1966, MHRH, vol. 1.

8. Holloway to Macpherson, November 12, 1966; Holloway to Compton Mackenzie, January 25, 1967; Holloway to Roger Senhouse, January 30, 1967, MHRH, vol. 1.

9. Holloway to Mark Hamilton, March 7, 1967, MHRH, vol. 1.

10. Philip Jenkins, *Moral Panic: Changing Concepts of the Child Molester in Modern America* (New Haven, CT: Yale University Press, 1998); Chris Ashford, "Queering Consent: (Re)Evolving Constructions of the Age of Consent and the Law," in *Legal Perspectives on State Power: Consent and Control*, ed. Chris Ashford, Alan Reed, and Nicola Wake (Newcastle upon Tyne, UK: Cambridge Scholars Publishing, 2016).

11. Kenneth Macpherson to Lola Szaldits, September 18, 1968, MHRH, vol. 2.

12. Holloway to Lola Szaldits, October 8, 1968, MHRH, vol 2.

13. Holloway to Archie Douglas, August 13, 1975, MHRH, vol 8.

14. Mark Roberts, "Ian Greenlees and Norman Douglas," in *Norman Douglas: 6. Symposium, Bregenz und Thüringen, Vlbg., 15./16.10.2010*, ed. Wilhelm Meusburger (Bregenz, Austria: Norman Douglas Forschungsstelle, Vorarlberger Landesbibliothek, 2011).

15. Mark Holloway, "Norman Douglas," in *The Craft of Literary Biography*, ed. Jeffrey Meyers (London: Macmillan Press, 1985), 105.

16. Geoffrey Grigson, "Not Such a Bright Young Thing," *Country Life*, December 9, 1976, 1783, box 17, UCLA.

17. Constantine FitzGibbon, "Norman Douglas: Memoir of an Unwritten Biography," *Encounter*, September 1974, 35–37.

18. Mark Holloway, letter to the editor, and Constantine FitzGibbon response, in *Encounter*, December 1974, 93.

19. Elizabeth David, letter to the editor, *Encounter*, February 1975, 95.

20. Elizabeth David, "South Wind through the Kitchen," in *An Omelette and a Glass of Wine*, ed. Jill Norman (Guildford, CT: Lyons Press, 1987), 126.

21. Elizabeth David, "Have It Your Way," in *An Omelette and a Glass of Wine*, 120.

22. David, "South Wind through the Kitchen," 128.

23. Theodora FitzGibbon, *Love Lies a Loss: An Autobiography, 1946–1959* (London: Century Publishing, 1985), 92.

24. Rachel Hope Cleves, "Philotes in the Kitchen: Norman Douglas' Friendships with Faith Compton Mackenzie, Elizabeth David, Sybille Bedford and Theodora Fitzgibbon," in *Norman Douglas: 9. Symposium, Bregenz und Thüringen, Vlbg., 7./8.10.2016*, ed. Wilhelm Meusburger (Bregenz, Austria: Norman Douglas Forschungsstelle, Vorarlberger Landesbibliothek, 2017).

25. Roger Williams, *Lunch with Elizabeth David* (London: Little, Brown, 1999).

26. Review of *Lunch with Elizabeth David*, by Roger Williams, March 1, 2000, https://www.publishersweekly.com/978-0-7867-0707-2.

27. Flavio Giacomantonio, ed., *Old Calabria di Norman Douglas tra cultura e tradizione: Con selezione antologica* (Cosenza: Pellegrini, 1984).

28. Claudio Gargano, *Capri pagana: Uranisti e amazzoni tra Ottocento e Novecento* (Capri: Edizioni la Conchiglia, 2007), 146. In Gargano's original Italian, this sentence reads: "in lui, unico tra i tanti scrittori che alimentano il mito di un'Italia arcaica e sensuale, no c'è traccia di esotismo o di colore locale."

29. Ciro Sandomenico, *Norman Douglas: Una vita indecente* (Capri: Edizioni La Conchiglia, 1996), 22.

30. For Astarita's writings about Douglas, see Vincenzo Astarita, "Siren Land Today," in *Norman Douglas: 9. Symposium, Bregenz und Thüringen, Vlbg., 7./8.10.2016*, ed. Wilhelm Meusburger (Bregenz, Austria: Norman Douglas Forschungsstelle, Vorarlberger Landesbibliothek, 2017); Norman Douglas, *Guide Miopi: Nelson, Caracciolo e la caduta della Republica Partenopa nel 1799*, ed. V. Astarita (Monghidoro, Italy: Con-Fine Edizioni, 2016).

31. Jenkins, *Moral Panic*.

32. Kevin Ohi, "Molestation 101: Child Abuse, Homophobia, and the Boys of St. Vincent," *GLQ: A Journal of Lesbian and Gay Studies* 6, no. 2 (2000): 197.

33. See, for example, Jeffrey Meyers, *Somerset Maugham: A Life* (New York: Vintage, 2005), 66; Richard J. Ruppel, *Homosexuality in the Life and Work of Joseph Conrad: Love between the Lines* (New York: Routledge, 2008); Lorna Gibb, *West's World: The Extraordinary Life of Dame Rebecca West* (London: Macmillan, 2013).

34. Francis King, *The Ant Colony* (London: Constable, 1992), 183.

35. Alex Preston, *In Love and War* (London: Faber & Faber, 2014).

36. Personal conversation with Alex Preston, September 12, 2016.

37. Michael Allan, "Dear Doug! Norman Douglas—Eric, René, Emilio, Ettore," in *Norman Douglas: 4. Symposium, Bregenz und Thüringen, Vlbg., 20./21. 10. 2006*, ed. Wilhelm Meusburger (Bregenz, Austria: Norman Douglas Forschungsstelle, Vorarlberger Landesbibliothek, 2007), 80. Allan's co-editor, Arthur Wensinger,

has been a little more ambivalent. At the project's beginning, he wrote: "Needless to say, to reduce Norman Douglas to a pederast sex fiend is wildly off the mark. Or is it, entirely? Perhaps not altogether." Quote from *Norman Douglas: (1868 Thüringen–1952 Capri), Schriftseller,* ed. Helmut Swozilek (Bregenz, Austria: Vorarlberger Landesmuseum, 2001), 277.

38. *Norman Douglas Selected Correspondence,* ed. Arthur S. Wensinger and Michael Allan, vol. 7, *Straining Friendship to Breaking Point: Letters from John Mavrogordato to Norman Douglas and a Selection of Letters from Douglas to Mavrogordato* (Graz/Feldkirch, Austria: W. Neugebauer Verlag, 2014), 77.

Reflection IV

1. Janet Malcolm, "Susan Sontag and the Unholy Problem of Biography," *New Yorker,* September 23, 2019.

2. Michael H. Keller and Gabriel J. X. Dance, "The Internet Is Overrun with Images of Child Sexual Abuse: What Went Wrong?" *New York Times Magazine,* September 29, 2019.

Index

Forbes, 17th Lord of (James Ochoncar
 Forbes), 23
Ford, Ford Madox (né Hueffer), 93, 98–
 99, 109, 113, 233
Foreign Office, British, 38–39, 42–47
Forster, E. M., 18, 56, 130, 158
Foucault, Michel, 121, 217–18
Fountains in the Sand (Douglas), 102
France, 3, 57, 125, 136, 143, 165, 175, 200,
 223, 231, 236, 242, 251, 260. *See also*
 Amiens; Antibes; Brittany; Calais;
 Corsica; Étretat; Menton; Nor-
 mandy; Paris; Provence; Saint-Malo;
 Sanary-sur-Mer; Vence
Francesco, 210–11
Franco-Prussian War, 35
Frere, A. S., 274
Freud, Sigmund, 18, 85, 168
Fry, Stephen, 176
Fulham Chronicle, 120

Gabrielle (Gaby), 229
Gabriello, 202, 208
Gafsa, 102
Gaiola, 48–49
Gallipoli campaign, 119
Galsworthy, John, 109, 110, 113, 233
Garnett, David "Bunny," 113
Garnett, Edward, 113
Gastone, Gian, 156
gay literature, 8, 26, 113, 181. *See also*
 Uranians
gay rights, 6, 13, 27, 34, 97, 108, 134–35,
 167, 275
Genazzano, 209, 210
gender, 60, 135, 213. *See also* effeminacy;
 masculinity
Geneva, Lake, 183, 200, 232
Gennaro's, 114, 234
Gerald, 203

German language, 33
Germany, 28, 46, 73, 175, 231, 236, 243.
 See also Baden; Berlin; Karlsruhe;
 Munich
Gervasito, 230
Gide, André, 6, 108, 183
Gielgud, John, 270
gifts, 45, 61, 63, 64, 111, 120–21, 141, 169,
 200, 205, 209–11, 226
Gilbert, Morris, 235
Gilt, Hermann, 32
Giulio, 132
Glimpse of Greece, A (Hutton), 188–89,
 193
Gloeden, Wilhelm von, 97, 98, 102
Goa, 230
Goggin, Detective-Sergeant, 120–21
Golden Ass, The (Apuleius), 47, 168
Golding, Louis, 182, 261
Goldman, Emma, 222
Gorky, Maksim, 248
gossip, 65, 79, 181, 191, 228, 249, 262, 271
Grand Man (Cunard), 271–72
Grand Tour, 50, 82
Gray, Cecil, 251
Gray, John, 190
Great Britain, 50, 62, 157, 167, 169,
 221, 232, 241, 275. *See also* England;
 Guernsey; Scotland
Great Exhibition of 1851, 104, 106
Greece, 8, 38, 96, 119, 175, 189. *See
 also* ancient Greece; Athens; neo-
 Hellenism; Santorini
Greek Anthology, The, 36, 38, 79, 168,
 266. See also *Musa Paedika, The*
Greene, Graham, 13–14, 251, 259, 268
Greenlees, Ian, 197, 200, 242, 276
Gregorovius, Ferdinand, 75, 79
Gretna Green, 118, 122
Grigson, Geoffrey, 276